⁓ CATO ⁓
SUPREME COURT
REVIEW

2016—2017

CATO
SUPREME COURT
REVIEW

2016—2017

CENTER FOR CONSTITUTIONAL STUDIES

INSTITUTE
Washington, D.C.

THE CATO SUPREME COURT REVIEW (ISBN 978-1-944424-83-1) is published annually at the close of each Supreme Court term by the Cato Institute, 1000 Massachusetts Ave., N.W.,Washington, D.C. 20001-5403.

CORRESPONDENCE. Correspondence regarding subscriptions, changes of address, procurement of back issues, advertising and marketing matters, and so forth, should be addressed to:

Publications Department
The Cato Institute
1000 Massachusetts Ave., N.W.
Washington, D.C. 20001

All other correspondence, including requests to quote or reproduce material, should be addressed to the editor.

CITATIONS: Citation to this volume of the Review should conform to the following style: 2016-2017 Cato Sup. Ct. Rev. (2017).

INTERNET ADDRESS. Articles from past editions are available to the general public, free of charge, at www.cato.org/pubs/scr.

ISBN 978-1-944424-83-1 (print)
ISBN 978-1-944424-84-8 (digital)

Printed in the United States of America.

Cato Institute
1000 Massachusetts Ave., N.W.
Washington, D.C. 20001
www.cato.org

Published through the generosity of George M. Yeager

Contents

FOREWORD
Judicial Confirmations and the Rule of Law
Roger Pilon   ix

INTRODUCTION
Ilya Shapiro   1

ANNUAL B. KENNETH SIMON LECTURE

State Constitutions: Freedom's Frontier
Clint Bolick   15

ARTICLES

FIRST AMENDMENT CHALLENGES

Beyond Trademarks and Offense: *Tam* and the
   Justices' Evolution on Free Speech
Clay Calvert   25

Our Fellow American, the Registered Sex Offender
David T. Goldberg and Emily R. Zhang   59

PROPERTY, RELIGIOUS AND SECULAR

Religious Freedom and Recycled Tires:
   The Meaning and Implications of *Trinity Lutheran*
Richard W. Garnett and Jackson C. Blais   105

From a Muddle to a Mudslide: *Murr v. Wisconsin*
Nicole Stelle Garnett   131

CONTENTS

TRICKY PRESIDENTIAL APPOINTMENTS

S.W. General: The Court Reins in Unilateral Appointments
  Thomas A. Berry   151

CASH & CRIME

Salman v. U.S.: Another Insider Trading Case,
    Another Round of Confusion
  Thaya Brook Knight   181

Nelson v. Colorado: New Life for an Old Idea?
  David G. Post   205

CREDIT & LABELS

Expressions Hair Design: Detangling the
    Commercial-Free-Speech Knot
  Mark Chenoweth   227

NEXT YEAR

Looking Ahead: October Term 2017
  Christopher Landau and Sopan Joshi   253

CONTRIBUTORS   293

FOREWORD

Judicial Confirmations and the Rule of Law

Roger Pilon*

The Cato Institute's Center for Constitutional Studies is pleased to publish this 16th volume of the *Cato Supreme Court Review*, an annual critique of the Court's most important decisions from the term just ended plus a look at the term ahead—all from a classical liberal, Madisonian perspective, grounded in the nation's first principles, liberty through constitutionally limited government. We release this volume each year at Cato's annual Constitution Day conference. And each year in this space I discuss briefly a theme that seemed to emerge from the Court's term or from the larger setting in which the term unfolded.

Unlike recent terms, the Court's October Term 2016 was remarkable for being largely unremarkable. With the seat of the late Justice Antonin Scalia remaining unfilled until Justice Neil Gorsuch was sworn in on April 10, little more than two months before the term ended, the Court decided only 62 cases after argument—the fewest ever—and no decision would count as extraordinary. Hence, this slimmer than usual *Review*.

The real action during the term lay beyond the Court, with the nomination of Judge Gorsuch and the confirmation hearings before the Senate Judiciary Committee that followed. Given his stellar credentials and Tenth Circuit record, his confirmation should have been unexceptional, as most such were in earlier days. (Indeed, even in appearance and demeanor he was straight out of Central Casting.) Instead, he was confirmed with nearly half the Senate voting no—a

* Vice president for legal affairs at the Cato Institute, founder and director of Cato's Center for Constitutional Studies, B. Kenneth Simon Chair in Constitutional Studies, and founding publisher of the *Cato Supreme Court Review*. I want to thank Cato summer intern Matt Robinson for his assistance with this piece.

party line vote with only three Democratic defections. And he endured hours of often aggressive grilling, much of it aimed at showing that he was not a "mainstream" nominee, notwithstanding that 97 percent of his 2,700 some decisions were unanimous and 99 percent of the time he was in the majority.

Ever since the brutal 1987 hearings for Judge Robert Bork, who paid the price for playing it straight—answering questions in detail, never equivocating or pretending to be someone he was not—judicial confirmation hearings have been stylized, questionably productive rituals, especially for Republican nominees. The Gorsuch hearings were no exception. Like other recent nominees of both parties, he said as little as needed to get by, and for perfectly legitimate reasons. He did not want to reveal how he might rule in future cases. More important, committing to certain positions as a condition for being confirmed would not only violate the judicial code of conduct but would be tantamount to deciding future cases in the hearings, by politics, rather than in the courtroom, by law. Indeed, in the run-up to and during the hearings, Democrats made much of the need for judicial independence of the president. Judges need also to be independent of Congress.

Meanwhile, as in other recent hearings, Democrats on and off the committee repeatedly charged Gorsuch with ruling for corporations and against workers, minorities, women, and, especially, the "little guy." Senator Dianne Feinstein, ranking minority member on the committee, put it plainly when she asked Gorsuch: "How do we have confidence in you, that you won't be just for the big corporations? That you will be for the little man?"

The implications of that view for the rule of law are stark. They amount to asking Lady Justice to remove her blindfold, to rule based not on the law but on who the parties are. Fortunately, and doubtless in anticipation of hearing it, committee Chairman Chuck Grassley began the hearings on just that point—fittingly, with a quote from a Scalia opinion. "It is the 'proud boast of our democracy that we have a government of laws and not of men,'" Scalia wrote. Drawn from the Massachusetts Constitution of 1780, that is a distinction between law and politics, for when all is politics, under the rule of man, nothing is law.

When the hearings concluded, it was more clear than ever that the Senate and, by implication, the nation are deeply divided not simply over politics but over the very meaning of the Constitution and the role of the courts under it—divisions that are far more pronounced and partisan than they've ever been. Democrats see the Constitution mostly as a "living" document, sufficiently open-ended and malleable to enable judges to "do justice"—as they see it. Republicans, by contrast, see the Constitution mainly as establishing a set of institutions, legal relationships, and rules that judges are to apply impartially in cases brought before them.

Given those starkly different views, and the implications for the rule of law, it would be useful to see how the Constitution itself contemplates the connection between politics and law. That will frame a brief look at how we got to where we are today with these confirmation hearings and a further and more important look at the substantive underpinnings of our deep divisions.

Politics and Law under the Constitution

In a limited constitutional republic like ours, the relation between politics and law is set, for the most part, by law—by the law of the Constitution. Drawing on reason and interest, the Framers drafted a constitution that became law through ratification—a *political* act that reflected the interests and will of the founding generation. Amended by subsequent acts of political will, the Constitution authorizes the political branches to act pursuant only to their enumerated powers or to enumerated ends. It further limits the exercise of those powers and the powers of the states either explicitly or by recognizing, with varying degrees of specificity, rights retained by the people. And by fairly clear implication, made explicit in the *Federalist* and shortly thereafter in *Marbury v. Madison*, the Constitution authorizes the judiciary to declare and enforce that law of authorizations and restraints consistent with the document itself.

Thus, the scope for "politics"—understood as the pursuit of individual or group interests through public or political institutions—is limited. Consistent with constitutional rules and limits, the people may act politically to fill elective offices. Those officers may in turn act politically to fill non-elective offices. But once elected or appointed, those officials may act politically only within the scope and limits set by the Constitution. In particular, in a limited republic like ours, not everything in life is meant to be subject to political or governmental determination. In fact, the founding and subsequent generations wanted most of life to be beyond the reach of politics, yet under the rule of law. In short, our Constitution does not say, "After periodic elections, those elected may do what they will or pursue any end they wish or any end the people want." On the contrary, it strictly limits, by law, the scope of politics. And it falls to the judiciary, the nonpolitical branch, to declare what the Constitution says that law and those limits are, thereby securing the rule of law.

The aim in all of this, then, is to constrain the rule of man—and politics—by the rule of law. The Framers understood that legitimacy begins with politics, with the people: "We the people . . . do ordain and establish this Constitution." But once ratification—the initial political act—establishes the rule of law, that law constrains politics thereafter. And it is the nonpolitical judiciary that declares and enforces that law. It is essential, therefore, that the judiciary act nonpolitically—not from will or interest but from reason, according to law, consistent with the first principles of the system. If it does not, then to that extent the rule of law is undermined and politics trumps law.

A Brief History of How We Got Here

Against that brief outline of the Constitution's ordering of politics and law, let us turn now to the judicial-selection process. In it, "raw" politics—the "horse-trading" we see in many areas of politics—has always played a part, and for good reason. It's built into the Constitution. At the federal level, at least, we don't select judges in the same way that we select civil servants. The *political* branches do the selecting: Presidents nominate and the Senate advises and consents, or not. And ultimately, of course, the selection of judges is political insofar as it rests with the people: They select the politicians who select the judges who in turn interpret and apply the constitutional provisions that empower and limit the politicians who selected them.

But while that raw politics has always been with us, it has also been supplemented from time to time with a politics animated by ideological considerations. The Gorsuch hearings revealed that clearly. For if judges, members of the *non*political branch, have a duty to say what the law is and apply it to cases before them—a principle older than *Marbury v. Madison*—then asking them to "do justice," regardless of what the law may say, is asking them to do nothing less than undermine the rule of law. (Recall Justice Oliver Wendell Holmes's retort when urged to "do justice": "My job is to apply the law.") Yet as noted above and illustrated further below, that is exactly what Democrats on the committee often expected Judge Gorsuch to do—not in terms, of course, but in effect. To be sure, they sometimes grounded their complaints in different readings of "the law"—and Republicans too sometimes misread the law, especially concerning the Ninth and Fourteenth Amendments and how the two go together through the Constitution's presumption of liberty. But in the main it was a repeated concern for "justice" over law that animated committee Democrats.

As mentioned above, hearings of the kind we've just seen were rare for most of our history. They've arisen mainly during the last three decades. Yet the *substantive* roots that help in part to explain them go far back. A particular but important such ground is the demise of the Fourteenth Amendment's Privileges or Immunities Clause in the *Slaughterhouse Cases* of 1873, which most scholars today believe were wrongly decided. As a result, the authority of judges to check the power of states over their own citizens remains confused to this day. But today's divisions arise far more broadly from the Progressive Era and its rejection of the Constitution's limited government principles, a vision that the New Deal Court institutionalized systematically in a series of decisions between 1937 and 1943, turning the Constitution on its head.

That constitutional revolution—eviscerating the doctrine of enumerated powers, bifurcating the Bill of Rights, creating a two-tier theory of judicial review, and jettisoning the nondelegation doctrine—was essentially a *political* settlement that followed Franklin Roosevelt's early 1937 threat to pack the Court with six new members. It set in train the modern redistributive and regulatory state, which in turn brought ever more complaints to the nation's courts, some unrelated to government growth and long overdue, as with civil rights, but many others the product of the burgeoning public sector. With legal realism, legal positivism, and other modern theories infusing those developments, the heady idea of judges "doing justice" followed quite naturally, surfacing especially in the post-War Warren and Burger Courts.

But "justice" of that kind offended many in the slowly emerging conservative movement, not only substantively but, even more, in its reflection of what they saw as "judicial activism"—judges deciding cases based not on the law but on their own, usually liberal, values.

Thus, in the 1960s Yale's Alexander Bickel wrote broadly of judicial review's "countermajoritarian difficulty"—questioning the legitimacy, in a democracy, of judges overriding democratic decisions. Discounting the "*majoritarian* difficulty" that so concerned the Framers—their fear of unrestrained legislative majorities—Bickel urged judges toward the "passive virtues" and "judicial restraint," influencing in the process people like Bork, Scalia, and other conservatives. Pointing to the separation of powers, these conservatives saw judges engaged in "lawmaking," which belonged properly to the legislative branches, not to the courts. They often overstated and misstated the problem, because they focused more on judicial behavior than on the Constitution, but their brief was not unfounded.

Looking back over this stretch, liberals, as pre-New Deal progressives came to be known, had the political and legal fields largely to themselves for decades. But that would change when the Reagan revolution came along. Focusing on the courts, the administration consciously supplemented the "raw" politics of judicial selection with an ideological politics, one informed by the principles of the regnant conservative and, to a lesser extent, libertarian movements. Thus, the 1986 hearings for Justice William Rehnquist to be the chief justice and Judge Scalia to fill the Rehnquist seat were the first to draw, in a full-fledged way, the ideological opposition of the long-dominant liberal movement. The issues were thus joined. Yet both nominees were finally confirmed on Constitution Day, 1986: Rehnquist 65-33, Scalia 98-0.

Those 1986 Rehnquist/Scalia hearings mark the beginning of what would be a series of ideologically contentious judicial confirmation battles. Often focused mainly on the proper role of the courts, competing conceptions of the law were always just below the surface, and sometimes above it. It took only a year for the most brutal of those battles to unfold. Fearing that replacing retiring Justice Lewis Powell with Judge Bork would tip the Court's balance too much in the conservative direction, the left, led by Senator Ted Kennedy, pulled out all the stops. Eminently qualified for the position, Bork nonetheless made the mistake of thinking that Democrats on the committee, and even some Republicans, were interested in discussing the niceties of constitutional law. Thus, he spelled out his own views in considerable detail, as mentioned earlier. Speaking truth to power, he was voted down, 58-42.

Months later, lessons learned, Judge Anthony Kennedy declined even to discuss *Griswold v. Connecticut*, the 1965 decision overturning the state's criminalization of the sale and use of contraceptives. He was confirmed 97-0. Four years on it was hardly so smooth when Judge Clarence Thomas went before the committee. Again, the left marshaled its forces, now against an African American who believed in natural law—disbelief in which was a charge Chairman Joe Biden had lodged against Bork. Despite Biden's critical discussion of Thomas's writings on natural rights and the emerging libertarian approach to constitutional interpretation, Thomas was narrowly confirmed by a vote of 52-48, with 11 Democrats voting yes, and two Republicans no.

Still, most Republicans continued to play by the old rules. In 1993, Judge Ruth Bader Ginsburg, whose history marked her clearly as a movement liberal, sailed through the Senate, 96-3, as did Judge Stephen Breyer a year later, 87-9. After a long stretch of no Court vacancies, however, it was again the Republicans' turn to make nominations: And again, Democrats on the committee rose to the occasion. The moderately contentious hearings for Judge John Roberts in 2005 led to his confirmation by a somewhat closer vote of 78-22, the 22 all Democrats. The hearings months later for Judge Samuel Alito were so brutal that his wife at one point walked out in tears. Despite his stellar credentials and solid Third Circuit record, he was confirmed by a much narrower vote of 58-42, with only 4 Democrats voting yes.

Perhaps as a sign of Republicans catching on to the game, the Senate votes since have been narrower. In 2009, Judge Sonia Sotomayor was confirmed 68-31, the 31 all Republicans, nine Republicans voting yes. A year later Elena Kagan was confirmed a bit more closely, 63-37, with 36 Republicans voting no, five voting yes. The record to date concludes with the much closer Gorsuch confirmation, 54-45, with all but three Democrats voting no.

Ideological Litmus Tests

Clearly, the trend has been in the direction of increasing polarity along partisan lines. One could say that Democrats have led the way, starting with their opposition to Rehnquist, exploding a year later against Bork. But Democrats will rightly answer that they were responding to the express ideological aim of the Reagan administration to select judges who understood and were part of the growing conservative and libertarian movements—as evidenced by the administration's frequent turn to the academy for nominees, not to the American Bar Association. On the other hand, conservatives will answer that they were simply responding to decades of ideological appointments by liberal Democrats aimed at upholding Great Society, New Deal, and Progressive Era programs—held by many conservatives and, especially, libertarians to be inconsistent with the Constitution's original understanding, notwithstanding claims by liberals about "settled law."

In the end, therefore, ideology has come to dominate the judicial confirmation process on both sides. Democrats make no effort to disguise it; Republicans sometimes do. Still, there are differences. Identity politics in the courtroom—finding for the "little guy," for example, when the law does not—is expressly result-oriented. Republicans, by contrast, focus primarily on judicial process, on applying the law, at least as they read it, whatever the result. That point was captured by Judge Gorsuch himself in his opening statement before the committee: "For the truth is, a judge who likes every outcome he reaches is probably a pretty bad judge, stretching for the policy results he prefers rather than those the law compels."

Concerning those differences, the Democratic view was never more undeniably evidenced than in the aftermath of the 2000 presidential election—driven, no doubt, by the Supreme Court's split decision in *Bush v. Gore*, which effectively settled the election. For nearly two years the Democrat-controlled Senate Judiciary Committee sat on most of President George W. Bush's first 11 appellate court nominees (two of those, Clinton holdovers renominated by Bush as a gesture, were confirmed immediately). Among those 11 were such legal luminaries as John Roberts, Jeffrey Sutton, and Miguel Estrada (who never did have a hearing, even after Bush renominated him two years later). It wasn't quality that concerned the Democrats. It was ideology, and expressly so.

Led by Senator Chuck Schumer, then-chairman of the Judiciary Committee's Subcommittee on Administrative Oversight and the Courts, now Senate minority leader, Democrats called explicitly for "ideological litmus tests" for judicial nominees. Claiming, not without reason, that judges are and perhaps should be "setting national policy," their express aim was to keep "highly credentialed, conservative ideologues" from the bench. Schumer was especially vexed, as he averred in a June 2001 *New York Times* op-ed, by "the Supreme Court's recent 5-4 decisions that constrain congressional power, probably the best evidence that the Court is dominated by conservatives." Thus the importance, Democrats said, of placing "sympathetic judges" on the bench, judges who share "the core values held by most of our country's citizens." In sum, law aside, it was all politics.

The stall lost steam once Republicans regained the Senate in 2003, but the themes Democrats had pressed in that 107th Congress continue to this day, as a few quotes from the Gorsuch hearings' opening statements will illustrate. Senator Feinstein, for example, voiced a common note when she said, "Our job is to assess how this nominee's decisions will impact the American people"—as if a judge should consider the policy implications of a law that, presumably, the legislature has already considered in passing it. Similarly, Senator Patrick Leahy said judges must "consider the effects of their rulings," then asked, "Will you elevate the rights of corporations over those of real people?" Citing former Senator Paul Simon, Senator Dick Durbin said that history will judge a judge by whether he restricts freedom or expands it, adding, "I don't mean freedom for corporations." The Democratic hostility to corporations throughout the hearings was striking. Nearly the whole of Senator Sheldon Whitehouse's opening statement, for example, was devoted to "cases that pit corporations against humans." From his statement one imagines that the Court has an abiding hostility toward humans.

Not surprisingly, originalism came in for criticism as well, even if it was often misunderstood. Thus, Senator Feinstein found it "really troubling" that judges should interpret constitutional text in light of the words' original public meaning, which she thought would mean "that judges and courts should evaluate our constitutional rights and privileges as they were understood in 1789" and "we would still have segregated schools and bans on interracial marriage." In fact, it was precisely when the words of the Equal Protection Clause were given their original public meaning that those practices could no longer survive. But on this point it was Senator Leahy who truly came up short when he contended that "originalism remains outside the mainstream of modern constitutional jurisprudence." He seems to have forgotten that it was his question that prompted Elena Kagan, in her hearings, to remark, "We are all originalists." The alternative, after all, is to read the text to say what it does not say—what a willful judge might want it to say.

In their statements, questions, and follow-up questions for the record, Democratic members covered the full range of "hot-button" issues—abortion, guns, women's issues, campaign finance, voting, employment discrimination, environmental regulation, privacy, immigration, LGBTQ issues, administrative law, and more. In each case, however, the interest was far more in the result than in the law that led to it—if at all in that. Senator Amy Klobuchar, for example, took exception to Gorsuch's suggestion "that the Court should apply strict scrutiny to laws restricting campaign contributions." So limiting Congress would be "in direct contradiction with the expressed views of the American people," she said, adding: "While polls aren't a judge's problem, democracy should be. When unlimited, undisclosed money floods our campaigns, it drowns out the people's voices. It undermines our elections and shakes the public's trust in the process." Whether true or not—I'm skeptical—such considerations are no part of a judge's duty. The part of McCain-Feingold at issue in *Citizens United* would have banned certain books and so it had to go pursuant to the law, namely, the First Amendment.

As a final illustration of the Democrats' thrust at these hearings, a point they made back at the beginning of the Bush 43 years—that judges are and perhaps should be "setting national policy"—was echoed by Senator Al Franken, who remarked that "the justices who sit on the Supreme Court wield enormous power over our daily lives." Senator Mazie Hirono made that same point: "The Supreme Court shapes our society," she said. They're right, of course. But rather than identify the problem that presents for our democracy— that we're being ruled by the nonpolitical branch—much less address the reasons underlying it—the massive growth of government since the Progressive Era, all of which eventually ends up for decision by the Supreme Court—Democrats want simply to have us ruled by *their* justices—provided these "policymakers" share "the core values held by most of our country's citizens."

The best evidence for this comes from the hearings themselves. Recall that what especially vexed Senator Schumer 16 years ago were "the Supreme Court's recent 5-4 decisions that constrain congressional power," the very power that over a century and more has given us the Leviathan that today so burdens the Court's docket. Well that most fundamental of constitutional issues—whether Congress has the constitutional authority to do all that it has done—barely surfaced in the Gorsuch hearings. In fact, I have found only one mention of the Commerce Clause, through which Congress has given us the modern regulatory state following the New Deal Court's opening of the floodgates. It is in Senator Mazie Hirono's subsequent "Questions for the Record." She raised the issue in connection with *Gonzales v. Raich*, the 2005 California medical marijuana case. Judge Gorsuch declined to respond directly because the answer would turn on particular facts. Perhaps Senate Democrats, especially after the Obamacare litigation, are now so confident that their power to legislate is plenary that the issue is no longer worth raising. But it remains the fundamental reason the battle for the Court today is so intense.

Republicans Respond

For their part, neither did committee Republicans raise the enumerated powers issue, understandably. Their job, after all, was to see the nomination through and hence to raise few problems. Thus, their focus was on criticizing the Democrats' lines of attack. Senator Orrin Hatch, for example, spoke of the conflict over judicial appointments as being "a conflict over the proper role of judges in our system of government," going on to draw a sharp distinction between impartial judges, who decide cases on the law, and political judges, who focus on the desired result and then fashion the means toward achieving it. In a similar vein, Senator Ted Cruz noted the "sharp disagreement about the very nature of the Supreme Court." Judges, he said, "are not supposed to make law. They are supposed to faithfully apply it." And Senator Mike Lee made a telling political point when he said that "our confidence in the American judiciary depends entirely on judges who are independent and whose only agenda is getting the law right."

But it was Chairman Chuck Grassley, perhaps anticipating Senator Lee's point, who set the stage for the hearings with an opening statement that spoke of liberty no fewer than seven times and of the separation of powers no fewer than ten. Thereby getting the law of the Constitution right, perhaps because he is not a lawyer and therefore is less likely to miss the forest for the trees, Grassley made it clear for all to hear that the Constitution's very purpose, the reason it was written by the Framers and ratified by the people, is to secure liberty.

And the means toward that end, more important even than the Bill of Rights, is found in "the design of the document itself," he continued. "It divides the limited power of government vertically, between the states and the federal government. And it distributes power horizontally, between the co-equal branches." With powers thus separated and the branches defined functionally, there is no authority for the political branches to go beyond the limited powers granted to them or the judicial branch to do anything other than say what the law is and apply it.

But because each branch has gone well beyond its allotted powers, venturing thus beyond the law established by the Constitution, what we see today and have seen for many decades is not the politics authorized and bounded by the Constitution but rather a politics unbound by law: a Congress addressing what it will, an executive regulating at will and ignoring legitimate law, and judges too often "doing justice" according to their own lights. Thus, the rule of law is now, to a disturbing extent, the rule of politics, the rule of man, and that bodes ill for liberty. That should concern every American, Republican and Democrat alike.

Introduction

*Ilya Shapiro**

This is the 16th volume of the *Cato Supreme Court Review,* the nation's first in-depth critique of the Supreme Court term just ended, plus a look at the term ahead. We release this journal every year in conjunction with our annual Constitution Day symposium, less than three months after the previous term ends. We are proud of the speed with which we publish this tome and of its accessibility, at least insofar as the Court's opinions allow. I'm particularly proud that this isn't a typical law review, whose submissions' esoteric prolixity is matched only by their footnotes' abstruseness. Instead, this is a book of essays on law intended for everyone from lawyers and judges to educated laymen and interested citizens.

And we're happy to confess our biases: We approach our subject from a classical Madisonian perspective, with a focus on individual liberty that is protected and secured by a government of delegated, enumerated, separated, and thus limited powers. We also maintain a strict separation of law and politics; just because something is good policy doesn't mean it's constitutional (see President Obama's executive actions on immigration) and vice versa (see President Trump's). Moreover, just because being faithful to the text of a statute might produce unfortunate results doesn't mean that judges should take it upon themselves to rewrite the law—as the new "junior justice," Neil Gorsuch, has already reminded us in his early writings. Accordingly, just as judges must sometimes overrule the will of the people—as when legislatures act without constitutional authority or trample individual liberties—resolving policy problems caused by poorly conceived or inartfully drafted legislation must be left to the political process.

* Senior fellow in constitutional studies, Cato Institute, and editor-in-chief, *Cato Supreme Court Review.* I dedicate this volume to Judge E. Grady Jolly, who this summer marked 35 years on the Fifth Circuit bench and is now taking senior status. It was my great good fortune to have clerked for Judge Jolly in 2003–04.

This was a term for legal nerds rather than political junkies, with plenty of interesting cases but not really any front-page news. (A transgender-bathroom-access case, *Gloucester County v. G.G.*, would've gotten plenty of attention, but it was ultimately remanded for reconsideration after the Trump administration rescinded the Obama-era guidance to which the lower court had simply deferred.) We had gotten used to the idea that every year the Supreme Court decides several of the biggest national political issues—we've seen six or seven consecutive "terms of the century"—but this year saw a regression to the mean.

Most of the reason for the low-key term is Justice Antonin Scalia's death in February 2016 and the delay in confirming a successor. Scalia's absence didn't change the result of that many cases—the previous term's *Friedrichs v. California Teachers Association* was by far the biggest exception (and the issue presented there, "agency fees" for public-sector-union nonmembers, will likely return to the Court next term)—but cert grants decreased in both quantity and quality. Now that the Court is back at full strength, cert grants are picking up in both number and profile; simple math tells you that getting four votes out of nine is easier than four out of eight. Already this summer we talked more about the travel ban, cell site location information, vendors for same-sex weddings, partisan gerrymandering, and sports betting in New Jersey—all cases granted in June—than anything that was decided this term.

The term's theme—to the extent this theme-searching exercise is productive—thus had little to do with the cases decided and everything to do with the culmination of the battle over the Scalia seat. More than a year after Scalia's death, the high court finally returned to a full complement of nine justices. But the newest justice's confirmation happened only after the Senate decided, on a party-line vote, to remove filibusters for Supreme Court nominations. The exercise of the "nuclear option" returns Senate procedures to what they were 15 years ago. Before 2003, the filibuster simply wasn't used for partisan purposes against nominees who had majority support. Now, a Senate majority will still be able to stall a nomination made by a president of the opposing party—we could see more Merrick Garlands—but a Senate minority will lack that power.

These developments sound like a big deal, but they were predictable given our political climate and won't actually change the operation of either the Court or the Senate. For every commentator who rues that our justices will now decline in quality, there's one who explains that this moment actually broke the fever of our toxic judicial politics. Given that judges are now selected for jurisprudential correctness (and on the left for demographic correctness) rather than party loyalty and cronyism, I can't imagine that nominees will be all that different. And opportunities for obstruction will continue too—pushed down to the "blue slip" and other arcane steps—even as control of the Senate remains by far the most important aspect of the whole endeavor.

The elimination of the filibuster for Supreme Court nominees was the natural culmination of a tit-for-tat escalation by both parties, with partisan disagreements over who started it. The Gorsuch denouement was retaliation for the Garland blockade, which in turn followed Harry Reid's nuking of filibusters for lower-court and executive-branch nominees in 2013, which came a decade after Reid used the tactic to block President George W. Bush's nominations (most notably Miguel Estrada, whom Democrats didn't want to set up for elevation as the first Hispanic justice not named Benjamin Cardozo).

At a certain point, it doesn't really matter who started it. The senatorial brinksmanship is all symptomatic of a much larger problem that began long before Ted Kennedy smeared Robert Bork: the Supreme Court's own self-corruption, aiding and abetting the warping of federal power by Congress and the executive branch. Living constitutionalists and their judicial-restraint handmaidens have politicized the law such that judges quail at enforcing the Constitution's structural limits and face attacks for not seeing statutes in a way that favors "the little guy." As we've gone down the wrong jurisprudential track since the New Deal, the judiciary now affects the direction of public policy more than it ever did—and those decisions increasingly turn on the party of the president who nominated the judge or justice. So of course confirmations will be fraught.

Given the highly charged battle we saw over Gorsuch—only three Democrats, from states Trump won "bigly" (Indiana, North Dakota, West Virginia), voted for him, and just one more, fellow Coloradan Michael Bennet, voted against filibuster—too many people will now think of the justices in partisan terms. That's too bad, but not a surprise when contrasting methods of constitutional and statutory interpretation largely track identification with parties that are (at least

3

in Congress) more ideologically coherent than ever before. Relatedly, confirmation hearings will continue to be kabuki theater, educational about various legal doctrines but illuminating little of the nominee's judicial philosophy. On the other hand, perhaps nominees will occasionally feel free to express themselves, knowing that they don't need any of the minority party's votes. I'm just glad we can stop talking about filibusters and nuclear options in this context.

In any case, the Court has effectively returned to the status quo we saw before Scalia's death. No two justices are the same, but Gorsuch can probably be expected to vote the same as Scalia on all the issues that broke down 5-4, including the cases (especially in criminal procedure) that joined the Court's left and right against the middle. More accurately, based on the one sitting's worth of cases in which he participated, Gorsuch will probably vote most often with Justice Clarence Thomas—so think about where you stand on cases where Scalia and Thomas diverged. Regardless, Gorsuch is the real deal. Those who hoped for (or feared) a smooth-writing textualist got what they expected. "Wouldn't it be a lot easier if we just followed the plain text of the statute?" he asked at his first argument, in the otherwise forgettable case of *Henson v. Santander*. He continued in that vein in his opinion in that case, where he noted that "we begin, as we must, with a careful examination of the statutory text." You may not agree with him on every case, but his opinions will be well-reasoned and clearly written. Gorsuch's mentor, Justice Byron White, liked to say that each new justice makes for a new court, and I welcome the breath of fresh air, intellectual rigor, collegiality, and constitutional seriousness that Justice Gorsuch is bringing.

Still, the Court's ideological dynamic—with four liberals, four conservatives, and a "swing" vote—is in its last stages. Whenever Justice Anthony Kennedy retires—there was no telegraph from Salzburg this summer—and whenever Justice Ruth Bader Ginsburg departs (unless she outlasts Trump and a Democrat is president), the Court will move right, with Chief Justice John Roberts at its center. But if and when there's a vacancy, there'll be no incentive for the president to moderate his choice of nominee. By filibustering the anodyne Gorsuch, the Democrats destroyed their leverage over the next nominee. It's not at all clear that "moderate" or "institutionalist" Republican senators like Susan Collins, Lisa Murkowski, or Lindsey Graham would've gone along with a "nuclear option" to replace Justice

Kennedy or Ginsburg with a nominee more controversial than Gor-such, but now they won't face that dilemma.

Moving to the statistics, the 2016–2017 term set a dubious record for low output—only 62 cases decided after argument—and approached the record-level unanimity from three years ago, when two-thirds of the cases produced no dissents and only 14 percent were split 5-4. Forty-one of the 69 cases decided on the merits (59 percent) ended up with unanimous rulings.[1] The previous term it was 48 percent, and the preceding five terms registered 41, 66, 49, 45, and 46, respectively (so you see the anomaly that was October Term 2013, which papered over real doctrinal differences). Six more cases were decided by 8-1 or 7-1 margins, which brings us to nearly 70 percent of the docket. Some of this can be attributed to Chief Justice Roberts's working hard to facilitate narrow rulings and thus avoid 4-4 splits, but this term (unlike the previous one), a diminished docket filled with fewer controversial cases is what really drove the Court to speak with more of one voice.

The term produced three actual 5-4 decisions, though it's fair to count four cases that went 5-3 as "5-4" for comparison with previous years. These included a couple of death-penalty cases, as well as the big property-rights ruling in *Murr v. Wisconsin*, but the overall rate (10 percent of the total) is one of the lowest in modern history. Only the previous term's five-percent rate of 5-4 splits was lower—but then when you add in the four 4-4s (in which Scalia would've broken the tie), this term is comparable.

The decrease in sharp splits naturally resulted in fewer dissenting opinions, 32, whereas in the previous term there were 50 (the yearly average going back to 2005–2006 is 52). Not surprisingly, the total number of all opinions (majority, concurring, and dissenting) was also low—139, down from 162 last term and far lower than the 12-year average of 172—and the average of 2.0 opinions per case was

---

[1] The total includes seven summary reversals (without oral argument), four of which were unanimous. It does not include two cases that were set for re-argument, presumably because they were split 4-4 and can now get Justice Gorsuch's tie-breaking vote. All statistics taken from Kedar Bhatia, Final Stat Pack for October Term 2016 and Key Takeaways, SCOTUSblog, June 28, 2017, http://www.scotusblog.com/2017/06/final-stat-pack-october-term-2016-key-takeaways. For detailed data from previous terms, see Statpack Archive, SCOTUSblog, http://www.scotusblog.com/reference/stat-pack.

similarly low. Justice Thomas per usual wrote the most opinions (31, including nine dissents), followed far behind by Justices Samuel Alito (18), Stephen Breyer (17), and Ginsburg (17). Justice Alito produced the most opinion pages (217), however, followed by Justices Thomas (189) and Breyer (180). This was all a far cry from the previous term, when Justice Thomas produced 341 opinion pages.

The Court reversed or vacated 56 lower-court opinions—79 percent of the 71 total, including the separate cases that were consolidated for argument—which is higher than last term and the last several recent years. Of the lower courts with significant numbers of cases under review, the U.S. Court of Appeals for the Ninth Circuit attained a 1-7 record (88 percent reversal), maintaining its traditional crown as the most-reversed court, followed by the Sixth and Federal Circuits (both 1-6, 86 percent reversal). State courts also fared poorly, attaining a 3-14 record (82 percent reversal). But really, whatever court you're appealing from, it's safe to say that getting the Supreme Court to take your case is almost the entire battle.

Less notable than some of the quirks described above is *which* justices were in the majority. Justice Kennedy kept his near-annual crown by being on the winning side in 69 of 71 cases (97 percent!) and 28 of the 30 divided cases (93 percent). Chief Justice Roberts regained his typical second place (93 percent) after having dropped to fourth last year, behind Justices Elena Kagan (now 93 percent) and Breyer (now 90 percent). Justice Thomas brought up the rear (82 percent and just 57 percent of divided cases).

Justice Kennedy also maintained his typical lead in 5-4 cases. Even though there were only seven of those, Kennedy was the only justice on the winning side of six. He was with the "liberals" in four of them and with the "conservatives" in the other two. In the remaining decision, in the racial gerrymandering case of *Cooper v. Harris*, Justice Thomas joined the "liberals" in a heterodox split (and without agreeing on the reasoning).

Thomas had enjoyed a long run of success in 5-4 cases—he was second to Kennedy in October Terms 2010–2013—but this year was ahead only of the chief justice and Justice Alito. Not surprisingly, Thomas was also the justice most likely to dissent (18 percent of all cases and 43 percent of divided cases). He also maintained his status as the leading "lone dissenter"—since 2005–2006 he's averaged 2.2 solo dissents per term, more than double his closest colleague—writing two such dissents, as did Justice Ginsburg. Justices Breyer and Sotomayor each wrote one. Chief Justice Roberts and Justice Kagan have still *never* written one of those during their entire tenures (12 and 7 terms, respectively). And neither yet has Justice Gorsuch, but he's still gotten off to a flying start on his writing. Setting aside his single opinion for the Court, in June alone he wrote more separate opinions than Justice Kagan did in her first two terms.[2]

More news comes from judicial-agreement rates. Two terms ago, the top six pairs of justices most likely to agree, at least in part, were all from the "liberal bloc." The three that tied for first all involved Justice Breyer—perhaps an unlikely "Mr. Congeniality." This term there seems to be no rhyme or reason to the top pairings, but number one is amazing: Justices Thomas and Gorsuch agreed completely *in every single case* (17 of them). They were followed by Justices Alito and Gorsuch at 94 percent (16 of 17 cases), followed by Justices Ginsburg and Sotomayor (93 percent), Breyer and Kagan (93 percent), and then Thomas/Alito, Roberts/Kennedy, Roberts/Alito, and Sotomayor/Kagan in a virtual tie at 91 percent. The rest of the pairings were below 90 percent. Justices Sotomayor and Gorsuch voted together less than anyone else (in 10 of 17 cases, or 59 percent). The next three lowest pairs all involve Justice Gorsuch, with Justices Ginsburg, Breyer, and Kagan, respectively (each at 65 percent). The least-agreeable pair in the non-Gorsuch division consisted of Justices Thomas and Ginsburg (65 percent).

My final statistics are more whimsical, relating to the number of questions asked at oral argument. Without Justice Scalia on the bench as the Supreme Court's most frequent interlocutor, it fell on others to pick up the slack. Justice Breyer asked more than 20 questions per argument and was among the top three questioners two-thirds of the time, more than all his colleagues except Justice Sotomayor (73 percent). Sotomayor, who had been just behind Scalia the last few terms, was about a question per argument behind Breyer. Justice Gorsuch was respectably in the middle of the pack, with 14 questions per argument—though he did beat Sotomayor's short-lived record for most questions asked during his first argument. Justice Ginsburg again asked the first question most often (in 30 percent of cases),

[2] See Adam Liptak, Confident and Assertive, a New Justice in a Hurry, N.Y. Times, July 4, 2017, at A13.

followed by Justices Sotomayor and Kennedy (22 percent). Justice Thomas, who some thought might fill in for his departed friend, resumed his silent ways.

Moving closer to home, Cato filed amicus briefs in 13 merits cases on issues ranging from the separation of powers to free speech (both commercial and disparaging) and property rights. Improving on a 4-4 performance in an unusual previous term—when we still beat the government handily—Cato achieved a 9-4 showing, besting the combined Obama-Trump effort of 8-12. Cato also effectively drew votes from across the judicial spectrum, winning 10 votes from each of Chief Justice Roberts and Justice Kagan, 9 votes from Justice Breyer, and 8 votes each from Justices Kennedy, Alito, and Ginsburg.

Donald Trump's inauguration also marked the official end of the Obama era at the Supreme Court. A pair of unanimous losses brought the administration's total to 48, more than a quarter of all cases it argued and approximately 50 percent higher than both the Bush and Clinton teams. President Obama's total winning percentage of under 47 percent was also significantly lower than both of his predecessors, who finished at 60 and 63 percent respectively. Of course, the Trump administration is off to an even less auspicious start, with a 1-9 record and five unanimous losses in just half a term. (The apportionment of cases on either side of the inauguration may be somewhat artificial, given that most or all of these relatively low-profile Supreme Court arguments were handled by career lawyers, not political appointees, and the government's position didn't change with the change of administration.)

The reason President Obama did so poorly is because he saw no limits on federal—especially prosecutorial—power and accorded himself the ability to enact his legislative agenda when Congress refused to do so. If President Trump wants to improve the government's legal record, I humbly suggest that his lawyers follow Cato's lead, advocating positions (and advising executive actions) that are grounded in law and that reinforce the Constitution's role in securing and protecting liberty.

Here I should make one final note about the Gorsuch nomination-announcement ceremony. The then-judge mentioned two figures who had occupied the seat he now fills: Justice Scalia, of course, but also Justice Robert Jackson. Jackson was one of the best writers the Court has ever seen, also served as attorney general and Nuremberg prosecutor, and was the last justice appointed who didn't graduate from law school. He's famous especially for two opinions: (1) the 1952 *Steel Seizures Case*, in which the Court rejected President Truman's attempt to nationalize the steel industry (where Jackson's concurrence became the legal standard for evaluating executive actions); and (2) *Korematsu v. United States* (1944), in which the Court allowed the war-time internment of Japanese Americans (Jackson dissented). It's no coincidence that the silver-haired nominee name-checked Jackson, and that should hearten those dismayed by a politics gone off the rails. When push comes to shove, the elegant Justice Gorsuch will help preserve our republic.

Turning to the *Review*, the volume begins as always with the previous year's B. Kenneth Simon Lecture in Constitutional Thought, which in 2016 was delivered by Justice Clint Bolick of the Arizona Supreme Court. Before his appointment to the bench, Bolick headed up the Goldwater Institute's litigation program—and earlier, he had co-founded the Institute for Justice—so it's no surprise that the subject of his remarks was the use of *state* constitutions to protect liberty. He explains that "even as the national constitution moved to the fore . . . many essential liberties were protected by state constitutions or not at all." Economic liberties, such as the right to earn an honest living, enjoy far better explicit coverage in many state charters than in our national one. Ironically, the "earliest clarion call for freedom advocates to repair to state constitutions came not from the right but the left," from Justice William Brennan in the late 1970s and early 1980s. Justice Bolick's engaging and pithy lecture blends theory and practice—with examples drawn from cases he himself handled—and concludes appropriately with a discussion on the role of judges in enforcing those long-neglected state-constitutional provisions.

Then we move to the 2016–17 term, starting with what is undoubtedly the most colorful case, *Matal v. Tam*. This is the case of the Asian-American electric-rock band that was denied trademark registration of their name, The Slants, because it "disparaged" Asian-Americans. The rockers' explanation that they were just trying to "take back" the slur went nowhere with the Patent and Trademark Office, so of course several years of litigation ensued before they were vindicated. University of Florida professor Clay Calvert—who was part of Cato's satirical brief on behalf of "a basket of deplorable people and organizations"—provides a thorough examination of the issues involved.

Tam "vindicates and reaffirms key First Amendment principles regarding both offensive expression and viewpoint discrimination," he writes. The fate of the Washington Redskins' trademarks also hung in the balance, so the team filed a brief with an 18-page appendix of registered marks that are far more offensive than "The Slants."

Stanford Law School's David Goldberg and his recently graduated former student Emily Zhang contribute an engaging piece on a case they worked on together through Stanford's Supreme Court clinic. Goldberg himself argued *Packingham v. North Carolina*, in which a unanimous Court held that even sex offenders have First Amendment rights. In addition to explaining the case and how it treated the role of social media in society, the authors show that *Packingham* raises profound issues about the treatment of sex offenders more broadly. "All of which is to say that we likely have reached a new day," Goldberg and Zhang write. "Courts will expect to see more challenges to restrictions on registrants that marshal the true facts and then ask judges to decide under equal-protection-infused understandings of state constitutions and the Ex Post Facto, Due Process, and other clauses."

We then move to an article on the term's big religious-liberty case, *Trinity Lutheran v. Comer*, authored by Notre Dame professor Rick Garnett and law student Jackson Blais. This was supposed to be a politically fraught culture-war case, so much so that, even though it was granted in January 2016, it wasn't argued until April 2017— presumably on the assumption that a ninth justice would be needed to break the tie. As it turned out, the Court ruled 7-2 in the church's favor, finding it problematic that Missouri had denied access to a playground-resurfacing subsidy solely because of religious status. "By taking seriously the fact that 'Trinity Lutheran is a member of the community too,'" Garnett and Blais conclude, "the justices appropriately pushed back against the notions that church-state separation precludes cooperation and that maintaining a secular government requires what Father Richard John Neuhaus called a 'naked public square.'"

Following Rick Garnett is his wife! Nicole Stelle Garnett is also a law professor at Notre Dame and serves on our editorial board. She writes on *Murr v. Wisconsin*, which, like *Trinity Lutheran*, was granted before Justice Scalia's death but argued more than a year later. *Murr* did, however, break down on conventional ideological lines, with

Justice Kennedy joining the liberal bloc to rule against property own-ers in this dispute over the regulatory burdens imposed on a choice piece of land. The "regulatory takings" doctrine is a thorny one. "On the one hand, the Court has long insisted that state laws define the contours of property rights," Garnett writes. "On the other, it also has admonished that state laws for other than traditional health and safety reasons will be treated as takings for which the regulated property owners are entitled to compensation." But apparently not when a nebulous multifactor balancing test is applied on the shores of St. Croix River.

Next we have young legal scholar Tommy Berry, who is now with the Pacific Legal Foundation but wrote his essay while a Cato legal associate. Berry covers the most important case of the term that no-body's heard about, *NLRB v. S.W. General*. Here the Supreme Court struggled to interpret the Federal Vacancies Reform Act, which sets the rules concerning who can serve as an acting official, for how long, and under what authority. At a time when political battles emerge over even the most obscure Senate-confirmed positions, understand-ing the FVRA's dictates has never been more important. Indeed, this obscure statute is the reason why Noel Francisco stopped serving as acting solicitor general the moment he was nominated to fill that position permanently. As Berry puts it, in *S.W. General*, "the Supreme Court has indisputably reined in the power of the president to by-pass the Senate in appointing acting officers."

From an obscure but significant case we turn to a high-profile case that resulted in an unsatisfying punt. *Salman v. United States* was supposed to simplify the complicated and convoluted jurisprudence surrounding insider trading, but all it succeeded in doing was to further muddy the waters. My colleague Thaya Brook Knight, as-sociate director of financial regulation studies at Cato, breaks down the three theories of insider-trading criminality before unpacking *Salman*. Ultimately, the continued lack of a unified theory of who's been harmed when traders benefit from inside information makes insider-trading law unworkable. "The core problem with devising good insider-trading law," she offers, "is that the central function of insider trading—introducing material information to the market—is good." The Court here clarified a small issue—whether an insider could gift information to curry favor—but left unexplained *why* such trading is illegal.

Then we have an essay by David Post, law professor emeritus at Temple University and a Cato adjunct scholar. He writes on *Nelson v. Colorado*, a case in which the Court again slapped down an outlier state statute. Here, Colorado required people who had been wrongly convicted to pursue a new legal claim under the state Exoneration Act to recover money paid as punishment, restitution, and other fees. Being ultimately found not guilty wasn't enough; you had to affirmatively prove your innocence to recover your funds. "It is entirely understandable that Colorado would want to restrict the award of special compensation to those who can show that they were actually innocent of the crimes charged, not merely 'legally innocent,'" Post explains, but surely recovering your own property is a different situation. This may seem "in some ways a very small case," but it's important for protecting basic due process and the presumption of innocence.

Our final contribution regarding the past term comes from Mark Chenoweth, a Washington lawyer who's served in all three branches of government, on a dispute over whether a particular law had anything to do with the First Amendment. Specifically, is telling merchants how they can advertise different prices for paying cash rather than credit "economic regulation" (to which courts are alas deferential) or a speech restriction (which would subject the law to heightened judicial scrutiny)? Readers of this publication are no doubt aware that credit-card companies charge businesses a small percentage of each card transaction. Most retailers pass along most of that cost to consumers—so cash-payers subsidize their plastic-wielding brethren—but some have two sets of prices. New York, where *Expressions Hair Design v. Schneiderman* originates, is one of 10 states that allow "discounts" for cash but not "surcharges" for credit. Of such semantics are constitutional cases made!

The volume concludes with a look ahead to October Term 2017 by Chris Landau, the head of appellate litigation at Kirkland & Ellis, and his colleague Sopan Joshi, who was one of Justice Scalia's last clerks. As of this writing, before the term starts, the Court has 31 cases on its docket—one other case was dismissed over the summer after the parties in interest changed—a bit low given recent history but certainly above where we were at this point last term. And this term will be anything but a snooze. Here are some of the issues: partisan gerrymandering (*Gill v. Whitford*), the "travel ban" executive order (*Trump v. International Refugee Assistance Project*), whether bakers can be forced to make wedding cakes for same-sex couples (*Masterpiece Cakeshop v. Colorado Civil Rights Commission*), warrantless searches of cellphone-location data (*Carpenter v. United States*), and sports betting in New Jersey (*Christie v. NCAA*). There's something for everyone, really, and that's before the Court takes up (again) the question of compelled "agency fees" assessed against union nonmembers in the public sector—the previous iteration of which fizzled 4-4 when Justice Scalia died—and the structural challenges to the Consumer Finance Protection Board and administrative law judges at the Securities and Exchange Commission. "These are unconventional times," Landau and Joshi conclude, "and the Supreme Court may be headed for an unconventional term."

* * *

This is the 10th volume of the *Cato Supreme Court Review* I've edited, and the third with Trevor Burrus as managing editor. Trevor has been a huge help over the years with both the *Review* and our amicus brief program, so I'm delighted to give credit where it's due. I'm also most thankful to our authors, without whom there would literally be nothing to edit or read. We ask leading legal scholars and practitioners to produce thoughtful, insightful, readable commentary of serious length on short deadlines, so I'm grateful that so many agree to my unreasonable demands every year.

My gratitude goes also to my colleagues Bob Levy and Walter Olson, who provide valuable counsel and editing in legal areas less familiar to me. My new colleague (and old friend) Clark Neily has stepped in to lead Cato's criminal-justice efforts; he edited one article in this volume and I look forward to working with him more in future. Our research assistant, Anthony Gruzdis, managed to avoid the sophomore slump last year and is an MVP not only on Cato's softball team, but here too. Anthony kept track of legal associates Tommy Berry, Meggan DeWitt, Frank Garrison, Matt Larosiere, David McDonald, and Devin Watkins—we welcomed a new class midway through the production process—and interns Jack Brown, Patrick Moran, and Matthew Robinson, who in turn performed many thankless tasks without complaint. Neither the *Review* nor our Constitution Day symposium would be possible without them.

Finally, thanks to Roger Pilon, who founded Cato's Center for Constitutional Studies when fresh from doing good at the Reagan administration and established this journal a decade later. Roger has advanced constitutionalism and the rule of law for decades, with an integrity and intellectual honesty that even Cato's harshest critics acknowledge and respect. He's not just a great boss and mentor, but a good friend.

I reiterate our hope that this collection of essays will secure and advance the Madisonian first principles of our Constitution, giving renewed voice to the Framers' fervent wish that we have a government of laws and not of men. In so doing, we hope also to do justice to a rich legal tradition in which judges, politicians, and ordinary citizens alike understand that the Constitution reflects and protects the natural rights of life, liberty, and property, and serves as a bulwark against the abuse of government power. In these heady times when the people feel betrayed by the elites—legal, political, corporate, and every other kind—it's more important than ever to remember our proud roots in the Enlightenment tradition.

We hope that you enjoy this 16th volume of the *Cato Supreme Court Review*.

State Constitutions: Freedom's Frontier

*Clint Bolick**

We gather today to celebrate the 229th anniversary of the signing of the most magnificent national freedom charter every created—appropriately enough in an institution dedicated to the eternal preservation of the Constitution and the principles on which it rests.

And yet, when we speak of *the* Constitution, no matter how much we properly revere it, we often overstate its intended importance in the American legal order. For in our federal system, we have not one but 51 constitutions. It is part of the masterpiece of federalism that each of us in the 50 states can look for the protection of our rights not to one constitution but two. Indeed, state constitutions were intended to be primary, not secondary. Early Americans looked mainly to their state constitutions to protect their rights. Only after the Fourteenth Amendment was ratified in 1868 could they look to the national constitution for protection against most state violations of their rights.

But even as the national constitution moved to the fore—particularly the rights protected in the Bill of Rights, plus equal protection and due process—many essential liberties were protected either by state constitutions or not at all. Freedom of enterprise, for instance, was left unprotected by the U.S. Supreme Court, even though many state courts applied their own constitutions to strike down excessive economic regulations.[1]

Yet today, state constitutions are relegated to an afterthought. Constitutional law classes rarely mention them. Litigators rarely invoke

*Justice, Arizona Supreme Court. This is a slightly revised version of the 15th annual B. Kenneth Simon Lecture in Constitutional Thought, delivered at the Cato Institute on September 15, 2016.

[1] See, e.g., Clint Bolick, Death Grip: Loosening the Law's Stranglehold Over Economic Liberty (2011) (discussing the failure to protect freedom of enterprise under the national constitution starting with *The Slaughter-House Cases*, 83 U.S. 36 (1873)).

them. State courts often interpret them as if they were mere append-ages of the national constitution.

Moreover, despite their professed commitment to federalism, many conservative and libertarian litigation groups focus almost exclusively on the national constitution, except when they have no other choice. That emphasis is profoundly unfortunate, for two reasons. First, it overlooks the vast untapped potential of state constitutions as bulwarks for freedom. Second, it concentrates resources in judicial terrain that may grow increasingly hostile to freedom in the years to come. So even as we pause to celebrate the remarkable resiliency of our nation's constitutional charter, so should we look anew to the state constitutions that were intended to provide the first line of defense against overreaching government.

I. The Advantages of State Constitutions

For freedom advocates, state constitutions provide significant advantages over their national counterpart. Indeed, if this talk had a subtitle, it would be "if only," as in, "if only the United States Constitution had so many of these features." Although the national constitution has many nifty qualities from a freedom perspective, many individual rights and constraints on government power in the U.S. Constitution have been winnowed by federal courts. And they pale in comparison to provisions for freedom available in state constitutions.

I call these superior features of state constitutions the Fabulous Five. Foremost among them is that all state constitutions provide protections of individual rights and constraints on government power that are completely unknown to the U.S. Constitution. I will discuss some of those provisions later on, but among those that are common to many state constitutions are explicit rights to privacy, debt limits, and prohibitions against gifts of public funds. For freedom advocates, exploring state constitutions is akin to being a kid in a candy store. And like the proverbial unseen tree falling silently, the freedom provisions of state constitutions are equally silent when they are unlitigated.

Second, many state freedom provisions that are similar to provisions in the U.S. Constitution are written more broadly. Even when such provisions are identical to those in the U.S. Constitution, state courts are free to interpret them differently than federal courts, but only in one direction: state courts may apply state constitutional provisions as more protective of freedom than their federal counterparts, but not less. I call this the freedom ratchet: the U.S. Constitution provides the floor beneath individual rights, while state constitutions can provide greater but not lesser protection.

Third, state courts have the final word on state constitutional interpretation. In other words, if you prevail on a state constitutional issue, the other side has no recourse to the U.S. Supreme Court, unless of course the state court interpretation violates the U.S. Constitution or valid federal laws. That is reason enough for freedom advocates to always consider filing constitutional cases in state courts and to always assert independent state constitutional grounds in addition to federal constitutional grounds when doing so.

Fourth, state constitutions often provide greater access to the courts than does the national constitution, at least as interpreted by the U.S. Supreme Court. For instance, many state constitutions do not contain "case or controversy" requirements. Perhaps most important, unlike federal courts, most state courts recognize taxpayer standing to challenge unconstitutional government spending.

Finally, state constitutions often are far more easily amended than the national constitution. If you've ever aspired to constitutional authorship, I suggest you look at amending state constitutions rather than attempt the Sisyphean task of amending the U.S. Constitution. Arizonans have added several freedom provisions to our Constitution in recent years, including a prohibition against racial preferences in government employment, education, and contracting; provisions protecting rights to healthcare autonomy and rights of terminally ill patients to use experimental drugs; and a provision authorizing the legislature or the people to forbid the use of state funds to implement federal laws or programs they believe exceed constitutional boundaries.

State constitutions, like the national constitution, were intended to protect individual rights and restrain government power. Their potential to do so is vast and largely unrealized, yet hardly unrealizable.

II. Learning from Justice Brennan

The earliest clarion call for freedom advocates to repair to state constitutions came not from the right but the left, in a pair of penetrating law review articles by U.S. Supreme Court Justice William

H. Brennan. Justice Brennan was not only a highly effective jurist but a brilliant legal strategist. By 1977, the Warren Court with Brennan as its chief architect had experienced a very successful run, fundamentally reshaping American jurisprudence in a wide array of areas, most notably the rights of criminal defendants. But Brennan correctly sensed that change was coming. With President Richard Nixon's appointment to the Court of so-called law-and-order strict constructionists, the jurisprudential tide was turning. Writing in the *Harvard Law Review*, Brennan declared that "[t]he legal revolution which has brought federal law to the fore must not be allowed to inhibit the independent protective force of state law—for without it, the full realization of our liberties cannot be guaranteed."[2] Where federal courts retreated from judicial frontiers, Brennan urged liberal advocates to turn instead to state courts.

They did, and with gusto. Only nine years later, when Brennan wrote his second article on the subject, he could report at least 250 state court decisions that had interpreted their state constitutional rights more broadly than their national counterparts.[3] Most of the decisions were in the realm of criminal procedure, but others encompassed free-speech guarantees and educational equity. In this second article, Brennan's call to arms was even more urgent, and grounded in decidedly different rhetoric addressed to liberals and conservatives alike. He applauded state courts for "construing state constitutional counterparts of provisions of the Bill of Rights as guaranteeing citizens of their own states even more protection than the federal provisions, even those identically phrased."[4] Brennan declared, "Every believer in our concept of federalism, and I am a devout believer, must salute this development in our state courts."[5]

Fast forward 30 years to today. I submit that we conservatives and libertarians may find ourselves in a "Brennan moment." For the past quarter-century, since the confirmation of Justice Clarence Thomas in 1991, we have enjoyed a renaissance in the jurisprudence of original meaning. I know that many will argue about whether the glass is

---

[2] William J. Brennan Jr., "State Constitutions and the Protection of Individual Rights," 90 Harv. L. Rev. 489, 489 (1977).

[3] William J. Brennan Jr., "The Bill of Rights and the States: The Revival of State Constitutions as Guardians of Individual Rights," 61 N.Y.U. L. Rev. 535, 548 (1986).

[4] *Id.* at 495.

[5] *Id.* at 502.

half-empty or half-full, and all of us would quibble over doctrinal details. But none of us would trade the federal jurisprudence of today for that of 1991. We have made significant progress for liberty in areas as diverse as freedom of speech, religion, and association; federalism; private property rights; Second Amendment rights; racial classifications; school choice; and the limits of federal power under the Commerce Clause.

But prospects for future freedom gains are uncertain. Justice Antonin Scalia's intellect and his role as an ardent proponent of constitutional textualism will be sorely missed. Justice Anthony Kennedy's pivotal vote is increasingly uncertain, as evidenced by his 2016 decision to uphold racial preferences at the University of Texas, after decades of voting to strike such preferences down. Chief Justice John Roberts disappointed freedom advocates by voting to uphold Obamacare. And of course we cannot be certain of President Donald Trump's commitment to appoint justices and judges dedicated to the rule of law.[6]

So the time has come for freedom advocates to devote greater attention to state constitutions. Some of the issues on which we have experienced great success in the federal courts cannot, of course, be equally advanced in state courts. But many, such as freedom of speech and religion, private property rights, and equal protection can be. And as I noted earlier, largely unexplored state constitutional frontiers abound in other areas, including economic liberty and taxpayer protections. Brennan's epiphany about the independent vitality of state constitutions is as relevant and resonant for today's freedom advocates as it was nearly four decades ago.

III. My Own Experience and Beyond

My own epiphany about state constitutions occurred early in my career. Like most lawyers, I never took a course in state constitutional law and hadn't a clue what treasures those mysterious documents contained. But I was about to be schooled on them in what was to be the most important case of my young career.

I went to law school in large part to advance educational freedom, especially through school vouchers, and was determined to defend voucher programs against inevitable legal challenges

---

[6] But the appointment of Justice Neil Gorsuch is a promising start!

by those invested in the status quo. Trouble was, there were no voucher programs to defend.

That changed in 1990 with the enactment of the Milwaukee Parental Choice Program. Initially it was tiny, limited to one percent of the school district's students who could use a fraction of their state education funds to attend nonsectarian private schools. Still, we knew a legal challenge was imminent. But what would be the grounds for attack? For years we had prepared for a challenge under the First Amendment's Establishment Clause, but the program excluded religious schools. So the challengers had to look not to the U.S. Constitution but to the Wisconsin Constitution.

There they found three causes of action: the educational-uniformity clause, the so-called public purpose doctrine, and the "private or local bill" clause, which the challengers asserted the program violated because it was passed as part of the state budget rather than as a stand-alone bill. I had never heard of any of these provisions, and I had all of a couple of weeks to fathom and argue them.

For the next two years, we battled over those provisions, winning in the trial court, losing in the court of appeals. The private or local bill clause, in particular, became the bane of my existence. Ultimately, in 1992, we prevailed in the Wisconsin Supreme Court by the resounding vote of 4-3,[7] which marked the start of a vibrant national movement to expand precious educational opportunities for children who desperately needed them.

In the midst of that grueling struggle, an odd thing happened: I fell in love with my *bête noire*, the private or local bill clause. Once I allowed myself to get past my adversarial disdain and see it in its natural splendor, I found the stuff of which libertarian dreams are made, a constitutional provision aimed at one of the most odious yet ubiquitous legislative practices: logrolling. Properly applied, the local or private bill clause, contained in numerous state constitutions, requires narrow-interest bills to stand on their own and be voted on separately, in the light of day. No more bridges to nowhere. No more larded up appropriations bills. No more earmarks. If only the U.S. Constitution contained such a provision! Having grasped the potential of the private or local bill clause, I made a mental vow

---

[7] Davis v. Grover, 480 N.W.2d 460 (Wis. 1992).

to one day wield it to good effect in litigation—a promise my colleagues eventually kept.

But that was not for many years. A far more pressing issue emerged requiring recourse to state constitutional protections, with results that illustrate perhaps better than any other the importance and potential for state constitutional guarantees. That issue was eminent domain. Under the guise of economic development, local governments around the country were using eminent domain in reverse-Robin Hood fashion, taking property from less well-connected owners and giving it often to developers tight with local officials.

The Fifth Amendment, of course, forbids that practice, limiting eminent domain to "public use." But a body of thought has emerged from the Supreme Court holding that the Constitution is self-amending, and that the justices' role is to discover and announce when that happens. Sure enough, the Court discovered that the Fifth Amendment's "public use" limitation had transmuted into the far more forgiving "public benefit." So when my colleagues challenged the taking of Suzette Kelo's little pink house in New London, Connecticut, under the Fifth Amendment, they faced a decidedly uphill task. And we all know the outcome: the neighborhood was bulldozed, the supposed public benefit never materialized, and we all suffered an erosion of our precious liberties.[8]

But at the same time the fight against eminent domain was being fought and lost in federal courts, my former colleagues and I were waging a similar battle in Arizona state courts on behalf of Randy Bailey, who owned Bailey's Brake Service in Mesa. Randy inherited the business from his dad and wanted to pass it along to his son. But the city had other ideas: it wanted to take Randy's shop and several homes so that the owner of a hardware store could expand his business. Under the *Kelo* decision, Randy surely would have come away empty-handed in federal court. But in state court, Randy had a powerful weapon: Article II, § 17 of the Arizona Constitution.

That provision states, "Private property shall not be taken for private use." Not only that, but it states, "Whenever an attempt is made to take private property for a use alleged to be public, the question whether the contemplated use be really public shall be a judicial question, and determined as such without regard to any legislative assertion that

---

[8] Kelo v. City of New London, 545 U.S. 469 (2005).

the use is public." Although the courts previously had not vigorously applied that standard, in Randy's case they did.[9] So while Suzette and her neighbors tragically lost their homes, you can still buy brakes at Bailey's Brake Service at Country Club and Main in Mesa.

That decision, in my view, illustrates what federalism and state constitutionalism are all about. And it's the kind of decision that can be contagious; indeed, several other state courts have applied their eminent domain provisions more broadly than the U.S. Supreme Court to protect private property rights.[10]

In other areas too, state court decisions have expanded the boundaries for freedom. In Arizona, my former colleagues and I dusted off the Gift Clause of the state constitution, which forbids gifts of public funds to private individuals, corporations, or associations by subsidy or otherwise.[11] At the time, Arizona cities were competing for sales tax revenues by subsidizing retail shopping centers. A Chicago developer landed a nearly $100 million taxpayer subsidy to construct a Phoenix mall that was supposed to be so grandiose that we dubbed it the "Taj Mah-Mall." In its 2010 decision in *Turken v. Gordon*, the Arizona Supreme Court ruled that payments to private companies are unconstitutional unless supported by tangible, enforceable consideration, thus bringing the costly subsidy wars to an end.[12] Dozens of other states have gift clauses in their constitutions, which are rarely deployed despite a plethora of state and local subsidies.

A recent decision by the Texas Supreme Court has special meaning for me because it involves a right to which I devoted much of my

---

[9] Bailey v. Myers, 76 P.3d 898 (Ariz. App. 2003).

[10] See, e.g., Mt. Valley Pipeline, LLC v. McCurdy, 793 S.E.2d 850 (W. Va. 2016) (holding that a natural gas pipeline did not constitute a public use because defendant was "unable to identify even a single West Virginia consumer, or a West Virginia natural gas producer who is not affiliated with [defendant], who [would] benefit"); Kirby v. N.C. DOT, 786 S.E.2d 919 (N.C. 2016) (holding that the state's designation of private property as part of a highway corridor, heavily restricting owners' right to develop, constituted a taking requiring just compensation); City of Norwood v. Horney, 853 N.E.2d 1115 (Ohio 2006) (In the first state supreme court case addressing the use of eminent domain for private development after *Kelo*, the court unanimously held that economic benefit to the government and community alone was not enough to constitute public use, that eminent-domain cases require heightened scrutiny, and that the use of the term "deteriorating area" as a taking standard was void for vagueness).

[11] Ariz. Const. Art. IX, § 7.

[12] 224 P.3d 158 (Ariz. 2010).

litigating career, but a right that the federal courts have almost completely buried: freedom of enterprise. Even though economic liberty was meant to be a foundational freedom protected by the Fourteenth Amendment's Privileges or Immunities Clause, federal courts have largely abdicated their responsibility to protect it, no matter how sweeping, destructive, or protectionist the regulation.[13]

In *Patel v. Texas Department of Licensing and Regulation*, the Court independently interpreted the state constitution to require greater justification for professional licensing, striking down regulations on eyebrow threading.[14] In a concurring opinion, Justice Don Willett articulated perfectly the necessity of state constitutionalism:

> Today's case arises under the Texas Constitution, over which we have final interpretive authority, and nothing in its 60,000-plus words requires judges to turn a blind eye to transparent rent-seeking that bends government power to private gain, thus robbing people of their innate right—antecedent to government—to earn an honest living. Indeed, even if the Texas Due Course of Law Clause mirrored perfectly the federal Due Process Clause, that in no way binds Texas courts to cut-and-paste federal rational-basis jurisprudence that long post-dates enactment of our own constitutional provision, one more inclined to freedom.[15]

Those stirring words are both an exposition of the boundless realm of the possible as well as a call to action.

What then are the frontiers for freedom advocacy under state constitutions? They depend, of course, on the particulars of specific state constitutions and the opportunities they afford to protect freedom. They also depend on how much erosion our rights sustain under the federal constitution, and whether state constitutions can fill the void. The possibilities run the gamut from rights protections—in such areas as free speech, religious liberty, criminal procedure, privacy, freedom of association, private property rights, economic liberty, gun ownership, due process, and equal protection—to structural limits on government power, such as separation of powers, spending limits, gift clauses, and anti-monopoly provisions.

---

[13] See, e.g., Clint Bolick, Death Grip: Loosening the Law's Stranglehold Over Economic Liberty (2011).

[14] 469 S.W.3d 69 (Tex. 2015).

[15] *Id.* at 98.

IV. The Judge's Role

Thus far I have emphasized the role of freedom advocates in bringing state constitutional actions. I will conclude by briefly discussing the role of judges in that context, a subject to which I hope to return in greater depth soon.

Judges are (or ought to be) bound by the rule of law. Even in my short time on the Arizona Supreme Court, I can attest that taking the rule of law seriously means departing frequently from personal policy preferences. We are not policymakers. That role is played by the political branches, within their constitutional boundaries.

But as state court judges, we swear oaths to two constitutions, and we ought to take each seriously. When a state constitutional issue is presented to us, that oath, in my view, requires us to interpret what the words of our state constitution say and mean—not what the federal courts have interpreted national constitutional provisions to mean. Unless our state constitutional provisions derive from the national constitution, what similar provisions of the national constitution mean is largely irrelevant to our task, and federal court interpretations even more so. In particular, while federal courts have determined that provisions of the U.S. Constitution have "evolved"—that is, have amended themselves to permit greater government power or protect fewer individual rights—there is no reason to assume that state constitutional provisions have experienced similar metamorphosis.

Each state has developed its organic law to reflect its own values and aspirations. The meaning of that law often is evident from its text and its history, but rarely from reference to federal jurisprudence. That is what is meant by independent interpretation of state law. As state judges, we are oath-bound to determine what our state constitutions mean. Quite often, they mean to protect freedom.

As a justice, I draw inspiration, and take my marching orders, from Article II, Section 1 of our Arizona Constitution: "A frequent recurrence to fundamental principles is essential to the security of individual rights and the perpetuity of free government." If we take those words seriously, and strive to give them their intended meaning, we will, despite all odds, leave to our children and grandchildren a nation more free than the one we inherited.

Beyond Trademarks and Offense: *Tam* and the Justices' Evolution on Free Speech

*Clay Calvert**

When the Supreme Court steps up to the plate in a case like *Matal v. Tam* involving free-speech protection of offensive expression, the justices have options about just how hard to swing the judicial bat.[1] First Amendment advocates, of course, hope they'll swing for the fences and crush free-expression grand slams. *Cohen v. California*, protecting the display of an offensive jacket in a courthouse corridor and propelled by memorable lines like "one man's vulgarity is another's lyric," was one such home run, soaring over a dissent and past the outfield wall of censorship.[2] Other times, the Court merely drops a bunt and barely advances the First Amendment score, if at all.

In *Tam*, the Supreme Court threw out the "disparagement clause" of the Lanham Act, the federal trademark law, because trademarks are private speech and thus regulating them based on government determinations of offensiveness violates the First Amendment. The solid outcome here—a virtual triple, as described later—contrasts with the narrow, incremental results in some other recent First Amendment cases that reached the Court.

---

* Professor & Joseph L. Brechner Eminent Scholar in Mass Communication and Director of the Marion B. Brechner First Amendment Project at the University of Florida. Also part of the Brief of Amici Curiae Cato Institute and a Basket of Deplorable People and Orgs. in Support of Petitioner, Lee v. Tam, No. 15-1293. Note that PTO Director Michelle Lee resigned shortly before the case was decided, with Joseph Matal now serving as acting director, so *Lee v. Tam* became *Matal v. Tam*.

[1] Admittedly, a baseball analogy featuring the Court batting strikes out against Chief Justice John Roberts's testimony during his confirmation hearings that "it's my job to call balls and strikes, and not to pitch or bat." Todd S. Purdum & Robin Toner, Roberts Pledges He'll Hear Cases with 'Open Mind,' N.Y. Times, Sept. 13, 2015, at A1.

[2] 403 U.S. 15, 25 (1971).

Consider *Federal Communications Commission v. Fox Television Stations*, a case regarding fleeting expletives and momentary nudity on broadcast television.[3] The Supreme Court had an opportunity to score two runs for the First Amendment—to abolish the FCC's regulatory authority over broadcast indecency (thereby reversing the aging 1978 *Pacifica* decision arising from the George Carlin filthy-words case[4]) and to strike down its definition of indecency as unconstitutionally vague. But the Court waved off both pitches.

Instead, it resolved the case "on fair notice grounds under the Due Process Clause."[5] The Court determined that the FCC had impermissibly changed its indecency policy to target fleeting expletives and isolated sexual images without giving networks Fox and ABC proper notice of the switch. As for the free speech issue, the Court simply reminded the FCC—perhaps with an eyebrow arched—that the commission should feel "free to modify its current indecency policy in light of its determination of the public interest and applicable legal requirements."[6]

Did the FCC heed that suggestion? No. Although it put out a notice for public comment about its indecency policy shortly thereafter and said it would target only egregious indecency incidents,[7] it failed to take substantive action. Today, the FCC's indecency policy remains what it was when the Court decided *Fox Television Stations* five years ago. The First Amendment issues are left waiting for another day and another case, perhaps the product of Chief Justice John Roberts's general penchant for minimalism and avoidance.[8]

Or take—with more relevance, as it happens, for *Tam*—the Court's 2015 decision in *Walker v. Texas Division, Sons of Confederate Veterans*.[9]

---

[3] 567 U.S. 239 (2012).

[4] Federal Communications Commission v. Pacifica Foundation, 438 U.S. 726 (1978).

[5] Fox Television Stations, 567 U.S. at 258.

[6] *Id.* at 259.

[7] See Press Release, Federal Communications Commission, FCC Reduces Backlog of Broadcast Indecency Complaints by 70% (More Than One Million Complaints); Seeks Comment on Adopting Egregious Cases Policy (Apr. 1, 2013), https://apps.fcc.gov/edocs_public/attachmatch/DA-13-581A1.pdf.

[8] See generally Clay Calvert & Matthew D. Bunker, Fissures, Fractures & Doctrinal Drifts: Paying the Price in First Amendment Jurisprudence for a Half Decade of Avoidance, Minimalism & Partisanship, 24 Wm. & Mary Bill of Rts. J. 943, 957 (2016) (analyzing "how philosophies of minimalism and avoidance have detrimentally affected First Amendment doctrines since Justice Kagan joined the Roberts Court").

[9] 135 S. Ct. 2239 (2015).

The odious speech there consisted of a proposed specialty license plate bearing the Confederate battle flag. Its censor, in turn, was the Texas Department of Motor Vehicles Board, which rejected the plate because "many members of the general public find the design offensive."[10] Would the Court hit a First Amendment homer and declare this a seemingly easy case of viewpoint discrimination violating core free-speech principles?

No. Instead, the five-justice majority—a bloc of four liberal-leaning justices (Stephen Breyer, Ruth Bader Ginsburg, Sonia Sotomayor and Elena Kagan) joined by Clarence Thomas—completely whiffed. Falling back on something called the government-speech doctrine, the majority held that messages on specialty license plates are speech of the government, not the private groups—in *Walker*, the Sons of Confederate Veterans—that design and sponsor them. And when the government speaks, the First Amendment has little application; the government can say what it likes, delete messages it doesn't like, and engage in viewpoint discrimination. As Justice Breyer wrote for the majority, "government statements (and government actions and programs that take the form of speech) do not normally trigger the First Amendment rules designed to protect the marketplace of ideas."[11] Labeling a mode of expression "government speech" gives the government a free pass to discriminate against viewpoints it deems noxious.

Justice Samuel Alito, joined in dissent by Chief Justice Roberts and Justices Antonin Scalia and Anthony Kennedy, bristled at applying the government speech doctrine to Texas's specialty plates. Alito opined that the messages "proposed by private parties and placed on Texas specialty plates are private speech, not government speech. Texas cannot forbid private speech based on its viewpoint. That is what it did here."[12] For him, expanding the government-speech doctrine to cover specialty plates "establishes a precedent that threatens private speech that government finds displeasing."[13]

At best, *Walker* proved a fleeting, feel-good win for those who find Confederate-flag imagery racist. That's because the script flipped soon thereafter in North Carolina. The *Walker* majority's holding

---

[10] *Id.* at 2245.

[11] *Id.* at 2245–46.

[12] *Id.* at 2263 (Alito, J., dissenting).

[13] *Id.* at 2254.

that specialty plates are government speech sustained the Tar Heel State's offering a "Choose Life" specialty plate but denying a pro-choice alternative.[14] In the simplest of stereotypes, the political left used the government speech doctrine to thwart a Confederate flag license plate in Texas, while the political right later used it to stifle a pro-choice plate in North Carolina. It was political tit-for-tat. At worst, then, *Walker* gave government entities an elastic mechanism for sanctioning viewpoint discrimination and dodging First Amendment challenges.

Then along came *Matal v. Tam*. It brought back the arguments about government-assisted speech in a context that invited the Court to (1) roll back, or at least cabin and confine, *Walker*'s government-speech doctrine; or (2) revisit the issue of whether viewpoint discrimination (normally verboten) becomes acceptable in that setting.

The U.S. Patent and Trademark Office (PTO) has statutory power to reject registration for marks that "may disparage . . . persons, living or dead, institutions, beliefs, or national symbols, or bring them into contempt, or disrepute."[15] For example, the PTO used this power to rebuff the effort of an Oregon-based Asian-American band called The Slants to register its name as a mark, finding that the name, as a reference to slanted eyes, had been employed to disparage Asian-Americans. Slants frontman, Simon Tam, countered that the band was reappropriating the term, wresting away its power, sting, and stigma from hate mongers.

What is "reappropriation"? In academic parlance, it's "the process of taking possession of a slur previously used exclusively by dominant groups to reinforce a stigmatized group's lesser status."[16] The Slants explain their meaning more lyrically in "From the Heart," a tune about fighting the PTO on the aptly titled album *The Band Who Must Not Be Named*:

Sorry if we try too hard
To take some power back for ours.
The language of oppression

---

[14] ACLU of North Carolina v. Tennyson, 815 F.3d 183 (4th Cir. 2016).

[15] 15 U.S.C. § 1052(a) (2017).

[16] Adam D. Galinsky et al., The Reappropriation of Stigmatizing Labels: The Reciprocal Relationship between Power and Self-Labeling, 24 Psychol. Sci. 2020, 2020 (2013).

Will lose to education
Until the words can't hurt us again.

So sorry if you take offense,
But silence will not make amends.
The system's all wrong
And it won't be long
Before the kids are singing our song.[17]

In December 2015, the U.S. Court of Appeals for the Federal Circuit, sitting *en banc*, ruled in The Slants' favor and struck down the disparagement clause, holding that "the First Amendment forbids government regulators to deny registration because they find the speech likely to offend others."[18] The appellate court found not only that the clause was viewpoint-based and could not pass muster under the rigorous strict-scrutiny standard of review,[19] but also that it failed under the more relaxed intermediate-scrutiny test governing commercial speech. The government petitioned the Supreme Court to hear the case, and The Slants, despite the Federal Circuit ruling in their favor, did likewise. The band argued the "issue is undeniably important. The Court is very likely to address it in the near future, in another case if not in this one. Meanwhile, respondent Simon Tam waits in limbo. His trademark rights will not be secure until the Court resolves this issue once and for all."[20]

In September 2016, the Supreme Court agreed to hear what was then known as *Lee v. Tam*. It framed the issue simply as whether the disparagement clause "is facially invalid under the Free Speech Clause of the First Amendment."[21] With The Slants case on its docket, the Court

[17] The Slants, From the Heart, on The Band Who Must Not Be Named (In Music We Trust Records, 2017). Take a listen and look on YouTube at https://www.youtube.com/watch?v=pwfEgcRXJjM.

[18] In re Tam, 808 F.3d 1321, 1358 (Fed. Cir. 2015).

[19] Strict scrutiny requires the government to prove that it has a compelling interest to support a statute and that the statute is narrowly tailored to serve that interest. See Brown v. Entm't Merchs. Ass'n, 564 U.S. 786, 799 (2011).

[20] Brief for Respondent at 1, On Petition for a Writ of Certiorari to the United States Court of Appeals for the Federal Circuit, Lee v. Tam, No. 15-1293 (June 20, 2016).

[21] Question Presented, Matal v. Tam, No. 15-1293 (Sept. 29, 2016), https://www.supremecourt.gov/qp/15-01293qp.pdf.

denied a petition one week later in *Pro-Football, Inc. v. Blackhorse*. That case centered on the PTO's cancellation of six registered marks involving variations of the NFL football team name Washington Redskins as disparaging to Native Americans. The outcome of the Redskins' battle thus would hinge on the result in The Slants case.

Saving its *Tam* decision until the penultimate week of its term, the Court on June 19, 2017 delivered what would have amounted to a First Amendment home run if not for some unfortunate four-to-four fracturing among the justices on logic and reasoning regarding viewpoint discrimination. Call it a triple.

All eight justices (newbie Neil Gorsuch played no part) agreed on the pro-free-speech outcome—that the disparagement clause, as Justice Alito wrote in announcing the Court's judgment, "offends a bedrock First Amendment principle: Speech may not be banned on the ground that it expresses ideas that offend."[22] That's an extremely close paraphrase of the Court's reasoning nearly 30 years earlier protecting flag-burning as political speech.[23] It's also a clear winner for The Slants, the Redskins and other provocatively named groups seeking federal trademark registration like Dykes on Bikes,[24] as well as more generally for free-speech advocates everywhere. Indeed, shortly after the ruling, Simon Tam called it "a win for all marginalized groups. It can't be a win for free speech if some people benefit and others don't. The First Amendment protects speech even that we disagree with."[25]

---

[22] Matal v. Tam, 137 S. Ct. 1744, 1751 (2017).

[23] See Texas v. Johnson, 491 U.S. 397, 414 (1989) ("If there is a bedrock principle underlying the First Amendment, it is that the government may not prohibit the expression of an idea simply because society finds the idea itself offensive or disagreeable.").

[24] Like The Slants, the San Francisco Dykes on Bikes Women's Motorcycle Contingent had fought lengthy registration battles with the PTO, which contended that "dykes" disparages lesbians. Somewhat echoing The Slants argument regarding reappropriation, Dykes on Bikes filed a friend-of-the-court brief in *Tam* arguing that "[a] trademark allows Dykes on Bikes to identify as a group by using language that invokes the members' own identities. That ability to associate individual identity with group identity and communicate a message unique to that group is central to the First Amendment." Brief of Amicus Curiae San Francisco Dykes on Bikes Women's Motorcycle Contingent, Inc., Matal v. Tam, No. 15-1293, 2017 U.S. LEXIS 3872, at 10–11 (June 19, 2017).

[25] Joe Coscarelli, Why the Slants Took a Fight over Their Band Name to the Supreme Court, N.Y. Times, June 19, 2017, https://www.nytimes.com/2017/06/19/arts/music/slants-name-supreme-court-ruling.html.

Thus, the constitutional outcome in *Tam* is not groundbreaking. Rather, it is principles-affirming: there is no categorical carve-out from First Amendment protection for either offensive or hateful speech, and viewpoint discrimination—something Justice Kennedy took pains to reinforce in a concurrence—is anathema to the First Amendment unless the government is speaking.

A close read of the trio of opinions in *Tam* reveals, however, at least seven other points that may affect future rulings in First Amendment disputes. Before addressing those items, a quick breakdown of the three opinions provides critical context:

1. Justice Alito wrote for a unanimous Court in some parts (most significantly, regarding government speech), for seven justices in another, and—critically—on behalf of only four justices (himself, Roberts, Thomas, and Breyer) in several sections;

2. Justice Kennedy agreed with the judgment but wrote a concurrence, joined by Justices Ginsburg, Sotomayor, and Kagan, centering on viewpoint discrimination and contending that a tighter focus on that concept would have eliminated the need for the other four justices to address other issues; and

3. Justice Thomas joined Alito's opinion in all but one rather non-crucial part and wrote separately to reiterate his prior position that commercial speech cases should be evaluated under strict, not intermediate, scrutiny.

As this breakdown suggests, the biggest rift in reasoning was between the Alito bloc on the one hand and the Kennedy bloc on the other. Although all eight justices agreed the law was viewpoint based, the former group delved into questions that the latter, by maintaining a crisper focus on viewpoint discrimination, would have jettisoned. Indeed, as argued later, Kennedy's concurrence provides a more clear, elegant articulation of when a statute is viewpoint based and, in turn, of the power of the doctrine against viewpoint discrimination to shut down other long-shot, statute-saving arguments.

Packingham v. North Carolina—another First Amendment free-speech decision issued the same day as *Tam*—displayed a nearly identical fracturing.[26] In *Packingham*, the Court struck down a state statute that banned registered sex offenders from using online social media services such as Facebook. Delivering the Court's opinion, Justice Kennedy once again was joined by Justices Ginsburg, Sotomayor, and Kagan, as well as Breyer. Similarly, Justice Alito was joined again by Roberts and Thomas, this time in a concurrence objecting to the Kennedy bloc's "unnecessary rhetoric" and "undisciplined dicta" about the importance of preserving the Internet and social media networks as venues for expression.

In brief, Kennedy and Alito each authored opinions in *Tam* and *Packingham* that agreed with a pro-free-speech result. Yet the Kennedy-authored opinions in both *Tam* (a concurrence) and *Packingham* (the Court's opinion) (1) were joined by all of the ostensibly liberal-leaning justices (save for Breyer in *Tam*), and (2) failed to gain traction with a three-justice bloc of ostensible conservatives (Alito, Roberts, and Thomas). Kennedy's penchant for grandiose statements about the importance of free speech—something predating *Tam* and *Packingham*[27]—may have driven a wedge between him and, as explained shortly below, the typically less free-speech friendly Alito.

The seven points—not necessarily in order of importance—from *Tam* that might affect future First Amendment speech cases in contexts beyond trademark law are these: (1) Justice Alito actually can pen an opinion protecting offensive expression; (2) Justice Breyer doesn't always go off into the balancing weeds of proportionality or denigrate fundamental First Amendment doctrines; (3) nary a justice

---

[26] 137 S. Ct. 1730 (2017).

[27] Kennedy often extols the value of free expression with rhetorical flourishes. See, e.g., Williams-Yulee v. Fla. Bar, 135 S. Ct. 1656, 1682 (2015) (Kennedy, J., dissenting) ("First Amendment protections are both personal and structural. Free speech begins with the right of each person to think and then to express his or her own ideas. Protecting this personal sphere of intellect and conscience, in turn, creates structural safeguards for many of the processes that define a free society."); United States v. Alvarez, 567 U.S. 709, 727 (2012) ("The remedy for speech that is false is speech that is true. This is the ordinary course in a free society. The response to the unreasoned is the rational; to the uninformed, the enlightened; to the straight-out lie, the simple truth."); Ashcroft v. Free Speech Coalition, 535 U.S. 234, 253 (2002) ("The right to think is the beginning of freedom, and speech must be protected from the government because speech is the beginning of thought."); Int'l Soc'y for Krishna Consciousness, Inc. v. Lee, 505 U.S. 672, 701 (1992) (Kennedy, J., concurring) ("The First Amendment is often inconvenient. But that is beside the point. Inconvenience does not absolve the government of its obligation to tolerate speech.").

fell to the pox of political correctness, even though the outcome of the Redskins case was resting in the balance and the floodgates were predicted to burst open with disparaging registered marks; (4) there was united pushback against the government-speech doctrine, stretching it beyond *Walker*; (5) the commercial-speech doctrine, premised on intermediate scrutiny review, someday may yet fall by the wayside; (6) while the whole Court agrees that viewpoint discrimination is wrong, justices conceptualize it differently and assign it differing degrees of importance; and (7) faith among the justices in the venerable marketplace-of-ideas theory remains remarkably strong in the digital age. Here's a more extended take on each item.

Alito Rides to the Defense of Offense

In *Snyder v. Phelps,* the Supreme Court came to the defense of the Westboro Baptist Church and ruled for its right to engage in anti-gay, anti-family, and anti-military speech near a funeral for a U.S. soldier killed in Iraq. Only one justice dissented: Samuel Alito. "Our profound national commitment to free and open debate is not a license for the vicious verbal assault that occurred in this case," he wrote, explaining why he would have ruled for the plaintiff's tort claims against Westboro.[28]

One year prior, in *United States v. Stevens,* the Court nullified as overbroad a federal law targeting so-called crush videos depicting the killing and mutilation of animals. There again, only one justice dissented: Samuel Alito. "The Court strikes down in its entirety a valuable statute . . . that was enacted not to suppress speech, but to prevent horrific acts of animal cruelty—in particular, the creation and commercial exploitation of 'crush videos,' a form of depraved entertainment that has no social value," Alito opined.[29]

Alito also authored a dissent—this one joined by Justices Scalia and Thomas—in *United States v. Alvarez*. The Court there applied the "most exacting scrutiny" to declare unconstitutional the Stolen Valor Act, which made it a federal crime to lie about having won a Congressional Medal of Honor. "The lies covered by the Stolen Valor Act have no intrinsic value and thus merit no First Amendment protection unless their prohibition would chill other expression that falls

[28] Snyder v. Phelps, 562 U.S. 443, 463 (2011) (Alito, J., dissenting).
[29] United States v. Stevens, 559 U.S. 460, 482 (2010) (Alito, J., dissenting).

within the Amendment's scope," Alito wrote.[30] Foreshadowing the Alito-versus-Kennedy opinions in *Tam* and *Packingham*, Alito's *Alvarez* dissent took aim at the Kennedy-authored plurality opinion.

I asserted several years ago that it seemed Alito was "trying to change . . . First Amendment jurisprudence when it comes to offensive speech that he perceives to be of low value . . . in order to meet his own subjective standards of decency, civility, and substantive importance of expression."[31] Or, as Professor Mary-Rose Papandrea more recently and succinctly put it, "Alito does not have a track record as a particularly speech-protective Justice."[32]

But in *Tam*, he proved quite capable of writing an opinion protecting offensive speech that won over, in various parts, a majority and plurality of his fellow justices. That's excellent news from a free-speech perspective, but does it mean that Alito has changed his First Amendment stripes?

That's highly doubtful. Alito's opinion in *Tam*, I suspect, was really about thwarting political correctness, even if the disparagement clause had been on the books since 1946, decades before "PC" became a term. This anti-PC motivation is evident when Alito derisively dubs the statute "a happy-talk clause" and when he attacks the government's argument that it "has an interest in preventing speech expressing ideas that offend." Quoting Oliver Wendell Holmes Jr., Alito retorts that "[s]peech that demeans on the basis of race, ethnicity, gender, religion, age, disability, or any other similar ground is hateful; but the proudest boast of our free speech jurisprudence is that we protect the freedom to express 'the thought that we hate.'"[33] Alito's defense of Confederate flags on specialty license plates in his *Walker* dissent similarly reflects an anti-political-correctness stance; he was defending the right to display a polysemic symbol vilified by the political left.

---

[30] United States v. Alvarez, 567 U.S. 709, 739 (2012) (Alito, J., dissenting).

[31] Clay Calvert, Justice Samuel A. Alito's Lonely War against Abhorrent, Low-Value Expression: A Malleable First Amendment Philosophy Privileging Subjective Notions of Morality and Merit, 40 Hofstra L. Rev. 115, 169 (2011).

[32] Mary-Rose Papandrea, Free Speech Foundations Symposium: The Government Brand, 110 Nw. U. L. Rev. 1195, 1197 (2016).

[33] Matal v. Tam, 137 S. Ct. 1744, 1764 (2017) (quoting United States v. Schwimmer, 279 U. S. 644, 655 (1929) (Holmes, J., dissenting).

For Alito, battling perceived political correctness in *Tam* and *Walker* is a far more important—and decidedly different—cause than safeguarding speech that (1) harms a grieving father—a private figure, no less—at his son's funeral (*Snyder*); (2) depicts helpless animals victimized by humans' sadistic sexual fetishes (*Stevens*); and (3) degrades the honor, as embodied by medals, of some of the bravest individuals who heroically fought enemy forces in the nation's wars (*Alvarez*). Those factual differences are probably pertinent for Alito in distinguishing *Tam* and *Walker* from *Snyder*, *Stevens*, and *Alvarez*. In brief, Alito's First Amendment stance in *Tam* may not cut across the free-speech playing field.

Breyer for Once Hews to Traditional Doctrinal Lines

In multiple free-speech cases such as *Alvarez* and *Reed v. Town of Gilbert*,[34] Justice Breyer demonstrates aversion to adhering to traditional doctrinal rules and labels while, instead, embracing a jurisprudence of proportionality. As a recent article puts it, Breyer "appears to distrust the Court's typical strict scrutiny framework for evaluating freedom of speech cases, including certain disputes where viewpoint discrimination is at issue. Frequently, he prefers employing a 'proportionality' balancing test for the vast majority of cases, refusing to place a heightened burden upon the statute at issue."[35] Professor Mark Tushnet contends that Breyer is engaged in a "project of partial de-doctrinalization."[36]

Breyer's 2015 concurrence in *Reed*, which struck down a content-based sign ordinance under strict scrutiny, is illustrative. Although agreeing with the result, Breyer rejected the "mechanical use of categories" like strict scrutiny and content discrimination.[37] In their place, he argued for "a more basic analysis, which . . . asks whether the regulation at issue works harm to First Amendment interests that is disproportionate in light of the relevant regulatory

[34] 135 S. Ct. 2218 (2015).

[35] Benjamin Pomerance, An Elastic Amendment: Justice Stephen G. Breyer's Fluid Conceptions of Freedom of Speech, 79 Alb. L. Rev. 403, 506 (2016).

[36] Mark Tushnet, Justice Breyer and the Partial De-Doctrinalization of Free Speech Law, 128 Harv. L. Rev. 508, 514 (2014).

[37] Reed, 135 S. Ct. at 2236 (Breyer, J., concurring).

objectives."[38] The term content discrimination, for Breyer, sometimes merits treatment merely "as *a rule of thumb*, finding it a helpful, but not determinative legal tool, in an appropriate case, to determine the strength of a justification."[39]

Such squishiness surfaced again in 2015 when Breyer concurred with a five-justice majority in *Williams-Yulee v. Florida Bar* that a rule banning judges from personally soliciting funds for their election campaigns survived strict scrutiny.[40] Referencing the traditional categories of constitutional review of strict scrutiny, intermediate scrutiny, and rational basis, Breyer wrote that he viewed the "Court's doctrine referring to tiers of scrutiny as *guidelines* informing our approach to the case at hand, *not tests* to be mechanically applied."[41] In fact, attacking the established doctrinal approach was the only reason Breyer wrote separately in *Williams-Yulee*: his concurrence was two sentences long and made no other points.

One thus can't be faulted for believing that if Breyer someday has his way, he might import into free-speech cases the same balancing approach to the undue-burden standard he embraced in 2016 in the abortion-restriction case of *Whole Women's Health v. Hellerstedt*.[42] Writing there for a five-justice majority, Breyer held that courts must "consider the burdens a law imposes on abortion access together with the benefits those laws confer."[43] Justice Thomas derided this tack as a "free-form balancing test."[44]

In the realm of free expression, Breyer's *Hellerstedt* iteration of the undue-burden test might mean weighing the benefits of a restriction on speech against the burdens the regulation imposes on both speakers and audiences to, respectively, convey and receive the speech via other nonrestricted alternative means. In other words, it might be fairly close to a proportionality analysis.

But in *Tam*, Breyer toed traditional doctrinal lines safeguarding offensive speech and prohibiting viewpoint discrimination. He didn't

---

[38] *Id.* at 2235–36.

[39] *Id.* at 2235 (emphasis added).

[40] 135 S. Ct. 1656 (2015).

[41] *Id.* at 1673 (Breyer, J., concurring) (emphasis added).

[42] 136 S. Ct. 2292 (2016).

[43] *Id.* at 2309.

[44] *Id.* at 2324 (Thomas, J., dissenting).

wander off to write a concurrence; in fact, he joined all parts and sections of the opinion authored by Alito. Perhaps most remarkable, he joined the section of Alito's opinion in which Alito, who had dissented in *Walker*, bluntly described the Breyer-authored majority opinion in that case as likely marking "the outer bounds of the government speech doctrine."[45] The only thing Breyer did not do in *Tam* was join the more decisive, case-killing approach to viewpoint discrimination adopted in Justice Kennedy's concurrence. It may be that Kennedy's more definitive doctrinal methodology to viewpoint discrimination in *Tam* is what caused Breyer—unlike fellow liberal-leaning Justices Ginsburg, Sotomayor, and Kagan—not to join Kennedy.

Political Correctness Loses Its Appeal

Looming in the *Tam* courthouse, acknowledged or not, was the controversy over a half-dozen then-canceled trademarks for the Washington Redskins football team. The fate of those marks would turn on the result in *Tam*, so it was not surprising that a friend-of-the-court brief was filed in the case by several Native American organizations on behalf of the government. That brief asserted, among other things, that the "use of 'REDSKINS'—like other racially disparaging sports mascots—inflicts real injury. These mascots demean and dehumanize the target group; they foster misinformation and inappropriate stereotype; and they hinder development of self-esteem and other preconditions for social success."[46]

Professor Adam Epstein once contended that "if there is a current professional team name that has sparked legal controversy over the issue of politically incorrect nicknames, it is the Washington Redskins football team."[47] Thus, if the 1995 battle for Major League Baseball's crown between the Atlanta Braves and Cleveland Indians was the "Politically Incorrect World Series,"[48] then the fight in *Pro-Foot-*

---

[45] Matal v. Tam, 137 S. Ct. 1744, 1760 (2017).

[46] Brief of Amici Curiae Native American Organizations in Support of Petitioner, Matal v. Tam, 137 S. Ct. 1744 (2017).

[47] Adam Epstein, Maryland Sports Law, 15 U. Denv. Sports & Ent. L.J. 49, 56 (2013).

[48] Michelle B. Lee, Section 2(A) of the Lanham Act as a Restriction on Sports Team Names: Has Political Correctness Gone Too Far?, 4 Sports Law. J. 65, 65 (1997).

ball, Inc. v. Blackhorse[49] was shaping up as the legal Super Bowl over impolite marks.

When the Supreme Court ruled for The Slants, it therefore was not surprising one scholar claimed "the Court struck a blow against political correctness."[50] But it was hardly the first time the Court had done that.

Specifically, all of the justices involved in *Tam*—save Alito—ruled in 2011 for the right of Westboro Baptist Church members to use politically incorrect statements such as "God Hates Fags," "Thank God for Dead Soldiers," and "Pope in Hell."[51] That's a trio of targets—the LGBTQ community, military, and Catholic church—of a combined sensitivity not far off from that of Asians or Native Americans. Sensitivity over the nation's racial history was also in play in *Walker*, although a bare majority there squelched the offending imagery. Speech inviting offense was nothing new.

In late June 2017, the battle over registering the Redskins' various marks concluded. The U.S. Justice Department filed a letter on June 28, 2017, with the U.S. Court of Appeals for the Fourth Circuit (where *Pro-Football, Inc. v. Blackhorse* was pending) and asked the court, in light of the Supreme Court's decision in *Tam*, to enter judgment in favor of Pro-Football.[52] The next day, Amanda Blackhorse's attorney filed a similar letter.[53]

Thus, in the early months of Donald J. Trump's tenure as an oft-politically incorrect and name-calling provocateur president, the Court confirmed that under our system, there is no right to be free of offensive expression. And while political turmoil still roils the nation's capital, its pro football team can—at least in the merchandising space—rest a tad easier after *Tam*.

---

[49] 112 F. Supp. 3d 439 (E.D. Va. 2015), cert. denied, 137 S. Ct. 44 (2016).

[50] Noah Feldman, Supreme Court Doesn't Care What You Say on the Internet, Bloomberg View (June 19, 2017), https://www.bloomberg.com/view/articles/2017-06-19/supreme-court-doesn-t-care-what-you-say-on-the-internet.

[51] Snyder v. Phelps, 562 U.S. 443, 448 (2011).

[52] Letter from Mark R. Freeman, U.S. Dep't of Justice Appellate Staff, Civil Division, to Patricia S. Connor, Clerk of the U.S. Court of Appeals for the Fourth Circuit (June 28, 2017), http://www.politico.com/f/?id=0000015c-f0a0-d1e3-a97d-f9f436400001.

[53] Letter from Jesse A. Witten, Counsel for Appellees Amanda Blackhorse et al., to Patricia S. Connor, Clerk of the U.S. Court of Appeals for the Fourth Circuit (June 29, 2017), http://was.247sports.com/Bolt/Native-American-tribespeople-drop-case-regarding-Redskins-name-53381907.

Beating Back the Government-Speech Doctrine

The government-speech doctrine, Professor Mark Strasser points out, is not merely new—it dates back fewer than 30 years to the Court's decision in *Rust v. Sullivan*, which upheld a program that denied federal funding to entities that perform abortions[54]—but also underdeveloped.[55] Indeed, Professor Papandrea asserts the doctrine is plagued by a "brief and troubled history."[56]

Yet this nascent canon is simultaneously formidable and dangerous. As I recently wrote, it is "a powerful weapon in a state's arsenal for expression—one deployable both for promoting the government's own viewpoint and, conversely, for squelching the views of others with which it disagrees"[57] provided they can be identified as an extension of the government's own expression. As the Supreme Court encapsulated it in 2009, "the Free Speech Clause restricts government regulation of private speech; it does not regulate government speech."[58]

The government-speech doctrine, if applied to trademarks, would permit the PTO to blatantly discriminate against viewpoints when denying registration. The PTO could unabashedly bully marks that supposedly disparage groups by not registering them, while conversely promoting marks that laud, praise, or compliment those same groups by granting them registration.

Before the June 2017 ruling in *Tam*, but subsequent to the Court's using the government-speech doctrine in *Walker* to censor the Confederate flag, lower courts concluded that the following constitute government speech: (1) a public school program allowing private businesses to hang self-promotional, school-partnership banners from school fences—picture outfield walls at baseball fields—in exchange for monetary donations;[59] (2) the words on food trucks

---

[54] 500 U.S. 173 (1991).

[55] Mark Strasser, Government Speech and Circumvention of the First Amendment, 44 Hastings Const. L.Q. 37, 38 (2016).

[56] Papandrea, *supra* note 32, at 1198.

[57] Clay Calvert, The Government Speech Doctrine in Walker's Wake: Early Rifts and Reverberations on Free Speech, Viewpoint Discrimination, and Offensive Expression, 25 Wm. & Mary Bill of Rts. J. 1239, 1243 (2017).

[58] Pleasant Grove City v. Summum, 555 U.S. 460, 467 (2009).

[59] Mech v. Sch. Bd. of Palm Beach Cnty., 806 F.3d 1070 (11th Cir. 2015), cert. denied, 137 S. Ct. 73 (2016). Classifying the banner program as government speech allowed the school district to deny banners to an individual who wanted to promote his math-

(including the names of businesses painted on them) taking part in a government-sponsored summer-lunch program held on government-owned property;[60] and (3) privately produced tourist guides and informational brochures distributed at rest stops and welcome centers owned by Virginia along its highways.[61]

It is not shocking, then, that one of the most important doctrinal issues in *Tam* was whether federally registered trademarks constitute government speech. The PTO argued that federal registration of marks transforms private expression into government speech—despite the fact that marks are not only created by private entities, but also used by those entities to identify themselves, their goods, and their services. Classifying federally registered trademarks as government speech would allow the PTO to deny registration to The Slants mark and, critically, to dodge all First Amendment-based challenges to its decision.

Under the PTO's logic in *Tam*, when you see Nike's omnipresent registered "swoosh" trademark on Nike running shorts ("Norts," as my undergrads dub them), it is the government—not the maker of athletic apparel and footwear—that is speaking. The government's argument in *Tam* thus sounded somewhat preposterous, but the Court in *Walker* opened the gate for it by holding that the messages on specialty license plates are those of the government, not those of either the private entities that design and create them or the private individuals who choose to display them.

Prior to *Walker*, the Court in 2009 held in *Pleasant Grove City v. Summum* that permanent monuments displayed in public parks constitute government speech, regardless of whether the monuments are designed, built, and donated by private entities.[62] In that case, a

---

tutoring business but who had previously worked as a porn star. In brief, the person's prior occupation was successfully used against him and his current, decidedly non-pornographic speech without raising a First Amendment issue.

60 Wandering Dago, Inc. v. Destito, No. 1:13-cv-1053, 2016 U.S. Dist. LEXIS 26046 (N.D.N.Y. Mar. 1, 2016). Labeling such expression government speech allowed the government to deny a permit, based on its alleged offensiveness, to the Wandering Dago food truck.

61 Vista-Graphics, Inc. v. Va. Dep't of Transport., No. 16-1404, 2017 U.S. App. LEXIS 5452 (Mar. 29, 2017).

62 555 U.S. 460 (2009). See Patrick M. Garry, *Pleasant Grove City v. Summum*: The Supreme Court Finds a Public Display of the Ten Commandments to Be Permissible Government Speech, 2008-2009 Cato Sup. Ct. Rev. 271 (2009).

religious entity called Summum sought to erect a stone monument bearing its "seven aphorisms" in a public park in Pleasant Grove City, Utah. When the city rejected Summum's request, the religious order sued, claiming violation of the Free Speech Clause and pointing out that the city had previously accepted a donated monument featuring the Ten Commandments in the same park. Summum contended that public parks are traditional public fora for expression—something that the Court has long acknowledged—and that viewpoint discrimination in such venues violates the First Amendment.

Without dissent, the Court rejected Summum's arguments. Justice Alito, penning the Court's opinion, rebuffed the public forum argument, citing spatial concerns that "public parks can accommodate only a limited number of permanent monuments."[63] While parks constitute sacred First Amendment space known as traditional public fora for some types of ephemeral expression—speeches, marches, rallies, and concerts—they don't where permanent monuments are involved. As Alito put it, "it is hard to imagine how a public park could be opened up for the installation of permanent monuments by every person or group wishing to engage in that form of expression."[64] Consider, in other words, grounds so crowded and cluttered by monuments that no space remains for bike paths, ball fields, swing sets, and the occasional amphitheater.

Beyond the spatial issue, Alito pointed to another factor—public perception—suggesting that donated, park-located monuments are government speech. "Public parks are often closely identified in the public mind with the government unit that owns the land," he wrote, adding that:

> Government decisionmakers select the monuments that portray what they view as appropriate for the place in question, taking into account such content-based factors as esthetics, history, and local culture. The monuments that are accepted, therefore, are meant to convey and have the effect of conveying a government message, and they thus constitute government speech.[65]

[63] Summum, 555 U.S. at 478.
[64] *Id.* at 479.
[65] *Id.* at 472.

But even in *Summum*, the government-speech doctrine rested on a shaky foundation. Alito, for example, openly acknowledged "there may be situations in which it is difficult to tell whether a government entity is speaking on its own behalf or is providing a forum for private speech."[66] Justice Breyer, who later wrote for the majority in *Walker*, delivered a concurrence, stressing—per his propensity for doctrinal squishiness addressed earlier—his "understanding that the 'government speech' doctrine is a rule of thumb, not a rigid category."[67] And Justice David Souter, citing the doctrine's relative recency, cautioned that "it would do well for us to go slow in setting its bounds, which will affect existing doctrine in ways not yet explored."[68]

But in *Walker*, the five-justice majority threw caution to the wind. In holding that specialty license plates are government speech, it ignored the fact that, unlike in *Summum*, there was no spatial scarcity problem. A seemingly vast number of specialty plates could coexist happily on Texas's registered vehicles; this was not a public park with finite acreage. In fact, when *Walker* was decided, more than 350 different specialty plates were on vehicles registered in the Lone Star State.[69]

Instead of focusing on *Summum's* scarcity concern, the Breyer-authored majority identified three factors—history, perception, and control—leading it to find that specialty plates are government speech. The first factor was the historical use of the medium as a means for expression. Specifically, Breyer wrote that "the history of license plates shows that, insofar as license plates have conveyed more than state names and vehicle identification numbers, they long have communicated messages from the States."[70]

The second variable—this one borrowed from *Summum*—was public perception regarding who is speaking: the government or a private entity? In *Walker*, Breyer found that because Texas not only issues all specialty plates, but also emblazons each with "Texas" at the

---

[66] *Id.* at 470.

[67] *Id.* at 484 (Breyer, J., concurring).

[68] *Id.* at 485 (Souter, J., concurring).

[69] Walker v. Texas Div., Sons of Confederate Veterans, 135 S. Ct. 2239, 2255 (2015) (Alito, J., dissenting).

[70] *Id.* at 2248.

top, viewers likely perceive them as "government IDs."[71] Citing nary a shred of evidence to support the claim, Breyer also reasoned that "a person who displays a message on a Texas license plate likely intends to convey to the public that the State has endorsed that message."[72]

Finally, the *Walker* majority considered the amount of control Texas exerts over specialty plates. Breyer determined that "Texas maintains direct control over the messages conveyed on its specialty plates" because its Department of Motor Vehicles Board "must approve every specialty plate design proposal before the design can appear on a Texas plate."[73]

Justice Alito, joined by the more conservative justices not named Thomas, scoffed at this approach, contending that the majority's "capacious understanding of government speech takes a large and painful bite out of the First Amendment."[74] Alito asserted that any person sitting by a Texas highway and watching cars speed by with specialty plates "bearing the name[s] of a high school, a fraternity or sorority, the Masons, the Knights of Columbus, the Daughters of the American Revolution, a realty company, a favorite soft drink, a favorite burger restaurant, and a favorite NASCAR driver" would not believe that such sentiments were those of Texas but rather the cars' owners.[75]

Tam marked the first time since *Walker* that the Court revisited the government-speech doctrine. Significantly, all eight justices participating in *Tam* joined the part of the opinion addressing government speech, thus presenting a unified front on this malleable doctrine. And although the justices did not jettison the government-speech doctrine to the dumpster of failed First Amendment principles, they made several efforts seemingly designed to curb its use. How did they do that?

First and foremost, the Court flatly rejected the government's contention that trademark registration converts private marks into government speech. As if channeling his snarky inner-Scalia, Alito posed twin rhetorical questions: "if trademarks represent

---

[71] *Id.* at 2249.

[72] *Id.*

[73] *Id.*

[74] *Id.* at 2255 (Alito, J., dissenting).

[75] *Id.*

government speech, what does the Government have in mind when it advises Americans to 'make.believe' (Sony), 'Think different' (Apple), 'Just do it' (Nike), or 'Have it your way' (Burger King)? Was the Government warning about a coming disaster when it registered the mark 'EndTime Ministries'?"[76] The queries pounded home Alito's point that if registered marks are government speech, then the government "is unashamedly endorsing a vast array of commercial products and services."[77]

Alito also engaged in some slippery-slope logic about the danger of calling registered marks government speech: "If federal registration makes a trademark government speech and thus eliminates all First Amendment protection, would the registration of the copyright for a book produce a similar transformation?"[78] Such an outcome would, akin to the PTO's attack on The Slants for disparaging Asians, give the U.S. Copyright Office power to discriminate against original works of authorship that disparage groups. It could, for example, easily deny copyright registration to Bruce Springsteen's lyrics for "Born in the U.S.A." because the song's protagonist is sent off "to a foreign land to go and kill the yellow man."

Beyond simply ruling against the PTO, the Court also signaled that the government-speech doctrine must be reeled in. Notably, it dubbed the doctrine "susceptible to dangerous misuse," thereby necessitating the Court to "exercise great caution before extending our government speech precedents"[79] such as *Summum* and *Walker*. And when it came to *Walker*—the opinion on which the PTO most heavily relied—Alito remarked that *Walker* "likely marks the outer bounds of the government speech doctrine."[80] Additionally, none of the three factors deployed in *Walker*—history, perception, and control—militated in favor of classifying registered trademarks as government speech, Alito wrote.

Perhaps more subtly limiting the doctrine's future scope was an Alito-created example suggesting it only applies and permits

[76] Matal v. Tam, 137 S. Ct. 1744, 1759 (2017).
[77] *Id.*
[78] *Id.* at 1760.
[79] *Id.* at 1758.
[80] *Id.* at 1760.

viewpoint discrimination when, in fact, it is the government that genuinely creates and conveys a message:

> During the Second World War, the Federal Government produced and distributed millions of posters to promote the war effort. There were posters urging enlistment, the purchase of war bonds, and the conservation of scarce resources. These posters expressed a viewpoint, but the First Amendment did not demand that the Government balance the message of these posters by producing and distributing posters encouraging Americans to refrain from engaging in these activities.[81]

Initially, this example is critical because it intimates that the government-speech doctrine is confined to scenarios in which the government itself produces and conveys a message related to its own interest. Furthermore, Alito's example smacks of gravitas—World War II, the military, national security, and urgently safeguarding the very future of the United States—whereas *Walker*, setting aside a Confederate-flag plate, involved the relative frivolity of specialized license plates supporting, among other things, multiple college sports teams and playing golf.[82]

Additionally, the message on wartime posters regarding army enlistment and war bonds directly ties to a specific government purpose or end that it hopes to achieve—winning a war. A specialty plate bearing the phrase "Rather Be Golfing" clearly does not seem to achieve any government purpose unless, perhaps, the government

---

[81] *Id.* at 1758.

[82] As Alito rhetorically asked in *Walker*:

> If a car with a plate that says "Rather Be Golfing" passed by at 8:30 am on a Monday morning, would you think: "This is the official policy of the State – better to golf than to work?" If you did your viewing at the start of the college football season and you saw Texas plates with the names of the University of Texas's out-of-state competitors in upcoming games—Notre Dame, Oklahoma State, the University of Oklahoma, Kansas State, Iowa State—would you assume that the State of Texas was officially (and perhaps treasonously) rooting for the Longhorns' opponents?

Walker v. Texas Div., Sons of Confederate Veterans, Inc., 135 S. Ct. 2239, 2255 (2015) (Alito, J., dissenting).

wants to generate revenue for itself from public courses. But that possibility is about as much of a legal stretch as was the PTO's argument in favor of government speech in *Tam*. Alito's example thus intimates that only when truly serious matters are at stake and, in turn, only when the government is the entity that actually creates and conveys the message for its own purpose, does it get a pass, via the government-speech doctrine, on the general rule against viewpoint discrimination.

Furthermore, Justice Kennedy's concurrence in *Tam* buttressed Alito's efforts to confine the government-speech doctrine. Specifically, Kennedy called it a "narrow" exception to the general rule against viewpoint discrimination, contending such narrowness is necessary "to prevent the government from claiming that every government program is exempt from the First Amendment."[83] Kennedy had joined Alito's dissent in *Walker*, so it is not surprising they were on the same page in this facet of *Tam*.

Ultimately, if the Court threw caution to the wind in *Walker* by unleashing the government-speech doctrine to sweep up specialty license plates that are designed, sponsored, and displayed by private entities and individuals, then in *Tam* it signaled a desire to keep the doctrine tightly tethered. Alito, who dissented against the use of the doctrine in *Walker*, thereby exacted a small measure of revenge in *Tam*.

Walker might turn out to be a dangerous but feel-good (at least for its liberal-bloc majority) one-off ruling to stop politically incorrect Confederate flags. Yet it remains good law today, even in the face of a unanimous effort to halt its momentum in *Tam*.

Putting the Commercial Speech Doctrine into Play Again

It wasn't until the 1970s that the Supreme Court extended formal First Amendment protection to truthful advertisements for lawful goods and services. Yet, the Court consistently treats commercial speech less favorably than other types of expression such as political speech. The Court does so by measuring the validity of restrictions on commercial speech against an intermediate—rather than

---

[83] Matal v. Tam, 137 S. Ct. 1744, 1768 (2017) (Kennedy, J., concurring).

strict—scrutiny test that affords greater deference to the government.[84] In brief, it generally is easier for the government to regulate ads for products and services than for it to regulate speech about other matters.

Justice Thomas, however, has long objected to this second-tier treatment of commercial expression. One scholar notes that Thomas has "clearly staked out his claim as a First Amendment defender in his commercial speech opinions."[85] As Thomas opined in 2001, "I continue to believe that when the government seeks to restrict truthful speech in order to suppress the ideas it conveys, strict scrutiny is appropriate, whether or not the speech in question may be characterized as 'commercial.'"[86]

Tam provided Thomas with another opportunity to make this point. That's because the government argued that trademarks are commercial speech—basically just names by which companies promote themselves. Applying the usual intermediate-scrutiny test for commercial-speech cases, a bloc of four justices in *Tam*—Alito, Roberts, Breyer, and Thomas—held that the disparagement clause failed to meet this standard. That conclusion is unremarkable.

Thomas, however, penned a concurrence. He agreed the disparagement clause was "unconstitutional even under the less stringent test" for commercial-speech cases, but he also reiterated his position that strict scrutiny provides the appropriate test in such disputes.[87]

---

[84] The U.S. Supreme Court fashioned a four-part test for commercial speech that requires courts to

> determine whether the expression is protected by the First Amendment. For commercial speech to come within that provision, it at least must concern lawful activity and not be misleading. Next, we ask whether the asserted governmental interest is substantial. If both inquiries yield positive answers, we must determine whether the regulation directly advances the governmental interest asserted, and whether it is not more extensive than is necessary to serve that interest.

Central Hudson Gas & Electric Corp. v. Pub. Servs. Comm'n, 447 U.S. 557, 566 (1980); see also Lorillard Tobacco Co. v. Reilly, 533 U.S. 525, 572 (2001) (Thomas, J., concurring) (describing "the intermediate scrutiny of *Central Hudson*").

[85] David L. Hudson, Jr., Justice Clarence Thomas: The Emergence of a Commercial-Speech Protector, 35 Creighton L. Rev. 485, 486 (2002).

[86] Lorillard Tobacco Co. v. Reilly, 533 U.S. 525, 572 (2001) (Thomas, J., concurring).

[87] Matal v. Tam, 137 S. Ct. 1744, 1769 (2017) (Thomas, J., concurring).

Although Thomas has yet to convince his fellow justices this should be the case, Alito's plurality opinion in *Tam* provides support for that prospect in the future.

In particular, Alito observed that "the line between commercial and non-commercial speech is not always clear, as this case illustrates."[88] Such murkiness is unsurprising, largely because the Court has never satisfactorily defined commercial speech in the first place. As one scholar bluntly wrote last year, "No one knows exactly what commercial speech is."[89]

The Court even passed on the opportunity to define it 14 years ago in a case involving Nike that blended commercial speech elements with political expression.[90] There, the Court initially decided to hear the case, but then dismissed it, invoking the rarely used notion that its writ of certiorari had been "improvidently granted."

Despite the definitional difficulties, the commercial versus noncommercial distinction can be pivotal—even outcome-determinative—because a statute is more likely to be struck down under strict scrutiny than intermediate scrutiny. Alito's frank acknowledgement in *Tam* that the nation's high court sometimes has trouble separating commercial and noncommercial speech further opens the door for scrapping what may be a false dichotomy.

Finally, Justice Kennedy's *Tam* concurrence further chops away at the notion that commercial-speech regulations are always subject only to intermediate scrutiny. As Kennedy wrote, "discrimination based on viewpoint, including a regulation that targets speech for its offensiveness, remains of serious concern in the commercial context" and thus "necessarily invokes heightened scrutiny."[91] In other words, a statute restricting commercial speech is subjected to something more than just intermediate scrutiny when the regulation is viewpoint-based. Kennedy explained that neither the term nor category of commercial speech provides "a blanket exemption from the First Amendment's requirement of viewpoint neutrality."[92]

---

[88] *Id.* at 1765 (Alito, J., joined by Roberts, C.J., and Thomas and Breyer, JJ.).

[89] Tamara R. Piety, The First Amendment and the Corporate Civil Rights Movement, 11 J. Bus. & Tech. L. 1, 4 (2016).

[90] Nike, Inc. v. Kasky, 539 U.S. 654 (2003).

[91] Matal v. Tam, 137 S. Ct. 1744, 1767 (2017) (Kennedy, J., concurring).

[92] *Id.*

This logic builds on Kennedy's 2011 majority opinion in *Sorrell v. IMS Health Inc.*[93] The Court there struck down a Vermont statute banning pharmacies from selling, for marketing purposes, records revealing the prescribing histories of individually identifiable doctors. Those records could be freely sold to others, but not to data-harvesting pharmaceutical marketers who, in turn, would use the information to try to sell particular drugs to specific doctors. Kennedy found this disparate treatment of pharmaceutical marketers troubling, reasoning the statute "disfavors marketing, that is, speech with a particular content. More than that, the statute disfavors specific speakers, namely pharmaceutical manufacturers."[94] The law thus warranted heightened scrutiny—scrutiny greater than the usual intermediate standard for commercial speech—because it targeted particular speakers (pharmaceutical salespeople) and their viewpoints in using that information. The majority, however, backed down from actually applying strict scrutiny (or something like it) in *Sorrell* because it reasoned the statute couldn't even pass muster under the lesser intermediate-scrutiny test.[95]

In summary, the trio of opinions in *Tam* authored by Justices Thomas, Breyer, and Kennedy collectively indicates that the future of an intermediate-scrutiny-based commercial-speech doctrine is perhaps tenuous. And when *Tam* is viewed more broadly, it illustrates different definitional difficulties—one in distinguishing government speech from private expression, the other in deciding what is commercial speech—now plaguing two relatively recent doctrines.

Viewpoint Discrimination: Contested Meaning and Effect

Although all eight justices in *Tam* agreed that the disparagement clause unconstitutionally discriminated against a viewpoint, they split 4-4 on when viewpoint discrimination exists and when it is fatal to a statute. Justice Kennedy, joined by Justices Ginsburg, Sotomayor, and Kagan, provided—in my view—a sharper, more textbook-like definition and emphasized the statute-killing power of the rule against viewpoint discrimination. Justice Alito, joined by Justices

---

[93] 564 U.S. 552 (2011).

[94] *Id.* at 564.

[95] As Justice Kennedy wrote, "the outcome is the same whether a special commercial speech inquiry or a stricter form of judicial scrutiny is applied." *Id.* at 571.

Roberts, Thomas, and Breyer, took a more muddled approach. Because this rift may affect future cases, it helps to explore it in greater detail, starting with Kennedy's opinion and then Alito's take.

What is viewpoint discrimination? For Kennedy, it is a subset or subtype of a larger category of discrimination called content-based discrimination. In brief, content-based discrimination targets a specific subject matter, while viewpoint discrimination slices and dices within that subject matter and, as Kennedy wrote, singles "out a subset of messages for disfavor based on the views expressed."[96] Put slightly differently by Kennedy, a viewpoint-based law impermissibly attempts "to remove certain ideas or perspectives from a broader debate" about a subject.[97] The First Amendment mandates viewpoint neutrality by the government—the converse of viewpoint discrimination.

The classroom example I use to illustrate this point compares two hypothetical laws restricting speech about abortion. Abortion, to use Kennedy's words, is "the relevant subject" in both laws. One law restricts *all speech* about abortion and thus reflects content-based discrimination. The other law restricts only *pro-choice speech* about abortion (but not pro-life speech or other perspectives on abortion), thereby embodying viewpoint discrimination.

Applying this logic to the disparagement clause, Kennedy explained that the subjects targeted were "persons, living or dead, institutions, beliefs, or national symbols." About such subjects, however, the clause permitted registration only for "a positive or benign mark but not a derogatory one. The law thus reflects the Government's disapproval of a subset of messages it finds offensive. This is the essence of viewpoint discrimination."[98] As applied to The Slants case, the clause allowed registering marks lauding Asian-Americans, but not ones disparaging them. It was that simple.

The impact of such viewpoint discrimination was, in turn, outcome determinative for the Kennedy bloc. Viewpoint discrimination, he emphasized, is "so potent that it must be subject to rigorous constitutional scrutiny," regardless of whether the speech offends audiences or is classified as commercial. "To the extent trademarks

---

[96] Matal v. Tam, 137 S. Ct. 1744, 1766 (2017) (Kennedy, J., concurring).

[97] *Id*. at 1767.

[98] *Id*. at 1766.

qualify as commercial speech, they are an example of why that term or category does not serve as a blanket exemption from the First Amendment's requirement of viewpoint neutrality," Kennedy wrote.[99]

That was an important point that divided the Court. Justices Kennedy, Ginsburg, Sotomayor, and Kagan believe that viewpoint-based laws targeting commercial speech are subject to "rigorous" scrutiny. Thus, they did not join in the part of Justice Alito's opinion in which he, Roberts, Thomas, and Breyer analyzed the disparagement clause under the deferential intermediate scrutiny that typically applies in commercial-speech cases.

Kennedy identified only one exception to the principle that viewpoint discrimination is verboten—namely, when the government-speech doctrine applies. As he put it, "the Court's precedents have recognized just one narrow situation in which viewpoint discrimination is permissible: where the government itself is speaking or recruiting others to communicate a message on its behalf."[100] Because that lone exception to the rule against viewpoint discrimination did not apply in *Tam*, The Slants prevailed and the PTO lost.

The bottom line for the Kennedy bloc in *Tam* is that the presence of viewpoint discrimination, coupled with the absence of government speech, rendered "unnecessary any extended treatment of other questions raised by the parties." The quoted part of that sentence jabs at the ink spilled by Alito, Roberts, Thomas, and Breyer in considering the government's back-up, ill-fated arguments that *Tam* should have been treated either as a government-subsidy case or under a proposed new doctrine for "government-program" cases.

Justice Alito's analysis of viewpoint discrimination is more problematic for two reasons. First, and as noted above, although Alito found that the disparagement clause discriminated on the basis of viewpoint, he nonetheless analyzed it under the intermediate-scrutiny test for commercial speech cases rather than a more rigorous standard. His choice didn't affect the outcome in *Tam* because the Alito bloc found that the clause failed even under intermediate scrutiny. It does, however, reflect a key difference between the Kennedy and Alito blocs going forward regarding the correct standard when

[99] *Id.* at 1767.
[100] *Id.* at 1768.

a law targeting commercial speech also discriminates on the basis of viewpoint.

Second, Alito failed to provide a clear formula for determining when a law is viewpoint-based. He simply wrote that "[o]ur cases use the term 'viewpoint' discrimination in a broad sense"; the disparagement clause was viewpoint-based because "[g]iving offense is a viewpoint."[101] Alito then cited a laundry list of cases, including the Court's flag-burning decision of *Texas v. Johnson*[102] and its ruling protecting pornographer Larry Flynt's ability to luridly poke fun at Reverend Jerry Falwell in *Hustler Magazine v. Falwell*,[103] standing for the proposition that an idea cannot be censored simply because it offends.

My worry is that Alito muddled two distinct doctrinal strands—one generally prohibiting censorship based on offensiveness and one banning viewpoint discrimination—in finding that "giving offense is a viewpoint." Consider *Cohen v. California*, the "Fuck the Draft" opinion noted at the start of the essay and a quintessential offensive speech case. The statute there targeted "offensive conduct," and the Court framed the issue as whether California could "properly remove this offensive word from the public vocabulary."

But if offense equals a viewpoint, as Alito has it in *Tam*, then it's surprising the Court in *Cohen* failed to analyze the California statute as an instance of viewpoint discrimination. There was, most notably, no examination by the Court of whether a person could freely say pro-draft messages in a courthouse but not make anti-draft statements. That's how a viewpoint-discrimination analysis likely would have unfolded in *Cohen*.

Instead, the Court focused on (1) the need to protect the emotive—not simply cognitive—function of speech, (2) the self-help remedy for those offended of averting their eyes from Paul Robert Cohen's jacket-worn message, and (3) the vagueness problems with defining offensiveness. Justice John Marshall Harlan II remarked for the majority on this last point that

---

[101] *Id*. at 1763 (plurality op.).
[102] 491 U.S. 397 (1989).
[103] 485 U.S. 46 (1988).

while the particular four-letter word being litigated here is perhaps more distasteful than most others of its genre, it is nevertheless often true that one man's vulgarity is another's lyric. Indeed, we think it is largely because governmental officials cannot make principled distinctions in this area that the Constitution leaves matters of taste and style so largely to the individual.[104]

The Court in *Cohen*, however, did recognize that offensiveness could serve as an excuse for discriminating against a viewpoint. As Harlan pointed out, "we cannot indulge the facile assumption that one can forbid particular words without also running a substantial risk of suppressing ideas in the process. Indeed, governments might soon seize upon the censorship of particular words as a convenient guise for banning the expression of unpopular views."[105]

In other words, offense and viewpoint are *not* always the same. The word "fuck" is what gave offense in *Cohen*, not Paul Robert Cohen's anti-draft viewpoint. Taking offense at a word ("fuck") is not the same as discriminating against the viewpoint in which that word is used ("fuck the draft"). "Fuck," standing alone without "the draft," is not a viewpoint. Giving or taking offense therefore is not always a viewpoint.

For Alito, *Tam* was more about protecting offensiveness than it was about prohibiting viewpoint discrimination. Alito's discussion of viewpoint discrimination in Part III, Section C—a section the Kennedy bloc did not join—covered only two paragraphs before Alito segued out by citing a list of right-to-offend cases, including *Johnson* and *Falwell*.[106] It's as if Alito tossed in a few sentences about viewpoint discrimination as a sop to Kennedy, who engaged in a lengthy analysis of that problem.

Perhaps most telling is the fact that Alito omitted any reference to viewpoint discrimination in announcing the Court's judgment at the opening of the opinion. He wrote only that the disparagement clause "violates the Free Speech Clause of the First Amendment. It offends a bedrock First Amendment principle: Speech may not be banned

---

[104] Cohen v. California, 403 U.S. 15, 25 (1971).

[105] *Id*. at 26.

[106] *Cohen v. California* is conspicuously missing from this list of cases.

on the ground that it expresses ideas that offend."[107] For Alito, *Tam* was about protecting offensive expression from the forces of political correctness.

Contrast that with the second paragraph of Justice Kennedy's concurrence, which reads: "As the Court is correct to hold, [the disparagement clause] constitutes viewpoint discrimination—a form of speech suppression so potent that it must be subject to rigorous constitutional scrutiny. The Government's action and the statute on which it is based cannot survive this scrutiny."[108] For Kennedy, *Tam* was about preventing viewpoint discrimination in the marketplace of ideas.

This may all seem like two sides of the same legal coin. I doubt, however, that Justice Kennedy thought so when he engaged in the kind of lengthy and thoughtful analysis of viewpoint discrimination that Justice Alito's opinion lacked.

Faith in the Marketplace of Ideas

Back in 1919, Justice Oliver Wendell Holmes Jr. imported the marketplace-of-ideas theory of free expression into First Amendment jurisprudence in *Abrams v. United States*.[109] Writing in dissent, Holmes contended that

> when men have realized that time has upset many fighting faiths, they may come to believe even more than they believe the very foundations of their own conduct that the ultimate good desired is better reached by free trade in ideas—that the best test of truth is the power of the thought to get itself accepted in the competition of the market.[110]

Nearly a century later, Justice Kennedy favorably invoked the marketplace metaphor in *Tam* to explain why viewpoint discrimination is wrong and why, in turn, the disparagement clause is

---

[107] Matal v. Tam, 137 S. Ct. 1744, 1751 (2017).

[108] *Id.* at 1765 (2017) (Kennedy, J., concurring).

[109] 250 U.S. 616 (1919).

[110] *Id.* at 630 (Holmes, J., dissenting).

unconstitutional. "By mandating positivity, the law here might silence dissent and distort the marketplace of ideas," Kennedy opined.[111]

Similarly, Kennedy's criticism of removing "certain ideas and perspectives from a broader debate" reflects the notion that the consummate marketplace of ideas is a forum for debating all ideas and perspectives. The participants in this ideal marketplace are also rational and thoughtful, with Kennedy confidently suggesting that an initial hostile reaction to a message "may prompt further reflection, leading to a more reasoned, more tolerant position." Ultimately, Kennedy closed his concurrence with a deep bow to faith in marketplace discussion rather than to trust in the government:

> A law that can be directed against speech found offensive to some portion of the public can be turned against minority and dissenting views to the detriment of all. The First Amendment does not entrust that power to the government's benevolence. Instead, our reliance must be on the substantial safeguards of free and open discussion in a democratic society.[112]

Some, of course, will consider such assuredness in the marketplace of ideas hopelessly naïve. We live in an era in which instantaneous outrage (not reason or reflection) rules in response to offending tweets and "free and open discussion" is replaced by often unhinged—albeit, certainly free and open—verbal confrontation. What's more, marketplace competition of ideas hasn't driven out the falsity that is fake news—the great political and journalistic panic of 2016–17—and replaced it with the truth. Many would also argue the marketplace of ideas already is badly distorted by the forces of concentrated, corporate media ownership, so what's the harm in a little government intervention when it comes to registering trademarks?

But the Court's continuing invocation of the metaphor is testament, against all else, that it is an aspirational model for which society should strive and upon which the government should not encroach or interfere. It may be a flawed theory, but it clearly captures

---

[111] Matal v. Tam, 137 S. Ct. 1744, 1766 (2017) (Kennedy, J., concurring).
[112] *Id.* at 1769.

why the government cannot jettison ideas and perspectives it disdains from the hurly-burly of today's speech environment.

Final Thoughts

Although the Court in *Tam* struck down the Lanham Act's disparagement clause, it did not address the constitutionality of another facet of the same statute that allows the PTO to deny registration to marks featuring "immoral, deceptive, or scandalous matter."[113] This clause has been used by the PTO to reject registration for sexually themed trademarks such "1-800-JACK-OFF" and "JACK-OFF" for a dial-a-porn company,[114] as well as the phrase "Cock Sucker" accompanying a drawing of a crowing rooster for a company selling—you guessed it—rooster-shaped chocolate lollipops.[115]

Unpacking the phrase "immoral, deceptive, or scandalous matter" is important. Prohibiting registration for deceptive marks is not problematic because the First Amendment does not safeguard commercial speech that is false or misleading. But refusing registration for immoral or scandalous marks is troubling, given the subjective, value-laden judgments regarding the meaning of those words. In particular, the PTO's use of "scandalous" is often interchangeable with the term "vulgar,"[116] which circles back to the Supreme Court's observation in *Cohen* that "one man's vulgarity is another's lyric."[117] A facial challenge on void-for-vagueness grounds to the part of 15 U.S.C. § 1052(a) targeting immoral and scandalous marks thus might provide another route for further rolling back the PTO's authority over offensive speech.[118]

---

[113] 15 U.S.C. § 1052(a) (2017).

[114] In re Blvd. Entm't, Inc., 334 F.3d 1336 (Fed. Cir. 2003).

[115] In re Fox, 702 F.3d 633 (Fed. Cir. 2012).

[116] Megan M. Carpenter & Mary Garner, NSFW: An Empirical Study of Scandalous Trademarks, 33 Cardozo Arts & Ent. L.J. 321, 335 (2015) (noting that "[t]he term 'scandalous' has been held to encompass matter that is merely 'vulgar,'" and adding that "the Federal Circuit has held that dictionary definitions alone can be sufficient to establish scandalousness where multiple dictionaries indicate a word is vulgar and the applicant's mark indicates the vulgar meaning of the word").

[117] 403 U.S. 15, 25 (1971).

[118] See Grayned v. City of Rockford, 408 U.S. 104, 108 (1972) (calling it "a basic principle of due process that an enactment is void for vagueness if its prohibitions are not clearly defined" such that they fail to "give the person of ordinary intelligence a reasonable opportunity to know what is prohibited").

On the one hand, the Supreme Court in *Tam* virtually teed up such a future challenge. That's because Justice Alito, in a part of the opinion joined by all of the justices except Thomas, dropped a footnote pointing out that "the PTO has acknowledged that the guidelines 'for determining whether a mark is *scandalous* or disparaging are somewhat vague and the determination of whether a mark is *scandalous* or disparaging is necessarily a highly subjective one.'"[119]

On the other hand, the Supreme Court's current test for obscenity is replete with moralistic terms such as "prurient interest" and "patently offensive."[120] Additionally, "prurient interest" is defined by the Court with the equally subjective and moralistic notion of "a shameful or morbid interest in sex."[121] And, as noted earlier, the Court recently dodged a First Amendment challenge to the FCC's problematic definition of indecency.[122] In brief, the Court demonstrates some tolerance for subjectivity and ambiguity when it comes to regulating sexual matters. Thus, whether a challenge to the PTO's authority over immoral and scandalous marks would be successful with the Supreme Court is unclear, but Alito's footnote in *Tam* certainly encourages the effort.

Although *Tam* addressed a federal statute, the Court's ruling has direct implications for state trademark laws too. That's because dozens of state statutes also target disparaging trademarks and mirror the language of the federal disparagement clause struck down in *Tam*. For instance, Florida Statute § 495.021(b) allows Sunshine State officials to deny registration to any mark that "consists of or comprises matter which may disparage . . . persons, living or dead, institutions, beliefs, or national symbols, or bring them into contempt, or disrepute." Statutes in other populous states such as California and New York contain the same language.[123] These laws are now ripe for First Amendment challenges, with *Tam* serving as precedent for holding them unconstitutional.

---

[119] Matal v. Tam, 137 S. Ct. 1744, 1756, n.5 (2017) (emphasis added) (quoting In re In Over Our Heads, Inc., 16 USPQ 2d 1653, 1654 (TTAB 1990) (brackets and internal quotation marks omitted)).

[120] Miller v. California, 413 U.S. 15, 24 (1973).

[121] Brockett v. Spokane Arcades, Inc., 472 U.S. 491, 504 (1985).

[122] *Supra* notes 3–8 and accompanying text.

[123] Cal. Bus. & Prof. Code § 14205 (2017); N.Y. Gen. Bus. § 360-a (Consol. 2017).

Ultimately, from a free-speech perspective, there is much to praise about the ruling in *Tam*. It vindicates and reaffirms key First Amendment principles regarding both offensive expression and viewpoint discrimination. It also rebuffs the government-speech doctrine in the realm of trademarks, while attempting to curb its expansion elsewhere. Furthermore, facets of the opinions of Justices Alito, Thomas, and Kennedy collectively raise questions about the future of an intermediate-scrutiny-based commercial speech doctrine. Additionally, *Tam* reinforces the Court's continued respect for the marketplace of ideas. What's more, Justice Alito came to the aid of offensive expression, while Justice Breyer didn't stray off the beaten doctrinal path. That's just about a First Amendment home run, with the unfortunate 4-4 split among the justices regarding viewpoint discrimination the only item keeping the ball inside the fence for a triple.

Our Fellow American, the Registered Sex Offender

David T. Goldberg* and Emily R. Zhang**

In the memorable closing scene of *The Producers*, the protagonists find themselves in a court of law, their can't-miss scheme thwarted by the unexpected theatrical success of *Springtime for Hitler*, the musical. The jury returns, and as all rise, the foreperson announces the verdict in *People v. Bialystock and Bloom*: "Your honor, we find the defendants *incredibly* guilty."

So too with North Carolina General Statutes Section 14-202.5, which bars people on the state's sex offender registry from accessing social-networking websites. Although the opinion in *Packingham v. North Carolina* did not use those exact words—Justice Anthony Kennedy's aversion to "ly" adverbs is well known—its verdict on North Carolina's ban was to the same effect. The Court described the law as a more flagrant violation than the measure struck down in *Jews for Jesus*, which earned its place in the canon of easy First Amendment cases by outlawing all "First Amendment activity."[1] Indeed, the three-justice *Packingham* concurrence took the view that the case was so easy that the majority should have simply struck down Section 202.5 as facially unconstitutional and then stopped talking.

* Instructor, Stanford Law School Supreme Court Litigation Clinic. Before that, Goldberg taught for a decade at the University of Virginia, where he cofounded and codirected that law school's Supreme Court Litigation Clinic.

** Ph.D. candidate in political science at Stanford University. Graduated from Stanford Law School in 2016.

The authors represented petitioner before the U.S. Supreme Court, as counsel and a law student member of the Stanford Supreme Court Litigation Clinic team. We thank J.R. Packingham, Glenn Gerding, the students on both the Stanford and UVA teams (Trevor Ezell, Samson Schatz, and Grace Zhou; Jackie Bechera, Monica Raymond, Emily Riff, and Dan Stefany), Dan Ortiz, Mark Stancil, John Elwood, Toby Heytens, Pam Karlan, Jeff Fisher, Sean Donahue, and David Post.

[1] Bd. of Airport Comm'rs of Los Angeles v. Jews for Jesus, Inc., 482 U.S. 569 (1987).

As we explain below, we don't disagree. Under settled doctrine, *Packingham* is as easy a First Amendment case as the Court will see—made easier still by the Roberts Court's recent muscular free-speech pronouncements. Nor was it the "new media" watershed that some seemed to think. Harry Kalven famously suggested that Americans owed "our" expanded free-speech rights to "the Negro"—that the Warren Court's righteous sympathy for civil rights led it to deepen and broaden protections for free speech.[2] But "we" don't owe "our" rights to Lester (a.k.a. J.R.) Packingham. It is inconceivable that a democratic majority would impose a restriction anything like Section 202.5 on "us." It is likewise beyond doubt that our right to speak over the dominant communications medium of our age is anything but fully protected.

But the First Amendment question *Packingham* raised of whether "they"—the class of people Section 202.5 targets, registered sex offenders—have the same rights as "us," was a nail-biter. Before Section 202.5 was toast, it was the toast of North Carolina. The law passed unanimously and was held constitutional "in all respects" by two courts.[3] And numerous other laws in North Carolina and across the country exclude "them" from streets, parks, and public places.

These laws have provoked barely a judicial peep. Indeed, these rapidly cumulating, ever-heavier burdens have taken on a life of their own. They have come to be understood by legislators and judges as a sign that people on sex-offender registries have a degraded citizenship status, and that there is no real constitutional limit on the disabilities that may be imposed in the interest of community safety. Twenty-five years ago, convicted child molesters were feared and loathed no less than now, but "sex offender" was not a legal category; and 15 years ago, "registration" was nothing but a description of the informational obligations imposed on people convicted of certain crimes. Now, registrant status is a gateway to routine, substantive, and decades-long impositions on basic liberties. And it is that force, which we (and others before us) call "sex offender exceptionalism," that *Packingham* was up against.

Although the U.S. Supreme Court has never upheld registration-based burdens, its opinions (much more than its holdings) have

---

[2] Harry Kalven, The Negro and the First Amendment 6 (1965).

[3] Packingham v. North Carolina, 368 N.C. 380, 381 (N.C. 2015).

played a complex, surprisingly important, and largely ignoble role in shifting this baseline. The Court has been none too careful about distinguishing between people who are required to register and "predators" who exhibit an uncontrollable and undeterrable proclivity to offend. When the plurality opinion in *McKune v. Lile* first said that "[s]ex offenders are a serious threat in this Nation," it was talking about individuals with a medically recognized disorder.[4] But the Court, by repeating that dictum in very different contexts—along with its deeply problematic evidentiary basis—has infected the entire registrant population with ticking-human-time-bomb dangerousness.

In upholding J.R. Packingham's First Amendment right to access social networking websites, the Court has broken free of this self-perpetuating cycle of cross-citations. The majority opinion is, for understandable reasons, fairly quiet about this, but the reasoning and language of the decision signaled an important departure from the habits of thinking that supported zoning people like J.R. Packingham out of the Constitution.

But on that point, troublingly, *Packingham* was more a 5-3 decision than an 8-0. Justices Samuel Alito and Clarence Thomas, as well as Chief Justice John Roberts, seemed willing to open a registered sex offender hole in existing doctrine by permitting punishment to be imposed for speech that neither causes nor was intended to cause harm, simply because the speaker is a registrant. And the concurrence's attempt to perpetuate "facts" about registrants' recidivism recycled from prior opinions—alongside some fresh anecdotes—prompted an unprecedented *Washington Post* "fact check" of a Supreme Court opinion.

So what will *Packingham* mean? While it is no Magna Carta for registrants, there is reason for optimism. The combination of this decision, the outside fact check, and broader societal shifts may lead legislatures and courts to think twice about imposing or rubber-stamping onerous and degrading restrictions, which reflect and reinforce the notion that registrants are permanent outcasts.

The dustup over the reliability and accuracy of the statistics in the *Packingham* concurrence highlights the need for an entirely different kind of caution than that opinion insisted on. Justice Alito insisted

---

4 536 U.S. 24, 32 (2002)

that the Court must be careful about the "implication of its rhetoric," but the path from *McKune* to *Packingham* shows that it must be more careful about its facts. It is a given that the Court's role in our system requires it literally to "find" facts—to look far beyond the record for information bearing on the broad legal questions it decides. But this imbroglio highlights both the Court's underappreciated power, through repetition and its own authority, to *create* facts and the dangers that this power poses.

I. Background: How Packingham Became *Packingham*

J.R. Packingham's journey to the U.S. Supreme Court began with his July 2010 victory in a less august tribunal: Durham County Traffic Court. When a traffic citation was dismissed, he decided to share the good news on Facebook:

> Man God is Good! How about I got so much favor they dismissed the ticket before court even started? No fine, no court costs, no nothing spent . . . . . . Praise be to GOD, WOW! Thanks JESUS!

While it would never be part of the case, it is relevant to Mr. Packingham's journey through America's judicial system that this invocation of the deity was no mere figure of speech. He is a person of deep religious faith, who generally believes that everything happens for a purpose, which turns out to be an excellent disposition to have if you're a Supreme Court litigant.

But Mr. Packingham was not looking to become a litigant that day and would not have become one but for the exertions of Corporal Brian Schnee of the Durham Police Department. Schnee had recently learned about an arrestee who had been charged with violating a 2008 law that made it a felony for persons on the state's Sex Offender and Public Protection Registry to "access" a "commercial social networking website."[5] Schnee was "intrigued."[6] So, sitting at his desk

---

[5] Transcript of Hearing, Vol. I, at 10–11, State v. Packingham, Apr. 5, 2011 (10-CRS-57146).

[6] *Id.* at 11.

one evening, he compiled a list of registrants in Durham County and began to search for them on Facebook and MySpace.[7]

He searched for the name "Lester Packingham," which landed him on J.R.'s father's page, which led to J.R.'s page and to the celebratory post.[8] J.R. Packingham had been a registrant for eight years because of a one-count guilty plea for taking indecent liberties with a minor when he was in college. That conviction, for which the judge had imposed a suspended sentence and a relatively brief period of supervised release, had occurred well before Section 202.5 was passed and before many of North Carolina's other restrictions on registrants were put in place. When he put up the fateful Facebook post, Packingham was not incarcerated, on probation, or on post-release supervision.

Trained detective that he was, Schnee checked the traffic court records to verify that J.R. Packingham was in fact the man responsible for the incriminating post. After he had confirmed that it was the same man, police went to Packingham's apartment to arrest him and execute a warrant enabling them to seize his computer drives. Law enforcement also subpoenaed account records from Facebook.

None of this activity turned up anything more incriminating than the original post—which became the basis for charging him with a single felony count of unlawful accessing. It soon became clear that the main issue would be the First Amendment; guilt under the statute was not seriously an issue. Packingham moved to dismiss the indictment on constitutional grounds. He and another man facing trial before the same judge for violating Section 202.5 were given a hearing, at which they identified a dizzying array of websites to which Section 202.5 might apply. The state, which in theory has the burden of justifying its law, put on no evidence at all. Nonetheless, the judge's common sense favored the prosecution, and the motion was denied. Packingham's case went to trial before a jury. The state presumably liked its chances of conviction, but it plainly recognized that jurors might see things differently than had the judge. So, in her summation, the prosecutor urged the jury not to think about all the

---

[7] *Id.* at 12. It's hard to believe now, but MySpace passed Google as the most visited website in the United States in 2006, and had more users than did Facebook until well into 2008.

[8] *Id.* at 75–77.

more narrow laws North Carolina *could have* enacted, but only to do their duty and convict under this one.[9] It worked. The judge imposed a suspended sentence, and Packingham appealed the conviction, persuading the state's intermediate court, but not its supreme court, that Section 202.5 was unconstitutional.

II. An Incredibly Unconstitutional Abridgment of First Amendment Rights

We'll now explain why, under First Amendment precedent both venerable and recent, *Packingham* was such an easy case. First, and unlike many of the Supreme Court's recent free-speech-protecting decisions, *Packingham* involved . . . speech. A time traveler from a different First Amendment era might have genuine difficulty understanding what data-mining, a trademark, advertisements of haircut prices, or campaign contributions have to do with the freedom of *speech*.[10] Not so here. The speech that led to Packingham's conviction was at the First Amendment's core. While the post may have been quotidian, by exclaiming "God is Good!" to celebrate the dismissal of the citation, Packingham was both commenting on a government proceeding and expressing his religious views. Contrast this with the speech that recent decisions have protected: the right to falsely represent one's military service, play luridly violent video games, broadcast unlawfully recorded conversations, and distribute depictions of unlawful animal cruelty.[11]

Nor did *Packingham* have another factor that can make for a hard First Amendment case: the presence of real or intended harm. The Court's first Facebook case, *Elonis v. United States*, involved a defendant whose vituperative posts about his ex-wife, expressed in the form of graphically violent rap lyrics, had indisputably made her fearful.[12] The Court vacated his conviction, holding—on very

---

[9] Trial Transcript, Vol. I, at 253–54, State v. Packingham, May 29, 2012, Durham County, N.C. (10-CRS-57148).

[10] See Sorrell v. IMS Health Inc., 564 U.S. 552 (2011); Matal v. Tam, 137 S. Ct. 1744 (2017); Expressions Hair Design v. Schneiderman, 137 S. Ct. 1144 (2017); and Citizens United v. FEC, 558 U.S. 310 (2010), respectively.

[11] See United States v. Alvarez, 132 S. Ct. 2537 (2012); Brown v. Entm't Merchants Ass'n, 564 U.S. 786 (2011); Bartnicki v. Vopper, 532 U.S. 514 (2001); and United States v. Stevens, 559 U.S. 460 (2010), respectively.

[12] 135 S. Ct. 2001 (2015).

free-speech-y statutory grounds—that proof of *mens rea* was required for a threat to be punishable. And in *Snyder v. Phelps*, the Court overturned a tort judgment for the Westboro Baptist Church's intentional—and repugnant—infliction of emotional distress on the family of a fallen soldier by picketing his funeral with signs declaring he had deserved to die.[13] To complete the picture, Packingham's was not a "partial sanction" situation. North Carolina did not restrict access to trademark registration or refuse government funding. It imposed criminal punishment without requiring proof of either an "evil-doing hand" or an "evil mind."

To be sure, *Packingham* is not the easiest possible case. North Carolina did not impose criminal punishment because the defendant had said "Thank you, Jesus" as opposed to "Praise Satan." Regardless of its content, the post was evidence of what was prohibited: the accessing of social networking websites. However, North Carolina was not concerned that physical "accessing" would overburden internet bandwidth, but rather that it would enable communication and the receipt of information—in other words, speech. It would be a free-speech restriction to prohibit reading the *New York Times* (or nytimes.com) on the theory that information could be gathered from it and put to criminal use. And it would be no less an abridgment to criminalize the "act" of picking up the newspaper to prevent that from happening.

It also doesn't make a First Amendment difference that North Carolina's ultimate purpose was to prevent crime. The Court has recognized two distinct "crime" exceptions to the First Amendment's otherwise categorical protections. The Constitution does not protect speech that is criminal in itself: if treason or criminal price-fixing is accomplished through words, that doesn't impair the government's power to punish those misdeeds. Nor does the First Amendment protect words that do not in themselves cause harm but are "integral to a criminal transaction": soliciting a hitman may be criminalized, and so may using Facebook to plot a getaway. J.R. Packingham's post (or his accessing, for that matter) cannot possibly be fit into those exceptions.

The power that North Carolina sought to exercise was in many respects the very one that the Court rejected in its early 20th-century

---

[13] 562 U.S. 443 (2011).

cases: by keeping people "like" J.R. Packingham from communicating or gathering information, social harm can be avoided. But the Supreme Court held decades ago that the First Amendment does not allow the government to prevent litter by prohibiting leafleting. And the "clear and present danger" doctrine seems especially appropriate to cases like these—and plainly fatal to Section 202.5. As expounded in the Court's later cases, the government *may* hold a speaker liable for what might happen as a result of his speech, but *only* if it demonstrates that he intended those unlawful consequences and that they were likely and imminent.[14] Section 202.5 requires no such showing, and J.R. Packingham's case lacked all three constitutionally required elements.

It might understandably be interjected that these rules can't *really* apply when the harm targeted is serious—preventing litter is one thing, but sexual abuse of a minor is another. The Court's precedents have this answer: "No." The Court in *Ashcroft v. Free Speech Coalition* confronted the same theory and same governmental purpose advanced here for speech suppression.[15] The government defended the federal statutory prohibition on "virtual child pornography" (that is, images that appear to depict actual children engaged in sexual activity, but in fact show computer-generated ones) by pointing to express congressional findings that possessing such materials would enable predatory pedophilic behavior—both by overcoming young targets' resistance (showing sexual contacts with adults to be "normal") and by making prosecutions for possessing true child pornography impossible to win.[16]

The Court would have none of that. *Ashcroft* told the government it had the First Amendment backward: it could not punish an innocent, fully protected activity on the theory that *someone* with a criminal purpose could put it to bad ends. The government may not criminalize possession of comic books merely because they might facilitate criminal abuse by someone inclined to do so. The way to go is to prosecute those who use it (or attempt to) for criminal purposes.

And there were still more First Amendment winds at *Packingham*'s back. A central theme of the Roberts Court's jurisprudence

[14] See Hess v. Indiana, 414 U.S. 105, 108–09 (1973).

[15] 535 U.S. 234 (2002).

[16] *Id.* at 263.

has been that judicial balancing and judicially established exceptions are "dangerous" to the free-speech guarantee.[17] The Court has expressed hostility to arguments that different types of speakers, kinds of speech, and media of speech warrant different treatment. The Court declined to treat speech by corporations differently from that of natural persons;[18] a majority of justices have expressed second thoughts about treating zoning restrictions on adult bookstores as "content neutral";[19] and similar regret has been expressed about special doctrines for broadcasting and commercial speech.[20] *United States v. Stevens* can be read as the Court's commitment device for avoiding new exceptions.[21] And *Reed's* refusal to exempt truly benign content-based distinctions from exacting scrutiny reflects just how rigidly the Court is holding itself to those rules.[22] Section 202.5's imposition of speech burdens purely on the basis of the identity of the speaker were vulnerable in light of the Court's increasingly noisy rumblings against speaker-based discrimination.

In addition, the state court's decision upholding Section 202.5 was riddled with problems. The North Carolina Supreme Court's primary rationale—that Section 202.5 regulated conduct—was plainly wrong; the state disavowed it at the certiorari stage. And the court's alternative suggestion that Section 202.5 could properly be analyzed under the Supreme Court's standards for "time, place, and manner" regulations ran into persistent difficulty. The essence of that doctrine is that normal, even-handed government activity will require that *some* speech be suppressed. That two parades can't march on the same street on the same day may necessitate a permit regime, but not a rule that a certain subset of speakers may never parade there. Moreover, social networking websites are very different "places."

---

[17] Stevens, 559 U.S. at 470.

[18] Citizens United v. FEC, 558 U.S. 310 (2010).

[19] City of Los Angeles v. Alameda Books, 535 U.S. 425, 448 (2002) (Kennedy, J., concurring) ("[The] fiction that such ordinances are content-neutral . . . is perhaps more confusing than helpful. These ordinances are content-based and we should call them so.").

[20] See, e.g., FCC v. Fox Television Stations, 556 U.S. 502, 530, 535 (2009) (Thomas, J., concurring) (declaring interest in "reconsidering" *Red Lion Broadcasting Co. v. F.C.C.,* 395 U.S. 367 (1969), which imposed a different standard for broadcast speech); Greater New Orleans Broad. Ass'n v. US, 527 U.S. 173, 197 (1999) (Thomas, J., concurring).

[21] 559 U.S. at 470.

[22] Reed v. Town of Gilbert, 135 S. Ct. 2218 (2015).

Facebook alone contains more people than any single continent. The canonical time, place, and manner case, *Ward v. Rock Against Racism,* limited how loud music could be played in a single venue in a single public park, and the dissent thought even that decision "eviscerate[d] the First Amendment."[23]

In any event, the upshot of the Court's improbable doctrinal stretches would still have been "intermediate" scrutiny—not no scrutiny. The central requirement of that test is that the law not suppress substantial quantities of speech that do not implicate the governmental purpose, and the Court's recent decision in *McCullen v. Coakley* had applied that requirement with real bite.[24] Here, the vast majority of what Section 202.5 suppressed is patently unrelated to the government's harm-prevention purpose.

Moreover, the North Carolina Supreme Court had included assertions that helped ensure that its opinion would be viewed as unserious. Assessing the requirement that "ample alternative channels" remain open, that court urged Mr. Packingham to look on the bright side: *New York Times*, Facebook, and Twitter might be off-limits, but not wral.com (local Raleigh news) or pauladeen.com, which did not permit minors to create accounts. And of course, he could express himself through phone calls and email. In an era when the president is announcing Supreme Court nominations on Twitter, these assertions would prove to be a millstone around the neck of Section 202.5. But it was not entirely the state court's fault—what *could* it have said to establish that there are meaningful alternatives?

Finally, and as a matter of legal realism, Section 202.5 was the kind of law the justices are comfortable striking down. Only a handful of other jurisdictions had attempted anything similar, and the law was, on its own terms, obviously ineffectual and lacking in common sense. The law contained an express—but inexplicable—exemption for "stand-alone" photo-sharing and "chat" sites, even though

---

[23] Ward v. Rock Against Racism, 491 U.S. 781, 812 (1989) (Marshall, J., dissenting). Justice Kennedy at oral argument asked the state for the best case support for upholding a law like Section 202.5; and when the state gave its answer, *"Burson v. Freeman,"* which upheld a 75-foot buffer around a polling place on Election Day, the justice could not help but say "If you cite *Burson*, I think -- I think you lose" (a comment that the superstitious co-author strained to forget as he awaited the Court's decision). Transcript of Oral Arg. at 40, Packingham v. North Carolina, 137 S. Ct. 1730 (2017) (No. 15-1194).

[24] 134 S. Ct. 2518, 2535–41 (2014).

pedophiles have long used the former, and the latter have been found to pose far greater dangers than sites like Facebook. And for obvious reasons, the law was most likely to catch a person like J.R. Packingham, who was saying things publicly, than a registrant who was up to no good (or a nonregistrant predator who used the sites to "harvest" information about teenagers). Those on petitioner's side in the Supreme Court were genuinely surprised that North Carolina's brief did not even muster an *anecdote* in defense of Section 202.5—not a single case in which a registrant's prohibited access had been used to enable a crime or even an instance in which an individual's other nefarious activities were uncovered through a Section 202.5 arrest and ensuing search of computer drives.

If that were not enough, North Carolina—in an attempt to minimize what Section 202.5 forecloses—argued that Section 202.5 would not have prevented J.R. Packingham from having a *friend* post his message on Facebook. That led our side to ask (rhetorically), wouldn't that also mean that a registrant with predatory intent could, without running afoul of Section 202.5, ask a friend to print out profile pages of the members of the local high school cheerleading squad? To our considerable surprise, the answer from the state was that that would be okay too.

III. Sex Offender Exceptionalism: A Caste of Thousands?

With all this going for *Packingham*, it would be tempting to say—as did Bialystock and Bloom over champagne at intermission— "What could possibly go wrong?" But here too, that seemingly rhetorical question has an answer: "sex offender exceptionalism."[25] The Supreme Court could have simply concluded that basic First Amendment rules do not apply to a measure that suppresses the rights of the particular group burdened by Section 202.5.

Such worry might seem far-fetched. There is no end of authority for the proposition that those whom we hate get full First Amendment protection. Indeed, some say that is the whole point of the First Amendment. The right of true-believing Nazis to parade amid the homes of Holocaust survivors in Skokie, Illinois is not even an interesting First Amendment question. And the Supreme Court recently

---

[25] We borrow this term from the title of Corey Rayburn Yung, Sex Offender Exceptionalism and Preventive Detention, 101 J. Crim. L. & Criminology 969 (2011).

announced—albeit in a conspicuously divided opinion—that the government commits an "independent constitutional wrong" when it draws speaker-based distinctions.[26] Presumably "the class" of persons targeted by Section 202.5 have no less a "right to use speech to strive to establish worth, standing, and respect" than, say, the artificial persons whose equal rights *Citizens United* vindicated.[27]

Moreover, Packingham's side could (and did) take solace from the Court's decisions in *Simon & Schuster v. Members of N.Y. State Crime Victims Board*[28] and *Ashcroft*.[29] The former held unconstitutional a law that, like Section 202.5, disadvantaged a particular class of speakers defined by a prior criminal conviction: it imposed special burdens on their making money by selling their crime stories. That measure—in an augur of the emotive naming conventions that would prevail in sex-offender legislation—was known as the "Son of Sam" law and apparently had been prompted by rumors that David Berkowitz, the serial killer who had terrorized New York City in 1977, was interested in a book deal. The *Simon and Schuster* opinion did not take long before it likened him—for First Amendment purposes—to Henry David Thoreau, Malcolm X, and Saint Augustine, whose memoirs had recounted their criminal exploits.[30] The *Ashcroft* decision was likewise a valuable data point for the "no exceptions" side. The plaintiff in that case was the "Free Speech Coalition" (producers of adult pornography), but, in vindicating the First Amendment, the Court did not shrink from the reality that there exists "subcultures" of persons—pedophiles—who could and would use virtual child pornography to overcome resistance of young victims.[31]

---

[26] Citizens United, 558 U.S. at 340–41.

[27] *Id.*

[28] 502 U.S. 105 (1991).

[29] Ashcroft v. Free Speech Coalition, 535 U.S. 234 (2002).

[30] Simon & Schuster, 502 U.S. at 121–22. Amazingly, David Berkowitz, the "Son of Sam"—still serving the over-300-year sentence imposed at a time when transistor radios were many New Yorkers' primary source of information—has a vital internet presence. He experienced a religious conversion in 1987 and now calls himself the "Son of Hope." Supporters have created a site that contains his religious-themed videos, along with an apologetic account of his murder spree.

[31] Ashcroft, 535 U.S. at 245. Neither decision was directly controlling. *Simon & Schuster* addressed content-based distinction between crime memoirs and other writings. The law in *Ashcroft* did not single out pedophiles, but rather prohibited all virtual child pornography.

But sex offender exceptionalism is what the state argued, unapologetically. North Carolina's brief asserted that it was a First Amendment "virtue, not a vice" that Section 202.5 targeted the free speech rights of only a "small percentage of the population."[32] "Sex offenders, in particular," the state explained, "have been subjected to a variety of registration, reporting, and residency restrictions, that could not have been imposed on the public at large."[33] And "courts have upheld" these laws "based on the predictive judgment that sex offenders are far more likely to commit future crimes than other citizens."[34] To the reader in search of a limiting principle, the state offered this not-very-reassuring one: the government's "leeway" in "dealing with" the constitutional rights of "this class of individuals" does "not mean, of course, that States may without cause deprive convicted persons of all their First Amendment rights."[35]

Bedrock constitutional principles are sometimes honored in the breach. That the civil rights movement had broadened First Amendment rights for everyone was only part of Harry Kalven's celebrated thesis. His full statement was that "the Negro" was "winning back" for "us" what "the Communists" had seemingly lost.[36] As he and others have long noted, the vaunted "clear and present danger" test was first announced in cases that did not protect the speech rights of those with revolutionary views; and the standard failed—in dramatic fashion—in *Dennis v. United States*,[37] in which the Court applied it to uphold the McCarthy-era campaign to extinguish the Communist Party. Nor, as Mary Ann Case points out, should it be forgotten that Justice John Marshall Harlan's legendary *Plessy* dissent, after remonstrating that "there is no caste here," went on to say "[except] the Chinese," who are "a race so different from our own that we do not permit those belonging to it to become citizens."[38]

---

[32] Brief for Respondent at 11, Packingham v. North Carolina, 137 S. Ct. 1730 (2017) (No. 15-1194).

[33] *Id.* at 19.

[34] *Id.*

[35] *Id.* at 19–20.

[36] Kalven, *supra* note 2, at 6.

[37] 341 U.S. 494 (1951).

[38] Plessy v. Ferguson, 163 U.S. 537, 561 (1896). Indeed, Professor Case made this very point in contrasting Justice Kennedy's sensitive and respectful account in *Lawrence v. Texas* of the lives of gays and lesbians to his harsh words about individuals convicted

A. Civil Death by 1000 Cuts?

North Carolina's plea for exceptionalism drew on both of these strands. First, it suggested that registered sex offenders are so different from "us" that they might be "stranger[s]" to the Constitution.[39] The state cited the very regularity with which registrants are subject to restraints that "could not have been imposed on the public at large," and the ease with which "courts have upheld" these restraints as evidence of their degraded citizenship status.[40] Second, it pointed to the reason for this: like Communists in the mid-20th century (but unlike, say, Jehovah's Witnesses), sex offenders are not only despised, they are feared. They are perceived to be so dangerous, so intent on causing harm (or constitutionally incapable of stopping themselves), and so stealthy in evading detection that their mere presence among the ordinary citizenry is an emergency condition, the sort of "ticking time bomb" or "clear and present danger" before which ordinary constitutional rules recede.

As a descriptive matter, North Carolina was not wrong that states *do* impose on registrants a vast array of oppressive restrictions that they could not—and would not—impose on any other free citizens. Under other provisions of North Carolina law, the same class of people (sometimes a subset of them) is excluded from churches, the grounds of the General Assembly, the state fair, and public schools and universities, not to mention shopping malls, all because of the concern that minors might at some point be present there.[41] Registrants nationwide are prohibited—either for life or for decades after completing their sentences—from living, working, or just being near such places. These burdens are qualitatively different from the

---

of sexual offenses in *McKune v. Lile.* "This coupling of the extension of protection to a newly respectable group with a more thoroughgoing willingness to fence out and treat harshly other groups still viewed as outcast," she observed, "is a common and much remarked on phenomenon." Mary Ann Case, Of "This" And "That" in Lawrence v. Texas, 55 Sup. Ct. Rev. 75, 99 n.107 (2003).

[39] Romer v. Evans, 517 U.S. 620, 635 (1996).

[40] This line of argument has more than faint echoes of the ultimate target of Justice Harlan's *Plessy* dissent—the majority opinion in *Dred Scott v. Sandford,* 60 U.S. 393, 409 (1857), which had treated the indignities piled on free African Americans as proof that, as a matter of constitutional law, their rights "might [be]. . .withh[e]ld or grant[ed] at [the] pleasure" of the majority.

[41] N.C. Gen. Stat. § 14-208.18(a). Some of these provisions were enjoined in Does v. Cooper, 148 F. Supp. 3d 477 (M.D.N.C. 2015) while *Packingham* was pending.

collateral consequences of convictions for other crimes (which are themselves often mean-spirited and counterproductive). Elected representatives freely refer to registrants in dehumanizing terms ("toxic waste"),[42] express glee at their hardships,[43] seek re-election based on toughness against them—and when their toughness is called into question by TV provocateurs, they have been known to convene a special session to take action.[44]

Nor was the state wrong about how overwhelmingly and readily these laws have been upheld by many courts. The North Carolina Supreme Court upheld a town's ban of registrants from its parks, rejecting a challenge by a man who had suffered a stroke who asked that his mother be allowed to push his wheelchair through the park across the street from where they lived.[45] Although it was "stipulated that the park . . . contain[ed] no amenities for children," the court of appeals reasoned, that "by restricting only registered sex offenders from entering public parks . . . the ordinance promotes the general welfare and safety of Woodfin's citizens, which is a legitimate government purpose."[46] And in *Grady v. North Carolina*,[47] a North Carolina appellate court held, even after the Supreme Court's decision

---

[42] See, e.g., Doe v. Pataki, 940 F. Supp. 603, 621–22 (S.D.N.Y. 1996), rev'd in part, 120 F.3d 1263 (2d Cir. 1997) (noting that, during the debate on New York's Megan's Law, state legislators referred to convicted sex offenders as "depraved," "animals," and "the human equivalent of toxic waste" (emphasis omitted)).

[43] See Jesse James Deconto, Arrested for Going to Church, Charlotte Observer, Aug. 22, 2009, http://www.bishop-accountability.org/news2009/07_08/2009_08_22_Deconto_ArrestedFor.htm (quoting state Sen. David Hoyle, Dem., sponsor of the North Carolina law as saying, "as far as I'm concerned, they've lost all their rights—to go to church ... to go to McDonald's to get a cheeseburger if they've got the slides. They have made that choice. They have imposed that on themselves. I didn't.").

[44] See Recent Legislation, 119 Harv. L. Rev. 940, 942 (2006) (explaining that stringent Alabama legislation was passed at special session convened one week after the host of "The O'Reilly Factor" described the state's laws governing sex offenders as evidence it didn't "seem to care about" protecting children); Bonnie Rochman, Should Sex Offenders Be Barred from Church?, Time, Oct. 14, 2009, http://www.time.com/time/nation/article/0,8599,1929736,00.html (quoting sponsor of North Carolina law as saying, "We feel it is a good law. When a person takes advantage of a child, I don't worry about their constitutional rights.").

[45] Standley v. Woodfin, 362 N.C. 328, 333 (N.C. 2008).

[46] Standley v. Woodfin, 186 N.C. App. 134, 138, 164 n.9 (Ct. App. 2007).

[47] 135 S. Ct. 1368 (2015).

in *United States v. Jones*,[48] that lifetime 24-hour-satellite-monitoring of certain registrants did not even count as a "search" for Fourth Amendment purposes.

Before he hit "post" on his fateful Facebook announcement, J.R. Packingham had been compelled to quit a job in a shopping mall kiosk because there was a daycare facility on the premises; he had had to move when he was informed that his apartment was too close to another facility. He surely had felt the sting of these laws in less direct ways. Indeed, the premise of these measures is that registrants are nothing but dangerous and that their presence in a place pollutes it for everyone else.

But in addition to these perils for Mr. Packingham, this landscape created problems for *Packingham*. If, as courts and legislators widely assume, registrants may readily be excluded from the "streets and parks" and public places that "time out of mind, have been used for purposes of assembly, communicating thoughts between citizens, and discussing public questions,"[49] then why not Facebook? If these exclusions are permissible, does that mean that registrants are not a part of the "public" or the "citizen[ry]" whose "privileges, immunities, rights, and liberty" the Constitution protects?[50] More than any First Amendment doctrine, this logic of status-based degradation posed the most serious threat to Packingham's challenge.

How likely was it that the Supreme Court would be swayed by the logic of these other "perfectly constitutional" infringements? Does the record of relative futility really mean that these laws are perfectly constitutional? If so, how did this come to pass? How did we get to the point where basic liberties of free people to live, work, and go about their business are routinely subject to legislative extinction? Relatedly, how did we get to the point at which it is permissible to view every person on a registry as if he were like the defendant in the 1997 case of *Kansas v. Hendricks*, a member of the truly tiny class

---

[48] 565 U.S. 400 (2012) (holding that the attachment of a GPS device to a vehicle is a search within the meaning of the Fourth Amendment).

[49] Hague v. CIO, 307 U.S. 496, 515 (1939).

[50] Somewhat incongruously, registrants—and other felons—are not stripped of the franchise in North Carolina, though, lest they forget their status, the state does have a special law requiring that they notify the school principal if their polling place is in a school. N.C. Gen. Stat. § 14-208.18 (e).

of persons whose personality disorder compels them to commit sexual acts against children?[51]

As a matter of doctrine, the U.S. Supreme Court had not, before *Packingham*, passed upon second-generation state laws that imposed substantive burdens on liberty based on registrant status. Indeed, its precedents show signs that it would not endorse exceptionalism. But the Court has played an outsized and lamentable indirect role in the "signal bleed"[52] that has led to the widespread belief among legislators and reviewing courts that such laws are sensible and unassailable, and increasingly that the liberties of registrants are matters of grace and not right.

B. The Supreme Court's Responsibility

When we say the U.S. Supreme Court has played an important role in this development, it is not because of what the Court's decisions have held, but rather what the Court's opinions have taught. In terms of holdings, the two most relevant Supreme Court decisions—*Smith v. Doe*[53] and *Connecticut Department of Public Safety v. Doe*[54]—sustained registration and community notification laws only after highlighting their purely procedural character. *Smith* observed that the Alaska law did "not restrain activities sex offenders may pursue but leaves them free to change jobs or residences."[55] For its part, the *Connecticut* Court denied non-dangerous registrants' claim to an individualized hearing on the ground that public dissemination of registrant status was not a representation of individual dangerousness.[56]

Indeed, the case that brought the Court closest to unvarnished "sex offender exceptionalism" before last term was when it summarily reversed the North Carolina courts' decision in *Grady*.[57] The Court had upheld federal registration a handful of times, but also struck it

---

[51] 521 U.S. 346 (1997).
[52] United States v. Playboy Entm't Group, Inc., 529 U.S. 803, 807 (2000).
[53] 538 U.S. 84 (2003).
[54] 538 U.S. 1 (2003).
[55] Smith, 538 U.S. at 100.
[56] 538 U.S. at 7.
[57] 135 S. Ct. 1368 (2015).

down once,[58] as it had with civil commitment.[59] (Indeed, as we note below, one of the registration cases, the 2013 opinion in *United States v. Kebodeaux*[60] took a no-drama approach to the very same empirical questions that drew attention to the *Packingham* concurrence.) And while less directly relevant, the decisions in *Ashcroft*,[61] *Kennedy v. Louisiana*,[62] and *Stogner v. California*[63] at least stand against the suggestion that, in the Supreme Court, all laws might go silent once sexual harm to minors is a part of a case.

But to focus only on the holdings of these cases—*Smith* decided no more than that the particular registration obligations imposed in the 1994 Alaska statute did not violate the Ex Post Facto Clause—is to ignore the myriad other ways the Court's output can shape the course of the law. And in this arena, those effects have been powerful and lamentable.

A fuller reckoning begins with Justice Kennedy's plurality opinion in *McKune v. Lile*, which offered a litany of deeply problematic factual assertions about "sex offenders" that continue to shape legal decisions to this day.[64] Indeed, many of the same assertions prompted the *Washington Post*'s fact check after *Packingham*.[65] The *McKune* passage, laden with citations to a variety of Justice Department sources, appeared to indicate that recidivism by sex offenders was different in kind from the ordinary recidivism problems that the criminal justice system must deal with. The opinion cited one "estimate" that placed the "rate of recidivism of untreated offenders. . . as high as 80%."[66] It

[58] Carr v. United States, 560 U.S. 438 (2010).

[59] Compare Kansas v. Crane, 534 U.S. 407 (2002) with Kansas v. Hendricks, 521 U.S. 346 (1997).

[60] 133 S. Ct. 2496 (2013).

[61] 535 U.S. 234 (2002).

[62] 554 U.S. 407 (2008).

[63] 539 U.S. 607 (2003).

[64] 536 U.S. 24 (2002).

[65] Michelle Ye Hee Lee, Justice Alito's Misleading Claim about Sex Offender Rearrests, Wash. Post, June 21, 2017, https://www.washingtonpost.com/news/fact-checker/wp/2017/06/21/justice-alitos-misleading-claim-about-sex-offender-rearrests; see also Ira Mark Ellman & Tara Ellman, "Frightening and High": The Supreme Court's Crucial Mistake about Sex Crime Statistics, 30 Const. Comment. 495 (2015).

[66] McKune, 536 U.S. at 32–33 (citing U.S. Dept. of Justice, Bureau of Justice Statistics, Sex Offenses and Offenders (1997); U.S. Dept. of Justice, Bureau of Justice Statistics, Recidivism of Prisoners Released in 1983 (1997)).

then identified two other documents as establishing that convicted sex offenders are "much more likely than any other type of offender to be rearrested for a new rape or sexual assault."[67] The "estimate," as critics would later show, was essentially rubbish; it had appeared in a "practitioner's guide" and was little more than the sales pitch of someone marketing his treatment services to corrections officials. The second "factual" assertion was so incomplete as to be seriously misleading. The "likel[ihood]" alluded to was an order of magnitude lower than the 80 percent figure the opinion actually mentioned, and "more likely" did not mean what one might expect. The underlying data did show the rates at which persons previously convicted of sex offenses were rearrested on sexual charges to be higher than the rates at which persons released after incarceration for nonsexual offenses were rearrested on sex crime charges. But the data *also* showed sexual offenders' same-offense and general recidivism rates to be *lower* than others, and further, that released burglars accounted for a larger *number* of sexual offense arrests than those who served time for sexual offenses (though the opinion did not mention a "frightening" problem of sexual assaults by convicted burglars).[68]

These errors and imprecisions, however unfortunate, appeared in *McKune* to address matters that were (or seemed) far removed from the constitutionality of broad-based, life-long disabilities for registrants. They were offered in an opinion upholding a program that the Court believed was meant to *help* those convicted, by offering what the dissenters in *Hendricks* had clamored for: in-prison treatment. It did so by aggressive means, leveraging the state's power over conditions of confinement to reward those who participated in the program (or disadvantage nonparticipants) and requiring participants to honestly account for their misdeeds—but refusing to guarantee immunity for those disclosures, ostensibly for therapeutic reasons. The result in *McKune* may have been (almost certainly) wrong as a matter of constitutional law, but it was by no means unreasonable—or vindictive. The same seems to be true of Justice Kennedy's litany of "facts" about "sex offenders." It was offered to make a point—that the government has a "vital interest" in providing treatment—that

---

[67] *Id.* at 33.

[68] U.S. Dept. of Justice, Recidivism of Prisoners Released in 1983, Bureau of Justice Statistics 6 (1997).

had scant real relevance to the Self-Incrimination Clause question presented and was not one on which there was disagreement. (Lile, the convicted rapist, *wanted* the treatment—but also immunity.) And when Justice Kennedy looked about for support for his relatively anodyne point, he went where most justices would have gone—to an amicus brief filed by the solicitor general, from which he lifted nearly all the still-controversial citations, characterizations, and assertions.[69]

But the *McKune* dictum should not be let off *too* easily. The Supreme Court should vet statistics or quasi-statistics far more carefully—and so should the solicitor general. Mere carelessness is not the whole story. Justice Kennedy did not just cite the statistics in a footnote. He placed them at the beginning of the legal reasoning section of the opinion. Moreover, he introduced them with the following pronouncement: "Sex offenders are a serious threat in this Nation" and described the Kansas program as reckoning with the "frightening and high risk of recidivism" within this offender "group."[70] The first statement was a paraphrase of the solicitor general's introduction, which had started "[s]exual offenders inflict a terrible toll each year on this Nation," in the apparent belief that this aspect of the case might help an underwhelming self-incrimination argument over the finish line.[71]

Nonetheless, *McKune* was nobody's epochal case. Indeed, even the *Doe* cases are more fairly described as the ones that brought the loaded gun on stage that others would later discharge. The holdings of both cases were relatively narrow and quite plausibly correct under applicable Supreme Court precedent. The claim in *Connecticut Department of Public Safety v. Doe*—that those required to register were entitled under due process to an individualized determination of dangerousness before the state published their registration information on the internet—seemingly was doomed by the decision in *Paul v. Davis*:[72] there is no constitutional "liberty interest" that prohibits the government from releasing stigmatizing information. If

---

[69] Brief for the United States as Amicus Curiae Supporting Petitioners, McKune v. Lile, 536 U.S. 24 (2002) (No. 00-1187).

[70] McKune, 536 U.S. at 32, 34.

[71] *Supra* note 69, at *2.

[72] 424 U.S. 693 (1976).

government defamation is not unconstitutional, then disclosure of truthful information —the fact of conviction—through a state-registry website could not be a deprivation of liberty warranting special procedures. This was all the more so, as the Court explained, because the criminal proceedings that result in convictions are, by constitutional design, public. And if that were not enough, Connecticut had included a disclaimer on the registry website that denied the premise of the plaintiffs' claim that inclusion on the registry was tantamount to a determination that a person was currently dangerous. The website, Connecticut explained, explicitly announced the opposite: that it made no representation either way of any registrant's individual danger, meaning that the further process plaintiffs sought would be pointless.

In *Smith v. Doe*, the path to victory was almost as unpromising. To begin, the ship had already sailed for declaring registration obligations broadly unconstitutional. Congress had enacted and amended a federal statute before the Supreme Court took the *Doe* cases (on petitions from states—with John Roberts representing Alaska); and, by then, 50 states had established registries. In theory, the Ex Post Facto Clause challenge in *Smith* should have been "easier" to win in that it would not require invalidating the law, only its application to earlier-convicted persons. But in reality, such claims introduce an element of fortuity. If having a registry is sensible and constitutional, a patchwork regime in which those with pre-statute convictions are "grandfathered in" but neighbors are informed that a later-convicted registrant has moved next door, is not really an appealing middle ground.

Moreover, the nature of the showing under the Ex Post Facto Clause is itself a strange one: the ultimate question is whether the state has improperly labeled a truly "punitive" regime as "civil or regulatory." Indeed, *Smith* could easily have been decided along the lines proposed in Justice David Souter's concurrence, which rested exclusively on "the presumption of constitutionality normally accorded a State's law [which entitles it to] . . . the benefit of the doubt in close cases like this one."[73] But that was unlikely to, and did not, happen. Having decided to hear the case, the Court did not limit itself to the provision before the Court, and in the face of a vigorous dissent,

[73] 538 U.S. at 110 (Souter, J., concurring).

the majority had strong incentive to make the challenged law look important and wise—not merely constitutionally permissible.

Both *Doe* opinions deployed the questionable language from *McKune*, which took on an entirely different character in the new context. In these cases, the Court was no longer addressing treatment of an individual serving a prison sentence, but rather a class of people—registrants—who *had been released*. If *they* truly are likely to recidivate at alarming rates upon release, that sounds like a present danger, not (as in *McKune*) a debater's point in argument about the Self-Incrimination Clause. Worse still, to say that "[s]ex offenders are a serious threat in this Nation" is to say that these people, widely referred to as "registered sex offenders," pose an ongoing threat, necessitating preventative measures. The solicitor general's *McKune* brief had at least referenced the "terrible toll" that *offenses* inflict, focusing on the consequences of actual crimes (committed overwhelmingly by non-registrants) rather than potential ones.

The Court's dismissiveness in both *Doe* opinions of individualized determinations of risk has sent a strong and dangerous message. In the course of concluding (plausibly) that individual determinations were not required for Connecticut's regime and that their absence did not make Alaska's law *ex post facto*, the Court signaled that it was generally permissible to treat registrants as a group, indeed a group *defined by* a similarly high individual risk of recidivism. But that is wrong twice over. First, none of the statistics the Supreme Court has cited have purported to describe rates for registrants, a highly heterogeneous group created by state law. Indeed, that was the forgotten linchpin of the *Connecticut* analysis: group averages say nothing about the dangerousness of individual members. Second, if registrants as a collective did have a higher average rate of recidivism, what would that show? If you, reader, were grouped with the likes of Hendricks, then your "group" would manifest an elevated (average) risk of offending.[74] The ensuing legal climate—where the public and their legislators say "predator" and "sex offender" and then enact

---

[74] The government's brief in *Smith v. Doe* began "[t]hey are the least likely to be cured"; "[t]hey are the most likely to reoffend"—quotations from a conference. There is no explanation on what "cure" means or which other offenders are more likely to be "cured." See Brief for United States as Amicus Curiae, Godfrey v. Doe, No. 01-729 at 1 (quoting comments from 1998 "Conference on Sex Offender Registries").

laws that burden *registrants*, citing high rates of recidivism—owes much to these Supreme Court-encouraged blurrings.

Third, the *Smith* opinion modeled a formalism and a certain cold-bloodedness that has infected courts confronting challenges to later, truly draconian laws. Rather than seeing the case as a "close one," the *Smith* majority sought to demolish every objection raised. There was not a hint of sympathy for the plight of registrants like the lead plaintiffs, who had offended many years earlier and had done hard work to reconnect with their families and persuade courts that they individually posed no real danger. The Court further suggested that posting on the internet was no different from going to a record archive and dismissed as "conjecture" what the justices surely knew to be the case[75]—that being publicly labeled a "sex offender" would worsen any registrant's job and housing prospects or worsen their lives. (The court cited an absence of record evidence on this point—an ironic assertion given the loose and unsupported "facts" it repeated from *McKune*.[76]) Indeed, the Court, relying on the public-private distinction that is a favorite of Justice Kennedy's (and presumably of our Cato readers, too), brushed aside the prospect of vigilante violence because the state's website warned against "the use of displayed information 'to commit a criminal act against another person.'"[77] Indeed, the Court evinced an almost Panglossian optimism: the public would know just the facts of registrants' offense; registrants who were not fearsome would be treated accordingly, notwithstanding the "sex offender" label and their ostensible "high risk of recidivism."

Finally, the *Smith* opinion did little to highlight the peculiar nature of what it was deciding and not deciding.[78] Since the *ex post facto* doctrine in *Smith* pivoted around a very unusual issue—whether the law was "punitive" or "regulatory"—there was a great danger that a "nonpunitive" holding will be taken to mean "generally appropriate" or "constitutional." Thus, the principle that laws which impose

[75] Smith, 538 U.S. at 100.

[76] *Id.*

[77] *Id.* at 105.

[78] Justice Souter tried to do so in both cases. Connecticut, 538 U.S. at 9 (Souter, J., concurring) (highlighting that decision did not "foreclose" a substantive due process or equal protection challenge to Connecticut's statute); see also, generally, Smith, 538 U.S. 107–110 (Souter, J., concurring).

disabilities or are needlessly excessive are not *necessarily* condemned as "punitive" under the Ex Post Facto Clause can sound like "laws may impose disabilities" or be excessive. The fact that "no one factor necessarily condemns a measure as *ex post facto*" can sound like "nothing condemns a law that operates on registrants." And just the simple fact that *ex post facto* claims are resolved by a balancing test can sound like the interests of "sex offenders" in, say, using a park may be properly "balanced" against the interest in protecting children from assault.

The *Doe* cases might be likened to *Clinton v. Jones*,[79] another instance when the Court's vision of what would happen as a result of its decision was wildly off the mark. There, the Court's confidence that civil litigation would not disrupt the presidency soon gave way to televised impeachment hearings. In the *Doe* cases, the Court seemed to envision registration (and public disclosure) as the stopping point, utterly failing to foresee that registrant status would become a legal category, on which transient anxieties and antipathies could find ready legislative expression. The latest panic—for example, might predators use drones to watch children?[80]—may be addressed through a law that imposes a restriction, along with a cross-reference to the registration chapter. Whether or not the Court should have foreseen in 2003 that the world it seemed to approve, where registrants would be "living where they wanted," would devolve into one where registrants are regularly subject to government-enforced homelessness, it exhibited a troubling insouciance about how its opinions could and likely would be understood. And, of course, the Court supplied a set of citations around which subsequent legal developments have long gravitated. Once the Supreme Court has recognized these alarming "facts" about registrants, what lower court will question them?

IV. The Supreme Court Decides: Thank God for the First Amendment

Packingham v. North Carolina arrived against this backdrop of casual but consequential Supreme Court statements about "sex offenders" and registrants. The ideas the majority opinion pronounces the

---

[79] 520 U.S. 681 (1997).

[80] See, e.g., Peter N. Borden, The Peering Predator: Drone Technology Leaves Children Unprotected from Registered Sex Offenders, 39 Campbell L. Rev. 167 (2017).

most are the less remarkable parts of the opinion. Instead, the principle that the opinion vindicates with little fanfare—that the First Amendment provides equal free-speech protection—is its most important contribution.

As befits a case so overdetermined, the First Amendment analysis in Justice Kennedy's majority opinion goes by in the blink of an eye. In one sentence, the Court assumes, but declines to decide, that the "time, place, and manner" intermediate scrutiny test applies; and in another sentence, the opinion states that Section 202.5 cannot meet that test. At various other points along the way, the majority grazes at the smorgasbord of other principles that condemn the law. At one point, the Kennedy five, citing *Ashcroft v. Free Speech Coalition*, announce that the case is controlled by the "well established . . . general rule" that the government "may not suppress lawful speech as the means to suppress unlawful speech. That is what North Carolina has done here. Its law must be held invalid."[81] At another juncture, the opinion says that Section 202.5's unconstitutionality follows *a fortiori* from *Jews for Jesus*: If a law prohibiting "all protected expression" at a single airport is not constitutional, "it follows with even greater force that North Carolina may not enact this complete bar to the exercise of First Amendment rights on social networking sites."[82]

Packingham will perhaps be most noted (and most widely cited) for its musings about the internet and social media. Whatever subtle signals the opinion sends about sex offender exceptionalism, all its rhetorical high notes sound in internet triumphalism. Indeed, the opinion reads like the remarks of someone who, invited to deliver an address about the rights of registered sex offenders, announces "I'd like to talk to you today about the social history of the Internet . . ." and plunges on from there. The opinion name-checks the Electronic Frontier Foundation's superb amicus brief three times—and, of course, acknowledges the excellent brief from Mr. Packingham's friends at the Cato Institute—but not the fact-rich brief submitted by the National Association for Rational Sex Offender Laws. And with paeans to the internet's "vast potential to alter how we think, express

---

[81] Packingham v. North Carolina, 137 S. Ct. 1730, 1738 (2017) (internal citations omitted).

[82] *Id.* at 1733.

ourselves, and define who we want to be,"[83] it earned a "like" from *Wired* magazine.[84] If gems like that were not enough, the Court suggests that its long and frustrating quest to identify and taxonomize "public forums" has reached its terminus: "While in the past there may have been difficulty in identifying the most important places (in a spatial sense) for the exchange of views, today the answer is clear. It is cyberspace . . . and social media in particular."[85]

But none of this broke new ground. That *Packingham* may be remembered as a "new media" speech case and sees itself as "address[ing] the relationship between the First Amendment and the modern Internet" is amusing.[86] The proposition that speech on the internet should receive full First Amendment protection was forcefully established almost 20 years ago in *Reno v. ACLU*,[87] when the internet truly was "new [and] protean."[88]

By contrast, early on during oral argument in *Packingham*, Justice Elena Kagan casually outed the elephant in the room by referring to President Trump's unbridled use of Twitter.[89] While we may not be able to imagine with specificity how the internet will be used in our future—encyclopedic knowledge, singularity, or a purely cloud-based U.S. Supreme Court?—the importance of the internet and its role as the dominant communications medium (among other things) is no longer uncertain as it was in *Reno*. The first part of the opinion may therefore be understood as a *Reno treppenwitz*: the language Justice Kennedy wished had accompanied the truly visionary and path-breaking decision. The fact that the following was said 20 years too late makes it all the more true: "The nature of a revolution in thought can be that, in its early stages, even its participants may be unaware of it."[90]

---

[83] *Id.* at 1736.

[84] Issie Lapowsky, The Supreme Court Just Protected Your Right to Facebook, Wired, Jun 19, 2017, https://www.wired.com/story/free-speech-facebook-supreme-court.

[85] Packingham, 137 S. Ct. at 1735.

[86] *Id.* at 1736.

[87] 521 U.S. 844 (1997).

[88] Packingham, 137 S. Ct. at 1736.

[89] Transcript of Oral Arg. *supra* note 23, at 27–28.

[90] Packingham, 137 S. Ct. at 1736.

Although the opinion does not break new ground on the techno-logical boundaries of the First Amendment, that does not mean it is unimportant. But discerning the opinion's contributions requires attention to something mostly unsaid in the opinion: its almost com-plete, if exceptionally understated, embrace of the proposition that registrants are entitled to full citizenship rights.

First and most important, the Court decided the case according to usual First Amendment rules, applying the *same* principles that would govern any other law. That might itself be "cause for dancing in the streets"[91]—at least those streets which do not pass within 300 feet of a school or licensed daycare facility. While the legal analysis in Justice Kennedy's *McKune* opinion kicks off with "sex offenders are a serious threat in this Nation" (uh oh), his *Packingham* opinion begins with "the fundamental principle of the First Amendment that all persons have access to places where they can speak and listen."[92] All persons. Section 202.5 may be said to be much more unconstitu-tional than the measure in *Jews for Jesus* only if the First Amendment rights burdened by the two laws—those of registrants and those of "all of us"—are made of the same stuff.

Second, on a rhetorical level, the opinion exhibits similar progress. It twice describes those whose First Amendment rights are abridged by Section 202.5 as "persons who have completed their sentences" and elsewhere describes them plainly as "convicted criminals" and "registered sex offenders," as opposed to "sex offenders"—a term that appears some 17 times in Justice Alito's concurrence (alongside references to "abusers" and "predators"). By contrast, the concur-rence sees today's registrant as tomorrow's "repeat sex offender," and everyone with a prior conviction—including, presumably, Henry David Thoreau and Martin Luther King Jr.—as a "potential recidivist."

Apart from labels, the Court made several substantive moves that warrant notice. First, although the Court unsurprisingly did not take up the invitation to announce when and whether speaker-based dis-crimination triggers strict scrutiny, it surely rejected North Caro-lina's position in the "virtue or vice" debate. The Court pointedly

[91] Harry Kalven, Jr., The New York Times Case: A Note on "The Central Meaning of the First Amendment," 1964 Sup. Ct. Rev. 191, 221 & n.125.

[92] Packingham, 137 S. Ct. at 1735.

refused to say that Section 202.5 is or could be analyzed as a garden-variety time, place, or manner regulation. It said only that the state had failed the test that the standard imposes.[93]

Third, the opinion made no mention of the statistics and the "facts" about "sex offenders" that have caused so much trouble. Though well short of a mea culpa, this silence—along with the notable outside fact-checking on this subject—offers up the hope that the cycle has been broken. Indeed, the opinion refuses to say anything about how dangerous "sex offenders" are. The closest it gets is its statement of how repugnant sexual *offenses* are—a statement supported with a citation not to *McKune* but rather to *Ashcroft*, which, of course, struck down a statute on First Amendment grounds—followed by an acknowledgment that *"valid* laws" to protect children from sexual abuse may be enacted.[94]

Fourth, the Court recognized, though less forcefully than did Judge Jay Bybee's opinion for the Ninth Circuit in *Doe v. Harris*,[95] that registrants who are not under criminal justice supervision are free people who do not owe their liberties to the government (or to the grace of the legislative majorities). It is significant as a principle that prisoners "have" First Amendment rights and there is no tradition of imposing speech-based disabilities as a consequence of conviction; in practice, those rights may be and almost always are traded off to accomplish "penological objectives."[96] But registrants who have finished their sentence stand on the same footing as individuals who have exited the criminal justice system after convictions for nonreportable offenses or those of us who have no criminal justice history.

Fifth, the Court observed that "even convicted criminals—and in some instances especially convicted criminals," may have important things to say on social media—"in particular if they seek to reform and to pursue lawful and rewarding lives."[97] That in itself is a milestone. This brief nod stops well short of the heartfelt welcome

---

[93] *Id.* at 1737.

[94] Ashcroft, 535 U.S. at 245.

[95] Doe v. Harris, 772 F.3d 563, 570–72 (9th Cir. 2014) ("Doe and Roe were convicted of sex-related crimes more than two decades ago and have completed their terms of probation and parole. . . . [They] are no longer on the 'continuum' of state-imposed punishments.").

[96] Pell v. Procunier, 417 U.S. 817, 822 (1974).

[97] Packingham, 137 S. Ct. at 1737.

into the political community that *Lawrence v. Texas* and *Obergfell v. Hodges* extended to other Americans formerly disdained as "sexual deviants." But acknowledging that there are registrants who seek "lawful and rewarding lives"—and are entitled to that pursuit—is entirely new terrain. In no other majority opinion has the Court recognized the individual humanity and agency of persons on registries or the possibility that they are "especially" in need of enforceable constitutional rights. Nor has the Court previously pronounced itself "troubled" or "unsettle[ed]" by the imposition of disabilities on people who have been convicted of registrable offenses.

Finally, the Court's discussion of the alternatives at North Carolina's disposal impressively (but imperfectly) avoids sex offender exceptionalism. As did *Ashcroft*, *Packingham* expressly affirms the fundamental principle that crime prevention must be pursued through the enactment of laws that target and punish wrongdoers (but that speech undertaken for criminal purposes is unprotected). It left no doubt that the mere presence of minors on the same platform was not enough to impose punishment and that valid laws must instead target activities, such as using a website to gather information about a minor or to contact a minor, which "often presage[] a sexual crime"—though here the Court arguably faltered, seeming to suggest that these conditions might be applied to registrants only.[98]

Taking these omissions and assumptions together, the Court effectively held—even without saying so as directly as Judge Bybee did—that registrants are not second-class citizens and that they are entitled (presumptively) to full free-speech rights.[99] There is reason for wishing that *Packingham* were an even more visible "milestone on the path to a more decent, tolerant, progressive society,"[100] but it is a solid victory for the important principle of free-speech equality and a welcome step away from meanness and intolerance.

---

[98] *Id.*

[99] Harris, 772 F.3d at 572 ("We accordingly agree with the district court that registered sex offenders who have completed their terms of probation and parole 'enjoy[ ] the full protection of the First Amendment.'") (citation omitted).

[100] Bd. of Trustees of Univ. of Ala. v. Garrett, 531 U.S. 356, 375 (2001).

V. The Concurrence: Taking Exception to "No Exceptions"

That Justice Alito concurred only in the judgment was not necessarily a surprise. He has been the least enthusiastic participant in the Roberts Court's fast-moving First Amendment march. And as in other cases, Justice Alito's theme was restraint. In *Snyder v. Phelps*, as the lone dissenter on a Court that seldom breaks 8-1, he had admirably interrupted the majority's civics lesson to highlight the real harm inflicted and to ask why the Court was so certain the First Amendment required this harm to go unremedied.[101]

But Justices Alito, Roberts, and Thomas did not *dissent* in this case. They too acknowledged that Section 202.5 was so unconstitutional they were "compelled" to strike it down.[102] But they were unwilling to say that the criminal punishment in J.R. Packingham's case went beyond the First Amendment pale. It may fairly be said that on the question of sex offender exceptionalism, the *Packingham* Court voted 5-3, not 8-0. That is extraordinary given that this law would be a flagrant, not a subtle, violation of free-speech rights if applied to anyone else, including to any other class of people who are believed to re-offend or offend at a higher-than-average rate. Indeed, the concurrence used the same *McKune/Smith* litany of facts—partly, perhaps, to make things uncomfortable for their author, who wrote for the Court in *Packingham*.

But while the concurrence chided Justice Kennedy for going further than necessary, the "caution" it championed was of a very odd sort. First, Justice Alito avoided opining on the constitutionality of the criminal prosecution actually before the Court. Instead, the concurrence imposed the broadest possible construction on Section 202.5—one the state's attorney general emphatically disavowed—and then decided that the law, thus construed, was facially unconstitutional.

The concurrence's legal conclusions were not incorrect. The question of statutory interpretation on which Justice Alito and the state's attorney general disagreed was whether Section 202.5's definition of "commercial social networking web sites" might be read as applying "only" to "true social networking sites" or whether sites such as WebMD and the *Washington Post* were prohibited. The concurrence was right that the statutory language could really only be read the

---

[101] 562 U.S. 443, 464–66 (2011) (Alito, J., dissenting).

[102] Packingham, 137 S. Ct. at 1743 (Alito, J., concurring).

second way. And it was also right that Section 202.5 was "substantially overbroad" and therefore merited facial invalidation. But in taking an approach that avoids a difficult constitutional question by reaching a *broader* constitutional question, one likely loses the right to criticize others' failures of restraint.[103] If, as here, doing so also entails overruling a state's construction of its own law, the Felix Frankfurter bobblehead on one's desk may begin to wag its finger.[104]

There is a second way in which the concurrence's accusations rings hollow. On the concurrence's telling, the majority had committed itself to "caution" based on the judiciary's relative lack of experience with internet-related First Amendment issues, only to break faith with that pledge by according broad (that is, standard) First Amendment protection to social media speech. But the majority opinion suffers from no such internal inconsistency: the "caution" Justice Kennedy championed related to according *exceptions* to settled First Amendment rules on the basis of the novelty of the medium. That, of course, is essentially the opposite of the kind of "caution" Justice Alito urged, which counsels hesitation before fully *protecting* speech (or recognizing free-speech rights) in novel settings. Whether one approach or the other is "restrained" depends on the baseline (and on what sort of "judicial activism" one seeks to guard against).

On this point, Justice Kennedy's opinion in *Packingham* is consistent with itself and with the stance taken in many other cases—that judges risk impermissibly picking winners when they fashion exceptions to the First Amendment rule. Two of the concurring justices have elsewhere been eloquent proponents of that view. The chief justice in *Stevens* considered the judiciary's deciding case-by-case what categories of speech should go unprotected to be "startling and dangerous."[105] And in *Reed*, Justice Thomas found that exempting political signs and temporary directional signs from an otherwise

---

[103] See Plaut v. Spendthrift Farm, Inc., 514 U.S. 211, 218 (1995) (courts should begin with narrowest constitutional ground).

[104] We do not suggest that the majority opinion was especially narrow. The bases on which it struck down J.R. Packingham's conviction would apply to anyone prosecuted under Section 202.5, so that was a facial invalidation too. It is not clear what would be gained by allowing North Carolina to enact a less overbroad, but still facially unconstitutional law.

[105] 559 U.S. 460, 470 (2010).

general prohibition triggered strict and fatal scrutiny.[106] Justice Alito has more frequently championed the different kind of judicial restraint urged in their *Packingham* concurrence—one that highlights modesty vis-a-vis legislatures.

But this was a strange case to beat that drum. In *Alvarez*, for example, Justice Alito could point to a tradition of prohibiting false speech about military honors. In *Snyder*, he highlighted that the funeral picketers' "outrageous conduct caused [the father of the deceased soldier] great injury," and that the Court should allow this acknowledgment of wrong to stand. By contrast, the legislative freedom that the majority opinion in *Packingham* was accused of needlessly foreclosing was the power to enact a law that would keep "predators" from accessing a "teen dating website."[107] But no law targeting only registrants is needed to suppress that behavior. The instinct driving this hypothetical is that *adults* have no legitimate reason to be on a teens-only site. And a law that prohibited adults generally from doing some creepy thing could of course be applied to registrants and would punish predators, the vast majority of whom will be non-registrants.[108] The state would not be "powerless."[109] (Indeed, "powerless" is not the word that comes to mind in describing North Carolina's relationship with persons on its registry.[110])

While discussing the two extreme cases—inherently innocent activity (no predator is looking for teenagers on WebMD) and plainly, or at least presumptively, inappropriate activity (visiting a teen-dating site)—the concurrence did not directly address the truly important First Amendment question the *Packingham* case presented: whether the presence, in some metaphysical way, of minors on a website—including one with 2 billion active users—is enough to make the vast

---

[106] 135 S. Ct. 2218, 2224 (2015).

[107] Packingham, 137 S. Ct. at 1743 (Alito, J., concurring).

[108] See Dallas v. Stanglin, 490 U.S. 19, 20–21 (1989) (upholding licensing regime that allows age restrictions for admission to dance halls for teenagers).

[109] Packingham, 137 S. Ct. at 1738 (Alito, J., concurring).

[110] Of course, the law would not actually stop anyone from visiting the sites. It could deter them, but only if the risk of detection and penalty were high enough, at which point the motivated predator could go elsewhere. But that is no different from how Section 202.5 worked—and failed to.

array of entirely innocent uses, like that here, proscribable.[111] The very notion that the concurrence seems comfortable accepting—that vast swaths of protected free speech could be punished based on the possibility that individuals *could* abuse their rights for a nefarious purpose—is what the First Amendment strongly rejects. (Indeed, it is a notion that ordinary criminal law principles would reject: reading the *New York Times* could not be punished as attempted bank robbery simply because the newspaper contains articles that a safe-cracker might find useful.)

This is where sex-offender exceptionalism enters the equation. The concurrence's reasons for implying that J.R. Packingham *did* do something punishable rely not on facts of this case, but rather on citations to *McKune* and *Connecticut Department of Public Safety v. Doe* (and *United States v. Kebodeaux*), said to establish that "sex offenders" are a "serious threat" to children and "more likely than" anyone else "to be rearrested" for a rape or assault. (Indeed, the concurrence is adamant that "repeat sex offenders pose an especially grave risk."[112])

The concurrence does not engage with the bases for these assertions, or with the serious and specific criticisms leveled against them. None of the underlying reports, for example, has anything to say about *registrants*, as opposed to persons committed to medical treatment programs for pedophiles or sentenced to federal prison. Updated statistics from the Justice Department report cited in *McKune* find that sex crime re-arrest rates were higher for those who committed sex offenses (as a whole, irrespective of the particular underlying offense) than for non-sex offenders. But those previously convicted of non-sex offenses committed the overwhelming number (87 percent) of sex crimes committed by all recidivists.[113] That finding is consistent with the widely recognized reality that the vast majority of sexual offenses are committed by those without prior convictions and that the vast majority of sexual assaults against minors are

---

[111] The difference between a law prohibiting speaking on Facebook and one prohibiting speech in North Carolina based on the "presence" of minors is that the percentage of minors in North Carolina is higher.

[112] Packingham, 137 S. Ct. at 1739 (Alito, J., concurring).

[113] Patrick A. Langan et al., Recidivism of Sex Offenders Released from Prison in 1994, Bureau of Justice Statistics 24 (2003), https://www.bjs.gov/content/pub/pdf/rsorp94.pdf.

perpetrated by family members and others whom they know, not predatory strangers like Hendricks or Lile.

It was enough for the concurrence that these "facts" have made it into the U.S. Reports. But it is not every day that a Supreme Court opinion is subject to a newspaper fact check. And it was disconcerting to see the highly trouble-making *McKune* dicta play a prominent role in a separate opinion whose thesis is that "[t]he Court should be more attentive to the implications of its rhetoric."[114] Indeed, the concurrence's inclusion of *Kebodeaux* in its litany deserves special mention. Justice Stephen Breyer's opinion for the Court in that case did acknowledge the same Justice Department report in *Smith* and did note that "[t]here is evidence that recidivism rates among sex offenders are higher than the average for other types of criminals."[115] But the opinion's next sentence observed that "[t]here is conflicting evidence on the point" and cited research supporting the opposite.[116] In the face of that opinion, to continue treating "frightening and high" recidivism as a Supreme Court-established fact and to claim *Kebodeaux* as fresh reinforcement, as the concurrence did, was something worse than a missed opportunity.

Moreover, the concurrence went further than just committing the same old offense of citing prior Supreme Court dicta without seriously interrogating their accuracy. It undertook its own Westlaw research to find lurid cases to show that social networking websites are—or at least can be—used in sexual offenses against minors (though several of these anecdotal examples appear to involve perpetrators who were not previously on registries).[117]

Finally, and still more troubling, the concurrence attempted to enlist academic "research" on its side, citing an article entitled "Online 'Predators' and Their Victims."[118] In fact, as the title's use of quotation marks suggests, and other research (cited in the *Packingham* briefs) confirms, academics who are experts on internet victimization of youth have been persistent, rigorous, and forceful critics of the assumptions underlying North Carolina's law and the concurring

---

[114] Packingham, 137 S. Ct. at 1743 (Alito, J., concurring).

[115] Kebodeaux, 133 S. Ct. at 2503.

[116] *Id.*

[117] Packingham, 137 S. Ct. at 1740 n.3 (Alito, J., concurring).

[118] *Id.* at 1740 n.2 (Alito, J., concurring).

opinion.[119] They have urged that "it is important for the public and officials [including Supreme Court Justices, presumably] to know that policies targeted at registered sex offenders are aimed at a very small part of the problem."[120] Indeed, the concurrence might have been reassured that their "findings (based on studying trends in arrests of 'online predators') do not suggest that the Internet is more dangerous than other environments that children and adolescents frequent."[121] Had Justice Alito's opinion commanded a majority, that important empirical reality would no longer matter. The opinion's pronouncement that "it is easier for parents to monitor the physical locations that their children visit and the individuals with whom they speak in person than it is to monitor their internet use" would effectively be the law of the land.[122]

VI. Conclusion: *Packingham's* Significance (?)

If the trajectory of *McKune* and *Doe* teaches anything, it is that Supreme Court opinions do not always mean what they hold or were intended to say. At the very least, much has happened since 2003 that the justices did not foresee or intend to approve. But the content and rhetoric of their opinions, in concert with cultural and political forces far removed from One First Street, N.E., helped bring sex offender exceptionalism to the First Amendment's door.

What will happen with *Packingham*? We first address some of the decision's potential implications for new media and the First Amendment rights of all of us. Then, we consider whether *Packingham's* discernable though muted turn from sex offender exceptionalism might signal a more general upturn in the status of registrants— or whether it is merely a case where a mighty force met its match, a First Amendment exceptionalism. Finally, we highlight a somewhat different *Packingham* effect, one attributable to the increased attention to the Supreme Court's ways of finding relevant facts and the

---

[119] See, e.g., Janis Wolak et al., Univ. of New Hampshire Crimes Against Children Research Center, Trends in Arrests of "Online Predators" 2 (2009) ("There was no evidence that online predators were stalking or abducting unsuspecting victims based on information posted at social networking sites. . . . Few of those arrested for online predation were registered sex offenders." (4 percent)).

[120] *Id*. at 9.

[121] *Id*. at 8.

[122] Packingham, 137 S. Ct. at 1743 (Alito J., concurring).

very real institutional difficulties that *Packingham*—and subsequent nonjudicial "fact checks"—have surfaced.

A. First Amendment and New Media

As we explained above, there was nothing new that needed to be said about the First Amendment to adjudge Section 202.5 (very) unconstitutional. Much of what sounded new or important is fairly described as commentary on the master text. *Reno* is the Magna Carta for the freedom of speech on the internet. That decision looks more impressive, even prophetic, with 20 years' hindsight.[123]

But *Packingham*'s significance for First Amendment law and "our" free-speech rights should not be too deeply discounted. First, the decision appears to signal a welcome development for a doctrine that has long vexed First Amendment doctrine: forum analysis. It is pretty clear that the *Jews for Jesus* case *became* an easy one because the justices were unexcited about deciding whether or not the airport terminal was a "public forum" (and if so, what kind). So the Court took the route—or exit ramp—favored by the *Packingham* concurrence: make the measure so silly that the justices' substantive disagreements would no longer matter. When the Court did address that question, in splintered fashion, in *International Society for Krishna Consciousness, Inc. v. Lee*,[124] Justice Kennedy lamented how utterly unmoored from both practical reality and its original purposes the public forum doctrine had become. Originally formulated—by Professor Kalven (!)—to describe a general limitation on the government's authority to regulate speech, the doctrine, he argued, had devolved into a favorite tool for those seeking to justify exclusions of First Amendment activities from public property. Further, Justice Kennedy contended that special First Amendment places should instead be identified functionally, without requiring a historic pedigree or a governmental dedication.[125] In other words, what matters

---

[123] See Noa Yachot, The "Magna Carta" of Cyberspace Turns 20: An Interview with the ACLU Lawyer Who Helped Save the Internet, ACLU Blog, June 23, 2017, https://www.aclu.org/blog/speak-freely/magna-carta-cyberspace-turns-20-interview-aclu-lawyer-who-helped-save-internet (noting that when the case was argued in the Court, "only one of the justices had ever been online and that several others were taken down to the court basement by their clerks and shown the internet.").

[124] 505 U.S. 672, 693–94 (1992).

[125] *Id.* at 694 (Kennedy, J., concurring).

most is whether a property is suitable for use by citizens to engage in speech activities. After many decades of spilled ink about whether a particular "forum" is "traditional,"[126] not to mention whether it has "a limited purpose,"[127] that is what the Court said in *Packingham.*

To be sure, *Packingham* did not—and could not—hold that Facebook.com is a "public forum." The doctrine was designed to restrain government from leveraging its powers as owner or trustee of property. Facebook is "public" in the sense that everyone (and their moms) are on it; but it is also the property of an (enormous) private corporation; and, broadly speaking, no one has a "First Amendment" right to post anything on Facebook if Facebook, Inc., does not want them there (think about restrictions on "offensive" posts). But the Court forcefully and admirably pronounced that speech-suppressive governmental interventions are least tolerated in "places" where Americans actually exercise their First Amendment rights.

In this regard, it is worth noting one last line of attack in North Carolina's argument that threatened real mischief—but that got no encouragement from the justices at oral argument and no mention in either opinion. In defending J.R. Packingham's conviction on appeal, the state pointed to language on the Facebook website (never introduced at trial), stating that registered sex offenders should not create accounts, and argued that he had no "independent First Amendment right" that Section 202.5 could abridge.[128] This late-breaking argument was not only improper, Packingham told the Court, it was also a red herring. It was undisputed that the state could prosecute—and had prosecuted—registrants under Section 202.5 for accessing social networking websites that have no such exclusionary policy (as appears to be true of Twitter, Linkedin, Snapchat, and the Facebook subsidiary Instagram). And if saying "God is Good" were a breach of contract with Facebook or a (metaphorical) trespass, that would make his case no different from those of litigants whose First Amendment rights were vindicated in *R.A.V. v. St. Paul* and *Virginia v. Black,* who burned crosses on the private property of African-American neighbors, or in *United States v. Stevens* and *Bartnicki v. Hopper,* whose

---

[126] See, e.g., Justice Alito's question during oral argument about how to translate Section 202.5 "into terms that would be familiar at the time of the adoption of the First Amendment." Transcript of Oral Arg., *supra* note 23, at 7.

[127] See, e.g., Rosenberger v. Rector & Visitors of the Univ. of Va., 515 U.S. 819 (1995).

[128] Brief for Respondent, *supra* note 32, at 53–54.

protected speech consisted, respectively, of depicting unlawful acts of animal cruelty and rebroadcasting illegally intercepted communications. Had the Court given any encouragement to the suggestion that the government has greater leeway, let alone plenary power, to regulate speech that occurs on property it does not control, *Packingham* would have been a First Amendment blockbuster—and not in a good way.

It is also likely that the opinion's exuberant celebration of social media's place in the First Amendment will exert influence in the "real world" deliberations of legislatures and courts. As the experience with *McKune* illustrates, the language of Supreme Court opinions can go viral. It is fair to say that Section 202.5 arose at the confluence of two moral panics: people are terrified about predators, and they are also highly anxious about what their own teenagers are saying and doing on social media. (Justice Alito's assertion—unadorned with cited authority—about parents' diminished ability to keep track of their kids reads like the lamentations of a worried dad.) And when their constituents are afraid, elected representatives are quick to take action. To the legislatures and judges who will deliberate over measures responding to future internet-related "crises," the grandfatherly assurances in Justice Kennedy's majority opinion could well provide a counterweight. "It's not as bad as it looks," the Court tells them—noting that "before it was the internet, it was the railroads"—and any "solution" is unlikely to make things better.[129]

B. Hope for Registrants

What hope, if any, does *Packingham* offer for the hundreds of thousands of Americans who find themselves on registries? On one reading, *Packingham* was a clash of exceptionalisms, pitting the judiciary's vast willingness to tolerate disfavored treatment for people with sex offense convictions against its longstanding readiness to probe the rationality of legislation when First Amendment freedoms (but only those) are burdened. It surely does not help that *Packingham*'s break with sex offender exceptionalism and its embrace of First Amendment rights for all were so understated. *Packingham*, as noted above,

---

[129] There is some danger that the opinion's language will be used to support absolutist arguments that one of this article's authors—the one who's not an ACLU lawyer—would wince at.

was no *Lawrence v. Texas* or *Romer v. Evans*, opinions that broadly challenged society to rethink irrational exclusions and the human toll of marginalization. Moreover, the fact that Justice Alito's harsh and unapologetic statements were expressed in a concurrence, rather than a dissent, may cloud the message still further—a signal that the Court's judgment is really about a silly law and is otherwise consistent with viewing the entire class of registrants as a threat.

In fact, it is not impossible that some states will attempt to blunt *Packingham*'s significance even for the First Amendment rights of those in J.R. Packingham's position. The Court's opinion rightly highlighted that Section 202.5 imposed on registrants burdens that no other free citizen—who had completed his prison sentence and term of supervised release—would be subjected to. It is thus theoretically possible that a state might attempt to impose a Section 202.5-like restriction by making "supervised release" permanent and imposing a social media ban as a mandatory condition. Such circumventions would not eliminate the constitutional violation, and they are unlikely to succeed. Indeed, the New Jersey Supreme Court rejected one such attempt, largely on state constitutional grounds, shortly before *Packingham* was decided.[130] Federal courts likewise have a long record of meaningfully scrutinizing restrictions on internet use by those under criminal justice supervision, albeit under a statutory provision that forbids "greater deprivation[s] of liberty than is reasonably necessary."[131]

We think that such pessimistic assessments miss much. First, the "signal bleed" that threatened the First Amendment claim can operate in both directions. If it is hard to articulate why park and Facebook restrictions should be different, the fact that the latter are now unconstitutional puts pressure on the premise that these other legislated disabilities are perfectly constitutional. And though the opinion could have said more, the Court's description of registrants as a segment of the populace that includes many ordinary people who want to get on with their lives surely takes some of the edge off the narrative of a single group-based "threat" to the nation.

Importantly, there is another way of understanding the case law that seemed to place so much wind at North Carolina's back. The

---

[130] J.I. v. New Jersey State Parole Bd., 155 A.3d 1008, 1023 (N.J. 2017).
[131] 18 U.S.C. § 3583(d)(2).

judicial success that laws like the one in *Woodfin* have enjoyed is less a sign that they—but not Section 202.5—are perfectly constitutional, but rather another "case of the missing amendments."[132] As Justice Antonin Scalia famously said, decrying the Court's willingness to entertain substantive due process arguments: "Our salvation is the Equal Protection Clause, which requires the democratic majority to accept for themselves and their loved ones what they impose on you and me."[133] That principle, whether or not fully judicially enforced, condemns laws that have grown up for the past two decades "singling out a certain class of citizens for disfavored legal status or general hardships."[134] Even though courts rarely strike down laws on that basis, their decisions applying other protections may—and should—be powerfully informed by these principles.

An interesting example is *United States. v. Brown*[135]—a decision issued after the national alarm about Communist threat began to recede. The Court held that a law barring Communists from holding union office was an unconstitutional bill of attainder. The government had said the law was like "a general rule to the effect that persons possessing characteristics which make them likely to incite political strikes should not hold union office, [which had] simply inserted in place of a list of those characteristics an alternative, shorthand criterion—membership in the Communist Party."[136] The "fallacy" *Brown* rejected—that treating "Communists" as "those persons likely to cause political strikes" was a mere "substitution of a semantically equivalent phrase"[137]—has been central to oppressive legislation targeting registrants: treating persons on the registry as the semantic equivalent for "predators" because they "as a group" are (believed to be) more likely to offend.

There are also important signs that the wave of panic and vituperation has crested. States have studied the actual effects of residency

---

[132] Akhil Reed Amar, The Case of the Missing Amendments: R.A.V. v. City of St. Paul, 106 Harv. L. Rev. 124 (1992).

[133] Cruzan v. Dir., Mo. Dep't of Health, 497 U.S. 261, 300–01 (1990) (Scalia, J., concurring).

[134] Romer, 517 U.S. at 633.

[135] 381 U.S. 437 (1965).

[136] *Id.* at 455.

[137] *Id.*

restrictions and have concluded that they are ineffectual at best.[138] Many in public safety have increasingly voiced opposition to ever-more intensive registration requirements, on the ground that they divert resources from what the laws are supposed to accomplish—that is, closely tracking the very small subset of individuals post-supervision whose behavior suggests an ongoing, substantial safety threat.[139] Even the mother of Jacob Wetterling—whose 1989 abduction at age 11 gripped the nation and whose name is memorialized in the federal statute mandating that states maintain registries—has spoken out against the harsh conditions that are now imposed.[140]

The results and tenor of judicial opinions considering non-free-speech challenges to restrictions seem to be shifting as well, in the direction of fairness, proportionality, and rationality. As noted above, the holdings of the Supreme Court's *Doe* cases were exceedingly narrow and fact-specific. They do not require that lower courts deciding challenges to residency restrictions, or even to present-day registration requirements, treat them as constitutional, even under the Ex Post Facto Clause. The multifactor balancing test relied on to uphold the law in *Smith* can produce very different results when the facts establish that the challenged restrictions are simultaneously draconian and ineffective. This is exactly what happened recently in the U.S. Court of Appeals for the Sixth Circuit in *Doe v. Snyder*: the court held numerous provisions of Michigan's law invalid on *ex post facto* grounds, highlighting evidence that these laws make it difficult for registrants to "find[] a home in which they can legally live or a job

---

[138] See, e.g., White Paper on the Use of Residence Restrictions as a Sex Offender Management Strategy, Colorado Sex Offender Management Board, Colorado Department of Public Safety (June 2009), http://www.csom.org/pubs/CO%20Residence%20Restrictions%202.pdf (noting that trend within Colorado and in other states in recognizing that restrictions are counterproductive).

[139] See, e.g., A Better Path to Community Safety: Sex Offender Registration in California, California Sex Offender Management Board at 5-6 (2014), http://www.casomb.org/docs/Tiering%20Background%20Paper%20FINAL%20FINAL%204-2-14.pdf (noting that California's system of lifetime registration produces a "very large" registry that has become "counterproductive" because law enforcement and the public cannot "differentiate between who is truly high risk and more likely to reoffend" and emphasizing the "need . . . to distinguish between sex offenders who require increased monitoring, attention and resources and those who are unlikely to reoffend").

[140] Jennifer Bleyer, Patty Wetterling Questions Sex Offender Laws, City Pages, Mar. 20, 2016, http://www.citypages.com/news/patty-wetterling-questions-sex-offender-laws-6766534.

where they can legally work" and keep the many registrants "who have children (or grandchildren) from watching them participate in school plays" or accompanying them to "public playgrounds."[141] The very recognition that many registrants are parents (and that many children have a parent who is on a registry) itself frustrates the narrative of "sex offenders" as a nonhuman "threat."

Of course, it is possible that by the time you read this or soon after, the Supreme Court will have granted review or even reversed that decision. Regardless, it is still a remarkable shift that Alice Batchelder, a conservative appellate judge, led the charge, and that, when the Court asked for the government's views, the acting solicitor general (in President Trump's Justice Department) indicated that he did not take issue with the holdings of federal circuit courts striking down liberty restrictions. Indeed, the government disputed Michigan's claim that *Smith* foreclosed the Sixth Circuit's consideration of the challenge to its registration laws, explaining that Michigan's regime was "altogether different from and more troubling than Alaska's first-generation registry law upheld in *Smith*."[142]

For these purposes, *Packingham*'s most significant contribution may prove to be not what the Court or the concurrence said on June 19—the day of the decision—but what appeared in the *Washington Post* soon thereafter. As we have discussed, the "fact check" awarded three "Pinocchios" out of a possible four to the discussion of recidivism in Justice Alito's concurring opinion. We have no interest in litigating that judgment (or the underlying, complex disputes about recidivism rates), and, in fairness, the statements the fact-checker highlighted had a long pedigree. But the *Post* highlighted, as had academic commentators,[143] that the ways in which those statistics were presented fostered misimpressions that recidivism rates are much higher than they actually are and obscured important realities about sexual offenses and people on registries. Those statements,

---

[141] 834 F.3d 696, 698 (6th Cir. 2016). See also *id.* at 702 for language from the court equating premises restrictions to "the ancient punishment of banishment," and for a map displaying visually the limited geographic areas in which registered sex offenders can live and work.

[142] Brief for the United States as Amicus Curiae 17, Snyder v. Doe, 834 F.3d 696 (6th Cir. 2016), petition for cert. filed, 2016 U.S. Briefs 768 (U.S. Dec. 14, 2016) (No. 16-768).

[143] See, e.g., Ellman & Ellman, *supra* note 65.

problematic on their own terms, are especially so in the use to which the opinions have put them.

Even more important than the underlying accuracy is the increasing public perception that the Supreme Court has not played it straight on these issues and that its litany of "facts" about registrants, in particular, is tainted. It seems highly improbable that courts going forward will be able to do what they have repeatedly done in the past—simply say that "Our General Assembly has recognized 'that sex offenders often pose a high risk of engaging in sex offenses even after being released from incarceration,'" followed by *"see also Conn. Dep't of Pub. Safety v. Doe,* 538 U.S. 1, 4 (2003) (discussing the threat posed by sex offenders); *McKune v. Lile,* 536 U.S. 24, 32–33 (2002) (plurality) (same)."[144]

All of which is to say that we likely have reached a new day. Courts will expect to see more challenges to restrictions on registrants that marshal the true facts and then ask judges to decide under equal-protection-infused understandings of state constitutions and the federal Ex Post Facto, Due Process, and other clauses.

C. *The Supreme Court's Alternative Facts*

Whatever *Packingham* spells for the future course of sex offender registration jurisprudence, the appearance of a *Washington Post* fact check of the opinion calls further attention to basic and truly difficult questions about how the Supreme Court goes about its work. Which facts should the Court consider when it decides cases and where and how should it find them?

Indeed, *Packingham* was the second flare-up relating to this difficulty in the 2016-17 term. In *Jennings v. Rodriguez,* a case that was argued in November of 2016 but set for re-argument, the solicitor general submitted a letter advising the Court that it learned that statistics it had supplied in *Demore v. Kim*[145]—on which the Court's opinion had relied—had misrepresented the average length of time that immigration detainees were being held without a hearing. These figures, compiled from executive branch data, had made their first appearance in the government's Supreme Court brief.

---

[144] Standley v. Town of Woodfin, 362 N.C. at 333.

[145] 538 U.S. 510 (2003).

Although the solicitor general played an indirect role, the *Packingham* problem seems even more intractable. The Court likes to be viewed as a tribunal deciding concrete cases between parties, but its distinct responsibility is to formulate legal rules that broadly settle important issues. In fulfilling that role, the Court surely needs facts beyond what the parties provide. Taking *Packingham* as an example, both opinions and both parties reached for facts far beyond the record. Petitioners drew in facts about how many people use Facebook, how often registrants commit bad acts after being released, how many individuals were prosecuted under Section 202.5, how hard or easy it is for parents or social networking websites to detect nefarious conduct online. And amici flooded the Court with facts about the internet, social media, and sex offender recidivism.

But how to accurately interpret and represent facts—especially those learned through social science research—is a feature, not a bug of the Supreme Court decisionmaking process. What started as little more than a rhetorical flourish became a "fact," whereupon it has significantly and unhelpfully affected the course of the law. Long after they have forgotten that equal-protection and substantive-due-process claims were not before the Court, or that Connecticut in *Doe* disavowed any claim that registrants were dangerous individuals, courts know that the U.S. Supreme Court stated, as a fact, that "sex offenders are a serious threat in this Nation."

If anything, the *McKune/Smith* experience exposes one strand of the *Packingham* concurrence to be mistaken: it turns out that supported assertions may cause broader harm than unsupported ones. The Court has special power, through paraphrasing of research and repeated (self) citations, to create facts that have a very special status in our legal system. While the Court cannot always help how litigants, lower federal courts, or the press miscite or abridge its opinions, the fact check might prompt the Court to ensure that at least it is not guilty of the same offense.

The Supreme Court responded to the *Washington Post* with a predictable statement: the Court "speaks through its opinions," which is plainly true and correct. But that is also a familiar slogan of a sort of "judicial exceptionalism," which chafes at the notion that judicial opinions could be treated like politicians' speeches or criticized by "lay" journalists, and presumes that there is some inherent misunderstanding (and unfairness) in "fact-checking" the Court. But given the Court's large and underappreciated power to create facts, there is no reason why fact-checkers should be scared off, least of all by the justices' inability to defend themselves. Part of the vibrant culture described in the *Packingham* opinion is a less deferential attitude toward assertions of institutional authority. On questions of fact, where the Court has considerable power but limited competence, that is likely a salutary development.

Religious Freedom and Recycled Tires: The Meaning and Implications of *Trinity Lutheran*

Richard W. Garnett* and Jackson C. Blais**

The story of constitutionalism and ordered liberty in the West features many dramatic clashes and confrontations between religious and political authority, between conscience and coercion.[1] At the same time, many of the American chapters of this story are Supreme Court decisions whose facts might seem pedestrian, even picayune: How many "talking wishing wells" and reindeer are necessary to purge a city's Christmas display of unconstitutional "endorsement" of religion? Or, what is the First Amendment significance of the differences among books, maps, and atlases—the last being, as Sen. Daniel Patrick Moynihan famously pointed out, "books of maps"?[2]

This year's marquee church-state case, *Trinity Lutheran Church of Columbia, Inc. v. Comer*, was about replacing the pea-gravel on a church-run preschool's playground with shredded scrap tires.[3] More specifically, it presented the question whether the Constitution allows the state of Missouri to refuse an otherwise-available reimbursement grant for this project simply because the applicant

* Paul J. Schierl/Fort Howard Corporation Professor of Law and Concurrent Professor of Political Science, University of Notre Dame.

** J.D. candidate, Notre Dame Law School, Class of 2019.

[1] See, e.g., Brian Tierney, Religion, Law, and the Growth of Constitutional Thought 1150–1650 1 (1982) ("It is impossible really to understand the growth of Western constitutional thought unless we consider constantly, side by side, . . . ideas about the church and ideas about the state."). See generally Richard W. Garnett, The Freedom of the Church, 4 J. Cath. Soc. Thought 59 (2007).

[2] 124 Cong. Rec. 25661 (1978). See also Daniel P. Moynihan, Government and the Ruin of Private Education, Harpers, Apr. 1978, at 36 ("Backward reels the mind. Books are constitutional. Maps are unconstitutional. Atlases, which are books of maps, are unconstitutional. Or are they? We must await the next case.").

[3] 137 S. Ct. 2012 (2017).

is a church. It is fair to say that, at least at first blush, the dispute is pretty far removed from, say, *Murder in the Cathedral*. As Chief Justice John Roberts admitted in the concluding section of his opinion for the Court, the government "ha[d] not subjected anyone to chains or torture on account of religion" and the consequence of the challenged state policy "is, in all likelihood, a few extra scraped knees."[4] However, the Court's decision is no less important for its prosaic particulars. It echoes and continues one of our longest running law-and-religion arguments and it has implications for similarly deep-rooted—and divisive—public-policy debates.

In *Trinity Lutheran*, the justices achieved substantial consensus regarding both a fundamental "basic principle"—that is, the First Amendment "protect[s] religious observers against unequal treatment"—and that principle's bottom-line application to the question before them.[5] At the same time, the justices' several opinions contain wrinkles and ambiguities and so provide reasons to ask whether the ruling is a "this day only" pronouncement about playgrounds;[6] an earthquake-like, "shambles"-leaving subversion of the "wall separating church and state";[7] or something else. Stay tuned.

I. Background and Context

Before turning to *Trinity Lutheran*'s details, it is worth identifying and explaining briefly three features of the case's legal, historical, and doctrinal contexts. First, the Court's doctrine having to do with government support for and funding of religious institutions and activities has evolved gradually, but significantly, since the early 1970s. The details of this development—one of the most noteworthy aspects

---

[4] *Id.* at 2024–25.

[5] *Id.* at 2019 (quoting Church of Lukumi Babalu Aye, Inc. v. Hialeah, 508 U.S. 520, 542 (1993)).

[6] See Marc O. DeGirolami, "Blaine Amendment" Case Decided, Seemingly without Reference to Blaine Amendments or Animus Inquiry, Law and Religion Forum, June 26, 2017, https://lawandreligionforum.org/2017/06/26/blaine-amendment-case-decided-without-reference-to-blaine-amendments-or-animus-inquiry.

[7] Erwin Chemerinsky, The Crumbling Wall Separating Church and State, SCOTUSblog, June 27, 2017, http://www.scotusblog.com/2017/06/symposium-crumbling-wall-separating-church-state.

of the late Chief Justice William H. Rehnquist's legacy[8]—have been presented and evaluated many times and in great detail.[9]

From the nation's beginning (and before), governments and religious institutions in this country have cooperated, regularly and frequently, in all kinds of ways, to promote the common good. The appropriate nature and permissible extent of this cooperation have always been and still are debated, but the "wall of separation" that Thomas Jefferson told the Danbury Baptists our Constitution "buil[t] . . . between Church & State" has only rarely—and never by the Court—been understood to rule out cooperation entirely.[10] The justices in the *Lemon* and *Nyquist* cases, and in many that followed through the mid-1980s, embraced and attempted to apply a rule of fairly strict "no aid" separationism, according to which policies that had the "principal or primary effect" of "advanc[ing] . . . religion" were unconstitutional establishments of religion.[11] Over time, however, the Court's focus shifted from the possibility of "advancement" to a requirement of government evenhandedness or neutrality. And, in a series of cases—most notably, the *Zelman* case, decided in 2002[12]—a slim but consistent majority of the Court developed and applied the rule that governs today, namely, "equal treatment is not establishment" when it comes to religion-neutral funding programs with valid public purposes.[13]

The second contextual feature is similar to the first. In both its Free Speech Clause and Free Exercise Clause doctrines, the Court made "neutrality" its constitutional touchstone. Time and again, the justices held that the government may not discriminate on the basis

---

[8] See generally, Richard W. Garnett, Chief Justice Rehnquist, Religious Freedom, and the Constitution, The Constitutional Legacy of William H. Rehnquist (Bradford Wilson, ed., 2015).

[9] See generally, e.g., Michael McConnell, et al., Religion and the Constitution 303–449 (4th ed. 2016); Nicole S. Garnett & Richard W. Garnett, School Choice, the First Amendment, and Social Justice, 4 Tex. Rev. L. & Pol. 301 (1999).

[10] Compare, e.g., James Madison, Memorial and Remonstrance against Religious Assessments (1785) with, e.g., Barnes v. First Parish in Falmouth, 6 Mass. 400 (1810). See also Thomas Jefferson, Letter to the Danbury Baptists (1802).

[11] Lemon v. Kurtzman, 403 U.S. 602, 612 (1971). See also Comm'n for Pub. Ed. and Rel. Liberty v. Nyquist, 413 U.S. 756 (1973).

[12] Zelman v. Simmons-Harris, 536 U.S. 639 (2002).

[13] Eugene Volokh, Equal Treatment Is Not Establishment, 13 Notre Dame J. L. Ethics & Pub. Pol'y 341 (1999).

of religion in the provision of benefits or the imposition of burdens[14] and may not exclude, censor, or disadvantage speech or speakers because of their religious "viewpoint."[15] In addition, the government is not required to exempt religious or religiously motivated activities from reach of "neutral," generally applicable, yet meaningfully burdensome regulations.[16]

The third aspect of *Trinity Lutheran*'s background to note at the outset is that almost 40 states—including Missouri—have provisions in their own constitutions that purport to prohibit or limit public funding of religious institutions and activities. The terms of these provisions differ in some ways; they were enacted and re-enacted at various times and in varying circumstances; and they have not been uniformly interpreted and applied by the relevant state courts. In both the popular and scholarly literature—as well as in many of the amicus curiae briefs filed with the Court in *Trinity Lutheran*—these provisions are known as "Blaine Amendments" or "Baby Blaines," after Senator James G. Blaine, who in 1875 proposed an amendment to the Constitution of the United States. The proposal, which failed, would have prohibited states from directing public funds or lands to the use or control of "religious sects or denominations."

In recent years, increased scholarly attention and criticism have been directed at Sen. Blaine's proposal and at state provisions that resemble it both textually and in terms of their inspiration and aims. It is clear that the proposal and these provisions reflect—significantly, even if to varying degrees—the anti-Catholicism, nativism, and nationalism of the 19th and early 20th centuries.[17] This should not be particularly surprising given that, "in a certain sense . . . anti-Catholicism is integral to the formation of the United States."[18] Indeed,

> anti-Catholicism in America was nothing new, and went well beyond the legal penalties imposed upon, and disabilities endured by, Catholics in the American colonies and states.

[14] See generally, e.g., Lukumi, *supra* note 5 and related text.

[15] See generally, e.g., Rosenberger v. University of Virginia, 515 U.S. 819 (1995).

[16] See generally, e.g., Employment Div. v. Smith, 494 U.S. 872 (1990).

[17] See generally, e.g., Richard W. Garnett, The Theology of the Blaine Amendments, 2 First Amd. L. Rev. 45 (2003).

[18] John T. McGreevy, "A History of the Culture's Bias," Remarks at the Anti-Catholicism: The Last Acceptable Prejudice Conference (May 24, 2002).

> From the Puritans to the Framers and beyond, anti-"popery"
> was thick in the cultural air breathed by the early Americans,
> who were raised on tales of Armadas and Inquisitions, Puritan
> heroism and Bloody Mary, Jesuit schemes and Gunpowder
> Plots, lecherous confessors and baby-killing nuns.[19]

To be sure, some scholars dispute the duration, extent, and virulence—or, in any event, the contemporary relevance—of anti-Catholic opinions and their influence on the various no-aid constitutional provisions.[20] These matters are discussed in more detail below. For present purposes, it is enough to note the existence of these provisions and the well-grounded claims about their purpose and motive, and to recall that the Supreme Court has held in several cases that laws "motivated by an improper animus or purpose"—including, of course, animus toward a particular religious community or tradition—are, for that reason, presumptively unconstitutional.[21]

With *Trinity Lutheran*'s scene-setting backdrop in place, we can move to the unfolding and resolution of the case.

II. The Facts and History of *Trinity Lutheran*

Trinity Lutheran Church Child Learning Center is a preschool and daycare center in Boone County, Missouri. It is operated by Trinity Lutheran Church, on church property. Also on church property is a colorful, inviting, well-equipped playground. Several years ago, however, the school's staff decided that rubber surfaces made from recycled scrap tires were better for children's knees and elbows than coarse pea gravel and grass. As Chief Justice Roberts put it, "[y]oungsters, of course, often fall on the playground or

[19] Richard W. Garnett, American Conversations with(in) Catholicism, 102 Mich. L. Rev. 1191, 1199 (2004) (reviewing John T. McGreevy, Catholicism and American Freedom: A History (2003)).

[20] See, e.g., Steven K. Green, Locke v. Davey and the Limits of Neutrality Theory, 77 Temple L. Rev. 913 (2004). All things considered, however, the weight of the evidence supports the conclusion that "the Blaine Amendments were designed to (and still do) impose special legal disadvantages on Catholics because their beliefs were feared or hated by a sufficient majority." Brief of Amici Curiae The Becket Fund et al. in Support of Respondent, Locke v. Davey 540 U.S. 712 (2004).

[21] See, e.g., United States v. Windsor, 133 S. Ct. 2675 (2013); Lukumi, *supra* note 5, at 547.

tumble from the equipment. And when they do, the gravel can be unforgiving."[22]

Because of these safety concerns, the church applied for a grant from the Scrap Tire Program, run by Missouri's Department of Natural Resources (DNR). This program awards reimbursement grants to qualifying nonprofits that upgrade playgrounds, and thereby ease burdens on landfills, using materials made from used tires. Funding is scarce, the program is competitive, and grants go to those who score the highest on the basis of a range of criteria. The church scored very well—5th out of 44—but was nevertheless denied, "simply because of what it is," the chief justice reported, "a church."[23] At the time the church's application was considered, he explained, the DNR had a "strict and express policy of denying grants to any applicant owned or controlled by a church, sect, or other religious entity."[24] The denial letter sent to Trinity Lutheran explained that this policy was based on, and required by, Article I, Section 7 of Missouri's constitution, which provides among other things that "no money shall ever be taken from the public treasury, directly or indirectly, in aid of any church, sect or denomination of religion."

The church took the matter to federal court and claimed that the rejection of its application pursuant to what the Supreme Court characterized as Missouri's "[n]o churches need apply" policy violated the First Amendment's Free Exercise Clause[25] and other state and federal constitutional provisions. According to the church, Missouri's policy forced the church to make a choice between abandoning its religious beliefs, mission, and character and foregoing an otherwise-available public benefit. The district court dismissed the case, relying on the Supreme Court's 2004 decision in *Locke v. Davey*, which upheld the constitutionality of a Washington state scholarship program that excluded students pursuing a "degree in devotional theology."[26] The district judge insisted that Missouri had

---

[22] Trinity Lutheran, 137 S. Ct. at 2017.

[23] *Id.* at 2023.

[24] In April 2017, the governor of Missouri directed the DNR to change the policy and allow religious nonprofits to compete for grants. The Court determined that the governor's announcement "does not moot this case." Trinity Lutheran, *id.* at 2019 n.1.

[25] See U.S. Const. amend. I ("Congress shall make no law respecting an establishment of religion, or *prohibiting the free exercise thereof* . . . .") (emphasis added).

[26] 540 U.S. 712 (2004).

done nothing to prevent church members from holding religious beliefs or to penalize them for exercising religious practices and that the DNR's decision did not reveal "hostility toward religion." The Free Exercise Clause, the court reasoned, speaks to restraints and compulsion in religious matters; it does not require governments to provide "affirmative benefit[s]" and it permits them to fastidiously avoid directly funding religious institutions.[27]

The court of appeals affirmed and for substantially the same reasons invoked by the district court: Given the Supreme Court's decision in *Locke v. Davey*, the First Amendment permits, but does not require, Missouri to fund reimbursement-grant applications from churches.[28] Judge Raymond Gruender, however, insisted in dissent that *Locke* can and should be read more narrowly, as a case involving the specific and historically fraught issue of funding for the religious training of clergy, and that the ruling "did not leave states with unfettered discretion to exclude the religious from generally available public benefits." Safe playgrounds, he observed, unlike theological formation, have "nothing to do with religion" and so Missouri's differential treatment of churches' grant applications cannot be defended as a safeguard against establishments of religion.[29]

III. The Court's Decision and the Justices' Opinions

On January 15, 2016, the Supreme Court granted Trinity Lutheran's petition for certiorari. A few weeks later, Justice Antonin Scalia died. Nearly a year after that—after the March nomination by President Barack Obama of Judge Merrick Garland to fill Justice Scalia's seat, the Senate Republicans' sustained refusal to act on that nomination, the November 2016 election of President Donald Trump, and the nomination to the Court in January 2017 by President Trump of Judge Neil Gorsuch—the church's case was set for oral argument. Despite a filibuster by Senate Democrats, Justice Gorsuch was confirmed on

---

[27] Trinity Lutheran Church v. Pauley, 976 F. Supp. 2d 1137, 1147 (W.D. Mo. 2013).

[28] Trinity Lutheran Church v. Pauley, 788 F.3d 779, 785 (8th Cir. 2015). Although the court referred to Trinity Lutheran's challenge as a "facial attack" on the relevant provision of Article I, Section 7, *id.* at 783, 785, Judge Gruender pointed out in dissent that the church repeatedly characterized its claim as an "as-applied challenge," *id.* at 790–91.

[29] *Id.* at 791, 793 (Gruender, J., dissenting).

April 7, and—with a full, nine-justice complement for the first time since Scalia's death—the Court heard the case 12 days later.

During the months of the eight-member Court, some wondered whether *Trinity Lutheran* would wind up on the list of 4-4, lower-court-affirming splits along partisan lines.[30] However, most observers concluded that the justices' questions and lawyers' answers during oral arguments pointed clearly to a win for Trinity Lutheran.[31] More than a few times, various justices—including Justices Elena Kagan and Stephen Breyer—pressed counsel for the DNR to explain why its policy—its understanding and application of Article I, Section 7—would not deny basic public services, like police and fire protection, to churches.[32] Justice Samuel Alito pursued a similar line, asking counsel for the DNR about a "security grant program . . . through the Department of Homeland Security . . . to harden . . . non-profit organizations" that are deemed high-risk targets for terrorist attacks or a program that "provide[s] . . . security enhancements at schools where there's fear of [a] shooting."[33] That the state's policy could prohibit financial support in such cases was clearly troubling to most members of the Court.[34]

---

[30] See, e.g., Ron Elving, "On the Docket, In Limbo: Scalia's Death Casts Uncertainty on Key Cases," NPR (Feb. 14, 2016), http://www.npr.org/2016/02/14/466752491/on-the-docket-in-limbo-scalias-death-casts-uncertainty-on-key-cases.

[31] The parties agreed, both in written filings and at oral argument, that the Missouri governor's announcement directing a change in policy did not moot the case. See Trinity Lutheran, 137 S. Ct. at 2019 n.1; Transcript of Oral Arg., at 23, 24 (Counsel for petitioner states that if "political winds change[d] . . . [the policy could] easily be changed back" and that "absent a ruling [at the Supreme Court] . . . , the old policy will be back in place."); *id.* at 52 (Counsel for respondent agrees that "there is no assurance that four years from now, with a change of administration, or at some point in the interim through a taxpayer standing suit, that there wouldn't be a . . . change back to the prior practice.").

[32] See, e.g., the account of the oral argument in Playground Scrap: The Supreme Court Appears to Side with a Church in a Funding Battle, The Economist (Apr. 19, 2017), https://www.economist.com/blogs/democracyinamerica/2017/04/playground-scrap.

[33] Transcript of Oral Arg. at 32, 33, Trinity Lutheran Church v. Comer, 137 S. Ct. 2012 (2017).

[34] Even Justices Sonia Sotomayor and Ruth Bader Ginsburg, who dissented, agreed that it "would violate the Free Exercise Clause" to "fence out religious persons or entities from a truly generally available public benefit" such as "police or fire protections." 137 S. Ct. at 2040 (Sotomayor, J., dissenting).

On June 26, 2017, the Court's 7-2 decision in favor of the church was announced, although it was somewhat overshadowed by fever-pitch speculation regarding Justice Anthony Kennedy's possible retirement and the justices' *per curiam* disposition of the challenge to President Trump's executive order restricting entry into the country for certain classes of foreign nationals.[35] The clarity of the church's win and the strong bottom-line consensus among the justices notwithstanding, the chief justice's opinion for the court, which five other justices joined either in full or almost entirely, both raised and left open questions. There were three complicating, concurring opinions filed as well as a lengthy and indignant dissent. It is worth addressing each opinion on its own before turning to the task of identifying the decision's meaning, implications, and limits.

A. *Chief Justice Roberts's Opinion for the Court: "Exclusion . . . is odious to our Constitution . . . and cannot stand"*

Part II of the chief justice's opinion sets out what the majority identified as the governing rules and controlling precedents. He observed laconically that "[t]he parties agree that the Establishment Clause . . . does not prevent Missouri from including Trinity Lutheran in the Scrap Tire Program."[36] That none of the justices in the majority saw any need to push back against this agreement is striking. It suggests that the evolution, described above, in the Court's approach to cases involving public support for, and cooperation with, religious institutions is fairly settled. The opinion moves quickly to the commands of the Free Exercise Clause, which "'protect[s] religious observers against unequal treatment' and subjects to the strictest scrutiny laws that target the religious for 'special disabilities' based on their 'religious status.'"[37] Given this command, "denying a generally available benefit solely on account of religious identity imposes a penalty on the free exercise of religion that can be justified only by a state interest 'of the highest order.'"[38] Laws that "single out the religious for

[35] Trump v. Int'l Refugee Assistance Program, Nos. 16-1436 & 16-1540 (June 26, 2017) (per curiam).

[36] Trinity Lutheran, 137 S. Ct. at 2019.

[37] *Id.* (quoting Lukumi, 508 U.S. at 533).

[38] *Id.* (quoting McDaniel v. Paty, 435 U.S. 618, 628 (1978) (plurality opinion) (quoting Wisconsin v. Yoder, 406 U.S. 205, 215 (1972))).

disfavored treatment," in other words, are crucially different from and much more suspect than those that are "neutral and generally applicable without regard to religion."[39] The majority concluded that Missouri's policy—that is, its interpretation and application of Article I, Section 7—is of the former kind. It "expressly discriminates against otherwise eligible recipients by disqualifying them from a public benefit solely because of their religious character" and "imposes a penalty on the free exercise of religion that triggers the most exacting scrutiny."[40]

The chief justice then addresses, and rejects, the state's argument that "merely declining to extend funds"—or, "declin[ing] to allocate a subsidy"—to Trinity Lutheran does not prohibit the church from engaging in any religious conduct or otherwise exercising its religious rights."[41] According to Missouri, a decision not to grant money that the state had no obligation to provide leaves the church entirely free to believe and profess religious truths and imposes no burden on religious exercise. The Court, however, frames the matter differently: "[T]he Department's policy puts Trinity Lutheran to a choice: It may participate in an otherwise available benefit program or remain a religious institution."[42] And, the chief justice insists, this is an imposition the Court's precedents almost never permit. It is not that the church is "claiming any entitlement to a subsidy" or that the state has "criminalized the way Trinity Lutheran worships"; instead, the "express discrimination against religious exercise here is . . . the refusal to allow the Church—solely because it is a church—to compete with secular organizations for a grant."[43]

Next, there is the matter of the Court's *Locke v. Davey* decision, which has already been mentioned and on which the lower courts relied. Again, in *Locke*, a (different) seven-justice majority, invoking the "play in the joints" between what the Establishment Clause allows and the Free Exercise Clause compels,[44] had permitted the state of Washington to deny an otherwise available college scholarship to

---

[39] *Id.* at 2020.
[40] *Id.* at 2021.
[41] *Id.* at 2022.
[42] *Id.* at 2021–22.
[43] *Id.* at 2022.
[44] Locke, 540 U.S. at 718.

a student who intended to train for the ministry and to pursue a degree that was "devotional in nature or designed to induce religious faith."[45] This case, the Court explained, is different. The student in *Locke* "was denied a scholarship because of what he proposed *to do*[]," not "because of who he *was*"; here, on the other hand, "Trinity Lutheran was denied a grant simply because of what it is—a church."[46] Indeed, the chief justice emphasized, Washington allowed religious students to receive scholarships, attend religious schools, and study religious subjects—just not to get a devotional-theology degree. Trinity Lutheran, on the other hand, is "put to the choice between being a church and receiving a government benefit. The rule is simple: No churches need apply."[47]

Having reached the conclusion that the choice demanded by Missouri's policy penalizes the free exercise of religion, the chief justice dropped a footnote that, *Carolene Products*-style, has drawn the close attention of scholars, commentators, and activists:[48]

> This case involves express discrimination based on religious identity with respect to playground resurfacing. We do not address religious uses of funding or other forms of discrimination.[49]

This note, which both unremarkably states the obvious and potentially unsettles the consensus, and which Justices Neil Gorsuch and Clarence Thomas declined to join, is discussed in more detail below.

The majority opinion concludes with the determination that the state's "policy preference for skating as far as possible from religious establishment concerns"—unlike the state of Washington's historically pedigreed aim of avoiding funding clergy-training—"cannot qualify as compelling" and so cannot justify the burden its discriminatory policy imposes.[50] "[T]he exclusion of Trinity Lutheran from a

---

[45] *Id.* at 716.
[46] Trinity Lutheran, 137 S. Ct. at 2023.
[47] *Id.* at 2024.
[48] See United States v. Carolene Products Co., 304 U.S. 144, 152 n.4 (1938).
[49] Trinity Lutheran, 137 S. Ct. at 2024 n.3.
[50] *Id.* at 2024.

public benefit for which it is otherwise qualified, solely because it is a church, is odious to our Constitution . . . and cannot stand."[51]

B. *Justice Thomas's Concurrence:* Locke *"Remains Troubling"*

Justice Thomas joined all of the Court's opinion except "Footnote 3," which was just quoted. In a short, three-paragraph concurring opinion, which Justice Gorsuch also signed, he re-affirmed his view that *Locke v. Davey* was wrongly decided: "This Court's endorsement in *Locke* of even a 'mil[d] kind' . . . of discrimination against religion remains troubling."[52] He welcomed the majority's "appropriately . . . narrow[]" reading of *Locke*, however, and underscored that the decision "did not suggest that discrimination against religion outside the limited context of support for ministerial training" would or should be "exempt from exacting review."[53]

C. *Justice Gorsuch's Concurrence: "General Principles, Rather Than Ad Hoc Improvisations"*

The Court's newest member, Justice Gorsuch, also joined all of the chief justice's opinion but Footnote 3. He set out the reasons—as he put it, "two modest qualifications"—for his reservations in a concurring opinion, which Justice Thomas also joined.[54] First, Justice Gorsuch expressed "doubts about the stability of . . . a line" between "laws that discriminate on the basis of religious *status* and religious *use*."[55] What is more, he suggested, it is not clear that the line should matter, given that the Constitution "guarantees the free *exercise* of religion, not just the right to inward belief (or status)."[56] He elaborated, "I don't see why it should matter whether we describe [a] benefit, say, as closed to Lutherans (status) or closed to people who do Lutheran things (use). It is free exercise either way."[57]

Next, Justice Gorsuch objected to the Court's anodyne, yet mysterious, observations in Footnote 3. On the one hand, it is generally and

51 *Id.* at 2025.

52 *Id.* at 2025 (Thomas, J., concurring in part).

53 *Id.*

54 *Id.* at 2025 (Gorsuch, J., concurring in part).

55 *Id.* (emphsis in original).

56 *Id.* at 2026.

57 *Id.*

not controversially the case that the Court addresses and resolves particular controversies involving particular players, facts, and circumstances. On the other hand, he cautioned "that some might mistakenly read [the footnote] to suggest that only 'playground resurfacing' cases, or only those with some association with children's safety or health, or perhaps some other social good we find sufficiently worthy, are governed" by the relevant rules and precedents. "[O]ur cases," he insisted, "are 'governed by general principles, rather than ad hoc improvisations[,]' . . . [a]nd the general principles here do not permit discrimination against religious exercise—whether on the playground or anywhere else."[58]

D. Justice Breyer's Concurrence: "Public Benefits Come in Many Shapes and Sizes"

Justice Breyer "agree[d] with much of what the Court sa[id] and with its result" but concurred only in the judgment.[59] As he had during the oral arguments, he emphasized the "particular nature of the 'public benefit' here at issue."[60] Seventy years earlier, in the landmark *Everson* ruling, the Court had observed that "'cutting off church schools from' such 'general government services as ordinary police and fire protection . . . is obviously not the purpose of the First Amendment."[61] And yet, by "cut[ting] Trinity Lutheran off from participation in a general program designed to secure or to improve the health and safety of children," Missouri is effectively doing the same thing. However, clearly aware of the possible implications and applications of the "general principles" cited by Justice Gorsuch, he wrote, "We need not go further. Public benefits come in many shapes and sizes. I would leave the application of the Free Exercise Clause to other kinds of public benefits for another day."[62]

---

[58] *Id.*

[59] *Id.* at 2026 (Breyer, J., concurring in the judgment).

[60] *Id.*

[61] *Id.* at 2027 (quoting Everson v. Board of Educ., 330 U.S. 1, 16 (1947)).

[62] *Id.*

E. Justice Sotomayor's Dissent: A "Constitutional Slogan" or a "Constitutional Commitment"?

Justice Sonia Sotomayor's dissenting opinion, which only Justice Ruth Bader Ginsburg joined, is bracing, unyielding, and nearly twice as long as the Court's. She read a version live from the bench and omitted the customary "respectfully" from the last line of her opinion.[63] An opinion by the late Justice Scalia that was similar in tone and urgency would probably have been widely characterized as "fiery," "blistering," or even "bitter." She warned that *Trinity Lutheran* is not "a simple case about recycling tires to resurface a playground" but is instead "about nothing less than the relationship between religious institutions and the civil government—that is, between church and state."[64] She charged the majority with "profoundly chang[ing]" that relationship, "slight[ing] both our precedents and our history," and "weaken[ing] this country's longstanding commitment to a separation of church and state beneficial to both."[65]

In a sense, Justice Sotomayor dissented twice. Recall, for starters, that the parties, the court of appeals, and the majority agreed, or at least assumed, that the Establishment Clause would allow Missouri to award a reimbursement grant to Trinity Lutheran for the purpose of resurfacing the Learning Center's playground.[66] The same is true

---

[63] *Id.* at 2041 (Sotomayor, J., dissenting).

[64] *Id.* at 2027.

[65] *Id.* Interestingly, Chief Justice Roberts's opinion for the Court nowhere specifically addressed these denunciations or the historical and precedential accounts that are offered in support of them. Had he or another justice done so, he could have demonstrated that Justice Sotomayor's effort to analogize late-18th century arguments about public funding for clergy training to the exclusion of a church-run preschool from a playground-resurfacing-grants program is, among other things, anachronistic.

[66] The district court's opinion commented that "using taxpayer-raised funds to refurbish Trinity's playground, no matter how innocuous, raises Establishment Clause concerns even if such use of funds would not violate the Establishment Clause." Trinity Lutheran, 976 F. Supp. 2d at 1150. However, that court continued, "the question of whether awarding a scrap tire grant directly to Trinity would violate the Establishment Clause is not at issue in this case, and so it is neither necessary nor appropriate to resolve this question here." *Id.* at 1151. Nonetheless, the court of appeals noted that "it now seems rather clear that Missouri could include the Learning Center's playground in a non-discriminatory Scrap Tire grant program without violating the Establishment Clause." Trinity Lutheran, 788 F.3d at 784. Judge Gruender, who dissented, agreed. *Id.* at 793 (Gruender, J., dissenting).

of nearly all the amicus briefs that were filed, on both sides.[67] In contrast, noting that "[c]onstitutional questions are decided by this Court, not the parties' concessions," she contended that "[t]he Establishment Clause does not allow Missouri to grant the Church's funding request because the Church uses the Learning Center, including its playground, in conjunction with its religious mission."[68]

The Court's precedents, she argued—running from *Everson* through today—establish a clear rule that "[t]he government may not directly fund religious exercise" and, she insisted, "[n]owhere is this clear rule more clearly implicated than when funds flow directly from the public treasury to a house of worship."[69] This is especially so given that the church had not provided, and—she asserted—could not provide, "assurances that public funds would not be used for religious activities."[70] After all, the church's own materials describe the Learning Center as "a ministry of the church" and its program—which its playground and other facilities, she suggests, serve—is "structured to allow a child to grow spiritually."[71] Underscoring this point—which seems consonant with Judge Gorsuch's reservation about a sharp distinction between "status" and "use"—she insisted that "[t]he Church's playground surface—like a Sunday School room's walls or the sanctuary's pews—are integrated with and integral to its religious mission."[72]

What can be seen as Justice Sotomayor's second dissent was her attack on the Court's conclusion that "the interests embodied in the Religion Clauses" do not justify "the line drawn in Missouri's Article

---

[67] But see, e.g., Brief of Amici Curiae American Civil Liberties Union, et al. in Support of Respondent, at 6 ("The Establishment Clause Prohibits the State from Awarding Direct Grants of Taxpayer Funds to Houses of Worship"); Brief of Amicus Curiae Lambda Legal Defense and Education Fund, Inc., in Support of Respondent, at 12, n.3.

[68] Trinity Lutheran, 137 S. Ct. at 2028 (Sotomayor, J., dissenting).

[69] *Id.* at 2028–29. Justice Sotomayor distinguished this rule from the line of cases "about indirect aid programs in which aid reaches religious institutions 'only as a result of the genuine and independent choices of private individuals.'" *Id.* at 2029 n.2 (quoting Zelman, 536 U.S. at 649).

[70] *Id.* at 2029. By failing to require such assurances, Justice Sotomayor wrote, the majority had departed from controlling precedents, including *Mitchell v. Helms*, 530 U.S. 793 (2000).

[71] *Id.* at 2027–28.

[72] *Id.* at 2029.

I, [Section] 7."[73] That is, any religion-based discrimination involved in Missouri's policy is, like the prohibition upheld in *Locke v. Davey*, the acceptable result of a permissibly separationist commitment. It is permissible, sometimes, for the law to "single[] out" religious individuals, entities, and activities for distinctive treatment—sometimes to accommodate, sometimes to exclude; what matters are "the reasons that it does so."[74] The decision reflected in Missouri's constitution and in the DNR's policy "has deep roots in our Nation's history" and "reflects a reasonable and constitutional judgment."[75]

The Court's judgment, and its focus on the issue of "discrimination," Justice Sotomayor contends, creates a "lopsided outcome" where "[t]he government may draw lines on the basis of religious status to grant a benefit to religious persons or entities but it may not draw lines on that basis when doing so would further the interests the Religion Clauses protect in other ways."[76] She asserted that the majority's decision, by undermining the separation between "the public treasury" and "religious coffers," "jeopardizes the government's ability to remain secular" and—responding explicitly to Justice Gorsuch's concurring opinion endorsing general principles of broader application—she warned of "what it might enable tomorrow."[77]

IV. *Trinity Lutheran's* Import and Implications

The observation is familiar that "where one stands depends on where one sits." The outcome in *Trinity Lutheran* was, again, not a surprise—at least, not after the oral arguments—and—given the

[73] *Id.* at 2031.

[74] *Id.* at 2032.

[75] *Id.* Part III-B of Justice Sotomayor's dissent presents these "deep roots," and the similar, longstanding provisions contained in many other state constitutions, in detail. *Id.* at 2032–38. "In the Court's view," she complained, "none of this matters." *Id.* at 2038. It should be noted, however, that her presentation of these "deep roots" is strikingly incomplete for failing to discuss fully these provisions' background, context, and aims.

[76] *Id.* at 2040 ("[T]he same interests served by lifting government-imposed burdens on certain religious entities may sometimes be equally served by denying government-provided benefits to certain religious entities.").

[77] *Id.* at 2041, 2040, 2041 n.14. On some justices' possibly revealing habit of using the term "coffers" to refer to the accounts of religious schools and other entities, see Richard W. Garnett & Benjamin P. Carr, Drop Coffers, 10 Green Bag 2d 299 (2007).

different places observers "sit"—neither is the fact that the result prompted a wide range of reactions from celebration to condemnation. Now, it could be that a ruling for the Church was overdetermined, given its "good facts" (playground safety and recycling) and framing (unyielding discrimination), the state's concessions at oral argument, the changes in the Court's membership since *Locke v. Davey* was decided, and the well-developed, ongoing shift away from strict, no-aid separationism in the Court's doctrine and legal scholarship. That said, given the various practices, precedents, and provisions set out in Justice Sotomayor's dissent—putting aside, for the moment, questions about their historical, constitutional, or moral merits[78]—it is striking and significant that a seven-justice majority, in a roiling political environment and a case that is at least adjacent to the culture-war arena, ruled that the Constitution requires the disbursal of funds to a church for its school.

The Court's judgment in *Trinity Lutheran* was the right one.[79] Indeed, one could argue that it is long overdue.[80] The majority was correct to treat the question presented as controlled primarily by the no-discrimination rule from cases like *Lukumi* and *McDaniel* and to reject an expansive reading of *Locke v. Davey*.[81] Douglas Laycock observed, not long after that ruling, that "the holding is confined to the training of clergy [and] to refusals to fund that are not based on hostility to religion," but he predicted with regret that these limitations would prove "illusory."[82] Perhaps not. Missouri's asserted

[78] See generally, e.g., Steven D. Smith, The Rise and Decline of American Religious Freedom (2014); Donald L. Drakeman, Church, State, and Original Intent (2010).

[79] See Richard W. Garnett, "Consensus & Uncertainty at the Supreme Court," Commonweal, Aug. 2, 2017 ("All things considered, the justices in the majority had the better of the argument."), https://www.commonwealmagazine.org/consensus-uncertainty-supreme-court.

[80] See, e.g., Garnett & Garnett, *supra* note 9, at 336 n.180, 338–39 n.195.

[81] Church of the Lukumi Babalu Aye, Inc. v. Hialeah, 508 U.S. 520 (1993); McDaniel v. Paty, 435 U.S. 618 (1978). Cf. Colo. Christian Univ. v. Weaver, 534 F.3d 1245, 1255 (10th Cir. 2008) ("The opinion . . . suggests, even if it does not hold, that the State's latitude to discriminate against religion is confined to certain 'historic and substantial state interest[s],' . . . and does not extend to the wholesale exclusion of religious institutions and their students from otherwise neutral and generally available government support.").

[82] Douglas Laycock, Comment, Theology Scholarships, the Pledge of Allegiance, and Religious Liberty: Avoiding the Extremes but Missing the Liberty, 118 Harv. L. Rev. 155, 184 (2004).

prophylactic interest in "achieving greater separation of church and State than is already ensured under the Establishment Clause"[83]—or, as the chief justice put it, in "skating as far as possible from religious establishment concerns"[84]—is, even if defensible, not weighty enough to justify its categorically exclusionary policy. And, contrary to Justice Sotomayor's overwrought denunciation,[85] to conclude as much is not at all to slight "this country's longstanding commitment to a separation of church and state" that is, properly understood, "beneficial to both."[86]

It is true that the separation—that is, the differentiation—between religious and political authority safeguards religious and political freedom. However, the maintenance of an appropriately secular government does not require the blanket exclusion of churches from generally available (and secular) public benefits or rule out cooperation between governments and religious institutions in advancing the common (and secular) good. It makes sense to protect religious liberty by preventing official interference with strictly religious affairs. It would be unconstitutional for Missouri to pick Trinity Lutheran's hymns or ordain its pastor, but it is—contrary to the narrative offered by Justice Sotomayor—well within our tradition to allow the church, like anyone else, to apply for help with playground safety.

Regardless of the merits or wisdom of its outcome, though, *Trinity Lutheran*'s meaning, applications, and implications are uncertain and sure to be contested. This is true both because of things said, and left unsaid, in the various opinions. Four matters are particularly worth addressing, even if only briefly: (1) whether "Footnote 3" of Chief Justice Roberts's opinion will have the effect of limiting the case's impact in school-choice litigation; (2) how to construe the justices' complete silence regarding the Blaine Amendments in general and Missouri's no-aid provision in particular, and what this silence means for future judicial inquiries into "animus"; (3) whether and to what extent "discrimination" by religious entities and employers

---

[83] 137 S. Ct. at 2024 (quoting Widmar, 454 U.S. at 276).

[84] *Id.* at 2024.

[85] See, e.g., 137 S. Ct. at 2041 ("Today's decision discounts centuries of history and jeopardizes the government's ability to remain secular.") (Sotomayor, J., dissenting).

[86] *Id.* at 2027.

constrains or is constrained by their receipt of public funding (note that concerns on this score were hinted at during oral argument and in the dissenting opinion and raised explicitly in at least one amicus brief); and (4) whether the distinction drawn in the case between religious "status" or "identity" ("who one is"), on the one hand, and religious exercise or uses ("what one does"), on the other, will or should be emphasized in future religious-freedom cases.

A. School Choice and "Footnote Three"

Throughout the *Trinity Lutheran* litigation and in the commentary and analysis before and since the ruling, the proverbial elephant in the room has been the implications of a win by the church for school-choice programs and education funding more generally.[87] Some courts, relying on broader readings of *Locke v. Davey* than the one given by the *Trinity Lutheran* majority, have rejected the argument that the Constitution requires the evenhanded inclusion and fair participation of religious schools in education-funding experiments. In several states, the existence and interpretation of Blaine Amendments and other no-aid provisions have functioned as barriers to such reform experiments. Given the "basic principle" invoked and applied by the Court, however, a state or local government should not be permitted to exclude a family from the benefits of a tuition-scholarship or tax-credit program simply because parents choose an otherwise qualified religious school as the provider of their child's education. As Justice Breyer noted in his concurring opinion, "[p]ublic benefits come in many shapes and sizes,"[88] including school vouchers.

But Justice Breyer also said he was "leav[ing] the application of the Free Exercise Clause to other kinds of benefits for another day."[89] Similarly, perhaps, Footnote 3 of the chief justice's opinion seemed to distinguish—for present purposes, anyway—between "express

---

[87] See, e.g., Valerie Strauss, Will the Supreme Court's Trinity Decision Lead to the Spread of School Voucher Programs?, Wash. Post., June 26, 2017, https://www.washingtonpost.com/news/answer-sheet/wp/2017/06/26/will-the-supreme-courts-trinity-decision-lead-to-the-spread-of-school-voucher-programs; Brief Amicus Curiae of the National Education Association in Support of Respondent, at 1; Brief for Amici Curiae Douglas County School District and Douglas County School Board in Support of Petitioner, at 1.

[88] 137 S. Ct. at 2027 (Breyer, J., concurring).

[89] *Id.*

discrimination based on religious identity with respect to playground resurfacing" and "religious uses or funding." Is the exclusion of religious schools from educational-choice programs meaningfully different from the former? Is the use of tax credits to help send a child to a parochial school an example of the latter?

Certainly, a number of footnotes have become famous and acquired precedential value. It is generally recognized that footnotes are parts of opinions and so should be regarded as part of the reasoning provided in support of a court's holding.[90] However, Footnote 3 is not part of the Court's opinion. Justices Gorsuch and Thomas expressly declined to endorse it and Justice Breyer concurred only in the judgment. It is not that these justices believe the footnote says anything wrong—the note's text is, as Justice Gorsuch concedes, "entirely correct."[91] What Justices Thomas and Gorsuch appear to reject is an understanding of the case that focuses more on its factual particulars than on the "general principles" applied to them and that "do not permit discrimination against religious exercise—whether on the playground or anywhere else."[92] And, the majority opinion, like Judge Gorsuch's concurrence, does indeed speak in terms of general, and generally applicable, nondiscrimination principles. The chief justice reports, for example, that Missouri "require[d] Trinity Lutheran to renounce its religious character . . . to participate in an otherwise generally available public benefit program, for which it is fully qualified."[93] Certainly, the dissenting justices were aware of "[t]he principle [the decision] establishes" and more worried about "what it might enable tomorrow" than about its particular application in the case.[94]

The meaning of *Trinity Lutheran* and the significance, if any, of Footnote 3 could become clearer soon. The day after the decision, the justices vacated and remanded, for further consideration in light of *Trinity Lutheran*, cases from Colorado and New Mexico in which state courts had applied no-aid provisions of their constitutions to

---

[90] Cf. United States v. Denedo, 556 U.S. 904, 921 (2009) (Roberts, C.J., concurring in part and dissenting in part) ("[F]ootnotes are part of an opinion, too, even if not the most likely place to look for a key jurisdictional ruling.").

[91] 137 S. Ct. at 2026 (Gorsuch, J., concurring in part).

[92] *Id.*

[93] 137 S. Ct. at 2022.

[94] *Id.* at 2041 n.14.

restrict educational-choice programs.[95] Although there is plenty of room for informed speculation about the vote-securing reasons for Footnote 3 and the various justices' views regarding the reach and limits of the "general principles" applied in the case, it remains to be seen whether lower courts will be guided more by Justice Gorsuch's rejection of "ad hoc improvisations" or by Justice Breyer's emphasis on public benefits' "many shapes and sizes."

B. The Blaine Amendments and Unconstitutional "Animus"

There is, as was discussed earlier, a lively academic debate about the aims and causes of the so-called Blaine Amendments and about the relevance, if any, of the anti-Catholicism and nativism that most agree are at least part of these amendments' stories. The questions whether Missouri's particular provision should be regarded as a Blaine Amendment and whether that provision's particular history is tainted by prejudice are also disputed.[96] The commentary leading up to *Trinity Lutheran* regularly emphasized the Blaine Amendments' history, context, and purposes and treated the case as, at least in part, a case "about" them.[97]

Several justices have, in the past, at least acknowledged the Blaine Amendments controversy and the connections among American anti-Catholicism, the 19th century "School Wars," and the proposal and enactment of strict no-aid provisions.[98] Yet the controversy, these connections, and even the word "Blaine" are utterly absent from the various justices' opinions. The opinion of the Court does little more than report that the Missouri no-aid provision exists. Justice Sotomayor's dissent provides lengthy footnoted string-cites as

[95] See Erica L. Green, Supreme Court Ruling Could Shape Future of School Choice, N.Y. Times, June 27, 2017, https://www.nytimes.com/2017/06/27/us/politics/supreme-court-school-choice-ruling.html.

[96] Compare, e.g., Brief of Amici Curiae, Legal and Religious Historians, in Support of Respondent, at 16, with Brief of the Union of Orthodox Jewish Congregations of America as Amicus Curiae in Support of Petitioner, at 18.

[97] See, e.g., Philip Hamburger, Prejudice and the Blaine Amendments, First Things, June 20, 2017, https://www.firstthings.com/web-exclusives/2017/06/prejudice-and-the-blaine-amendments; Richard W. Garnett, Confronting a Nativist Past; Protecting School Choice's Future, SCOTUSblog, Aug. 10, 2016, http://www.scotusblog.com/2016/08/symposium-confronting-a-nativist-past-protecting-school-choices-future.

[98] See Mitchell v. Helms, 530 U.S. 793 (2000) (Thomas, J., plurality op.).

evidence that many other similar provisions exist, and have long existed, and—she contends—reflect "principles rooted in this Nation's understanding of how best to foster religious liberty."[99] The argument that Missouri's no-aid provision, or the Blaine Amendments generally, are rendered unconstitutional by virtue of their motives, history, or aims makes no appearance in the decision, even though it is impossible that the justices were unaware of it.[100]

In recent months, advocates and scholars challenging the Trump Administration's "travel ban" executive order have argued that legislation or official action resulting from hostility or "animus" toward or a "bare desire to harm" a religious minority or politically unpopular group is unconstitutional. That analogous arguments were raised, but ignored, in *Trinity Lutheran* could indicate reservations by some justices regarding judicial doctrines and tests that require close scrutiny and criticism of official actors' motives and aims.[101] To be sure, such doctrines and tests have developed and been deployed in several constitutional contexts, including cases applying the Equal Protection, Due Process, Free Exercise, and Establishment Clauses. And yet, reservations about this kind of inquiry seem warranted. Not only is the inquiry notoriously difficult, it can invite and reward arguments that attack the character or motives of one's opponents and contribute to what Steven Smith has called a "jurisprudence

---

[99] 137 S. Ct. at 2037 (Sotomayor, J., dissenting).

[100] See, e.g., Brief for the Cato Institute as Amicus Curiae Supporting Petitioners, at 4 (noting that a Missouri Senator, during the debate on the Art. I § 7 provision, argued that the Missouri Senate ought to "'say in plain English what is intended' by adding 'Catholic' to the [proposed amendment]."); Brief for The Union of Orthodox Jewish Congregations of America as Amicus Curiae Supporting Petitioners, at 4, 11 ("Missouri's Blaine Amendment [Art. I § 7] [] is one of the most restrictive versions of the original Blaine Amendment in the entire United States"); Brief for Council of Christian Colleges and Universities et al. as Amici Curiae Supporting Petitioners, at 19–20 ("Rather than embracing pluralism, [the approach of courts in expansively interpreting *Locke*] reflects a return to the forced orthodoxy and sectarian bias of the Blaine Amendment.").

[101] Cf. Caleb Nelson, Judicial Review of Legislative Purpose, 83 N.Y.U. L. Rev. 1784, 1859 (2008) ("It is safe to say that courts remain cautious about imputing impermissible purposes to duly enacted statutes; even when judges acknowledge both the relevance of legislative motivation to a statute's constitutionality and the judiciary's ability to investigate that motivation, they tend to resolve doubts in favor of presuming that the legislature behaved properly.").

of denigration"[102] and the "discourse of disrespect."[103] The Blaine Amendments' misguided and even bigoted premises and purposes, and the larger history of anti-Catholicism in America, should be confronted and regretted. But it might be better if legal challenges to no-aid provisions' application are resolved, as *Trinity Lutheran* was, on more narrow, simpler non-discrimination grounds.

C. *"Discrimination" by Religious Entities and Employers*

The freedom of religion includes, in some instances, the freedom to "discriminate." The Supreme Court affirmed as much unanimously five years ago in the *Hosanna-Tabor* case.[104] If this statement jars, it is probably because of the notoriously imprecise ways the term "discrimination" is used in contemporary political and legal discourse.[105] Protecting and promoting religious freedom, which American governments may and should do, includes not only tolerating but also preserving the right of religious institutions to engage in forms of "discrimination"—for example, using religious criteria in the hiring and firing of ministerial employers—that would and should be illegal when attempted by governments or commercial entities. A second elephant in the courtroom, then—a not-too-distant relation of the first—was the fear that a victory for the church in *Trinity Lutheran* would lead not only to a requirement that religious schools be allowed to participate in tuition-scholarship and tax-credit programs but also to massive subsidization of objectionable "discrimination" on religious and other grounds.

This fear was expressed most explicitly in an amicus brief filed by the Lambda Legal Defense and Education Fund that asked the Court to ensure that "adequate safeguards prevent channeling government aid to advance religious activities or to support harmful

---

[102] Steven D. Smith, The Jurisprudence of Denigration, 43 U.C. Davis L. Rev. 675 (2014).

[103] Steven D. Smith, Free Exercise Doctrine and the Discourse of Disrespect, 65 U. Colo. L. Rev. 519 (1994).

[104] Hosanna-Tabor Evangelical Lutheran Church and School v. EEOC, 565 U.S. 171 (2012). See generally Richard W. Garnett & John M. Robinson, Hosanna-Tabor, Religious Freedom, and Constitutional Structure, 2011–2012 Cato Sup. Ct. Rev. 307 (2012).

[105] See generally Richard W. Garnett, Religious Accommodations and—and among—Civil Rights: Separation, Toleration, and Accommodation, 88 S. Cal. L. Rev. 493 (2015).

discrimination."[106] In addition, Lambda Legal contended that "[t]he Establishment Clause prohibits government from providing direct aid to sectarian schools that use the funds or materials for religious purposes or engage in religious discrimination."[107] Now, although the larger issue is famously complicated, this claim seems to be in tension with the Court's state-action doctrine, and none of the justices in *Trinity Lutheran* addressed it directly.[108] The 1972 *Moose Lodge* decision held that a private club that discriminated against an African American because of his race was not a state actor simply because it received a license from the state's liquor board allowing the club to serve alcohol, and emphasized that the state was not "significantly involved with [the] invidious discrimination."[109] On the other hand, Lambda Legal highlights the statements from *Norwood v. Harrison*, decided the following year, that "the Constitution does not permit the State to aid discrimination" and "[a] State's constitutional obligation requires it to steer clear . . . of giving significant aid to institutions that practice racial or other invidious discrimination."[110]

In fact, Trinity Lutheran is not transformed into a constitutionally regulated "state actor" by receiving a reimbursement grant to upgrade its playground and the same thing is, or should be, true of a parochial school that receives funds through a school-choice program or that benefits from parents' tax credits. Putting aside the constitutional question, though, it is clearly the case that the "no public funds for discrimination" slogan carries significant rhetorical and political weight. Activists engaged in policy arguments are not likely to carefully distinguish governments' invidious uses of suspect or irrelevant criteria from religious institutions' efforts to hire for religious mission and act with religious integrity. The unconditional-conditions doctrine is, to put it mildly, murky, and its application to

[106] Brief for Lambda Legal as Amicus Curiae Supporting Respondents, at 4.

[107] *Id.* at 11.

[108] Justice Sotomayor, after expressing concern about what the Court's decision "might enable tomorrow," quoted the following passage from the Court's 1963 school-prayer decision, *Abington Township v. Schempp*: "[T]he Free Exercise Clause . . . has never meant that a majority could use the machinery of the State to practice its beliefs." 137 S. Ct. at 2041 n.14.

[109] Moose Lodge v. Irvis, 407 U.S. 163, 177, 173 (1972) (quoting Reitman v. Mikey, 387 U.S. 369, 380 (1967)).

[110] 413 U.S. 455, 465–67 (1973).

antidiscrimination regulations tied to direct or indirect public funding is uncertain. *Trinity Lutheran*'s rejection of discriminatory exclusion from funding programs could end up mattering very little if voters and elected officials decide that religious institutions' efforts to act with mission-integrity render them unworthy to receive public benefits or cooperate for the public good.

D. The Merits and Durability of a "Status"/"Use" Distinction

It was important to Chief Justice Roberts's argument—and, in particular, to his reading and application of *Locke v. Davey*—that Missouri's policy required discrimination "solely on account of religious identity" or "status."[111] As he saw it, Trinity Lutheran was disqualified from competing for a reimbursement grant not because of what it planned to do with the funds—that is, resurface its playground—but "simply because of what it is—a church."[112] It is not clear, as Justice Gorsuch pointed out in dissent, that this distinction is or should be so important. Moreover, it is not clear that the distinction explains why *Locke v. Davey* does not justify Missouri's policy. After all, Chief Justice Rehnquist's opinion for the Court in *Locke* upheld Washington's rule against using public scholarships for devotional-theology degrees not because the rule is about the "use" of funds but because of the historical pedigree of the specific use that Washington ruled out—the training of clergy.[113]

The Free Exercise Clause guarantees, as Justice Gorsuch emphasized, "the free *exercise* of religion, not just the right to inward belief (or status)."[114] To reduce religion to status, class, or "identity" is to lose, or at least to diminish, religious freedom. "Status" does not capture what the First Amendment's Religion Clauses should protect. Certainly, many religious believers would report that their religious beliefs are central to who they "are," but most would also say that their faith commitments require and inspire a range of actions, both pious and mundane, and are lived out in community and in public. The elaboration and application of the chief justice's distinction will and should be closely watched.

---

[111] Trinity Lutheran, 137 S. Ct. at 2019.

[112] *Id.* at 2023.

[113] See *id.*, at 2026 (Gorsuch, J., concurring in part).

[114] *Id.*

V. Conclusion

Trinity Lutheran represents a significant step in the gradual working out of several lines of First Amendment cases. By taking seriously the fact that "Trinity Lutheran is a member of the community too,"[115] the justices appropriately pushed back against the notions that church-state separation precludes cooperation and that maintaining a secular government requires what Father Richard John Neuhaus called a "naked public square." However, future cases involving official discrimination against religious entities, practices, and beliefs in the context of public-benefit and other programs will almost certainly involve more difficult and divisive facts. Whether the Court will allow governments to use funding, licensing, granting, contracting, and taxing as ways of leveraging their police and other powers into coercive control over religious schools and service providers is a crucial and coming-soon question.

---

[115] *Id.* at 2022 (Roberts, C.J., majority op.).

From a Muddle to a Mudslide:
Murr v. Wisconsin

Nicole Stelle Garnett*

Murr v. Wisconsin was not an easy case, but it was a straightforward one. That is, the answer to the question presented in the case was not self-evident, but the question itself was not complicated. *Murr* was a so-called "regulatory takings" case. The Fifth Amendment's Takings Clause provides "nor shall private property be taken for public purposes without just compensation." Compensation is always required when the government uses the power of eminent domain to take property for public uses. But in a line of cases dating to the early 20th century, the Court also has held that property regulations that go "too far" are tantamount to takings and require compensation.[1]

The regulatory takings doctrine seeks to articulate the line between the vast universe of constitutionally permissible regulations restricting the use of private property, many of which impose financial burdens on property owners, and regulatory outliers that impose burdens so severe that the Fifth Amendment's Takings Clause requires the government to compensate the owners for their losses. The protection provided by the Takings Clause is not robust. As Chief Justice William Rehnquist once said, he saw no reason why the Takings Clause, "as much a part of the Bill of Rights as the First Amendment or Fourth Amendment, should be relegated to the status of a poor relation."[2] *Murr* proved no exception. Indeed, it further undermined the already enfeebled constitutional rights enjoyed by property owners against regulatory excess.

---

*John P. Murphy Foundation Professor of Law, University of Notre Dame.
[1] Pennsylvania Coal Co. v. Mahon, 260 U.S. 393, 415 (1922).
[2] Dolan v. City of Tigard, 512 U.S. 374, 392 (1994).

In *Murr*, the Court squarely confronted tension inherent in the Court's regulatory takings canon. On one hand, the Court has long insisted that state laws define the contours of property rights.[3] On the other, it also has admonished that state laws that impose particularly harsh burdens on property owners for other than traditional health and safety reasons will be treated as takings for which the regulated property owners are entitled to compensation.[4] These two ideas are not easily reconciled. If state laws define the contours of property rights, it is reasonable to ask why state laws that restructure those contours—restricting or reshaping property rights—ought ever be considered compensable takings. In other words, if states have the power to define what property *is*, why can't they *redefine* what it is without compensating property owners? Conversely, giving states *carte blanche* to regulate away all the value of private property would render the protection provided by the Fifth Amendment's Takings Clause a dead letter.

Murr illustrates this conundrum. The Murrs, four siblings, received as a gift title to two adjoining lots on the St. Croix River that their parents had purchased at separate times in the 1960s. The parents built a cabin on one and kept the other as an investment property. The two lots have always been deeded and taxed separately, and remain so to the present.

But in 1975, a local zoning ordinance combined the lots. The effect, as the Murrs discovered in 2004 when they sought to sell the investment lot (valued at $410,000), was to prohibit them from doing so unless they sold the other lot and cabin with it. They argued that the law preventing them from selling or developing the undeveloped parcel effected a regulatory taking of their property, since it extinguished rights their parents had enjoyed. The Supreme Court disagreed on the ground that the economic impact of the regulation should be measured not by treating the lots separately but by considering them together. This conclusion sealed the Murrs' fate, since the total value of the lots together was only slightly lower than the two lots valued separately.

---

[3] Murr v. Wisconsin, 137 S. Ct. 1933, 1950 (2017) (Roberts, C.J. dissenting) ("Our decisions have, time and again, declared that the Takings Clause protects private property rights as state law creates and defines them.").

[4] Pennsylvania Coal, 260 U.S. at 415.

Commentators have for years complained that the Supreme Court's regulatory takings doctrine is an indeterminate muddle.[5] *Murr* need not have added to the confusion. The Court might reasonably have held, based on the principle that state law defines the contours of property rights, that the merged lots were the relevant parcel for regulatory takings analysis. Alternatively, it might have held that property rights are not so malleable that the state can erase them simply because title changes hands. Unfortunately, the *Murr* decision does more than simply compound the confusion of takings law. In an effort to reconcile the tension between state laws as the source of property rights and the Takings Clause's prohibition on regulatory takings, the majority took the opportunity not simply to answer the relatively straightforward question presented in *Murr*, but also to articulate a multifactor balancing test that seeks, for the first time, to define "property" as *a matter of federal constitutional law*. The factors in this new definition of property are not only subjective and malleable, but decidedly pro-government. As a result, the majority opinion transforms the "muddle" of regulatory takings law into a mudslide that threatens to undermine the very foundation of property rights. Thus, all property owners—not just the Murrs—lost in the litigation.

I. The Murrs' Merger Problem

The petitioners in *Murr* were four siblings who had received as gifts from their parents two adjacent lots (given the sophisticated names "Lot E" and "Lot F") along the St. Croix River in northwestern Wisconsin. The Murrs' parents purchased Lot F in 1960 and placed the title in the name of Mr. Murr's business, William Murr Plumbing, Inc., on the advice of their accountant. Soon after purchasing the property, they built a small vacation cabin on Lot F. Three years later, they purchased the adjacent Lot E, planning eventually to develop or sell it. For whatever reason, they did neither. Lot E remains undeveloped to this day, although most of the other lots in the subdivision have been developed with homes, many of which are occupied by year-round residents. In 1994, the Murr parents transferred title to

---

[5] See, e.g., Carol M. Rose, *Mahon* Reconstructed: Why the Takings Issue Is Still a Muddle, 57 S. Cal. L. Rev. 561 (1984).

Lot F and the cabin to their children as a gift. They transferred title to Lot E to the children the following year.

A decade later, the Murr siblings began to explore the possibility of selling Lot E, valued at $410,000, to fund upgrades to the family cabin. At this point, they learned that they were no longer legally entitled to sell or develop Lot E unless they sold Lot F and the cabin with it. The reason was that state and county regulations enacted in 1975 include identical provisions that automatically "merge" contiguous lots whenever they come under common ownership. Thus, Lots E and F were "merged" when the parents gave their children title to Lot F in 1995. These regulations also provide that lots merged under this provision "may not be sold or developed as separate lots" unless they have at least one acre of developable land. Unfortunately for the Murrs, Lot E does not. While the lot's size is approximately 1.25 acres, other regulations and topographical features restrict its developable space to less than an acre.

The fact that they no longer had a right to sell or develop Lot E must have come as quite a shock to the Murrs. Although the government claimed that the two lots had been legally "merged," the Murrs never received any notice of this action. Moreover, they continued to hold separate title to the lots and pay separate tax bills for them. Their parents obviously had the right to transfer Lot E individually, since the Murr siblings received title to the lot in exactly such a transfer. Moreover, the Murrs only had to look around the neighborhood to realize that their neighbors also had the right to develop and sell lots no bigger than Lot E, since most similar lots in the neighborhood are occupied by residences.

Unfortunately for the Murrs, the "merger" regulations extinguished rights their neighbors continue to enjoy. Before the gifts to the Murr siblings, when the lots were owned separately (by the Murr parents and the plumbing company), a grandfather clause in the regulations permitted their separate sale and development—probably because the government was concerned that eliminating these rights might be unconstitutional. But upon receiving the gift of the adjacent lots, the siblings lost valuable rights enjoyed by their parents (and virtually all of their neighbors) because the state law "merged" the two separate, legally distinct, parcels.[6]

---

[6] Murr, 137 S. Ct. at 1940–42.

The Murrs believed that the regulations extinguishing their rights to sell or develop Lot E separately from Lot F had confiscated their property rights, so they filed a regulatory takings action against the state of Wisconsin. Based upon prior precedent, they appeared to have a very strong case. Twenty-five years ago, in *Lucas v. South Carolina Coastal Council,* the Supreme Court ruled in favor of a developer in an almost identical situation. Mr. Lucas had purchased two beachfront parcels in a high-end residential subdivision, intending to build a home for himself on one and a home to sell on the other. Before he could do so, South Carolina enacted a coastal preservation law that prevented construction of any "permanent habitable structure" on Mr. Lucas's property, even though all the other lots in the subdivision had been developed with large homes.[7] After finding that the prohibition rendered the regulated parcels "valueless," a state trial court held that the regulation effected a taking. The South Carolina Supreme Court disagreed, holding instead that the regulation was a valid exercise of the police power "designed to prevent serious public harm."[8] The U.S. Supreme Court reversed. Writing for the majority, Justice Anton Scalia concluded that regulations that "den[y] all economically beneficial or productive use of land" are automatically compensable unless they inhere in the "restrictions that background principles of the state's law of property and nuisance already placed upon land ownership."[9] Except that the Murrs' lots were contiguous, and Mr. Lucas's were not, the Murrs' situation was analogous. They argued that the lot merger regulation had exactly the prohibited effect—that is, it "depriv[ed] . . . them of 'all, or practically all, of the use of Lot E because the lot cannot be sold or developed as a separate lot.'"[10] Therefore, they asserted, citing *Lucas,* they were categorically entitled to compensation for the value of Lot E.

The state of Wisconsin argued that the economic effect of the regulation on Lot E was irrelevant because the Murrs' no longer owned it separately from Lot F. The state claimed that the Murrs could not claim a "total taking" of their property since the regulation only slightly reduced the value of their property considered as a whole:

[7] Lucas v. South Carolina Coastal Council, 505 U.S. 1003, 1007 (1992).

[8] *Id.* at 1009–10.

[9] Lucas, 505 U.S. at 1029.

[10] Murr, 137 S. Ct. at 1941.

the Murrs could use, develop, and sell the merged Lot E/F. In such "diminishment-in-value" cases, the plaintiffs are not categorically entitled to compensation. Instead, courts must consider three factors first articulated in the 1978 case, *Penn Central Transportation Company v. City of New York*.[11] These factors are: (1) "the economic impact of the regulation on the claimant," (2) "the extent to which the regulation has interfered with distinct investment-back expectations," and (3) "the character of governmental action."[12]

Although the *Penn Central* factors have assumed talismanic significance in regulatory takings cases, their precise meaning remains unclear—other than that they strongly favor government regulations (for reasons that are not themselves self-evident). Not surprisingly, therefore, their application by the lower courts resulted in losses for the Murrs. The trial court agreed with the state that the relevant parcel for purposes of takings analysis was the merged Lot E/F rather than Lot E individually and that the Murrs had not been deprived of all economic value of their property since they retained many options for using their property, considered as a whole. In fact, comparing the value of the merged lots to the lots valued separately, the court concluded that the merger regulations devalued the Murrs' property by less than 10 percent.[13]

The Wisconsin Court of Appeals affirmed. It also rejected the Murrs' argument that it should analyze the effect of the regulations on Lot E only. Instead, it held that the takings analysis was "properly focused" on the regulations' effect "on the Murrs' property as a whole," that is, both lots together. The court concluded that the Murrs could not reasonably have expected to use the lots separately after they came under common ownership because they were charged with knowing how the merger law would affect their development rights. The "expectation of separate treatment became unreasonable," the court concluded, "when they chose to acquire Lot E in 1995, after their having acquired Lot F in 1994."[14] Using this framework, the court of appeals held that the merger regulations did not effect a taking. The court acknowledged the trial court's finding that

[11] 438 U.S. 104 (1978).

[12] *Id.* at 124–25.

[13] Murr, 137 S. Ct. at 1942.

[14] Murr v. State of Wisconsin, 359 Wis. 2d 675 (2014), at ¶ 30 (unpublished) (per curiam).

the regulations diminished the total value of the Murrs' property (that is, Lots E and F considered together) by less than 10 percent. After the Wisconsin Supreme Court declined to hear the case, the U.S. Supreme Court granted the Murr's petition for certiorari.

II. *Murr's* Mudslide

The outcome in *Murr* turned on whether the Court should assess the effect of the challenged regulations on Lot E alone or on the lots considered together. The Court answered by invoking the parcel-as-a-whole rule, first announced in *Penn Central*. There, the Court considered a regulatory takings challenge to a historic preservation law that prohibited the owner of New York City's Grand Central Station—the Penn Central Transportation Company—from erecting a high-rise office building above the terminal. Penn Central claimed that the regulation had taken 100 percent of its airspace, causing it to suffer a financial loss of hundreds of millions of dollars.[15] The Court rejected the claim that the regulation confiscated the whole of the airspace above the terminal. It reasoned instead that the impact of a regulation must be measured against the regulated "parcel as a whole," which, in *Penn Central*, was "the city tax block designated as the landmark site."[16] The Court characterized the historical preservation regulation as merely a use restriction on that parcel (that is, the ground and the air considered together). Since the regulation preserved Penn Central's original "investment backed expectations" (to operate a railway station), the Court concluded—despite the magnitude of the loss caused by the regulation—that Penn Central had not suffered a compensable regulatory taking.[17]

The parcel-as-a-whole rule seeks to prevent property owners from gaming the system by engaging in what Margaret Radin has called "conceptual severance"—that is, separating for regulatory takings analysis the portion of its property impacted by a regulation from the remaining portion that is unaffected by the challenged regulation.[18]

---

[15] Penn Central had entered into a contract worth hundreds of millions of dollars with a developer for the sale of the airspace, which was contingent upon securing regulatory permission to build a high rise above Grand Central.

[16] Penn Central, 438 U.S. at 130–31.

[17] *Id.* at 131–34.

[18] Margaret Jane Radin, The Liberal Conception of Property: Cross Currents in the Jurisprudence of Takings, 88 Colum. L. Rev. 1667, 1676 (1988). This is often referred to

Since, due to the *Lucas* holding, a property owner's likelihood of succeeding in a regulatory takings case increases dramatically if the regulation at question effects a "total" taking, property owners have an incentive to define the relevant private property affected by a regulation narrowly. As Chief Justice John Roberts observed in his dissent in *Murr*, "Because a regulation amounts to a taking if it completely destroys a property's productive use, there is an incentive for owners to define the relevant 'private property' narrowly. This incentive threatens the careful balance between property rights and government authority that our regulatory takings doctrine strikes . . . . And so we do not allow it."[19] The Court has reiterated in a number of subsequent cases that the impact of a challenged regulation will be measured against the regulated "parcel as a whole." It has also made clear that property owners cannot claim that a regulation effects a "total taking" of a portion of their regulated property as long as development is permitted on the remainder of it.[20]

The difficulty in *Murr*, however, was that the Court had to decide what the relevant parcel was—Lot E or the merged Lot E/F. The Supreme Court had never before confronted the question of what the relevant "parcel" is in a takings case when the government *changed* parcel boundaries (in the Murrs' case, by merging legally distinct lots). The answer to the question was critical—indeed, outcome-determinative: Either the Murrs had lost all value of Lot E or they had suffered a minor reduction in value in their property considered as a whole. Ultimately, the Court affirmed the Wisconsin Court of Appeals' ruling that the relevant parcel was the merged Lot E/F. It

---

as the "denominator problem" in regulatory takings law. See Keystone Bituminous Coal Association v. DeBenedictus, 480 U.S. 470, 497 (1987) ("Because our test for regulatory taking requires us to compare the value that has been taken from the property to the value that remains in the property, one critical question is determining how to define the unit of property 'whose value is to furnish the denominator of the fraction.'").

[19] Murr, 137 S. Ct. at 1952 (Roberts, C.J., dissenting).

[20] See Tahoe Sierra Preservation Council v. Tahoe Regional Planning Agency, 535 U.S. 302, 331 (2002) (refusing to allow property owners to "effectively sever" the 32 months during which a regulatory moratorium prevented all development in order to claim that the regulation effected a "temporary total taking" of their property); Palazzolo v. Rhode Island, 533 U.S. 606, 631–37 (2001) (holding that a wetlands regulation did not effect a total taking because development was permitted on an upland portion of the plaintiff's property).

therefore concluded that the Murrs had not suffered a regulatory taking.

On its face, there is nothing earth-shattering about the Court's *holding* in *Murr*. As Chief Justice Roberts observed in dissent:

> The Court today holds that the regulation does not effect a taking that requires just compensation. This bottom-line conclusion does not trouble me; the majority presents a fair case that the Murrs can still make good use of both lots, and that the ordinance is a commonplace tool to preserve scenic areas, such as the Lower St. Croix River, for the benefit of land owners and the public alike.[21]

Unfortunately, the path that the majority took to reach this, in my view, erroneous conclusion effectively rewrites the law of takings and replaces one of the few clarifying principles in the regulatory takings muddle—that state laws are the source of property rights—with a new balancing test that seeks to define the meaning of property for the first time as a matter of federal law. That new test is subjective and unpredictable, and it decidedly tips the scales in favor of the government, further undermining the Takings Clause's already limited protection against regulatory excess.

A. The Majority

Justice Anthony Kennedy's majority opinion began by reviewing the Court's regulatory takings canon, with a particular emphasis on the division between ad hoc and categorical review. As a general matter, Justice Kennedy observed, the Court has refrained from elaborating definitive rules that govern the analysis of takings claims. Instead, regulatory takings cases generally involve "ad hoc, factual inquiries, designed to allow careful examination and weighing all of the relevant circumstances."[22] This pattern was established in what is widely regarded as the Court's first regulatory takings case, *Pennsylvania Coal Company v. Mahon*, which announced the oft-repeated but completely unhelpful principle that "while property

---

[21] Murr, 137 S. Ct. at 1950 (Roberts, C.J., dissenting).

[22] *Id.* at 1942 (majority op.) (quoting Tahoe Sierra, 535 U.S. at 322).

may be regulated to a certain extent, if regulation goes too far it will be recognized as a taking."[23]

As Justice Kennedy observed, however, the Court has over the years articulated a number of principles that guide the analysis of whether a regulation "goes too far." Two of these principles were of particular relevance in *Murr*. The first is the rule articulated in *Lucas*: Except in certain narrow circumstances, such as nuisance abatement, a regulation which "denies all economically beneficial or productive use of land" is categorically compensable.[24] The second is the multi-part balancing test announced in *Penn Central*, which applies to "partial takings" or "diminution in value" cases: "[W]hen a regulation impedes the use of property without depriving the owner of all economically beneficial use, a taking still may be found based on a 'complex of factors,'" which include, "(1) the economic impact of the regulation on the claimant; (2) the extent to which the regulation has interfered with distinct investment-backed expectations; and (3) the character of the governmental action."[25]

As discussed previously, the merger rule challenged in *Murr* created confusion over which rule the Court should use to analyze the Murrs' regulatory takings claim: If the relevant parcel was Lot E alone, then the case would seem to involve a fairly straightforward application of the categorical prohibition on "total takings" announced in *Lucas*. The regulations that prevented the Murrs from developing or selling Lot E appeared to impose a total taking of Lot E, in which case the Murrs would be categorically entitled to compensation. If the relevant parcel was the "merged" Lot E/F, however, then the regulations did not effect a total taking, since the Murrs retained the right to develop and sell the "merged" parcel. In other words, if the merger regulation expanded the relevant parcel to include both lots, considered together, then the case was transformed from a total-takings claim, which the Murrs should win, into a diminution-in-value challenge, which the Murrs should lose.

The Murrs argument that they had suffered a total taking of Lot E was made stronger by the fact that their parents had the right to develop or sell Lot E before the transfer. In *Lucas*, Justice Scalia had

---

[23] Mahon, 260 U.S. at 415.

[24] Lucas, 505 U.S. at 1015.

[25] Murr, 137 S. Ct. at 1943 (citing Penn Central, 438 U.S. at 124).

clarified that the property owners cannot challenge regulations that "inhere" in the "background principles of . . . property and nuisance already placed upon land ownership."[26] This exception to the total takings rule makes sense—after all, property owners cannot lose rights they never had. But that does not mean that the Murrs could not challenge the merger rule merely because they assumed ownership subject to it. In fact, the Wisconsin Court of Appeals conclusion to the contrary squarely conflicted with the holding in the 2001 case *Palazzolo v. Rhode Island*. In that case, the U.S. Supreme Court rejected the claim that owners are barred from challenging regulations merely because they assume ownership subject to them. In *Palazzolo*, the plaintiff challenged wetlands regulations that prohibited him from developing much of his property. While the plaintiff assumed title to the property subject to the regulations, the previous owner had purchased the property before the regulations were imposed. The state of Rhode Island, citing *Lucas*, argued that the owner could not challenge the regulations since he knew or should have known about the development restrictions when he took title to the property. The Supreme Court disagreed, holding instead that states do not have unfettered discretion to "shape and define property rights."[27] In particular, the Court held that a state cannot construct legal rules that eliminate valid regulatory takings claims upon a transfer of ownership. Otherwise, the Court warned, "postenactment transfer of title would absolve the State of its obligation to defend any action restricting land use, no matter how extreme or unreasonable. A State would be allowed, in effect, to put an expiration date on the Takings Clause."[28]

The Murrs' predicament was similar to the facts in *Palazzolo*. After all, before the transfer, their parents enjoyed the right to develop and sell Lot E separately from Lot F. Their children lost this right solely because the title to the lots changed hands. Unfortunately, the majority in *Murr* did not see it this way. Instead, Justice Kennedy construed *Palazzolo* to open the door to a new federal definition of property, one unhinged from the Court's previous insistence that state law defines the contours of property rights. Citing *Palazzolo*,

[26] Lucas, 505 U.S. at 1029.

[27] Palazzolo v. Rhode Island, 533 U.S. 606, 626 (2001).

[28] *Id.* at 627.

Kennedy argued that the Court has "expressed caution [about] the view that property rights should be coextensive with those under state law."[29] He warned, "defining the parcel by reference to state law could defeat a challenge even to a state enactment that alters permitted uses of property in ways inconsistent with reasonable investment-backed expectations."[30]

Kennedy, therefore, refused to adopt either of the "formalistic rules" urged by Wisconsin or the Murrs to guide the parcel inquiry. Wisconsin's approach—to "tie the definition of the parcel to state law, considering the two lots here as a single whole due to their merger under the challenged regulation"—was flawed because it "simply assumes the answer to the question." The Murrs' approach—"a presumption that lot lines define the relevant parcel in every instance"—was flawed because it "ignored the fact that lot lines are themselves creatures of state law, which can be overridden by the State," and because it would require the Court to "credit the aspect of state law that favors their preferred approach (lot lines) and ignore that which does not (merger provision)."[31]

Kennedy concluded that no single consideration could be used to determine the relevant parcel in a regulatory takings challenge. Instead, he directed courts to consider an entirely new laundry list of inchoate, vague factors to decide the universe of property rights affected by a challenged regulation. The first consideration is the way that the law regulates the plaintiffs' property. While he insisted, citing *Palazzolo*, that "[a] valid takings claim will not evaporate just because a purchaser took title after the law was enacted," he also suggested that "[a] reasonable restriction that predates a landowner's acquisition . . . can be one of the objective factors that most landowners would reasonably consider in forming fair expectations about their property" in light of "background customs and the whole of our legal tradition."[32] The second consideration is the "physical characteristics of the landowner's property," including "the relationship of any distinguishable tracts, the parcel's topography, and the surrounding human and ecological environment." He suggested that "it

---

[29] Murr, 137 S. Ct. at 1938.

[30] *Id.* at 1943.

[31] *Id.* at 1947.

[32] *Id.* at 1945.

may be relevant that the property is located in an area that is subject to, or likely to become subject to, environmental or other regulation." The third consideration is how the challenged regulations affect not only the "value of the property under the challenged regulations," but also "the effect of burdened land on the value of other holdings." For example, he suggested, a use restriction may decrease the market value of the regulated property, but add value to the landowner's other holdings, such as "increasing privacy, expanding recreational space, or preserving surrounding natural beauty."[33] Rather ominously, Kennedy did not rule out the possibility that parcels that are clearly distinct legally under state law—including perhaps noncontiguous parcels—might be considered a single parcel in a regulatory takings case if the regulation of one parcel added "value" (including nonmonetary value) to the other.

Applying this new test, Kennedy concluded that the relevant parcel in the case was the "merged" Lot E/F. His reasoning was as circular and convoluted as the new test itself. First, he concluded that the Murrs' property should be treated as a whole because the state law that they were challenging treated it as a whole (and for a good reason). The "treatment of the property under state and local law," he concluded, "indicates petitioners' property should be treated as one when considering the effects of the restrictions." Kennedy emphasized the reasonableness of the merger provision, the prevalence of similar provisions in other states' laws, and the public-policy goals that merging small lots advanced—especially the elimination of substandard lots to encourage orderly and rational development. He also concluded that the Murrs' expectations were not unduly disrupted, since they voluntarily (albeit unknowingly) submitted to the merger regulation by assuming common ownership of both Lot E and Lot F. And, he observed that a contrary holding would throw into question numerous other merger and boundary-alteration provisions in state law, including some that allow informal adjustments with minimal government oversight.[34] Second, he opined that the Murrs should have expected their property to be regulated because it was the kind of property that often is regulated. The "physical characteristics of the property support its treatment as a unified parcel,"

[33] *Id.* at 1945–46.
[34] *Id.* at 1948.

he concluded, because the lots' "rough terrain and narrow shape make it reasonable to expect their range of potential uses might be limited."[35] He also opined, citing the history of land use regulation in the Lower St. Croix River area, that the lots' location along the river should have put the Murrs on notice that their property was likely to be regulated. Third, he concluded that the "prospective value that Lot E brings to Lot F supports considering the two as one parcel." He reasoned that the restriction on selling or developing Lot E was "mitigated by the benefits of using the property as an integrated whole, allowing increased privacy and recreational space, plus the optimal location of any improvements."[36]

Weighing the impact of the regulation against the totality of the Murrs' property, not surprisingly, resulted in a government victory. The majority concluded that the Murrs had not suffered a compensable taking: They were not categorically entitled to compensation under *Lucas* because the regulations had not deprived them of all the value of the combined parcels. And, they were not entitled to compensation under the *Penn Central* balancing factors because the regulation had, at most, minimally reduced the value of the parcels considered together. Indeed it was possible that the merger regulations increased the overall value of the Murrs' property.[37]

B. The Dissent

As noted previously, Chief Justice Roberts began his dissent by observing that he had no particular objection to the majority's holding that the merger regulation did not effect a taking of the Murrs' property. His dissent focused on the majority's decision to replace the presumption that state laws define the contours of property rights, which the Takings Clause in turn secures, with a new multifactor, takings-specific federal definition of property. "Our decisions have, time and again, declared that the Takings Clause protects private property rights as state law creates and defines them," Roberts argued. "By securing such *established* property rights, the Takings Clause protects individuals from being forced to bear the full weight of actions that should be borne by the public at large. The majority's

35 *Id.*
36 *Id.*
37 *Id.* at 1949–50.

144

new malleable definition of 'private property'—adopted solely 'for purposes of th[e] takings inquiry'—undermines that protection."[38]

The chief justice asserted that the Court should have adhered to the traditional approach, which relied on state law to define the boundaries of private property, and treated the question of whether the challenged regulation effected a taking as a separate issue. The Takings Clause, he urged, raises three distinct questions about regulatory action: The first is "what 'private property' the government's planned course of conduct will affect." The second is "whether that property has been 'taken for public use.'" And, if so, third, what compensation is due?

Murr was a "step one" case, which required the Court to identify the property interest at stake. Because the Takings Clause does not define "property," this first inquiry "requires looking outside the Constitution" to sources such as state law.[39] Admittedly, Roberts observed, the "enigmatic" parcel-as-a-whole rule "has created confusion about how to identify the relevant property in a regulatory takings case when the claimant owns more than one lot of land. Should the impact of the regulation be evaluated with respect to each individual lot, or with respect to the adjacent lots grouped together as one unit?"[40] Clearly, this "confusion" was at the heart of the dispute in *Murr*. But Roberts correctly faulted the majority's conclusion that the answer to the question "what is the relevant parcel?" requires a new federal definition of property. He urged a more "straightforward" approach: "State laws define the boundaries of distinct units of land, and those boundaries should, in all but the most exceptional circumstances, determine the parcel at issue."[41] Roberts rejected the majority's conclusion that reliance on state law to determine the contours of property rights creates an excessive risk of "gamesmanship." He reasoned, "States create property rights with respect to particular 'things.' And in the context of real property, those 'things' are horizontally bounded lots of land." Given this reality, he reasoned, courts are perfectly capable of sussing out strategic efforts to combine (on the part of states) or divide (on the part of property owners)

[38] *Id.* at 1950 (Roberts, C.J., dissenting) (citation omitted).
[39] *Id.* at 1951.
[40] *Id.* at 1952.
[41] *Id.* at 1953.

parcels to enhance the likelihood of succeeding in a regulatory takings case.

Roberts further criticized the majority for conflating the first inquiry in a takings case (determining the relevant universe of property rights at issue), with the second inquiry (determining whether a taking has occurred). In deciding that Lots E and F were a single parcel, as Roberts observed, the majority considered factors (such as the owners' regulatory expectations and the public-policy goals advanced by the regulations) that are irrelevant to the determination of the contours of the regulated property. These factors are properly considered after that determination has been made, when a court must decide whether a taking has occurred. By "cramming [these considerations] into the definition of 'private property,'" Roberts warned, the majority "undermines the effectiveness of the Takings Clause as a check on the government's power to shift the cost of public life onto private individuals."[42] As Roberts observed, while it is true that regulatory takings inquiries are usually ad hoc, the takings inquiry "presuppos[es] that the 'relevant private property' has already been identified." He continued, "while ownership of contiguous parcels may bear on whether a person's plot has been 'taken,' *Penn Central* provides no basis for disregarding state property lines when identifying the 'parcel as a whole.'"[43]

The majority's decision to depart from state property principles to determine the scope of the Murrs' property rights, Roberts urged, opens the door to precisely the kind of gamesmanship that supposedly motivated the majority's decision to adopt a federal constitutional definition of property. "Whenever possible, governments in regulatory takings cases will ask courts to aggregate legally distinct properties into one 'parcel' solely for purposes of resisting a particular claim." And since the majority's new definition of the parcel-as-a-whole turns in part on the reasonableness of the regulation at issue, the government's interest unfortunately will come into play twice—both when identifying the relevant parcel and when determining whether the regulatory burden is so excessive as to constitute a taking.[44] "The result," Roberts worried, "is clear double counting to

[42] *Id.* at 1954.

[43] *Id.*

[44] *Id.* at 1955.

tip the scales in favor of the government: Reasonable government regulation should have been anticipated by the landowner, so the relevant parcel is defined consistent with that regulation." What's more, "In deciding whether there is a taking under the second step of the analysis, the regulation will seem eminently reasonable given its impact on the pre-packaged parcel. Not, as the Court assures us, 'necessarily' in 'every' case, but surely in most."[45] Thus, the majority's "new framework compromises the Takings Clause as a barrier between individuals and the press of the public interest."[46]

Roberts concluded by analyzing the Murrs' takings claim under the traditional approach, which looks to state law to determine the contours of the property rights at issue. In his view, the case was a relatively straightforward one. Faulting the Wisconsin Court of Appeals for, much like the majority, adopting a "takings-specific approach to defining the relevant parcel," he argued that the case should be remanded to determine whether Lots E and F are legally distinct parcels using "ordinary principles of Wisconsin property law."[47] At that point, after the court determines the relevant parcel, the real work of determining whether a taking had occurred— a necessarily fact-intensive task requiring the exercise of reasoned judgment—would properly begin. But, he admonished, "basing the definition of 'property' on a judgment call, too, allows the government's interests to warp the private rights that the Takings Clause is supposed to secure."[48]

C. *Remediating* Murr's *Mudslide*

Chief Justice Roberts is undoubtedly correct that all private property owners, not just the members of the Murr family, lost in the *Murr* case. For the reasons set forth in his dissent, the majority's multifactor redefinition of private property undermines the Fifth Amendment's already limited protection against expropriative regulations. In the future, courts and regulators alike will undoubtedly read *Murr* as an invitation to reject regulatory takings claims challenging the high costs imposed by regulations that purport to advance the public

---

[45] *Id.* at 1955–56.
[46] *Id.* at 1956.
[47] *Id.*
[48] *Id.* at 1957.

interest. There is a serious risk that *Murr* transforms the Court's prior admonition that the Takings Clause exists to prevent the government from "forcing some people alone to bear public burdens which, in all fairness and justice, should be borne by the public as a whole" into mere hortatory fluff.[49] The factors that the opinion requires courts to apply to define the property rights at issue in a regulatory takings case are not only vague and subjective; they also favor government regulators over property owners since they import public policy considerations into the definition of private property itself. Essentially, to answer the question "what property does the plaintiff own?" courts must now engage in guesswork about whether a plaintiff should have anticipated a regulation and weigh the owner's loss against the public policy goals of a challenged regulation. Those factors ought to be irrelevant to determining the scope of ownership rights.

The chief justice also is right that a continued reliance on state laws to define the contours of property rights would have averted the *Murr* mudslide. The traditional approach would have been vastly preferable to the constitutional detour taken by the majority. But Roberts overestimates the extent to which relying on state laws to define property rights clarifies the takings muddle. For the reasons discussed previously, the question posed in *Murr* is endemic to the takings puzzle: If state laws secure property rights, why can they also violate them? Commentators have faulted Justice Scalia for misapprehending in *Lucas* the nature of "background principles of property and nuisance"—by assuming that these principles are fixed and static when in fact they are fluid and evolving.[50] Chief Justice Roberts similarly is too sanguine that there are sufficiently fixed "ordinary principles" of state property law to resolve contested questions about the nature and extent of property rights affected by a challenged regulation. After all, the Wisconsin courts purported to apply settled Wisconsin law in holding that the Murrs' lots should be considered one parcel, yet Roberts faulted them for adopting a "takings specific" definition of property. It is unclear what in the nature of "ordinary principles" of state property law prevents state courts from adopting such a definition, or, for that matter, any definition.

---

[49] Armstrong v. United States, 364 U.S. 40, 49 (1960).

[50] Louis A. Halper, Why the Nuisance Knot Can't Undo the Takings Muddle, 28 Ind. L. Rev. 329 (1995); William W. Fisher III, The Trouble with *Lucas*, 45 Stan. L. Rev. 1393 (1993).

And, while reliance on state law will lend more certainty in many takings cases—for example, the fact that the Murrs held separate title to Lots E and F and paid separate tax bills strongly suggests that the lots should be treated as legally distinct—it will not alone protect property owners from malleable rules that favor regulators. Moreover, even if state law provides a satisfactorily stable definition of property rights, the takings inquiry in diminution-in-value cases will continue to turn on the application of the elusive *Penn Central* factors, which themselves tip the scale in favor of regulators over property owners.

In his separate dissent in *Murr*, Justice Clarence Thomas questioned the wisdom of the entire regulatory-takings doctrine. He suggested that "it would be desirable for us to take a fresh look at our regulatory takings jurisprudence, to see whether it can be grounded in the original public meaning of the Takings Clause of the Fifth Amendment or the Privileges or Immunities Clause of the Fourteenth Amendment."[51] In my view, Justice Thomas is correct that a historically grounded "fresh look" is the only principled way to clear the takings muddle. *Murr* further muddies the takings waters, but the entire doctrine has long been riddled with inconsistencies and relies more on *ipse dixit* assertions than reasoned analysis. The parcel-as-a-whole rule is a case in point. It is not at all clear why the proportion of an owner's loss resulting from a regulation should matter more to the Court than the magnitude of the loss. For example, if a rancher owning 1,000 acres was prevented by an environmental regulation from using 100 of them for any purpose, he would probably lose a regulatory takings challenge. But if he owned only the 100 regulated acres, then he might well win one (unless the regulation fell under *Lucas*'s narrow nuisance exception). Yet the regulatory burden is the same.[52]

Thomas did not elucidate what a rigorous historical analysis of the original public meaning of the Fifth and Fourteenth Amendments might reveal about the regulatory takings problem. Many scholars have suggested that the Takings Clause as originally understood

[51] Murr, 137 S. Ct. at 1957 (Thomas, J., dissenting).

[52] See David A. Dana, Why Do We Have the Parcel-as-a-Whole Rule? 39 Vt. L. Rev. 617 (2015); Richard A. Epstein, Physical and Regulatory Takings: One Distinction Too Many, 64 Stan. L. Rev. Online 99 (2012).

provided no protection against regulatory takings at all.[53] I am a skeptic of this claim.[54] Even if I am wrong—and I am admittedly in the minority—Thomas suggests that the Fourteenth Amendment's Privileges or Immunities Clause may provide an alternative source of protection against regulatory excesses. Scholars have demonstrated that, by the antebellum period, courts had begun to develop a fairly robust jurisprudence delineating the line between valid and expropriative regulations.[55] These jurisprudential concepts might have found a home in the Privileges or Immunities Clause had it not been eviscerated in the *Slaughter House Cases*.[56] It is unclear whether analyzing problems like the one posed in *Murr* under the Privileges or Immunities Clause, as properly understood, would lend greater clarity to the regulatory takings issue. But it is hard to imagine that it could compound the confusion any more than current law does. Unfortunately, since Thomas appears to be alone in his curiosity about the matter, the takings waters likely will remain muddied for the foreseeable future.

---

[53] John F. Hart, Colonial Land Use Law and Its Significance for Modern Takings Doctrine, 109 Harv. L. Rev. 1252, 1252 (1996); John F. Hart, Land Use Law in the Early Republic and the Original Meaning of the Takings Clause, 94 NW. U. L. Rev. 1099 (2000); Michael Treanor, The Original Understanding of the Takings Clause and the Political Process, 95 Colum. L. Rev. 782 (1995).

[54] Nicole Stelle Garnett, "No Taking without a Touching?'" Questions from an Armchair Originalist, 45 San Diego L. Rev. 761 (2008).

[55] Eric R. Claeys, Takings, Regulations, and Natural Property Rights, 88 Cornell L. Rev. 1549 (2003).

[56] Michael Rappaport, Originalism and Regulatory Takings: Why the Fifth Amendment May Not Protect against Regulatory Takings, but the Fourteenth Amendment May, 45 San Diego L. Rev. 729 (2008).

S.W. *General*: The Court Reins In Unilateral Appointments

*Thomas A. Berry**

N.L.R.B. v. S.W. General, Inc.[1] represents the latest round in the long-running dispute over when and how the president can bypass the Senate in appointing executive-branch officers. Unlike the last Supreme Court case on this topic, *N.L.R.B. v. Noel Canning*,[2] this case concerned only statutory interpretation questions, not constitutional ones. Nonetheless, *S.W. General* is an important clarification of the law that governs acting officers, a law that will likely return to the Court before much longer.

This article will explore both the context of the statutory dispute and the future implications the decision may hold. First, I will give a brief history of the Appointments Clause and the various iterations of the Vacancies Act. That history culminates with the passage of the Federal Vacancies Reform Act (FVRA) in 1998, the statute at issue in *S.W. General*. Second, I will work through both the majority and dissenting opinions in *S.W. General*. This account will explain how the core of the disagreement came down to whether a single canon of interpretation—that reference to one thing in a class excludes all others (known by its Latin name *expressio unius*)—should have been applied.

Finally, after this rundown of the case itself, I will move on to examining three unsettled questions raised by the decision. First, what retroactive effect might it have on the actions of past acting officers

*College of Public Interest Law Fellow, Pacific Legal Foundation; former legal associate, Cato Institute. He contributed to an amicus brief filed by Cato in support of SW General at the Supreme Court, though his name could not appear on the brief because he was not yet a member of the bar. See Brief of Cato Institute as Amicus Curiae Supporting Respondent, N.L.R.B. v. S.W. General, Inc., 137 S. Ct. 929 (2017).

[1] 137 S. Ct. 929 (2017).

[2] 134 S. Ct. 2550 (2014).

who, we now know, were serving illegally? Second, how might the Court's final interpretation of one section of the FVRA affect *another* unsettled question regarding another important section of that same law? And third, are there constitutional problems with the FVRA itself (as suggested in a concurrence by Justice Clarence Thomas) that could arise in a future legal challenge?

I. Background

A. The Appointments Clause and the Vacancies Act

During the Constitutional Convention, there was a serious debate over the best method of appointment to both executive-branch offices and judicial positions. "One group of delegates, led by James Wilson, Nathaniel Gorham, Alexander Hamilton, and Gouverneur Morris, favored control of appointments by a strong executive. The opposing camp, led by Charles Pinckney, Luther Martin, George Mason, Roger Sherman, Oliver Ellsworth, and John Rutledge, favored legislative control of the appointment process."[3]

Each method had its passionate critics. In opposition to a plan that would have had the legislature select federal judges, James Wilson declared that "[e]xperience shewed the impropriety of such appointm[ents] by numerous bodies. Intrigue, partiality, and concealment were the necessary consequences."[4] On the other side, Roger Sherman argued against unilateral presidential appointments and in favor of senatorial appointments. The Senate, he contended, "would be composed of men nearly equal to the Executive, and would of course have on the whole more wisdom."[5] For this reason, he believed the Senate "would bring into their deliberations a more diffusive knowledge of characters."[6] And finally, Sherman predicted that "[i]t would be less easy for candidates to intrigue with [the Senate], than with the Executive Magistrate."[7]

Eventually, as with many other aspects of the Constitution, the two sides reached a compromise that was acceptable to both. The

[3] Adam J. White, Toward the Framers' Understanding of "Advice and Consent": A Historical and Textual Inquiry, 29 Harv. J. L. & Pub. Pol'y 103, 110–11 (2005).

[4] 1 The Records of the Federal Convention of 1787, at 119 (Max Farrand ed., 1911).

[5] 2 The Records of the Federal Convention of 1787, at 43 (Max Farrand ed., 1911).

[6] *Id.*

[7] *Id.*

president would select each nominee, but those nominees would only be installed in office after obtaining the "advice and consent" of the Senate.[8] Gouverneur Morris touted the strength of this dual-role system: "as the President was to nominate, there would be responsibility, and as the Senate was to concur, there would be security."[9] On September 17, 1787, the convention approved the final version of the Appointments Clause when the delegates approved the final draft of the Constitution, giving us the system of executive-branch appointment we retain today:

> [The President] shall nominate, and by and with the advice and consent of the Senate, shall appoint ambassadors, other public ministers and consuls, judges of the Supreme Court, and all other officers of the United States, whose appointments are not herein otherwise provided for, and which shall be established by law: but the Congress may by law vest the appointment of such inferior officers, as they think proper, in the President alone, in the courts of law, or in the heads of departments.[10]

But soon after, during George Washington's very first term, the executive branch confronted a problem that those at the convention never explicitly considered: what to do if an office unexpectedly falls vacant while the Senate is in session (when the Recess Apointments Clause cannot be invoked). Should the duties of that office go unperformed until a new nominee wins Senate confirmation, or could a system of temporary "acting" appointments somehow solve this problem? In 1792, the Second Congress chose the latter course, enacting a law declaring that in the case of a vacancy in any office

> whose appointment is not in the head [of that office's department], . . . it shall be lawful for the President of the United States, in case he shall think it necessary, to authorize any person or persons at his discretion to perform the duties of the said respective offices until a successor be appointed, or until such absence or inability by sickness shall cease.[11]

---

[8] The phrase "advice and consent" was first put before the convention in a proposal by the Committee on Compromise on September 4, 1787. See *id.* at 498–99.

[9] *Id.* at 539.

[10] U.S. Const. art. II, § 2, cl. 2.

[11] Act of May 8, 1792, ch. 37, § 8, 1 Stat. 281.3.

Three years later, the statute was amended so that "no one vacancy shall be supplied, in manner aforesaid, for a longer term than six months."[12]

This was the state of the law until 1868, when the first comprehensive "Vacancies Act" was passed.[13] This law expanded the number of offices that could be filled by acting officers, but also eliminated the power of the president to appoint "any persons" he wished. First assistants to an officer became the default acting-officer appointees, with presidential discretion to appoint instead someone currently serving in another Senate-confirmed office. Additionally, the Vacancies Act lowered the maximum tenure of acting officials dramatically, from six months to only 10 days.

The Vacancies Act was amended several times over the subsequent decades, but the core structure remained the same.[14] Eventually, however, a series of conflicts between the president and the Senate over temporary appointments convinced Congress that a major reform was needed. The result was the Federal Vacancies Reform Act (FVRA) of 1998,[15] the statute at issue in *S.W. General.*

The FVRA addressed two major flaws that had emerged in the Vacancies Act. First, when acting officers overstayed their time limitation, there were few practical consequences. The actions taken by an invalid acting officer still had the force of law, until—if push came to shove—a court found that the officer had overstayed his tenure. As a result, acting service beyond the time limitations in the act was widespread.[16] And to make matters worse, the U.S. Court of Appeals for the D.C. Circuit held in 1998 that even if an acting officer were found by a court to have served improperly, any subsequent legitimate officer could simply "ratify" the actions taken

[12] Act of Feb. 13, 1795, ch. 21, 1 Stat. 415.

[13] Act of July 23, 1868, ch. 227, 15 Stat. 168–69.

[14] The most significant changes were a steady lengthening of the tenure of acting officers. See Doolin Sec. Sav. Bank, F.S.B. v. Office of Thrift Supervision, 139 F.3d 203, 210 (D.C. Cir. 1998) (describing how the tenure of acting appointments was lengthened to 30 days in 1891 and then to 120 days in 1988).

[15] 5 U.S.C. § 3345 et seq.

[16] "[D]uring 1998 some 20% of the 320 advice and consent positions in the departments were being filled by temporary designees, most of whom had served beyond the 120-day limitation period of the Act." Morton Rosenberg, Congressional Research Service Report for Congress, The New Vacancies Act: Congress Acts to Protect the Senate's Confirmation Prerogative 1 (1998).

by the prior illegitimate acting officer, retroactively making those actions legally sound.[17]

Second, dozens of "delegation" statutes had proliferated over the decades, giving cabinet secretaries wide leeway to assign the duties of their departments to whomever they wished. As a result, those who were ineligible for appointment as acting officers under the terms of the Vacancies Act were frequently "delegated" the title and duties of precisely the same office, meaning the act's restrictions had become largely toothless.[18]

The FVRA attempted to solve these two problems by creating much more serious consequences for unauthorized acting service: with limited exceptions, actions taken by illegitimate acting officers were legally void and could not be retroactively "ratified" by later legitimate officers.[19] Further, the FVRA clarified that the delegation powers given to the cabinet secretaries could *not* be used to appoint acting officers.[20]

In addition to these two marquee changes, the FVRA also targeted the practice of giving nominees a "head start" in their job before Senate confirmation. With limited exceptions, the FVRA banned appointing the same person as both an acting officer and the nominee for Senate confirmation to be the permanent officer in the same position. It is a dispute over the extent of those limited exceptions that would lead to the *S.W. General* litigation.

---

[17] See Doolin, 139 F.3d at 212–14.

[18] The most high-profile instance of this maneuver, which helped to precipitate passage of the FVRA, was the delegation of power from the attorney general to Bill Lann Lee, making him acting assistant attorney general for the Civil Rights Division far longer than the time limitations of the Vacancies Act allowed. See Steven J. Duffield & James C. Ho, The Illegal Appointment of Bill Lann Lee, 2 Tex. Rev. L. & Pol. 335 (1998).

[19] See 5 U.S.C. § 3348(d)(1)–(2) ("An action taken by any person who is not acting [in compliance with the FVRA] shall have no force or effect" and "may not be ratified."). The legislative record makes clear that this change was a direct response to *Doolin*. See, e.g., 144 Cong. Rec. S6414 (stating that the FVRA "impose[s] a sanction for noncompliance," thereby "[o]verruling several portions of [*Doolin*]"); S. Rep. No. 105-250, at 5 ("The Committee . . . finds that th[e ratification] portion of [*Doolin*] demands legislative response.").

[20] See 5 U.S.C. § 3347.

B. Background of the S.W. General Litigation

When an ambulance company in Arizona entered into a dispute with its employees about annual bonuses, they likely did not anticipate that this would ultimately lead to the resolution of a textual debate that had lasted nearly two decades.

The ambulance company in question, S.W. General, had ceased paying certain "longevity bonuses" to its longer-tenured employees after the collective bargaining agreement that established those bonuses expired in December 2012. The employees believed that until the next collective bargaining agreement was put in place, they were entitled to continue receiving the bonuses under federal law.[21] And so in January 2013, as occurs in dozens of cases every year, the National Labor Relations Board (NLRB) issued a formal complaint alleging unfair labor practices.[22] Although the complaint was issued by a regional officer, all such complaints are filed under the authority of the general counsel of the NLRB, which is a Senate-confirmed position.[23]

At the time the complaint was issued, however, there was no Senate-confirmed general counsel. Instead, a longtime NLRB lawyer named Lafe Solomon was serving as the *acting* general counsel. Solomon believed himself to be validly serving pursuant to the FVRA, but S.W. General's response to the complaint alleged that he was not, and that the complaint was therefore unauthorized.[24] To understand S.W. General's argument, we have to get into the textual weeds.

The FVRA provides three alternate means to become an acting officer, which are referred to by their subsection numbers: (a)(1), (a)(2), and (a)(3). First, under subsection (a)(1), the "first assistant" to a vacant position can become an acting officer by default, immediately upon the vacancy occurring.[25] The term "first assistant" is never defined in the act itself, but most Senate-confirmed offices have a "deputy" or "assistant" who is designated by statute as the "first assistant" for FVRA purposes.

---

[21] Specifically, their claim was under sections 8(a)(1) and 8(a)(5) of the National Labor Relations Act, 29 U.S.C. § 158(a)(1), (5).

[22] See S.W. General, Inc. v. N.L.R.B., 796 F.3d 67, 72 (D.C. Cir. 2015).

[23] See 29 U.S.C. § 153(d).

[24] See S.W. General, 796 F.3d at 72.

[25] See 5 U.S.C. § 3345(a)(1).

Second, under subsection (a)(2), the president can choose any currently serving Senate-confirmed officer from any part of the executive branch to serve as the acting officer.[26]

Third and finally, under subsection (a)(3), the president can choose any employee *in the same department as the vacancy* to serve as the acting officer, provided that the employee's job is at the highest of the 15 levels in the civil service pay scale (an indication that the job has management-level responsibilities) and that the employee held that job for at least 90 days during the previous year.[27] Unlike those appointed under (a)(2), those appointed under (a)(3) are not required to have held Senate-confirmed positions.

When Ronald Meisberg resigned as NLRB general counsel in June 2010, Lafe Solomon was appointed acting general counsel under subsection (a)(3).[28] He had been director of the NLRB's Office of Representation Appeals for the previous 10 years, and thus met both the tenure and salary requirements.[29] He was ineligible for appointment under (a)(2) because his job was not a Senate-confirmed position, and ineligible under (a)(1) because he was not the first assistant to the general counsel.

Six months later, in January 2011, the president nominated Solomon to be the permanent general counsel.[30] This brings us to the part of the FVRA's text that is disputed: the so-called "disqualification clause," also referred to by its subsection number (b)(1). The core of the controversy boiled down to this single question: did this clause disqualify Solomon from serving as the acting general counsel from the moment he was nominated for the permanent position? The disqualification clause reads as follows:

> Notwithstanding subsection (a)(1), a person may not serve as an acting officer for an office under this section, if-
>
> (A) during the 365-day period preceding the date of the death, resignation, or beginning of inability to serve, such person-

---

[26] See 5 U.S.C. § 3345(a)(2).

[27] See 5 U.S.C. § 3345(a)(3).

[28] See S.W. General, 796 F.3d at 71.

[29] See *id.* at 73.

[30] See *id.* at 71.

    (i) did not serve in the position of first assistant to the office of such officer; or

    (ii) served in the position of first assistant to the office of such officer for less than 90 days; and

  (B) the President submits a nomination of such person to the Senate for appointment to such office.[31]

There is no dispute that Solomon had never served as first assistant and thus met the criterion of (A)(i). Further, there is no dispute that the president had submitted Solomon's nomination for the permanent position, thus meeting the criterion of (B). Instead, the dispute is what meaning, if any, to give to the first three words (often called the preamble) of this section: "Notwithstanding subsection (a)(1)."

Does this preamble mean the entire disqualification clause applies *only* to acting officers who received that position under (a)(1)? If so, Solomon was not disqualified, since he received his position as acting officer under (a)(3), not (a)(1). Alternatively, is the purpose of the preamble only to *emphasize* that the disqualification applies to the otherwise-automatic elevation of the first assistant? In that case, the disqualification would likewise apply to the two other (not emphasized) categories of (a)(2) and (a)(3), and Solomon would have been disqualified from the moment he was nominated for the permanent position.

Soon after the FVRA was passed, the Office of Legal Counsel (OLC) weighed in on this textual question. In a lengthy guidance on the effects of the FVRA, OLC took the former position, that the disqualification clause applies only to subsection (a)(1).[32] Even though OLC gave no hint of the reasoning that led to this conclusion, the executive branch took this recommendation into practice. This, presumably, is why President Barack Obama nominated Solomon for the permanent position without fear of disqualifying him as the acting officer.

But OLC opinions are not binding on the judicial branch, and until *S.W. General* this textual question had rarely been confronted in the courts.[33] An administrative law judge and the NLRB itself both

---

[31] 5 U.S.C. § 3345(b)(1).

[32] See Guidance on Application of Federal Vacancies Reform Act of 1998, 23 Op. O.L.C. 60, 64 (1999).

[33] Before *S.W. General*, only two federal district courts had examined the question. Both found that the disqualification clause applied to all three subsections. See Hooks

declined to address S.W. General's FVRA argument, and both ruled against S.W. General on the underlying labor-law issue.[34] S.W. General then appealed to the D.C. Circuit, which became the first court of appeals to grapple with this FVRA question.[35]

In August 2015, a unanimous three-judge panel of the D.C. Circuit agreed with S.W. General's textual argument. The court held that the "notwithstanding" preamble served only as a clarification, not as a limitation on the clause's overall scope.[36] The government asked the Supreme Court to take the case for review, which it did in June 2016. And that is how a dispute over just three words reached the U.S. Supreme Court.

II. The *S.W. General* Decision

On March 21, 2017, the Supreme Court ruled by a vote of 6–2 that the notwithstanding clause does *not* limit the reach of subsection (b)(1), and that Solomon was therefore ineligible for acting service and unauthorized to issue the complaint against S.W. General. Chief Justice John Roberts wrote the majority opinion, joined by Justices Anthony Kennedy, Clarence Thomas, Stephen Breyer, Samuel Alito, and Elena Kagan. Justice Sonia Sotomayor wrote a dissenting opinion, joined by Justice Ruth Bader Ginsburg. In addition, Justice Thomas wrote a concurring opinion, focusing not on the statutory interpretation question but on a constitutional issue that may be presented in a future case. In this section, I will summarize the competing statutory arguments of the majority and dissenting opinions. I will reserve a discussion of Justice Thomas's concurrence for a later section on the future implications of the case.[37]

---

v. Remington Lodging & Hospitality, LLC, 8 F. Supp. 3d 1178, 1187–89 (D. Alaska 2014); Hooks v. Kitsap Tenant Support Servs., Inc., No. 13-cv-5470, 2013 WL 4094344, at *2 (W.D. Wash. Aug. 13, 2013).

[34] See S.W. General, 796 F.3d at 72 (citing 360 N.L.R.B. No. 109 (2014)).

[35] After the D.C. Circuit issued its opinion but before the Supreme Court ruled on the appeal, the Ninth Circuit likewise held that the disqualification clause applied to all three subsections. See Hooks v. Kitsap Tenant Support Servs., Inc., 816 F.3d 550, 558–59 (9th Cir. 2016).

[36] See S.W. General, 796 F.3d at 78.

[37] See *infra* notes 95–113 and accompanying text.

A. The Majority Opinion

The core of the majority's reasoning was that the reference to (a)(1) can be fully explained by (a)(1)'s unique structure as a default rule, *not* by a desire to limit the scope of the disqualification. "The phrase '[n]otwithstanding subsection (a)(1)' does not limit the reach of (b)(1), but instead clarifies that the prohibition applies even when it conflicts with the default rule that first assistants shall perform acting duties."[38]

Several pieces of evidence led the Court to this conclusion. First was the implausibility of the government's textual argument when considering two crucial words coming *after* the "notwithstanding" preamble: "person" and "section." The prohibition begins with the phrase "a person may not serve," which, as the Court noted, naturally means that the prohibition "applies to any 'person.'"[39] Such broad language would be inapt if the prohibition applied to only first assistants, since "[i]mportant as they may be, first assistants are not the only 'person[s]' of the bunch."[40] And the prohibition continues with the phrase "as an acting officer for an office under this section," which would naturally mean that the prohibition applies to the *whole* section. But (a)(1) is only a subsection within a larger section that identifies all three types of acting officers. As the Court observed, "[w]hen Congress wanted to refer only to a particular subsection or paragraph, it said so."[41] For this reason, the Court reasoned that the prohibition refers "to the entire section—§3345—which subsumes all of the [three] ways a person may become an acting officer."[42] The Court bolstered this reasoning with the use of comparative textualism, which looks to see how the same words are used in other parts of the same law. The Court found that in each of the other instances where "person" and "section" were used, they referred to all *three* types of acting officers.[43]

---

[38] S.W. General, 137 S. Ct. at 938.

[39] *Id.*

[40] *Id.*

[41] *Id.* at 939.

[42] *Id.*

[43] See *id.* (noting that a later section of the law specifies how long "the *person* serving as an acting officer as described under *section* 3345 may serve in the office," and that still another clause refers to actions "taken by any *person* who is not acting under *section* 3345, 3346, or 3347") (emphasis added by the Court).

The Court then turned to another familiar textual question: did Congress have alternate means of expression available besides this broad language—words that would have unambiguously limited the disqualification to subsection (a)(1)? And the answer to that question was yes: "Replacing 'person' with 'first assistant' would have done the trick. So too would replacing 'under this section' with 'under subsection (a)(1).'"[44] As the Court has held in previous statutory interpretation cases, forgoing a "readily available and apparent alternative" strongly suggests that Congress meant the words it chose to have their natural meaning.[45]

With this broad meaning as the clear winner in everything *after* the preamble, the Court then turned to an analysis of the preamble itself—the only part of the clause that, in the government's view, pointed in the opposite direction. First, the Court noted that if the preamble were meant to *limit the scope* of the clause, then the choice of the word "notwithstanding" would have been inapt, because "[t]he ordinary meaning of 'notwithstanding' is 'in spite of,' or 'without prevention or obstruction from or by.'"[46] A notwithstanding clause is thus meant to *settle a conflict* between two provisions, not to *narrow the applicability* of a provision.[47] And the notwithstanding clause of (b)(1) does settle a conflict, because subsection (a)(1) flatly states that a first assistant "shall" become the acting officer in the event of a vacancy. The disqualification clause creates a new exception that conflicts with "shall;" in other words, it tells us that the "shall" in (a)(1) does not actually always mean "shall."[48]

But this explanation still leaves one puzzle: both subsections (a)(2) and (a)(3) *also* describe situations in which a person (seemingly without out exception) can become the acting officer. This means that logically speaking, the disqualification clause conflicts with those two

---

[44] *Id.*

[45] *Id.* (quoting Knight v. Commissioner, 552 U.S. 181, 188 (2008)).

[46] *Id.* (quoting Webster's Third New International Dictionary 1545 (1986); Black's Law Dictionary 1091 (7th ed. 1999)).

[47] "In statutes, the word [notwithstanding] 'shows which provision prevails in the event of a clash.'" *Id.* (quoting Antonin Scalia & Brian Garner, Reading Law: The Interpretation of Legal Texts 126–27 (2012)).

[48] See *id.* ("[The preamble] confirms that the prohibition on acting service applies even when it conflicts with the default rule that the first assistant shall perform acting duties.").

subsections as well. Yet the notwithstanding clause singles out only (a)(1). How should we explain this singling out, and is it meaningful to the operation of the FVRA? That is the major question on which the majority and dissent split, and it is the question the Court turned to in the remainder of its textual analysis.

1. The Notwithstanding Clause and the *Expressio Unius* Doctrine

The core of the government's argument was that "singling out subsection (a)(1) carries a negative implication: that 'Congress did not intend Subsection (b)(1) to override the alternative mechanisms for acting service in Subsections (a)(2) and (a)(3).'"[49] This is an application of an interpretive doctrine holding that what is *not* said can sometimes be as meaningful as what *is* said. That doctrine is known by its Latin name: *Expressio unius est exclusio alterius*, "'expressing one item of [an] associated group or series excludes another left unmentioned.'"[50] We use this general rule to make inferences in daily life: "If a sign at the entrance to a zoo says 'come see the elephant, lion, hippo, and giraffe,' and a temporary sign is added saying 'the giraffe is sick,' you would reasonably assume that the others are in good health."[51]

But *expressio unius* is not an absolute rule, and context determines whether it should be decisive. As Karl Llewellyn observed more than 60 years ago, the natural "parry" to the *expressio unius* canon is that in some statutes "[t]he language may fairly comprehend many different cases where some only are expressly mentioned by way of example."[52] The difficult work is determining, from context, whether a particular case has been singled out only for the purpose of example, or instead for the purpose of excluding the unmentioned cases.

In the majority's view, there is one very good reason to believe (a)(1) was singled out only for emphasis: singling out one potential conflict for explicit clarification would be expected if that conflict "was

---

[49] *Id.* at 939–40 (quoting NLRB Reply Brief 3).

[50] *Id.* at 940 (quoting Chevron U.S.A., Inc. v. Echazabal, 536 U.S. 73, 80 (2002)) (alterations in original).

[51] *Id.*

[52] Karl Llewellyn, Remarks on the Theory of Appellate Decisions and the Rules or Canons about How Statutes Are to Be Construed, 3 Vand. L. Rev. 395, 405 (1950).

particularly difficult to resolve, or was quite likely to arise."[53] As an illustration, the Court gave an everyday example of such a situation:

> Suppose a radio station announces: "We play your favorite hits from the '60s, '70s, and '80s. Notwithstanding the fact that we play hits from the '60s, we do not play music by British bands." You would not tune in expecting to hear the 1970s British band "The Clash" any more than the 1960s "Beatles." The station, after all, has announced that "we do not play music by British bands." The "notwithstanding" clause just establishes that this applies even to music from the '60s, when British bands were prominently featured on the charts. No one, however, would think the station singled out the '60s to convey implicitly that its categorical statement "we do not play music by British bands" actually did not apply to the '70s and '80s.[54]

In the Court's view, *expressio unius* would be inappropriate when interpreting the FVRA for the same reason that it would be inappropriate when interpreting this radio advertisement. Just as the '60s differ from the other two decades in quantity of British bands, so does (a)(1) differ from the other two subsections in an important respect: "Adding 'notwithstanding subsection (a)(1)' makes sense because (a)(1) conflicts with (b)(1) in a unique manner. The former is mandatory and self-executing: The first assistant 'shall perform' acting duties."[55] By contrast, "subsections (a)(2) and (a)(3) just say that the President 'may direct'" persons to perform acting duties.[56] "The natural inference, then, is that Congress left these provisions out of the 'notwithstanding' clause because they are different from subsection (a)(1), not to exempt [them] from the broad prohibition" of the disqualification clause.[57]

This argument against the *expressio unius* canon likely determined the Court's decision, because the government relied almost exclusively on *expressio unius* for its textual case. Once the Court rejected *expressio unius*, it was almost certain to affirm the D.C. Circuit's

---

[53] S.W. General, 137 S. Ct. at 940.

[54] *Id.*

[55] *Id.*

[56] *Id.*

[57] *Id.* at 940–41.

reading and rule for S.W. General. But for good measure, the Court did not stop there, instead adding a few miscellaneous arguments to further bolster the case for a broad reading of the disqualification clause.

2. Structural and Extra-Textual Arguments

The Court's main structural arguments centered on a section of the FVRA that I have not yet mentioned: subsection (b)(2).

The disqualification clause is an exception to the president's general power to appoint acting officers. But in typical congressional fashion, the FVRA was also written with an *exception to the exception*, specifying a particular circumstance in which someone who would otherwise be disqualified by the clause may nonetheless serve. Subsection (b)(2) is that exception to the exception. It applies only if three criteria, listed separately, are all met. First, that "such person is serving as the first assistant to" the vacant office.[58] Second, that "the office of such first assistant is" itself a Senate-confirmed office.[59] And third, that "the Senate has approved the appointment of such person to such [first assistant] office."[60]

It is the first of these three criteria that provides further evidence that the disqualification clause applies more broadly than just the first assistants of (a)(1). For if it did not, "there would be no need to state the requirement . . . that 'such person is serving as the first assistant.'"[61] If everyone who might be disqualified necessarily served as a first assistant, this "makes the first requirement [for the exception to disqualification] superfluous."[62] This is a result that those on the Court "typically try to avoid."[63]

The other structural point made in the majority opinion is a rebuttal of an argument made in the dissent. But since the premise of that argument is more fully laid out in the dissent, I will reserve it for the upcoming discussion of the dissenting opinion.[64]

---

[58] 5 U.S.C. § 3345(b)(2)(A).

[59] 5 U.S.C. § 3345(b)(2)(B).

[60] 5 U.S.C. § 3345(b)(2)(C).

[61] S.W. General, 137 S. Ct. at 941.

[62] *Id.*

[63] *Id.* (citing Williams v. Taylor, 529 U.S. 362, 404 (2000)).

[64] See *infra* notes 74–78 and accompanying text.

The Court devoted the remainder of the opinion to a short discussion of extra-textual evidence.[65] But before it did so, it made clear that these factors would not be determinative: "The text is clear, so we need not consider this extra-textual evidence."[66] The Court declined to give weight to the legislative statements and drafting histories through which the two sides attempted to prove congressional intent, noting that "[w]hat Congress ultimately agrees on is the text that it enacts, not the preferences expressed by certain legislators."[67] And finally, the Court dismissed the OLC opinion on which the executive branch had long relied, since both OLC and a similar Government Accountability Office report "paid the matter little attention" and "made conclusory statements about subsection (b)(1), with no analysis."[68]

With the interpretive work done, applying the FVRA to Solomon's case took only a single paragraph. Since he had been ineligible to serve from the time he was nominated for the permanent position in 2011, the order he purported to issue against S.W. General in 2013 was invalid, and therefore vacated.[69]

B. The Dissenting Opinion

Justice Sotomayor's disagreement with the majority can be easily summarized: whereas the majority believed *expressio unius* was inapplicable to this case, the dissent believed it was determinative. The dissent summarized its own argument:

> A notwithstanding clause identifies a potential conflict between two or more provisions and specifies which provision will prevail. Under the familiar *expressio unius est exclusio alterius* interpretive canon, the choice to single out subsection (a)(1)—and only subsection (a)(1)—in this notwithstanding clause strongly suggests that the prohibition reaches, and conflicts with, subsection (a)(1), and only subsection (a)(1).[70]

---

[65] See S.W. General, 137 S. Ct. at 941–43.

[66] *Id.* at 942.

[67] *Id.* (citing Oncale v. Sundowner Offshore Services, Inc., 523 U.S. 75, 79 (1998)).

[68] *Id.* at 943.

[69] *Id.* at 943–44.

[70] *Id.* at 950 (Sotomayor, J., dissenting).

How did Justice Sotomayor reach the opposite conclusion as to whether *expressio unius* is applicable? At the heart of determining whether that canon should apply is the task of finding plausible explanations for *why* the legislature neglected to list the omitted examples. And while one explanation is present here—that the word "shall" appears only in (a)(1)—others are absent.

Most important, the number of other subsections with which (b)(1) might conflict are neither too *numerous* nor too *unpredictable* to expect drafters to list them. Indeed, the dissent emphasized how easy it would have been to name them all in a single sentence by doing so itself: "The omission of any reference to subsections (a)(2), (a)(3), and (c)(1), in spite of the parallel potential for conflict with those subsections, suggests that the omission was a 'deliberate choice, not inadvertence.'"[71] Because referencing the other subsections would have been just as easy as writing that sentence, the dissent concluded that "the clause's specific reference to subsection (a)(1) and only subsection (a)(1) strongly supports reading the attached prohibition to limit only subsection (a)(1)."[72]

Further, Justice Sotomayor found the presence of "shall" in (a)(1) and only (a)(1) to be an unconvincing explanation. As she pointed out, curtailing the default rule of (a)(1) and curtailing the presidential appointment powers of (a)(2) and (a)(3) both alter the operation of those respective subsections. The distinction between an automatic appointment and a conditional appointment "makes no difference when asking whether a conflict between subsections (b)(1) and (a)(1) would be harder to resolve without guidance than a conflict between subsection (b)(1) and the other subsections."[73]

The dissent then turned to a structural argument based on a clause that I have not yet discussed: subsection (c)(1). "Under subsection (c)(1), the President may designate a person whose term in an office has expired and who has been nominated to a subsequent term to serve as

---

[71] *Id.* (quoting Bruesewitz v. Wyeth LLC, 562 U.S. 223, 232–33 (2011)).

[72] *Id.* at 951 (citing Preseault v. ICC, 494 U.S. 1, 13–14 (1990)).

[73] *Id.* What the majority could have written in response is that the project of interpretation is not to find whether (b)(1) *actually* conflicted with (a)(1) more than it did with the other subsections, but instead whether it would have *seemed to the drafters* to have done so. In other words, a plausible account for a legislative drafting decision need not assume that legislative drafters are perfectly rational in the distinctions they draw.

the acting official."[74] In other words, (c)(1) deals with the particular situation where a vacancy arises not by death, illness, resignation, or firing, but instead by the expiration of an officer's term in office. In that situation, a *fourth* type of person becomes eligible for appointment as an acting officer, beyond the first assistant of (a)(1), the Senate-confirmed officer of (a)(2), and the high-ranking employee of (a)(3). This fourth type of person is the very person whose term has just expired, *provided that* the person has been nominated by the president for an additional term.

Here is the question: does the disqualification clause apply to acting officers appointed under (c)(1)? If it does, then the scope of (c)(1) is actually vastly smaller than it appears. By definition, those appointed acting officer under (c)(1) have also been nominated for the permanent position, meeting one of the criteria for disqualification under (b)(1). So unless an appointee somehow served as first assistant for 90 days and then subsequently started *and finished* a term as the officer lasting 275 days or less (thereby ensuring that the 90 days fell within the last 365), that appointee could not actually take advantage of (c)(1).[75] Therefore, if the disqualification clause applies to (c)(1), it would disqualify *nearly everyone* who could otherwise be appointed the acting officer under (c)(1).

This makes it much more likely that (b)(1) does *not* apply to (c)(1). But if it does not apply, that raises a problem for the majority's argument. If the "notwithstanding" clause is only a point of clarification and does not limit the broad meanings of "person" and "section," why should (b)(1) *not* apply to the acting officers appointed under (c)(1)? In other words, how can a principled line be drawn so that the clause applies to the (unmentioned) subsections (a)(2) and (a)(3) but not to the (similarly unmentioned) subsection (c)(1)?

For the majority, a separate canon of interpretation solves this problem, and determines that the disqualification clause should *not* apply to (c)(1): "'[I]t is a commonplace of statutory construction that the specific governs the general.'"[76] Even if the notwithstanding

---

[74] *Id.*

[75] See *id.* at 951–52 ("It is unlikely, even implausible, that a person who serves out a set term will have served as the first assistant to her own office during the year before her term expired.").

[76] *Id.* at 941 (majority op.) (quoting RadLAX Gateway Hotel, LLC v. Amalgamated Bank, 566 U.S. 639, 645 (2012)) (alterations in original).

clause were not in the statute at all—in which case both sides agreed that (b)(1) would apply to (a)(1), (a)(2), and (a)(3)—this canon would provide a reason to think (b)(1) does *not* apply to (c)(1). In the majority's view, "[t]he general prohibition on acting service by nominees yields to the more specific authorization allowing officers up for reappointment to remain at their posts."[77]

For the dissent, however, this line of reasoning undermined the breadth that the majority otherwise wished to give the words "person" and "section": "The Court's reasoning on this point undercuts its opening claim that the words 'person' and 'under this section' in subsection (b)(1) must refer to 'anyone who performs acting duties under the FVRA.'"[78] In the dissent's view, by relying heavily on the plain meaning of the words after the preamble, the majority inadvertently proved too much.

Finally, Justice Sotomayor concluded with a survey of legislative history and other extra-textual evidence, arguing that they too pointed toward a narrower reading of (b)(1).[79] But the majority's approach made the details of these disputes over competing floor statements inconsequential. *S.W. General* was unabashedly won and lost on purely textualist grounds. And this in itself, beyond the details of the case and the outcome of the textual analysis, should be a source of encouragement for many.

III. After *S.W. General*: Unanswered Questions

A. Retroactivity

After the *S.W. General* ruling, we can say two things with certainty. First, the NLRB order against S.W. General has been vacated. And second, no *future* acting officer appointed under (a)(2) or (a)(3) can serve in violation of (b)(1). But this leaves a crucial unanswered question: what is the status of past legal actions, made any time in the 19 years between passage of the FVRA and *S.W. General*, that we now know were illegitimate because taken by acting officers violating (b)(1)? What is the retroactive effect, if any, of the *S.W. General* decision?

The short answer, most likely, is very little. The D.C. Circuit briefly addressed this question in concluding its opinion:

[77] *Id.*

[78] *Id.* at 952 (Sotomayor, J., dissenting) (quoting *id.* at 938 (majority op.)).

[79] See *id.* at 953–54.

Finally, we emphasize the narrowness of our decision. . . . [W]e do not expect [this decision] to retroactively undermine a host of NLRB decisions. We address the FVRA objection in this case because the petitioner raised the issue in its exceptions to the ALJ decision as a defense to an ongoing enforcement proceeding. We doubt that an employer that failed to timely raise an FVRA objection—regardless whether enforcement proceedings are ongoing or concluded—will enjoy the same success.[80]

During oral argument at the Supreme Court, Justice Kagan asked the government's lawyer, Acting Solicitor General Ian Gershengorn, whether he agreed with the D.C. Circuit's suggestion. Gershengorn expressed more concern than the D.C. Circuit:

It does subject the past officials to substantial uncertainty. In truth, we don't know exactly the extent of it, because we don't know when we'll have defenses of waiver. . . . I'm in a tough position, because I don't want to argue too hard against defenses that we're going to want to assert later. But I do think what Judge [Karen] Henderson [author of the D.C. Circuit opinion] was talking about in particular was the NLRB situation . . . . We have not gone back and catalogued all of the potential ramifications, but we do think that with over 100 officials [appointed in the same manner as Solomon] over the course of 20 years, the effects of this are really quite significant.[81]

Whether Gershengorn's fears were well-founded is an open question, one that will only be resolved if and when the actions of these 100-odd officers are actually challenged in court. But it is telling that neither the majority nor dissenting opinion even mentioned this issue, a sign that the justices may have reached the unanimous conclusion that the D.C. Circuit was likely correct on the lack of retroactive repercussions.

B. *The Acting Service of "Ex Post Appointee" First Assistants*

Interpreting a complex statute is a bit like solving a crossword puzzle. As the answer to one question is filled in, that answer

---

[80] S.W. General, 796 F.3d at 82–83 (citing 29 U.S.C. § 160(e); Andrade v. Lauer, 729 F.2d 1475, 1499 (D.C. Cir. 1984)).

[81] Transcript of Oral Arg. at 17–19, N.L.R.B. v. S.W. General, Inc., 137 S. Ct. 929 (2017).

constrains the available solutions to other questions. And just as an early mistake in a crossword puzzle can lead to a cascade of errors, so can one false interpretation lead to other mistakes of interpretation in the same statute. The Supreme Court's decision reveals that this is exactly what happened in an OLC opinion nearly 20 years ago.

Consider this scenario: A Senate-confirmed officer unexpectedly leaves office while her first assistant position is vacant. The president would like to appoint Mr. Smith to serve as the acting officer, beginning immediately. Mr. Smith has never before served in government, however, and so is ineligible for appointment as the acting officer under either subsection (a)(2) or (a)(3). But the president takes advantage of the simultaneous vacancy in the first-assistant position and appoints Smith as the first assistant (which requires neither prior government service nor Senate confirmation), and then Smith is immediately elevated, becoming the acting officer under subsection (a)(1).

Intuitively, such a maneuver seems to be against the spirit of the FVRA. Most first-assistant positions may be filled by *anyone*, with no requirement of prior governmental service of any kind. But if anyone may become an acting officer by appointment as first assistant *after* a vacancy occurs (when the president knows that the appointee will automatically thus become the acting officer), the FVRA's limitations on who is eligible to be appointed under subsections (a)(2) and (a)(3) become almost meaningless. That is, whenever a first assistant position is vacant, the de facto prerequisites for appointment to serve as the acting officer become only whatever prerequisites are placed upon appointment to that office's *first assistant* position. Since Congress would not likely have created the detailed restrictions on service under subsections (a)(2) and (a)(3) if it intended this workaround, the practice of elevating *ex post* first assistants is in severe tension with the purpose of the law.

But this purposive argument does not settle the textual question. The text of subsection (a)(1) itself reads: "If an officer . . . dies, resigns, or is otherwise unable to perform the functions and duties of the office– the first assistant to the office of such officer shall perform the functions and duties of the office temporarily in an acting capacity."[82] The answer to whether a first assistant appointed *after* a vacancy arises can be elevated to acting officer depends on

---

[82] 5 U.S.C. § 3345(a)(1).

whether the phrase "first assistant to the office of such officer" includes first assistants appointed *after* a vacancy arises. The courts have never settled that question, but OLC has staked an opinion on it. *S.W. General* has now seriously called that OLC opinion into doubt.

In its initial 1998 guidance after the passage of the FVRA, OLC advised that someone appointed first assistant after a vacancy occurred could *not* become the acting officer:

> Question 13. If someone is designated to be first assistant after the vacancy occurs, does that person still become the acting officer by virtue of being the first assistant?

> Answer. While the Vacancies Reform Act does not expressly address this question, we believe that the better understanding is that you must be the first assistant when the vacancy occurs in order to be the acting officer by virtue of being the first assistant.[83]

In a 2001 opinion, however, OLC changed its mind:

> Having now specifically considered the question in light of both the Act's text and structure, we conclude that our initial understanding was erroneous. . . . Given the Act's text and structure, we now believe that the better understanding is that an individual need not be the first assistant when the vacancy occurs in order to be the acting officer by virtue of being the first assistant.[84]

OLC gave two arguments in support of its reversal. But of these two arguments, one depended entirely on the premise that the Supreme Court rejected in *S.W. General*.

OLC's argument centered around a conflict that its initial interpretation would have created with the disqualification clause at issue in *S.W. General*. Recall that a person is disqualified from serving as acting officer if he is nominated for the permanent position *and* "during the 365-day period preceding the date of the [vacancy], such person did not serve in the position of first assistant to the office of such

---

[83] 23 Op. O.L.C. at 63–64.
[84] 25 Op. O.L.C. 177, 179, 181 (2001).

officer."[85] In explaining the problem caused by this second requirement, OLC implicitly assumed that the disqualification clause applies only to acting officers appointed under (a)(1). That is why OLC
argued that this second requirement

> [would be] meaningless if an individual who was not the
> first assistant when the vacancy occurred is already flatly
> prohibited from serving in an acting capacity pursuant
> to subsection (a)(1), as we previously concluded. Indeed,
> [the requirement] was necessary only if an individual who
> becomes first assistant after a vacancy occurs could otherwise
> serve in an acting capacity pursuant to subsection (a)(1). If
> [this requirement] is to be given operative effect, which it
> must, our initial understanding of subsection (a)(1) must give
> way.[86]

If we assume that the disqualification clause applies only to subsection (a)(1), then OLC's argument makes sense. If the disqualification clause is limited to the universe of those who might become acting officers under (a)(1), then that universe seemingly must include
people who never served for a moment as first assistants *before* the
vacancy. Otherwise, the number of people actually disqualified by
this portion of the disqualification clause would be a null set; every
(a)(1) acting officer appointed for the permanent position would have
previously served as first assistant, and therefore would be immune
from this type of disqualification.[87]

But after *S.W. General*, we now know that the disqualification
clause applies to those who become acting officers under subsections (a)(2) and (a)(3) as well. As a result, this textual problem has
disappeared. The number of those who become acting officers under
(a)(1) having served no time as first assistant prior to the vacancy
could indeed be zero. That is because the portion of the disqualification clause at issue is targeted exclusively at those acting officers

---

[85] 5 U.S.C. § 3345(b)(1)(A)(i).

[86] 25 Op. O.L.C. at 180.

[87] This does not mean the *entire* disqualification clause would be a dead letter. The
clause also disqualifies those appointed to the permanent position who "served in the
position of first assistant to the office of such officer for less than 90 days" during the
preceding year. 5 U.S.C. § 3345(b)(1)(A)(ii). The problem that OLC identified is that
this would be left as the *only* portion of the disqualification clause to ever have opera-
tive effect.

who obtained that position through (a)(2) or (a)(3), and who therefore likely had not served as the first assistant prior to the vacancy.[88]

One of the two justifications for OLC's position has thus been entirely eliminated by the *S.W. General* decision. But OLC did give one additional textual argument, which is now likely to be at the center of any future litigation on this question.

In replacing the Vacancies Act with the FVRA, Congress amended the wording used in what is now subsection (a)(1). Instead of promoting the "first assistant to the officer" who died or resigned, the FVRA instead promotes "the first assistant to the *office*" of the officer who died or resigned.[89] OLC reasoned that the phrase that had formerly been used, the "first assistant to the officer who resigned," would naturally describe only one person, the first assistant at the time of the original vacancy. By *not* using that phrase, and instead choosing the broader phrase "first assistant *to the office* of the officer who resigned," the drafters of the FVRA would seem to have intended the language to have a broader scope. Building on this premise, OLC assumed that the only way to give the clause a broader scope was to include people holding the office of first assistant not just when the original Senate-confirmed officer resigned, but also at any time thereafter.[90]

But this argument is flawed as well, because a close reading of legislative history reveals a different reason for this broader language. The language was not changed to allow a first assistant to fill a vacancy immediately upon being appointed. Instead, it was most likely changed to deal with a different specific contingency.

Suppose that Mr. Jones is serving as an acting officer pursuant to the FVRA and Mr. Smith is later appointed as his first assistant. Sometime later, Acting Officer Jones dies or resigns as acting officer. In this situation, where Smith became first assistant *after* Jones began serving as acting officer, may Smith succeed to acting officer under (a)(1)? In other words, may one acting officer be succeeded by *another* acting officer under (a)(1)? The floor statements of Senator

---

[88] Splitting the disqualification clause into two subsections thus makes perfect sense: the portion disqualifying those who had never served as first assistants is targeted at (a)(2) and (a)(3) appointees, while the portion disqualifying those who had served as first assistants for less than 90 days is targeted at (a)(1) appointees.

[89] 5 U.S.C. § 3345(a)(1) (emphasis added).

[90] See 25 Op. O.L.C. at 179–80.

Fred Thompson (a sponsor of the FVRA) indicate that the broader language was meant to resolve *this* question (and only this question) in the affirmative. Describing the final version of the FVRA on the Senate floor, Senator Thompson said:

> The term "first assistant to the office" is incorporated into [the FVRA] rather than "first assistant to the officer." This change is made to "depersonalize" the first assistant. Questions have arisen concerning who might be the vacant officer's first assistant if the acting officer dies or if the acting officer resigns while a permanent nomination is pending. The term "first assistant to the officer" has been part of the Vacancies Act since 1868, however, and the change in wording is not intended to alter case law on the meaning of the term "first assistant."[91]

This statement suggests that when an *acting* officer leaves that role through death or resignation, she should be succeeded by the first assistant to the office *at that moment*, not by the person who was the first assistant at the time of the original vacancy. In other words, the "depersonalization" was meant to ensure that the first assistant to not only the original Senate-confirmed officer, but also to subsequent *acting* officers, would be eligible to become acting officer under subsection (a)(1).[92] But it does nothing to suggest that a first assistant appointed when an office is filled with *neither* a permanent officer *nor* an acting officer may immediately be elevated to acting officer.

After *S.W. General*, OLC's 2001 guidance rests on very shaky footing. Nonetheless, because of that guidance, elevating *ex post* first assistants to acting officer has been the practice of the executive branch

---

[91] 144 Cong. Rec. S12,822 (daily ed. Oct. 21, 1998).

[92] This understanding accords with Senator Thompson's similar statement in the Senate report that "[a]n acting officer may die or resign. *In that event*, the first assistant, if there *is* one, or a new presidential designee of a Senate-confirmed officer may become the acting officer." Comm. on Gov'tal Affairs, 105th Cong., S. Rep. No. 105-250, at 14 (1998) (emphasis added).

for three administrations.[93] After *S.W. General*, a challenge to this practice is likely not far off.[94]

C. *Justice Thomas's Concurrence: Is the FVRA Constitutional?*

S.W. General was a statutory interpretation case, and neither side raised a constitutional argument. But that did not stop Justice Thomas, in a concurrence, from flagging a serious constitutional concern with the FRVA itself, one that may well arise in a future case.

Thomas's concurrence began with a persuasive originalist argument that the Constitution's Appointments Clause applies to acting officers just as much as permanent ones: "Around the time of the framing, the verb 'appoint' meant '[t]o establish anything by decree,' or '[t]o allot, assign, or designate.' When the President 'direct[s]' a person to serve as an acting officer, he is 'assign[ing]' or 'designat[ing]' that person to serve as an officer."[95] For this reason, Thomas concluded that "[w]hen the President 'direct[s]' someone to serve as an officer pursuant to the FVRA, he is 'appoint[ing]' that person as an 'officer of the United States' within the meaning of the Appointments Clause."[96]

---

[93] To give just one example, this maneuver was recently used to install someone with no prior government experience as the acting assistant attorney general (AAG) for the Office of Civil Rights in the Department of Justice. When the prior acting AAG Molly Moran resigned, ACLU lawyer Vanita Gupta appears to have been appointed principal deputy AAG and acting AAG *simultaneously* on October 20, 2014, *after* Moran's resignation. I have not found any evidence that Moran remained acting AAG until moments after Gupta had officially become principal deputy AAG. See Department of Justice Press Release, Attorney General Holder Announces Vanita Gupta to Serve as Acting Assistant Attorney General for the Civil Rights Division (Oct. 15, 2014), https://www.justice.gov/opa/pr/attorney-general-holder-announces-vanita-gupta-serve-acting-assistant-attorney-general-civil ("Gupta begins at the department on Monday, Oct. 20.").

[94] The D.C. Circuit opinion in *S.W. General* (but not the Supreme Court's) briefly waded into this very question. Citing OLC's first (and later renounced) position, the D.C. Circuit noted that "[a]lthough we do not decide its meaning today, subsection (a)(1) may refer to the person who is serving as first assistant *when the vacancy occurs.*" S.W. General, 796 F.3d at 76 (citing 23 Op. O.L.C. at 64) (emphasis in original).

[95] S.W. General, 137 S. Ct. at 946 (Thomas, J., concurring) (citations omitted).

[96] *Id.* (alterations in original). There is, however, an original-practice argument that could be used to rebut Thomas's original-meaning argument. The Second Congress, which comprised many of the same people who had ratified the Constitution itself, passed an act granting the president the unilateral power to appoint acting officers, including for principal positions. See *supra* note 12 and accompanying text. This sug-

Here is the problem: The Appointments Clause only allows Congress to vest an appointment in "the president alone" if the appointee is an "inferior officer."[97] Principal officers must be confirmed by the Senate, and many of the positions that can be filled under the FVRA—most obviously cabinet secretaries—are indisputably principal officers.[98] How, then, could the FVRA's method of unilateral appointment to acting service in these principal positions comply with the Appointments Clause?

One possible solution is that the time limits the FVRA places on acting service might "downgrade" principal officers to inferior officers. A Senate-confirmed cabinet secretary is indisputably a principal officer. But an acting secretary, who knows that by law she may only serve while someone else is nominated to replace her (plus a seven-month grace period), is in a more constrained situation, perhaps one so constrained as to make her "inferior."[99]

Justice Thomas, however, quickly rejected this possibility. The fact that acting officers are appointed temporarily "does not change the analysis," Thomas argued, because "the structural protections of the Appointments Clause [cannot] be avoided based on such trivial distinctions."[100] As Thomas pointed out, the tolling of the FVRA's time limit during the pendency of a permanent nomination means that there is no hard upper limit to how long acting officers can theoretically serve. Lafe Solomon himself, because of the lengthy period of time his own nomination was stalled in the Senate, "served

---

gests that many of those who originally enacted the Appointments Clause did not consider it a bar to the unilateral appointment of acting principal officers. The most likely explanation for this is that they did not believe the Appointments Clause applied to acting appointments at all.

[97] U.S. Const. art. II, § 2, cl. 2.

[98] Thomas devoted the bulk of his concurrence to an analysis of whether Solomon's position—general counsel of the NLRB—is itself a principal officer position. See S.W. General, 137 S. Ct. at 946–48 (Thomas, J., concurring). Thomas concluded that the position is likely a principal one. *Id.* at 948. This particular question, though, is not relevant to the broader question of the FVRA's constitutionality.

[99] In the Cato amicus brief co-authored by Ilya Shapiro, Trevor Burrus, and myself, we suggested this potential solution without examining the question in depth. See Brief of Cato Institute as Amicus Curiae Supporting Respondent at 5 n.2, N.L.R.B. v. S.W. General, Inc., 137 S. Ct. 929 (2017).

[100] S.W. General, 137 S. Ct. at 946 n.1 (Thomas, J., concurring).

for more than three years in an office limited by statute to a 4-year term."[101]

Further, even a hard upper limit on acting service would not necessarily change the analysis. Although the Supreme Court held in 1988 that "limited tenure" is one factor indicating that an officer is inferior,[102] the Court held nine years later that an inferior officer is one "whose work is directed and supervised at some level by others who were appointed by Presidential nomination with the advice and consent of the Senate."[103] Whether time limits can make a position inferior depends on whether the later categorical test has fully replaced the earlier multifactor test, a question that the Supreme Court has never resolved.[104]

There is an additional argument by which the FVRA might be partially saved, however. When an acting officer is appointed under (a)(2), that acting officer has, by definition, already been confirmed by the Senate to some other executive-branch position. Subsection (a)(2) thus allows the president to unilaterally grant a new title (and with it, new powers and duties) to someone who has already been confirmed by the Senate to wield other powers. And in 1994, the Supreme Court held that another statute with a similar operation did not violate the Appointments Clause.

In *Weiss v. United States*, the Court examined a statute that allowed the Judge Advocate General of each branch of the armed forces to unilaterally appoint commissioned officers of the United States to be military trial judges in their respective branches.[105] Such officers would then hold the position of military judge "for a period of time

---

[101] *Id.*

[102] See Morrison v. Olson, 487 U.S. 654, 672 (1988).

[103] Edmond v. United States, 520 U.S. 651, 660 (1997).

[104] Justice Thomas, for his part, does believe that the later case overruled the earlier, and that the later is the correct test: "Although we did not explicitly overrule *Morrison* in *Edmond*, it is difficult to see how *Morrison*'s nebulous approach survived our opinion in *Edmond*. *Edmond* is also consistent with the Constitution's original meaning and therefore should guide our view of the principal-inferior distinction." S.W. General, 137 S. Ct. at 947 n.2 (Thomas, J., concurring). For a fuller discussion of this question, see Nick Bravin, Note, Is *Morrison v. Olson* Still Good Law? The Court's New Appointments Clause Jurisprudence, 98 Colum. L. Rev. 1103 (1998).

[105] 510 U.S. 163 (1994). The only limitation on which officers the Judges Advocate General could choose to appoint was that they must have been members of a state or federal bar.

[the Judge Advocate General] deems necessary or appropriate, and then they may be reassigned to perform other duties."[106]

As a preliminary matter, the Court agreed "that a military judge is an 'officer of the United States'" for purposes of the Appointments Clause.[107] But the position of a commissioned officer, from which all military judges were selected, was one requiring presidential nomination and Senate confirmation, meaning every military judge had already gone through this process once. The question, then, was whether the Appointments Clause "require[d] a second appointment before military officers may discharge the duties of such a judge."[108] The Court held that it did not.

The Court's reasoning on this point was obscure. In an 1893 case, the Court had held that when a statute grants a *particular* Senate-confirmed officer new duties, those duties must be "germane" to the office already held if they are to be performed without a second Senate confirmation.[109] In *Weiss*, the Court suggested that because Congress was not selecting particular military trial judges via statute but instead leaving their selection up to someone else, even this germaneness test may not be necessary to pass constitutional scrutiny.[110] Yet the Court then assumed, *arguendo*, that the germaneness test did apply (likely because there was unspoken disagreement among the justices in the majority as to whether it should apply) and found that the duties of a military trial judge passed this test anyway.[111]

Like the statute in *Weiss*, the FVRA's subsection (a)(2) allows someone (in this case the president) to temporarily grant the duties of a new office to a person who has already received Senate confirmation to another office. Even if the appointment of acting principal officers under (a)(1) and (a)(3) is constitutionally suspect, their appointment under (a)(2) may well survive a future challenge (especially if the duties of the acting office are "germane" to the office previously held

---

[106] *Id.* at 176.

[107] *Id.* at 173.

[108] *Id.* at 176.

[109] Shoemaker v. United States, 147 U.S. 282, 300–01 (1893).

[110] Weiss, 510 U.S. at 174.

[111] *Id.* at 174–76.

by the appointee). This would preserve at least one method of temporarily filling the highest ranks of government.[112]

These questions will form the fault lines of future litigation if, as Justice Thomas predicted, "[c]ourts inevitably will be called upon to determine whether the Constitution permits the appointment of principal officers pursuant to the FVRA without Senate confirmation."[113]

Conclusion

The dangers of the *expressio unius* canon are obvious: if applied incorrectly, a congressional attempt to strengthen the force of a provision through emphasis can result in precisely the *opposite* effect, weakening the provision by limiting it to only the example singled out.[114] In everyday language, we frequently single out particular examples for clarity and emphasis. But the *expressio unius* canon presents legislative drafters who wish to add such clarity with a dilemma: emphasizing one provision risks eliminating others. For this reason, the canon should only be applied if context shows that there is no real risk of undermining the intended breadth of a provision, a risk that was obviously present in *S.W. General*.

It's possible that in 50 years *S.W. General* will be remembered more as a useful citation in opposition to the *expressio unius* canon than it will for its effect on the presidential appointment power—though both aspects of the case are certainly important. As the title

---

[112] Thomas himself does not consider this possibility, discussing neither *Weiss* nor *Shoemaker* in his concurrence. This may be because Thomas focused on whether the Constitution barred Solomon's appointment in particular, and Solomon himself was appointed under (a)(3), not (a)(2).

[113] S.W. General, 137 S. Ct. at 949 (Thomas, J., concurring).

[114] Perhaps the most infamous occurrence of this was in *United Steelworkers of America, AFL-CIO-CLC v. Weber*, 443 U.S. 193 (1979). There, the Court held that Title VII of the 1964 Civil Rights Act did not ban employers from engaging in affirmative-action programs, even though the act flatly made it illegal for any employer "to deprive any individual of employment opportunities . . . because of such individual's race." See *id.* at 199 n.2. The *Weber* Court latched onto a clarifying provision "that nothing contained in Title VII 'shall be interpreted to *require* any employer . . . to grant preferential treatment . . . to any group because of the race'" of its members. *Id.* at 205–06 (emphasis added by the Court). The Court then stringently applied *expressio unius* to this provision, reasoning that "[t]he section does *not* state that 'nothing in Title VII shall be interpreted to *permit*' voluntary affirmative efforts to correct racial imbalances. The natural inference is that Congress chose not to forbid all voluntary race-conscious affirmative action." *Id.* at 206 (emphasis in original).

of this article suggests, the Supreme Court has indisputably reined in the power of the president to bypass the Senate in appointing acting officers. But to the extent that *S.W. General* may also rein in the *expressio unius* canon itself, that will be a less-anticipated but just as welcome result.

Salman v. U.S.: Another Insider Trading Case, Another Round of Confusion

Thaya Brook Knight[*]

Last term, the Supreme Court took up its first insider-trading case in 20 years, *Salman v. United States*.[1] Insider trading is an area of law crying out for clarification and simplification, so the Court's decision to hear the case was encouraging. Unfortunately, the opinion the Court issued in *Salman* answered only a very narrow question and answered it in the way most likely to lead to confusion and muddled opinions in the lower courts. Given that a conviction for insider trading can carry a penalty of a decade in prison, this decision is disappointing.

Salman involves three members of the same family: brothers Maher and Michael Kara, and their brother-in-law Bassam Salman. Maher worked for Citigroup's healthcare division. He passed nonpublic information he obtained through his employment to his brother, Michael, who traded on it and shared it with Salman, who also traded on it. It is not clear when Maher became aware that Michael was trading on the information. According to the record, he first shared information with Michael because Michael has a degree in chemistry and he was hoping that Michael could provide some insight into the companies he was handling. He later shared information with Michael as the brothers were considering treatment options for their dying father in the hope that some of the treatments he had encountered in his work might help their father's condition. Finally, and in the eyes of the law most damnably, Maher passed information along to Michael with the intention that Michael would trade

---

[*]Associate director of financial regulation studies, Cato Institute.
[1] 137 S. Ct. 420 (2016).

on it. He testified that he wanted to "help" his brother and "fulfill whatever needs he had."[2]

As I describe below, there are three theories of insider-trading law: classical, tipper/tippee, and misappropriation. *Salman* implicated the tipper/tippee theory, but the root of the problem is that none of these theories is clear on the harm that insider-trading law is trying to prevent. Without a unifying theory of harm, it is difficult to state a unifying theory of liability.

I. Theories of Insider-Trading Law

No federal statute prohibits insider trading. Instead, over the years courts have developed various theories of how what is known as "insider trading" operates as a kind of fraud. Fraud in connection with securities transactions *is* proscribed by statute. Under the Securities Exchange Act of 1934, it is unlawful to "use or employ, in connection with the purchase or sale of any security . . . any manipulative or deceptive device or contrivance in contravention of such rules and regulations as the [Securities and Exchange] Commission may prescribe as necessary or appropriate in the public interest or for the protection of investors."[3] Pursuant to this provision, the Securities and Exchange Commission (SEC) issued a rule that prohibits the use of "any device, scheme, or artifice to defraud . . . [or] to engage in any act, practice, or course of business which operates or would operate as a fraud or deceit upon any person, in connection with the purchase or sale of any security."[4]

The fact that any theory of insider trading must ultimately be tied back to some notion of "fraud" is one of the factors that has so tied the courts in knots over the years.[5] Underpinning any insider-

---

[2] *Id.* at 424.

[3] Securities Exchange Act, 15 U.S.C. § 10(b).

[4] 17 C.F.R. § 240.10b-5.

[5] The proscription on the use of deceit has been interpreted to extend beyond the scope of common law fraud, which requires that the plaintiff or government show that the defendant made a misleading statement, knew it was misleading, and intended for the victim to rely on the statement; then the victim did rely on it and as a result suffered a harm. While Rule 10b-5 certainly captures actions that would fall within this definition of fraud, the SEC has stated that it is a "broad remedial provision[] aimed at reaching misleading or deceptive activities, whether or not they are precisely and technically sufficient to sustain a common law action for fraud and deceit." In the Matter of Cady, Roberts & Co., 40 S.E.C. 907, 910 (1961).

trading case must be some argument that the conduct in question operated as a fraud on some identified person or persons. Naming the victim and working backward to construct the theory that demonstrates how the victim was defrauded has been a difficult process.

One of the chief problems is that an action for fraud typically seeks to redress harm to a participant in a particular transaction. To the extent that a securities transaction involves direct fraud, the victim and the harm are easy to identify. If a seller intentionally provides untrue and material information about a security to a potential buyer with the intent that the buyer rely on that information and therefore overpay, the transaction clearly involves fraud. In the case of insider trading, however, the insider typically has not communicated any information to the other party. Fraud is much trickier when the problem is a lack of communication. The question is therefore: who has an obligation to disclose such that a failure would constitute fraud? While each of the theories of insider trading offers an answer, none provides one that is fully satisfactory.

A. Classical Theory of Insider Trading

Under the classical theory of insider trading, an insider—someone who owes a duty to the company as an employee or director—obtains nonpublic information through her relationship to the company. Without disclosing the information to the public, she trades on this information and earns a profit.

One of the earliest cases to establish the crime of insider trading was *In the Matter of Cady, Roberts & Co.*, decided by the SEC.[6] In this case, a broker received information from his business partner, who sat on the board of a company about to announce its quarterly dividends. The broker traded on the dividend information before it was publicly announced. The SEC found the trade to be illegal because "[an] affirmative duty to disclose material information . . . has been traditionally imposed on corporate 'insiders,' particularly officers, directors, or controlling stockholders."[7] The SEC went on to note that it and "the courts have consistently held that insiders must disclose material facts which are known to them by virtue of their position

[6] 40 S.E.C. 907 (1961).
[7] *Id.* at 911.

but which are not known to persons with whom they deal and which, if known, would affect their investment judgment."[8]

The path from *Cady* could have been a broad one, and a simple one to administer. The rule could have been simply that it is illegal to trade on nonpublic information received from an insider. "Disclose" or "abstain" could have been the rule for everyone.

The notion that those involved in securities transactions must provide accurate information when it is "material" appears in other areas of securities law. In *TSC Industries v. Northway, Inc.*, and later in *Basic v. Levinson*, the Supreme Court held that a fact is material if there is a "substantial likelihood that the disclosure of the omitted fact would have been viewed by the reasonable investor as having significantly altered the 'total mix' of information made available."[9] Using this principle as a basis for asserting a unifying theme underlying securities law, the courts could have determined that withholding nonpublic material information is not permitted when engaging in a securities transaction or related activity, whether the activity is trading in the secondary market, issuing securities, or sending out proxy materials.

In *Chiarella v. United States*, the Court squarely considered this question: does a trade based on material nonpublic information qualify as insider trading if the information was not directly obtained by or through an insider?[10] In this case, the Court answered "no." Vincent Chiarella worked for a financial printer. In the course of his work, he came across documents related to a merger that had not yet been announced. Although the documents did not have the names of the companies on them, he was able to divine them through other information in the documents. He traded on this information and was charged with insider trading. In holding that Chiarella's actions did *not* constitute insider trading, the Court found that "[w]hen an allegation of fraud is based upon nondisclosure, there can be no fraud absent a duty to speak" and held that "a duty to disclose under § 10(b) does not arise from the mere possession of nonpublic market

[8] *Id.*

[9] TSC Industries v. Northway Inc., 426 U.S. 438, 449 (1976) (determining whether omitted information was "material" in the context of proxy disclosures); Basic v. Levinson, 485 U.S. 224, 231–32 (1988) (determining whether information was "material" such that its omission would trigger liability under Section 10(b)).

[10] Chiarella v. United States, 445 U.S. 222 (1980).

information."[11] Because Chiarella had no explicit duty to either of the companies involved in the merger, the Court found, his use of the information, without disclosure to the market, did not constitute insider trading. "[O]ne who fails to disclose material information prior to the consummation of a transaction commits fraud only when he is under a duty to do so."[12]

Whether a broader prohibition may have been more prudent either because it would be the better policy or because it would be easier to administer—and therefore more fair to market participants who must know when they are running afoul of the law—the Court clearly felt constrained by the language of Section 10(b). "Section 10(b) is aptly described as a catchall provision," the Court noted, "but what it catches must be fraud."[13]

In light of *Chiarella*, the rule guiding the classical theory of insider trading is that there is no universal duty to disclose nonpublic information when engaging in a securities transaction. Instead, liability exists only when the individual also breached some identified duty in failing to make a disclosure. The nature and scope of this duty was not definitively settled by the Court. Indeed, the Court noted that the government had put forward a theory under which Chiarella would be liable due to his duty as an employee of the financial printer. This theory had not been presented at trial, however, and because the Court could not "affirm a criminal conviction on the basis of a theory not presented to the jury," the Court could not "speculate upon whether such a duty exists, whether it has been breached, or whether such a breach constitutes a violation of § 10(b)."[14]

B. Tipper/Tippee Theory of Insider Trading

If there is to be a prohibition on insider trading, the prohibition must extend beyond the insider herself to be truly effective. Otherwise, the rule could be easily evaded. The insider could simply pass the information to a friend and say "trade on this and give me the profits." Or the insider could sell the information to willing traders. This theory of liability, under which the insider passes information

[11] *Id.* at 235.
[12] *Id.* at 228.
[13] *Id.* at 234–35.
[14] *Id.* at 236–37.

to a third party who then trades on it, is "tipper/tippee" liability. The insider is known in insider trading law as the "tipper" and the person to whom he passes the information is the "tippee."

Salman is a tipper/tippee case: Salman traded on tips received through a chain beginning with his brother-in-law Maher Kara, the insider at Citigroup. This theory adds a new wrinkle to the basic question underpinning all insider-trading cases. Instead of simply determining, as *Chiarella* requires, whether the person who originally obtained the information had an existing duty, a court must also determine whether and how the person who ultimately traded on the information became subject to such a duty. There are clear cases, of course. My first example is one. If the tipper asks the tippee to trade and give him (the tipper) the profits, the tipper is clearly attempting to obtain the same result as if he himself had made the trade. The rule rejected by *Chiarella*—that *any* trader must disclose or abstain—would have at least been easier to administer even if it still suffered from other flaws.

In 1983, the Court attempted to clarify this area of law in *Dirks v. SEC*.[15] This case did not involve a typical insider-trading transaction, however, because the insider disclosed the information to right a wrong, not to make money for himself or his friends. In *Dirks*, a corporate insider disclosed information to Raymond Dirks, a broker, about widespread fraud within the insider's company. His stated purpose in making the disclosure was for Dirks to investigate and ultimately uncover the ongoing fraud. Dirks did just that. He even went to the *Wall Street Journal* with the information and urged one of the editors to run a story. The editor declined, fearing a libel suit. Dirks also disclosed the information to many of his clients, who traded on the information. The fraud was eventually uncovered, charges were brought against the company's employees, and the *Wall Street Journal* ran a front-page story on it.[16] Dirks was censured by the SEC for insider trading because he had disclosed the information to his clients who then traded on it.

The Supreme Court ruled in Dirks's favor on appeal, substantially narrowing the holding of *Chiarella*. Not every breach of fiduciary

---

[15] 463 U.S. 646 (1983).

[16] See William Blundell, A Scandal Unfolds: Some Assets Missing, Insurance Called Bogus at Equity Funding Life, Wall St. J., Apr. 2, 1973, at 1.

duty is sufficient to support a charge of insider trading. "There must also be manipulation or deception . . . . Thus, an insider will be liable under Rule 10b-5 for inside trading only where he fails to disclose material nonpublic information before trading on it and thus makes secret profits."[17] It clearly troubled the Court that someone who was trying to uncover wrongdoing could, in the process, be deemed guilty of wrongdoing himself. The Court therefore rejected the government's proposed rule, that anyone who "knowingly receives nonpublic material information from an insider has a fiduciary duty to disclose before trading."[18] The correct reading of *Chiarella*, according to the Court, is that "only some persons, under some circumstances, will be barred from trading while in possession of material nonpublic information."[19]

The result, however, was to introduce a fair amount of muddiness into the legal waters. Instead of the potential bright-line rule that *Cady* could have presented—disclose or abstain—or even a broader rule set forth in *Chiarella*—if the information was obtained pursuant to a fiduciary duty, disclose or abstain—the post-*Dirks* rule is substantially more complex. Under *Dirks*, "the test is whether the insider personally will benefit, directly or indirectly, from his disclosure. Absent some personal gain, there has been no breach of duty to stockholders. And absent a breach by the insider, there is no derivative breach."[20] In what is arguably nonbinding *dictum*, the Court went on to say that, although it may be difficult to divine when the insider has indeed benefited from the disclosure:

> [t]here are objective facts and circumstances that often justify such an inference. For example, there may be a relationship between the insider and the recipient that suggests a *quid pro quo* from the latter, or an intention to benefit the particular recipient. The elements of fiduciary duty and exploitation of nonpublic information also exist when an insider makes a gift of confidential information to a trading relative or friend. The tip and trade resemble trading by the insider himself followed by a gift of the profits to the recipient.[21]

[17] Dirks, 463 U.S. at 654 (internal quotations and citations omitted).
[18] *Id.* at 656.
[19] *Id.* at 657.
[20] *Id.* at 662.
[21] *Id.* at 664.

This introduced the question at the heart of *Salman*. It is clear that any theory of tipper/tippee liability must extend beyond the exchange of cash. There is no material difference between the insider saying "trade on this and give me the profits" and saying "trade on this and give me a Porsche." But what of intangible benefits? For example, what if the insider says "trade on this and in exchange admit my kid to your exclusive school"? Or what if the insider receives nothing in return? What if, as the *Dirks* dictum states, the insider "makes a gift of confidential information"? Must tipper/tippee liability always involve some sort of quid pro quo?

An earlier case out of the U.S. Court of Appeals for the Second Circuit implied that the answer was "yes." *United States v. Newman* was part of a massive insider-trading investigation focused on a number of hedge funds.[22] The case itself centered on a chain of tippers and tippees; the inside information that formed the basis of the trades had passed through three to four people before it reached Todd Newman and his acquaintance at another firm, Anthony Chiasson. There was no evidence that Newman or Chiasson had provided any benefit to the tippers in a quid pro quo exchange for the information. It was also not clear, or at least not sufficiently proven, that Newman and Chiasson knew that the information they received had been obtained from someone who had breached a fiduciary duty. Newman and Chiasson were found guilty at trial, however, pursuant to a jury instruction that required a guilty verdict if the jury found the defendants "knew that the material, nonpublic information [on which they had traded] had been disclosed by the insider in breach of a duty of trust and confidence." On appeal, the Second Circuit surprised much of the legal and financial world by finding the lower court had erred. "In light of *Dirks*," the court noted, "we find no support for the Government's contention that knowledge of a breach of the duty of confidentiality without knowledge of the personal benefit is sufficient to impose criminal liability."[23] The rule as established by *Newman*, at least for the Second Circuit, seemed to be

---

[22] 773 F.3d 438 (2d Cir. 2014).
[23] *Id.* at 448.

that a conviction for insider trading requires the government to establish that the tipper received something of value from the tippee.[24]

Although the government asked the Supreme Court to review the *Newman* ruling, its petition was denied. Salman then attempted to use *Newman* to support his defense in the U.S. Court of Appeals for the Ninth Circuit. That court, however, both asserted its prerogative to establish its own precedent—independent from its sister circuit—and distinguished *Newman*. While *Newman* addressed the question of whether the government must prove some benefit to the tipper, it did not address the question of whether *Dirks* prohibited insiders from making gifts of information to "a trading relative or friend." Nothing of substantial value was given by any tippee for the information in *Newman*, and the chain of tippers and tippees included no close friends, only acquaintances. There was therefore no evidence to support an inference that the tippers had given information as true gifts to the tippees.

The facts in *Newman* were therefore materially different from those in *Salman*, where the insider asserted that he had given the information to a close relative to "benefit him." The question of whether insider-trading liability attaches when the information is given as a gift remained open. The question of whether the relationship between the tipper and tippee was relevant also remained open. The *Newman* court expressly considered the relationships among the individuals in the tipping chain. The relationships are relevant because they can, in the language of *Dirks*, serve as "objective facts and circumstances that often justify . . . an inference" that the tipper received something of value because there is a "relationship between the insider and the recipient that suggests . . . an intention to benefit the particular recipient."[25] In *Newman*, however, the Second Circuit found that the individuals in the tipping chain were acquaintances or, at best, family friends who occasionally socialized with one another, and not the kind of close friends contemplated by the *Dirks* dictum.

---

[24] It should be noted that while the Second Circuit can bind only itself and the courts within its circuit, it tends to be a leader in the area of securities law given its deep experience and well-developed law arising out of its jurisdiction over New York City.

[25] 463 U.S. at 664.

C. Misappropriation Theory

The last theory of insider trading is "misappropriation." This theory, unlike the other two, expressly attempts to identify the harm insider trading causes. Under this theory, the harm is that the insider misappropriates the company's information, and it is this theft that insider trading law seeks to redress. During oral argument in *Salman*, the government asserted a misappropriation theory of insider trading, claiming that Maher Kara had used secret information for his own benefit. Because Kara was not an insider at the companies on which his brother and brother-in-law traded, but at Citigroup, the government needed this theory to support its claim that the information nonetheless was tainted.

The last insider-trading case that the Court decided before *Salman*, *U.S. v. O'Hagan*, affirmed the misappropriation theory and with it the concept of the "temporary insider."[26] James O'Hagan was a partner at the law firm Dorsey & Whitney. His firm represented a company contemplating a takeover of another company, although O'Hagan himself was not involved in the matter. O'Hagan's position as a partner in the firm afforded him access to confidential information about the proposed tender offer, which he used to trade. He had embezzled funds from a client account and hoped to use the proceeds of his trade to cover the missing money.

One particularly tricky aspect of this case is the distance between the deception and the securities transaction. A person who merely misappropriated confidential information would not be guilty of a securities violation. Section 10(b) prohibits (1) the use of "any manipulative or deceptive device" (2) "in connection with the purchase or sale of any security." First, O'Hagan misappropriated confidential information. This is where the deceptive practice occurred. Then he used that information to trade. The trade itself involved no "deceptive device" beyond the use of material nonpublic information. Under *Chiarella*, the mere possession of material nonpublic information does not render a trade based on that information "deceptive." The theory allowing criminal liability to attach must therefore show something more.

The misappropriation theory as articulated in *O'Hagan* holds that "a fiduciary's undisclosed, self-serving use of a principal's information

[26] U.S. v. O'Hagan, 521 U.S. 642 (1997).

to purchase or sell securities, in breach of a duty of loyalty and confidentiality, defrauds the principal of the exclusive use of that information."[27] While the Court noted that "[a] fiduciary who pretends loyalty to the principal while secretly converting the principal's information for personal gain dupes or defrauds the principal,"[28] it later went on to assert that the harm Section 10(b) intends to prevent is not to the principal but to the market. According to the Court, "[t]he misappropriation theory is thus designed to protect the integrity of the securities markets against abuses."[29] Further, "[a]lthough informational disparity is inevitable in the securities markets, investors likely would hesitate to venture their capital in a market where trading based on misappropriated nonpublic information is unchecked by law"—especially as the advantage in such a case "stems from contrivance, not luck" and as such "it is a disadvantage that cannot be overcome with research or skill."[30]

Although the holding in *Chiarella* does not encompass a misappropriation theory, the *O'Hagan* Court was clear that it read *Chiarella* as expressly reserving the question of whether a noninsider could be liable for insider trading if he received the nonpublic information through a position of trust. Chiarella, recall, received the relevant information through his employment with a financial printer. Given the sensitive nature of the materials such a business handles, there would usually be an understanding between the printer and its clients that it would protect the information it receives. The Court in *Chiarella* did indeed note the possibility of asserting insider-trading liability on this basis. But, because the government had not presented the argument at trial, the Court was not able to consider it.

O'Hagan expanded the universe of potential tippers. Because some, but not all, people may freely trade on material nonpublic information, the question in any insider-trading case is to which group does the defendant belong? Those for whom trading is permitted, or those for whom trading is a felony? After *O'Hagan*, the latter group expanded

---

[27] *Id.* at 652. To further complicate matters, O'Hagan did not trade in the stock of the company his firm represented. Instead, he traded in the target company's stock. The Court nonetheless found that this trade constituted insider trading.

[28] *Id.* at 653–54 (internal quotations omitted).

[29] *Id.* at 653 (internal quotations omitted).

[30] *Id.* at 658–59 (internal quotations omitted).

beyond company insiders, as traditionally understood, to anyone with a particular relationship with the company.

II. And So We Come to *Salman*

Viewed in one light, *Salman* was simply closing the loop opened in *Dirks*. In *Dirks*, the Court considered, but was not presented with, the possibility that a tipper who makes a gift of information could be guilty of insider trading. *Newman* was viewed at the time as a potential departure from *Dirks* in the Second Circuit. The court devoted considerable attention to the question of whether there was a quid pro quo arrangement between tipper and tippee, noting as well that the tipper must receive a considerable personal benefit from the exchange. Any gift language in either *Dirks* or *Newman*, however, was arguably *dictum*. In *Dirks*, there was no allegation that the insider had given Dirks information because he wished to make him a present. The discussion of gifts is therefore not relevant to the holding. In *Newman*, the court found that the information provided neither to Newman nor to Chiasson was intended as a gift, and therefore in that case, too, any discussion of gifts was not relevant to the holding. As the Court noted in *Salman*, the gift of information from one brother to another, provided to "benefit" him and "provide for his needs" is "in the heartland of *Dirks*'s rule concerning gifts."[31] This is not to say that *Salman* rejects the premise that the insider must personally benefit from the disclosure. Instead it asserts that giving a gift can itself be a benefit to the tipper. The fact that "determining whether an insider personally benefits from a particular disclosure, a question of fact, will not always be easy for courts"[32] did not trouble the Court. "[T]here is no need for us to address those difficult cases today," the Court stated, "because this case involves precisely the gift of confidential information to a trading relative that *Dirks* envisioned."[33]

The actual holding of the case is quite narrow in light of existing precedent. It simply affirmed the *Dirks* dictum. And yet the resulting rule is incredibly complex. As the Court stated in the opening of the opinion, the rule is now:

---

[31] Salman v. United States, 137 S. Ct. 420, 429 (2016).

[32] *Id.* (quoting Dirks, 463 U.S. at 664).

[33] *Id.* (internal quotation marks omitted).

Section 10(b) of the Securities Exchange Act of 1934 and the Securities and Exchange Commission's Rule 10b-5 prohibit undisclosed trading on inside corporate information by individuals who are under a duty of trust and confidence that prohibits them from secretly using such information for their personal advantage . . . . These persons also may not tip inside information to others for trading. The tippee acquires the tipper's duty to disclose or abstain from trading if the tippee knows the information was disclosed in breach of the tipper's duty . . . . [L]iability for trading on inside information hinges on whether the tipper breached a fiduciary duty by disclosing the information. A tipper breaches such a fiduciary duty . . . when the tipper discloses the inside information for a personal benefit . . . . [A] jury can infer a personal benefit— and thus a breach of the tipper's duty—where the tipper receives something of value in exchange for the tip or makes a gift of confidential information to a trading relative or friend.[34]

To fully understand the crime, it may be useful to break it down into its elements. And there are many elements. Even the comparatively simple classical insider trading has six elements:

1. A person who is an insider, typically an officer or director,
2. obtains information that is
3. material and
4. nonpublic,
5. and executes a securities transaction
6. based on that information.

Under the misappropriation theory, the "insider" status is less clear and thus must include the following elements:

1. The individual held a position in which she owed a duty of trust and confidence to another and
2. obtained information by virtue of that position.

Finally, the tipper/tippee theory adds these elements:

1. The tipper/insider discloses the information
2. to obtain a benefit
3. that is personal.

[34] *Id.* at 423.

4. It can be something of value, or
5. the tip may constitute a gift.
6. The tippee knows the information was disclosed by
7. an insider
8. who obtained a benefit
9. that is personal
10. or provided the information as a gift, and
11. the tippee trades on the information.

On the one hand, the presence of so many elements works against the government since, to obtain a conviction, the government must prove each element beyond a reasonable doubt. But on the other, the existence of such complexity makes it more difficult for individuals and companies who are trying to avoid illegal acts in the first place.

This comes back to the central problem: insider-trading law has not clearly defined the harm it seeks to avoid. Consider, for example, a crime such as murder. The harm is abundantly clear. A person is dead. Whether the person's death is due to murder or to accident, manslaughter, or some other action, there is no serious disagreement over the fact that a person's untimely death is a tragedy to be avoided. Insider trading is entirely different.

III. Arguments for Restricting Insider Trading and Why They're Flawed

The core problem with devising good insider-trading law is that the central function of insider trading—introducing material information to the market—is good. It improves the market's ability to properly direct resources. Securities markets provide both a common meeting place for buyers and sellers and, crucially, a means of ensuring that resources are allocated to their best use. Basic economics teaches that the price that a buyer is willing to pay reflects that buyer's understanding of the thing's value (whether that "thing" is a security, a loaf of bread, or a taxi ride). The buyer will use the information available to assess what price she is willing to pay. The seller conducts a similar evaluation, using information about the thing to determine at what price he is willing to sell. Every time a price changes, other buyers and sellers incorporate the change into their own assessment of price. For example, consider a homeowner who believes his house to be worth $300,000. If a similar house in his neighborhood sells for

$600,000, he will assume that $300,000 is no longer the value of his house and will no longer sell at that price—even if he knows nothing more about the house that sold, the seller, or the buyer. He will assume that there is something about his house—the neighborhood, popular taste in housing styles, *something*—that doubled the value of his neighbor's house and therefore must increase the value of his own similar house. When a security is heavily traded, such price signals flow through the market constantly. Any trade made on the basis of material information provides such a signal.

As securities change in price, the market learns information about the underlying company. A company that is doing well will attract more money. Why should this be? Because, presumably, the company is doing something valuable. In the first two decades of life as a public company, Apple stock bumped along around $1 or $2 per share. By the end of 2007, it jumped to around $27. What did Apple do in 2007? It invented the iPhone. iPhones provide value to consumers who like having access to so much information and data in one place. Apple received more money from the market because it was using the money well. It hit a spike again in 2015, the year the iPad came out. As of April 28, 2017, it was trading at around $144. The pharmaceutical company Pfizer saw a massive increase in its stock price between 1996 and 1998—from around $12 to $44. What did it do in that time? It released the blockbuster heart medication Lipitor, which has contributed to a huge decrease in deaths due to heart disease. A properly functioning market will ensure that good ideas get funded and bad ideas are starved of precious resources.

Although introducing information into the market is important, something about insider trading seems to induce a strong negative reaction in many policymakers and commentators. Many see something "unfair" about the process. Beyond general fairness concerns, the argument typically assumes that if insider trading were permitted, investors would lose confidence in the market and would therefore abandon it. At oral argument in *Salman*, the deputy solicitor general opened by saying that permitting an insider to "parcel out" valuable information to family and friends "would be deleterious to the integrity of the securities markets" and "would injure investor confidence."[35]

---

[35] Transcript of Oral Arg. at 23–24, Salman v. United States, 137 S. Ct. 420 (2016).

Despite the advantages of introducing accurate information into the market, there may be a role for restrictions on insider trading. Unfortunately, the case law as it currently exists—constrained as it is by the need to tie any theory back to Section 10(b)—has not adequately explained either what constitutes insider trading or why what has been tagged "insider trading" should be punished as a felony. More unfortunately still, the Court missed an opportunity in *Salman* to provide either to the public.

A. Using Inside Information Is Cheating

One of the chief arguments against insider trading is that it constitutes a form of cheating. Business ethics professor Bruce W. Klaw has argued that insider trading constitutes cheating because the person trading on nonpublic information is gaining an advantage through the use of information that could not also be accessed by others "through their independent and otherwise lawful diligence."[36] Such arguments might be persuasive if there were a complete ban on the use of material nonpublic information in the securities markets—or at least on any information that could not be discerned through the careful use of data available to those who would collect and properly analyze it. But, under *Chiarella*, a taxi driver who overhears an indiscrete conversation between passengers may freely trade on the information even though the information came to him by luck. If the driver trades on the information, he is arguably deceiving the counterparty to his transaction because that person would likely demand a different price if she were aware of the information the driver has. *Chiarella*, however, explicitly rejected a "parity-of-information" rule.[37] Why is this trade less deceptive, though, than the same trade based on the same information, but with a company insider in the place of the taxi driver?

To be fair, Professor Klaw argues that *Chiarella* was improperly decided. It was "Chiarella's *access* to the dealbooks that was the

---

[36] Bruce W. Klaw, Why Now Is the Time to Statutorily Ban Insider Trading Under the Equality of Access Theory, 7 Wm. & Mary Bus. L. Rev. 275, 310 (2016) ("This Article would submit that the 'rule' violated by insider trading is the implied rule that 'thou shalt not trade in securities on the basis of information concerning that issuer unless such information could also be available to others through their independent and otherwise lawful diligence.'").

[37] See Chiarella, 445 U.S. at 233.

proximate and structural cause of his informational advantage, rather any true financial acumen or diligence on his part[,]" he notes. So a rule that would bar someone like Chiarella "from exploiting his position of access against his counterparties, whom he knew could not possibly lawfully access the same information, could have formed the basis for a limited rule about why, under the circumstance, he should have been under a unique obligation to abstain from trading."[38]

Perhaps this luck-based method of obtaining inside information does not concern the law because it is likely to happen so rarely. Someone may overhear a conversation in a taxi or an elevator, or may find a revealing memo accidentally dropped from a briefcase, but those opportunities are likely to happen once in a lifetime, if at all. The likelihood of someone trading on such information at any given time is so low that it is unlikely to deter others from entering the market. But even if it is likely to be rare, if the problem is that it is deceptive for one party to use secret information to gain an advantage over another, it should not matter how frequently such deception occurs.

Professor Klaw argues that insider trading constitutes cheating in part because the inside information cannot be gained through acumen or skill. But it may go too far to say that obtaining insider information requires no skill. In her book *Black Edge: Inside Information, Dirty Money, and the Quest to Bring Down the Most Wanted Man on Wall Street*, journalist Sheelah Kolhatkar recounts in great detail the lengths that hedge fund employees have gone to in order to cultivate just such information.[39] While there may be an easy and entirely fortuitous way to access such information—by belonging to the kind of family that has deep connections with industry titans or by going to the schools that foster such ties—such connections are likely to be limited by chance. Family ties to one industry do not guarantee similar ties in another unrelated field. Developing a professional network, however, is a skill at the heart of many occupations. Journalists, for example, require a broad web of sources to produce timely scoops. Anyone who must bring in

---

[38] Klaw, *supra* note 36, at 303–04.

[39] Sheelah Kolhatkar, Black Edge: Inside Information, Dirty Money, and the Quest to Bring Down the Most Wanted Man on Wall Street (2017).

clients must cultivate relationships with the right people. Those looking for work are frequently advised to work their networks. It is not entirely clear how developing sources as a journalist, for example, is fundamentally different from developing sources for market information. The difference is certainly not that only the former requires any "skill."

Existing law creates a strange paradox. Information that one party has but that is not available to the market broadly is permitted if it was attained by pure luck (as with our taxi driver) or if it was attained through *some* kinds of skill, but not through the skill of developing human sources of information. If a trader wants to watch the road outside a factory to glean information about a company's output, or study satellite pictures of parking lots to gauge retail activity, these sources of information, while not widely available, are nonetheless permissible for use in trading.

B. Investors Will Lose Confidence in the Market If They Believe that Insiders Are Using Nonpublic Information

Those who argue against insider trading on the basis of fairness often buttress their positions by noting the likely effect of insider trading on the markets. During oral argument in *Salman*, counsel for the United States stated that allowing corporate insiders to "parcel . . . out [material nonpublic information] to favored friends, family members, and acquaintances . . . would be deleterious to the integrity of the securities markets."[40] The idea is that if some market participants have information unavailable to others, investors will be wary and shy away from the markets, uncertain of whether they are being exploited.

But under the formulation expressed in *Salman*, what matters is that information is provided by an insider *in breach of a duty*. If the concern is the duty that has been breached, this may make sense. But to the extent that the concern is—as the deputy solicitor general argued—the integrity of markets and the willingness of investors to participate, then whether a duty was breached seems hardly relevant. If the breach of duty were truly the concern, a company could grant certain officers and directors leave to trade on inside information as a form of cheap compensation. But this

---

[40] Transcript of Oral Arg. at 23–24, Salman v. United States, 137 S. Ct. 420 (2016).

is not permitted because, in the end, the integrity of the market is ostensibly the concern. Yet such a stance disregards the value to the market of a high-ranking officer or director trading in the company's stock. Imagine if a CEO were to short her own company, or buy up additional shares in a spending spree. Either move would send a very strong signal to the market and help improve the existing information. If the concern is that some traders may have information unavailable to others, then whether that information was obtained through a breach of duty should be irrelevant.

C. Companies Have the Right to Exclusive Use of Their Information

A final argument for restricting insider information is perhaps the least persuasive, which is that companies have the right to exclusive use of their information. Under this formulation, which is the foundation of the misappropriation theory, insider trading is essentially theft. It is true that companies clearly have an interest in controlling the dissemination of their sensitive information. Whether the law should affirmatively protect that interest with the use of criminal sanctions is less clear.

Companies routinely keep news of a merger quiet until the transaction is complete. The concern is that the merger is premised on a particular stock price. Assuming the merger is a good one, the price of the merged company's stock should rise once the merger becomes public knowledge. Between the time that the merger is under consideration and the time it becomes public, therefore, the stock is underpriced. If the price would rise if the market knew about the merger, that means that the existing price is incorrect and does not reflect the true value of the company. Anyone who sells the stock without knowing about the merger is selling too cheaply. In some ways, the company's keeping the information private is a form of insider trading. Anyone who knows that a stock's value is likely to rise because of secret information, and therefore holds the stock with the expectation of profits once the information is disclosed, is making a trading decision based on material nonpublic information.

In *Salman*, the trades at issue involved just such a contemplated merger. At trial, Maher Kara testified about a contemplated merger that would proceed only if the information remained private and therefore only if the stock prices of the relevant companies remained stable. The company, a client of Citigroup's, insisted on the strictest confidentiality. Because Michael had become aware of the merger through information disclosed by Maher, he rightly commented that the company seemed "cheap."

Ultimately, however, the misappropriation theory proves too much because it is limited to misappropriation *for the purpose of trading* only. It is not difficult, however, to imagine other uses to which information might be put that would deprive the company of its exclusive use without involving a securities transaction. It is not even necessary to speculate or devise hypothetical situations; *Salman* itself includes such a use. Maher Kara testified that he had shared information with Michael for the purpose of exploring treatment options for their dying father. While this use is clearly sympathetic—it would seem cruel to punish two sons for using information at their disposal to try to save their father—it is just as clearly one with only a personal benefit to Kara. Neither Citigroup nor any of its clients benefited from the elder Mr. Kara receiving improved medical treatment.

So why must the harm be tied to a personal use that also involves a securities transaction? One answer may be that such a use risks affecting the company's position in the market. Activity unexplained by public information would hint to traders that there was some material nonpublic information to be had. The market might react and harm the company both through a price movement itself (if the price were to go down) and from the presence of a hint that might lead others to guess the secret information—for example, that a long-rumored merger was finally going ahead.

While the harm to the company would be clear, the fact that these trades might move the market suggests that the presence of the currently illicit trades would actually improve the market. Perfect information should lead to prices reflecting the actual value of a security. If a security is trading at an artificially high or low price, the market suffers. Introducing secret information sooner rather than later benefits the market as a whole (and the rest of society, which benefits from resources being directed to their best use), even if it disadvantages the company whose securities are being traded.

What if the trades do not move the market? In a very active security, one person trading may go entirely unnoticed, especially if that person is a step or two removed from the company itself. (A CEO's trades will never go unnoticed, of course.) These trades introduce no new information into the market because no one takes notice of them. In that case, however, it seems even harder to show that there is a harm to the company. A few trades that have no impact on price, and that might have happened anyway—just with a different buyer or seller—arguably incur no harm on the company itself.

There is a disconnect in this logic. If it is harmful to a company for its information to be used for a purpose it does not approve, if it loses the exclusive use of its information, the harm must exist even if the use is not trading in the company's securities. But if the harm exists only when it is tied to a securities transaction, why does a trade that has no impact on price harm the company? And in the case that the trade does move the price, why should the company's desire to have exclusive use of the information be protected by law? If the rapid dissemination of accurate information is a benefit to the market and society more broadly, why criminalize activity that forwards that interest? It would seem that a better approach would be to permit the company to take measures to protect its own information, but refrain from interfering when someone breaches that protection.

IV. A Better Solution

There is arguably no need for a law that proscribes insider trading. First, the introduction of accurate information into the marketplace is an inherent good. Restricting this flow of information through criminal law only serves to make markets less efficient and prices less accurate. Second, companies already have a strong incentive to protect their own information and the means to punish their own insiders who improperly disclose the information, including by using it to trade. Confidentiality provisions are common in employment agreements. These agreements can be enforced by the companies themselves—through threat of termination or by clawing back certain compensation from employees who violate the contract, or through litigation, which provides employers with remedies to help recoup the losses sustained through the employee's illicit disclosures. Employers are free to punish almost any unauthorized disclosure, including a disclosure to a friend or relative with the intent that the individual use the information to trade.

Despite these arguments against insider-trading law, it is unlikely that insider-trading law will be abandoned any time soon. There remains a strong sense among many that insider trading is "cheating."[41] A more rational, easily understood, and easily administered rule is needed.

Chief Justice Warren Burger's dissent in *Chiarella* presented one such rule. Burger noted that "neither party to an arm's-length business transaction has an obligation to disclose information to the other unless the parties stand in some confidential or fiduciary relation . . . [but] the rule should give way when an informational advantage is obtained, not by superior experience, foresight, or industry, but by some unlawful means."[42] Chiarella's conviction should stand, he reasoned, because the act of obtaining data from confidential client sources is itself unlawful.

Assuming that the various laws proscribing certain means of obtaining information are just—which may be a large assumption but is at least the subject of a separate inquiry—then dissuading individuals from employing those proscribed means to obtain information itself promotes a good. Unlawfully breaking into a company's headquarters or, more likely in 2017, servers and stealing information is clearly harmful because it violates the company's property rights. A law that enforces a company's agreements with its employees—including provisions against using confidential company data for personal reasons—similarly promotes the value of strong contract rights.

Such a substantial change in the law would be best attempted by Congress. The prohibition on insider trading could therefore be completely untethered from the language of Section 10(b) and its insistence on fraud, and written to address a specific harm.

To the extent that the harm investors fear is truly that they may be trading with someone who has access to information entirely unavailable to themselves, the proper rule is simply to bar any trading on material nonpublic information, no matter how it was obtained. This would of course cause some reduced flow of information into the market, but it would at least provide clear guidance for those wishing to avoid criminal liability. It would also require a firm commitment to the stated principle of protecting market integrity.

---

[41] The reason for such sentiment is the subject for another paper. It should be noted, however, that fully lawful means of trading often face similar emotional reactions. Consider, for example, sentiments surrounding high frequency trading: those who use such methods are often depicted as "cheaters" as well.

[42] Chiarella, 445 U.S. at 239–240 (Burger, C.J., dissenting).

The way things stand now, it is not entirely clear why investors would fear insiders' trading but would not fear other traders using equally secret information.

*　*　*

The Court in *Salman* clarified a small question of insider trading law—whether an insider could make a gift of information—but failed to provide any additional clarity on why such trading is illegal at all. While the process of developing rules through the common law system of legal precedents can be beneficial, in this case the mix of an underlying statute with a crime that has been built haphazardly on top of it has only resulted in confusion. Existing law, in part because it relies on a catch-all that must catch fraud, has followed a tortuous path. Justice requires that individuals be able to clearly understand what actions will result in criminal penalties. This clarity depends in part on a clear understanding of what harm is being prevented. This is what is meant by adhering to the "spirit of the law." It is not clear that insider trading must be criminalized at all. But if it must be, then the law should be written in a way that all market participants can clearly understand. This requires a clear statement of the harm to be avoided and a body of law devoted to avoiding that particular harm. That is far from what our current law provides.

Nelson v. Colorado:
New Life for an Old Idea?

*David G. Post**

Background[1]

In 2006, Shannon Nelson was convicted by a Colorado jury of two felonies and three misdemeanors arising from the alleged sexual and physical abuse of her children.[2] The trial court sentenced her to a prison term of 20 years to life. Pursuant to Colorado law, which provides that persons convicted of criminal activity are responsible, immediately upon their conviction, for certain costs and fees, the court ordered Nelson to pay the following: (1) $125.00 to the State's Victim Compensation Fund; (2) $162.50 to the Victims and Witnesses Assistance and Law Enforcement Fund; (3) $35.00 for court costs; (4) a "time payment fee" of $25.00; and (5) $7,845.00 in restitution, bringing the total owed to $8,192.50.[3]

Nelson was unable to pay the amount due; consequently, during her incarceration, the Colorado Department of Corrections periodically deducted money from her inmate account to satisfy the debt she owed to the state.

*Professor of law, Beasley School of Law, Temple University (retired); contributor, Volokh Conspiracy; adjunct scholar, Cato Institute. I want to thank Rob Johnson and Darpana Sheth of the Institute for Justice for involving me in their work on this case, which ultimately led to our filing an amicus brief in the Supreme Court, on behalf of the Institute for Justice and the Cato Institute, in support of petitioner Nelson.

[1] The factual background is taken from the Supreme Court decision in *Nelson v. Colorado*, 137 S. Ct. 1249 (2017), and the opinion below, *People v. Nelson*, 362 P.3d 1070 (Colo. 2015).

[2] Nelson's case was joined with a second case, *People v. Madden*, 364 P.3d 866 (Colo. 2015), raising the same issues under the same Colorado law. The two cases were decided together, and all references below in the singular to "Nelson's claim" should be understood to refer to Madden's as well.

[3] Nelson, 362 P.3d at 1071.

In 2009, the Colorado Court of Appeals reversed the judgment against Nelson, finding that the testimony of an expert witness at her trial had been improperly used, and remanded her case for a new trial.[4] A new jury was empaneled. It acquitted Nelson of all charges at the second trial, and she was released from state prison.

During Nelson's incarceration, the state had deducted just over $700 from her account; upon her acquittal and release, she wanted that money back. She filed a motion with the trial court, seeking its return on the ground that her acquittal eliminated whatever claim the state may have had to the funds. The trial court denied the motion, but the Colorado Court of Appeals again ruled in Nelson's favor, holding that all assessments of costs, fees, and restitution must be "tied to a valid conviction," absent which a court must "retur[n] the defendant to the *status quo ante*."[5] Accordingly, the court ordered the trial court to grant Nelson's refund motion.[6]

The state appealed, and the Colorado Supreme Court, over a vigorous dissent by Justice William Hood, reversed.[7] Relying on the principle that the allocation of public money is a legislative—not a judicial—prerogative, the court reasoned that the trial court had no inherent authority to refund Nelson's money and could only do so pursuant to express legislative direction:

> The General Assembly authorizes the collection, management, and distribution of the funds raised by costs, fees, and restitution pursuant to its power to define crimes and sentences, raise revenue, and make appropriations. These powers are inherently legislative, and a court may not intrude on the General Assembly's power by authorizing a refund from public funds without statutory authority to do so.[8]

---

[4] People v. Shannon Kay Gonser, n/k/a Shannon Nelson, No. 06CA1023, 2009 Colo. App. LEXIS 637 (Colo. App. Apr. 9, 2009).

[5] People v. Nelson, 369 P.3d 625, 628 (Col. App. 2013).

[6] *Id.* at 629

[7] Nelson, 362 P.3d at 1079.

[8] *Id.* at 1075–76. See also Colorado Const. Art. V §33 ("No moneys in the state treasury shall be disbursed . . . except upon appropriations made by law, or otherwise authorized by law.").

The court then found that Colorado's Compensation for Certain Exonerated Persons statute (commonly known as the "Exoneration Act"),[9] passed in 2013, contains the specific statutory authorization for the refund that Nelson sought. This law, the court held, "specifically addresses when a defendant who was wrongfully convicted may seek a refund of costs, fees, and restitution" and therefore "provides the proper procedure for seeking a refund."[10] Because no other statute addressed this question, the Exoneration Act was the *"exclusive* process for exonerated defendants seeking a refund of costs, fees, and restitution."[11] In response to Nelson's argument that a "failure to refund the money would violate state and federal constitutional guarantees of due process," the court found that the act "provides sufficient process for defendants to seek refunds of costs, fees, and restitution that they paid in connection with their conviction."[12]

Thus, if Nelson wanted a refund, she would have to file an Exoneration Act claim and proceed under that statute. Because she had not done so, "the trial court lacked the authority to order a refund of Nelson's costs, fees, and restitution based on her motion following her criminal trial."[13] As a result, the Colorado Supreme Court ordered the trial court to deny her motion for a refund with leave to file a claim under the Exoneration Act.

I. Colorado's Exoneration Act

Though it might appear as though the case was one in which the "litigants merely needed directions on where to ask for relief,"[14] several features of the Exoneration Act complicate the matter. Like more than half the states, Colorado provides a civil remedy through which individuals who have been "exonerated"—proven to be *"factually innocent* of any participation in the crime" with which they were charged and convicted[15]—can receive compensation from the

---

[9] Colo. Rev. Stat. § 13-65-101 et seq.

[10] Nelson, 362 P.3d at 1077–78.

[11] *Id*. at 1078 (emphasis added).

[12] *Id*. at 1071, 1078.

[13] *Id*.

[14] *Id*. at 1081 (Hood, J., dissenting).

[15] Colo. Rev. Stat. § 13-65-101(1)(a)(II) (emphasis added). See also § 13-65-102(4)(a) (declaring that an individual is "not eligible for compensation pursuant to [the Ex-

state for their wrongful incarceration. Recovery under this law is available only to persons who have served all or part of a term of incarceration pursuant to a felony conviction, and only to those whose conviction has been overturned for reasons *other than* a finding that the "evidence [was] legally insufficient to support the petitioner's conviction," or that there had been some "legal error unrelated to the petitioner's actual innocence."[16] Moreover, the burden of proving that she is actually innocent of all crimes for which she was incarcerated is on the Exoneration Act claimant, and the proof must be by "clear and convincing evidence."[17]

Successful claimants under the Exoneration Act receive a fixed payment of $70,000 for each year of incarceration (with additional amounts payable in certain specified circumstances[18]), tuition waivers at all state institutions of higher learning for all family members, along with—crucially, for this case—reimbursement for "any fine, penalty, court costs, or restitution" paid as a result of the wrongful conviction.[19]

It is safe to say that the Colorado legislators who passed the Exoneration Act did not have Shannon Nelson's particular situation in mind. The overriding purpose of the act was to provide special, and rather substantial, compensation to persons who have been especially ill-treated by the criminal justice system—compensation to which the individuals concerned would not, absent the act, be otherwise entitled. It is entirely understandable that Colorado would want to restrict the award of special compensation to those who can show that they were actually innocent of the crimes charged, and not merely "legally innocent" because their conviction had been overturned for "legal error." The conditions that the state imposed on would-be claimants under the act were meant to be difficult to fulfill; indeed, the legislature's own estimates of the financial consequences

---

oneration Act] if he or she does not meet the definition of actual innocence in section 13-65-101(1).").

[16] *Id.* § 13-65-101(1)(b).

[17] *Id.* § 13-65-102(6)(b) ("[T]he burden shall be on the petitioner to show by clear and convincing evidence that he or she is actually innocent of all crimes that are the subject of the petition, and that he or she is eligible to receive compensation pursuant to this article. A trial to a jury of six must result in a unanimous verdict.").

[18] *Id.* § 13-65-103(3).

[19] *Id,* § 13-65-103(2)(e)(V).

of the act assumed that only one person every five *years* would meet the act's requirements and qualify for a financial award.[20]

Nelson, however, wasn't seeking special compensation for the time she served in prison; she was merely seeking a return of money she had paid to the state as a consequence of her now-vacated conviction. But because the Exoneration Act—almost as an afterthought—*also* provided for reimbursement of funds previously paid by "exonerated" defendants, she would have to satisfy the act's stringent conditions in order simply to get her money back.

That hardly seems fair. It is difficult to imagine that any legislator could have known or intended enactment of the Exoneration Act to have the effect it had on individuals standing in Nelson's shoes, or intended the act to deny or delay reimbursements to individuals whose convictions are overturned without proof of their "actual innocence." Nelson is, in the eyes of the law, legally innocent—"presumed innocent"[21]—of the crime with which she was charged; her acquittal at her second trial means that the state failed to sustain its burden to prove, beyond a reasonable doubt, each and every element of the charged offense. The state's entitlement to the funds in question was based entirely on the earlier conviction. She may or may not be *actually* innocent as a matter of fact. The jury at her second trial was not asked to rule on that, and its verdict of acquittal does not speak to that question; it establishes only that the state had not sustained its burden of proving beyond a reasonable doubt that she was guilty of the crimes charged. Requiring her to prove that she is actually innocent could be a rather complex undertaking. But more important, why should she have to establish actual innocence to receive a refund of fees assessed upon her (now vacated) conviction? Once that conviction was overturned, she did not have to show that she was "actually innocent" to be released from prison—that is, to have her *liberty* restored. Why should she have to do so to have her *property* restored?

Instead of filing an action under the Exoneration Act, Nelson appealed to the U.S. Supreme Court, arguing that Colorado's

---

[20] Nelson, 137 S. Ct. at 1260 (Alito, J., concurring in the judgment) (citing Colorado Legislative Council Staff Fiscal Note, State and Local Revised Fiscal Impact, HB 13–1230, 2 (Apr. 22, 2013)).

[21] I discuss this concept and the role it played here in a later section of this essay.

requirement that she proceed under the Exoneration Act and prove her actual innocence by clear and convincing evidence before she could receive reimbursement violated her right to due process under the Fourteenth Amendment.

II. The Supreme Court Decision

In a 7-1 decision, the Supreme Court reversed the Colorado Supreme Court, agreeing with Nelson that Colorado's scheme "offends the Fourteenth Amendment's guarantee of due process."[22] Justice Ruth Bader Ginsburg (joined by Chief Justice John Roberts and Justices Anthony Kennedy, Stephen Breyer, Sonia Sotomayor, and Elena Kagan), wrote the majority opinion. Applying the "familiar procedural due process inspection instructed by *Mathews v. Eldridge*"[23] the Court considered three factors and found that all of them weigh decisively against the Colorado law:

1. *The private interest affected.* Nelson has an "obvious interest in regaining the money [she] paid to Colorado."[24] Once her conviction was erased, "the presumption of [her] innocence was restored. . . . Colorado may not presume a person, adjudged guilty of no crime, nonetheless guilty *enough* for monetary exactions."[25] "[T]o get their money back, defendants should not be saddled with any proof burden. Instead, . . . they are entitled to be presumed innocent."[26]

2. *The risk of erroneous deprivation of that interest through the procedures used.* Under Colorado's procedures the "risk of erroneous deprivation"—the "risk faced by a defendant whose conviction has already been overturned that she will not recover funds taken from her solely on the basis of a conviction no longer valid"—is substantial, both because "the Act conditions refund on defendants' proof of innocence by clear and convincing evidence" and because "the cost of mounting a claim under the Exoneration Act and retaining a lawyer to pursue it" will

---

[22] Nelson, 137 S. Ct. at 1252.

[23] *Id.* at 1255.

[24] *Id.*

[25] *Id.* at 1255–56 (emphasis added).

[26] *Id.* at 1256.

often be "prohibitive" in light of the relatively small amounts of money involved.[27]

3. *The governmental interest at stake.* This one was easy: Colorado simply "has *no* interest in withholding from Nelson . . . money to which the State currently has zero claim of right."[28]

In sum, the Court held that Colorado's scheme

> fails due process measurement because defendants' interest in regaining their funds is high, the risk of erroneous deprivation of those funds under the Exoneration Act is unacceptable, and the State has shown no countervailing interests in retaining the amounts in question. . . . [Colorado] may not impose anything more than minimal procedures on the refund of exactions dependent upon a conviction subsequently invalidated.[29]

Justice Samuel Alito concurred in the judgment and wrote separately. In his view, this case addresses "'state procedural rules which . . . are part of the criminal process,'"[30] making the *Mathews* balancing test inapposite. Instead, he would apply the more deferential framework set forth in *Medina v. California*, under which "a state rule of criminal procedure . . . violates the Due Process Clause of the Fourteenth Amendment only if it offends a fundamental and deeply rooted principle of justice," looking to "historical practice" for probative evidence of whether a procedural rule can be characterized as "fundamental."[31] He agreed, though, that even under *Medina*'s framework, the Exoneration Act procedures are inadequate:

> Under Medina, the Colorado scheme at issue violates due process. . . . The Act places a heavy burden of proof on defendants, provides no opportunity for a refund for defendants . . . whose misdemeanor convictions are reversed, and excludes defendants whose convictions are reversed for reasons unrelated to innocence. These stringent requirements all but guarantee that most defendants whose convictions

---

[27] *Id.* at 1256–57.

[28] *Id.* at 1257 (emphasis added).

[29] *Id.* at 1257–58.

[30] *Id.* at 1258 (Alito, J. concurring in the judgment) (citing Medina v. California, 505 U.S. 437, 443 (1992)).

[31] *Id.*

are reversed have no realistic opportunity to prove they are deserving of refunds. Colorado has abandoned historical procedures that were more generous to successful appellants and incorporated a court's case-specific equitable judgment. Instead, Colorado has adopted a system that is harsh, inflexible, and prevents most defendants whose convictions are reversed from demonstrating entitlement to a refund.[32]

Justice Clarence Thomas was the sole dissenter. His opinion (which I discuss in more detail below) can be summarized thus: once the state has lawfully taken Nelson's money from her upon her conviction, it's not *her money* anymore; it belongs, under Colorado law, to the state. Therefore, her due process challenge to the Exoneration Act refund procedures must fail, because those procedures, whatever burdens they may impose upon her, do not constitute a "depriv[ation] . . . of [her] property" within the meaning of the Fourteenth Amendment's Due Process Clause.

III. The Significance of the Decision

Few Supreme Court decisions, one would think, *directly* impact fewer people than this one. No other state requires—or, to my knowledge, has ever required—persons seeking a return of financial exactions levied on the basis of a subsequently invalidated criminal conviction to prove their actual innocence, let alone by clear and convincing evidence.[33] So the decision will have no direct impact on the law outside of Colorado.

And even within Colorado, the decision will have negligible effect. Shortly after the Supreme Court decided to review the case, Colorado enacted a new law that provides that a "defendant whose court-ordered fines, fees, costs, surcharges, restitution, interest, or other monetary amounts resulting from a criminal conviction . . . have been paid" can obtain, by motion at the trial court, reimbursement of that money in the event that the conviction "is vacated after post-conviction proceedings or overturned on appeal," or if "the charge on which the conviction was based is dismissed or the person is

---

[32] *Id.* at 1260.

[33] Petition for Writ of Cert., Nelson v. Colorado, at 9 ("Colorado appears to be the only state that requires defendants to prove their innocence before they can get a refund of monetary penalties when a conviction is reversed.").

acquitted of the charge after a new trial"—thus effectively nullifying the Colorado Supreme Court decision under review.[34]

Although the new statute, which does not take effect until September 1, 2017, does not technically moot Nelson's claim,[35] its enactment surely both supports the proposition that Nelson's legal predicament was the product of pure legislative inadvertence and further shrank the already-small universe of persons directly impacted by the decision. Indeed, it would not have come as a shock had the Court chosen to "DIG" the case—dismiss as improvidently granted—after passage of the new law.[36]

But while the decision will thus have little direct impact on individuals, or on the law regarding the return of fees and costs after invalidation of a criminal conviction, it may well have an impact—and possibly a substantial impact—on developments elsewhere in the law. My guess—and it can only be a guess at this point—is that *Nelson* will turn out to be important in the intensifying legal battles over civil forfeiture practices. These have become, in recent years, quite controversial and may well become the subject of a Supreme Court decision in the not-too-distant future.

Civil forfeiture is "a legal fiction that enables law enforcement to take legal action against inanimate objects for their participation in alleged criminal activity, regardless of whether the property owner is guilty or innocent—or even whether the owner is charged with a crime."[37] As Justice Thomas recently put it:

> Modern civil forfeiture statutes are plainly designed, at least in part, to punish the owner of property used for criminal purposes. See, *e.g., Austin v. United States*, 509 U. S. 602, 618–619 (1993). When a state wishes to punish one

[34] See An Act Concerning a Process for Repayment of Certain Criminal Monetary Amounts Ordered by the Court to Be Paid Following Conviction, Colo. Rev. Stat. § 18-1.3-703, http://extras.denverpost.com/app/bill-tracker/bills/2017a/hb_17-1071.

[35] See Nelson, 137 S. Ct. at 1254 n.4 (discussing new legislation).

[36] See Perry Grossman, Common High Court Ground: The Supreme Court Is Looking for Cases to Curb Abusive Law Enforcement Seizures," Slate, Apr. 28, 2017, http://www.slate.com/articles/news_and_politics/politics/2017/04/the_supreme_court_finally_found_an_issue_that_unites_them.htm.

[37] Institute for Justice, Policing for Profit: The Abuse of Civil Asset Forfeiture 10 (2d ed. Nov. 2015), https://ij.org/wp-content/uploads/2015/11/policing-for-profit-2nd-edition.pdf.

of its citizens, it ordinarily proceeds against the defendant personally (known as *"in personam"*), and in many cases it must provide the defendant with full criminal procedural protections. Nevertheless, . . . this Court permits prosecutors seeking forfeiture to proceed against the property (known as *"in rem"*) and to do so civilly. See, *e.g., United States v. James Daniel Good Real Property,* 510 U. S. 43, 56–57 (1993). *In rem* proceedings often enable the government to seize the property without any predeprivation judicial process and to obtain forfeiture of the property even when the owner is personally innocent. . . .

Civil proceedings often lack certain procedural protections that accompany criminal proceedings, such as the right to a jury trial and a heightened standard of proof.[38]

The use of civil forfeiture proceedings, under state and federal forfeiture statutes, exploded during the early 1980s as part of the "war on drugs," and it has become a commonly used weapon in the government's crime-fighting arsenal. As Rep. Tim Walberg (R-MI) put it recently: "civil forfeiture is big business for the government."[39] In Justice Thomas's words again:

[C]ivil forfeiture has in recent decades become widespread and highly profitable. . . . This system—where police can seize property with limited judicial oversight and retain it for their own use—has led to egregious and well-chronicled abuses.[40]

Whether civil forfeiture procedures comport with constitutional due process requirements is a question that is currently the subject of considerable attention in the lower federal courts and the subject of intense scholarly and public debate.[41] Justice Thomas, at least, has

---

[38] Statement of Justice Thomas Respecting the Denial Of Certiorari in Leonard v. Texas, No. 16-122 (Mar. 6, 2017), http://www.scotusblog.com/wp-content/uploads/2017/03/16-122-respecting-cert-denial.pdf.

[39] Tim Walberg, Stopping the Abuse of Civil Forfeiture, Wash. Post, Sept. 4, 2014, https://www.washingtonpost.com/opinions/tim-walberg-an-end-to-the-abuse-of-civil-forfeiture/2014/09/04/e7b9d07a-3395-11e4-9e92-0899b306bbea_story.html.

[40] See Statement, *supra* note 38.

[41] The literature on the civil forfeiture controversy is vast. See generally, Policing for Profit, *supra* note 37; Margaret Lemos & Max Minzner, For-Profit Public Enforcement,

clearly signaled a willingness to have the Court address the question directly.[42]

Nelson, of course, did not involve a civil forfeiture proceeding. But the question it raised has echoes in the forfeiture context: What process is due to an individual seeking, in a civil action, a return of property seized by the government? And, in particular, what role does the "presumption of innocence" play in deciding that question?

IV. The Presumption of Innocence

The "presumption of innocence" plays a curious role in the law, and it played a curious role in this case. There may well be no principle of law more familiar to most people—if only from the many TV shows and movies that have repeated the formulation—than the notion that a criminal defendant is "presumed innocent" of all charges, and that the government has the burden of proving guilt by proof "beyond a reasonable doubt." And there are few principles (if any) with deeper roots in the Anglo-American system of justice. As the Court wrote in *Nelson*, the presumption of innocence is "axiomatic and elementary," and "lies at the foundation of our criminal law," and is unquestionably a "principle of justice so rooted in the traditions and conscience of our people as to be ranked as fundamental." [43]

It was clearly critical to the resolution of this case. As the Court put it: "Once [Nelson's] conviction[ ] was erased, the presumption of [her] innocence was restored . . . Colorado may not presume a

---

127 Harv. L. Rev. 853 (2014); Stefan Cassella, Asset Forfeiture Law in the United States (2d ed., Juris 2012); Sarah Stillman, Taken, New Yorker, Apr. 12, 2013.

[42] *See* Statement, *supra* note 38:

> The Court has justified its unique constitutional treatment of civil forfeiture largely by reference to a discrete historical practice that existed at the time of the founding. . . . In the absence of this historical practice, the Constitution presumably would require the Court to align its distinct doctrine governing civil forfeiture with its doctrines governing other forms of punitive state action and property deprivation. . . . One unaware of the history of forfeiture laws and 200 years of this Court's precedent regarding such laws might well assume that such a scheme is lawless-a violation of due process. . . . I am skeptical that this historical practice is capable of sustaining, as a constitutional matter, the contours of modern practice."

[43] Nelson, 137 S. Ct. at 1256 & note 9 (internal citations and quotation marks omitted).

person, adjudged guilty of no crime, nonetheless guilty *enough* for monetary exactions."[44] "To get their money back, defendants should not be saddled with any proof burden. Instead, . . . they are entitled to be presumed innocent."[45]

The precise meaning of the presumption of innocence, though, is a bit more slippery than one might think. It is not, for instance, a true "presumption" at all, as that term is ordinarily used in the law. A true presumption is *evidentiary* in nature, a "rule affecting the finder of fact, under [which], if a basic fact (Fact A) is established, then the fact-finder must accept that the presumed fact (Fact B) has also been established."[46]

But the presumption of innocence does not operate this way. It *doesn't* have an evidentiary function, mandating a progression from proven fact to presumed fact. As the Court put it in *Taylor v. Kentucky*:

> It is now generally recognized that the "presumption of innocence" is an inaccurate, shorthand description of the right of the accused to "remain inactive and secure, until the prosecution has taken up its burden and produced evidence and effected persuasion; *i.e.*, to say in this case, as in any other, that the opponent of a claim or charge is presumed not to be guilty is to say in another form that the proponent of the claim or charge must evidence it." The principal inaccuracy is the fact that it is not technically a "presumption"—a mandatory inference drawn from a fact in evidence. Instead, it is better characterized as an "assumption" that is indulged in the absence of contrary evidence.[47]

---

[44] *Id*. at 1251 (emphasis in original).

[45] *Id*. at 1257.

[46] Weinstein's Federal Evidence § 301.02; accord, Lafave & Scott, Criminal Law § 8 (1972) (A presumption is generally used to describe the situation in which "a party having the burden of producing evidence of fact A, introduces proof of fact B," which proof then permits the jury to presume or infer the existence of fact A); Dean McCormick, Law of Evidence § 342 (2d ed., Edward Cleary, ed., 1972) (A presumption is generally used to describe the situation in which "a party having the burden of producing evidence of fact A, introduces proof of fact B," which allows the jury to presume or infer the existence of fact A; a presumption "in the legal sense" builds on this rudimentary concept by shifting the burden of producing evidence, as well as the burden of persuasion, on the question to the adversary.).

[47] Taylor v. Kentucky, 436 U.S. at 483 n. 12 (internal citations omitted). The Court's early confusion over the meaning of the presumption illustrates how slippery this concept can be. When it first recognized the constitutional status of the presumption,

The presumption of innocence, in other words, does *not* mandate, in the manner of a true presumption, that the fact-finder draw a *factual* inference—that is, that the defendant is *innocent in fact*—from the government's failure to produce contrary evidence. If anything, it is a kind of *anti*-presumption, *forbidding* the fact-finder from making certain inferences: for instance, inferring that the defendant performed the acts constituting the crime from any facts that are not introduced into evidence at trial, or simply from the defendant's having been arrested, detained, and charged with the commission of a crime.[48]

The so-called presumption of innocence is better characterized as an *assumption* of a defendant's legal innocence,[49] applied prophylactically in criminal proceedings because, in what is perhaps Blackstone's most famous maxim, "the law holds that it is better that ten guilty persons escape than that one innocent suffer."[50] It operates

---

the Court viewed the presumption of innocence as "an instrument of proof created by the law in favor of one accused, whereby his innocence is established until sufficient evidence is introduced to overcome the proof which the law has created." Coffin v. United States, 156 U.S. 432, 459 (1895). The *Coffin* formulation was the subject of scathing criticism from Professor James Bradley Thayer, the dean of U.S. evidence scholars at the time. See James Thayer, The Presumption of Innocence in Criminal Cases, 6 Yale L. J. 185 (1897), and James Thayer, A Preliminary Treatise on Evidence at the Common Law (1898). As the Court itself subsequently acknowledged, Thayer "ably demonstrated the error" the *Coffin* Court had made, "pointing out that the so-called 'presumption' is not evidence—not even an inference drawn from a fact in evidence—but instead is a way of describing the prosecution's duty both to produce evidence of guilt and to convince the jury beyond a reasonable doubt." Taylor, 436 U.S. at 483 n.12. A mere two years later, the Court retreated from its position that the presumption of innocence has an evidentiary function for the fact-finder. See Agnew v. United States, 165 U.S. 36, 51–52 (1897). See also, generally, William F. Fox, Jr., The 'Presumption of Innocence' as Constitutional Doctrine, 28 Cath. U. L. Rev 253 (1979).

[48] See Thayer, The Presumption of Innocence in Criminal Cases, *supra* note 47, at 188–89.

[49] A Mississippi case cited with approval by the Court in Taylor v. Kentucky—Carr v. State, 192 Miss. 152, 156 (1941)—was apparently among the first to use the phrase "the *assumption* of innocence" rather than the usual (though technically incorrect) "presumption." The Model Penal Code, promulgated in final form in 1962, also changes the crucial term from "presumption" to "assumption": "In the absence of such proof [beyond a reasonable doubt], the innocence of the defendant is assumed." Model Penal Code § 1.12(1) (1962). See also Fox, *supra* note 47, at 261 (noting that the Supreme Court "has long recognized that the presumption of innocence does not work as a true presumption").

[50] 4 William Blackstone, Commentaries, 358 (1765).

by allocating the burden of persuasion in criminal trials, requiring the government to bear the burden of proof with respect to each and every element of the charged offense; it "describes [a criminal defendant's] right to do nothing until the prosecution has met its burdens of production and persuasion":[51]

> [T]he general rule of our jurisprudence is, that the party accused need not establish his innocence; but it is for the government itself to prove his guilt before it is entitled to a verdict or conviction.[52]

And on "grounds of fairness and abundant caution," this presumption of innocence is "coupled with a separate special rule as to the *weight* of evidence necessary to make out guilt"[53]—the requirement of proof "beyond a reasonable doubt." It was, in Professor Thayer's words, "summed up and neatly put"[54] by Chief Justice Lemuel Shaw in an 1850 Massachusetts case:

> The burden of proof is upon the prosecutor. All the presumptions of law independent of evidence are in favor of innocence; and every person is presumed to be innocent until he is proved guilty. If upon such proof there is reasonable doubt remaining, the accused is entitled to the benefit of it by an acquittal.[55]

But all that leaves us with a question: Why is it being invoked *here*? Shannon Nelson—in *this* case—is not a criminal defendant, and she is no longer on trial. She was a criminal defendant, of course, twice. But there is no suggestion that in those trials she received anything

---

[51] Fox, The 'Presumption of Innocence' as Constitutional Doctrine, *supra* note 47, at 255 n. 8.

[52] U.S. v. Gooding, 12 Wheat. 460 (1827) (Story, J.).

[53] Thayer, The Presumption of Innocence in Criminal Cases, *supra* note 47, at 196 (emphasis added). See also *id.*, at 201-02 ("It seems to be true that the presumption of innocence, as applied in criminal cases, is a form of expression which requires to be supplemented by the rule as to the weight of evidence; that it is merely one form of phrase for what is included in the statement that an accused person is not to be prejudiced at his trial by having been charged with crime and held in custody, or by any mere suspicions, however grave; but is only to be held guilty when the government has established his guilt by legal evidence and beyond all reasonable doubt.").

[54] *Id.* at 196.

[55] Commonwealth v. Webster, 59 Mass. 295, 320 (1850).

less than the full protection of the "presumption of innocence"; in those trials, the burden had been correctly placed on the prosecutor to prove her guilt beyond a reasonable doubt. It's true that Colorado then placed the burden on *her* to prove her innocence in an Exoneration Act action; but that's a *civil* action in which she was the plaintiff, occurring after all criminal proceedings against her had been completed.[56] So why does due process require that she be permitted to invoke her "presumption of innocence" in a case where she is a claimant in a civil action against the state? If the presumption of innocence does no more than prescribe the burden of proof in a criminal proceeding, what relevance does it have for the case at hand?

Colorado pressed this very argument before the Court:

> The presumption of innocence applies only at criminal trials, not at hearings to establish compensation for defendants whose convictions have been overturned. *See Bell v. Wolfish,* 441 U.S. 520, 534 (1979) ("The presumption of innocence is a doctrine that allocates the burden of proof in criminal *trials*.").[57]

And Justice Alito's concurring opinion noted the apparent contradiction: the majority opinion "relies on a feature of the *criminal* law, the presumption of innocence," in holding that Nelson's payments must be refunded, while simultaneously denying that the case is "part of [Colorado's] *criminal* process" for purposes of determining the proper due process framework to apply.[58]

---

[56] See Nelson, 137 S. Ct. at 1255 (this case "concern[s] the continuing deprivation of property after a conviction has been reversed or vacated, with no prospect of reprosecution . . . [and] no further criminal process is implicated.").

[57] Nelson v. Colorado Brief for Respondent, Nelson v. Colorado, No. 15-1256, at 40 n. 19 (Dec. 14, 2016) (emphasis added), http://www.scotusblog.com/wp-content/uploads/2016/12/15-1256-respondent-merits-brief.pdf. The Court rejected Colorado's argument in these words:

> Colorado misapprehends *Wolfish.* Our opinion in that case recognized that "under the Due Process Clause," a detainee who "has not been adjudged guilty of any crime" may not be punished. 441 U.S., at 535-536; see *id.,* at 535-540. *Wolfish* held only that the presumption does not prevent the government from "detain[ing] a defendant] to ensure his presence at trial . . . so long as [the] conditions and restrictions [of his detention] do not amount to punishment."

Nelson, 137 S. Ct. at 1255 n.8.

[58] *Id.* at 1258 (Alito, J. concurring). Justice Alito, recall, see *supra* note 20, would have applied the more deferential *Medina* standard—in which due process requires only

That the Court rejected the argument, and denied the apparent contradiction, may prove significant in the civil forfeiture context if not elsewhere. The "presumption of innocence" to which the Court is referring—the one that was "restored" to Ms. Nelson after her prior conviction was overturned[59]—must encompass something more than the allocation of the burden of proof to the government in a criminal trial, because there is no longer any criminal trial on the horizon.

This has long been a secondary thread in "presumption of innocence" doctrine: the presumption encapsulates not just the requirement that the government prove guilt beyond a reasonable doubt in criminal trials, but more broadly it "describes our assumption that, in the absence of contrary facts, it is to be assumed that any person's conduct upon a given occasion was lawful."[60] Or, in the words of what was apparently the first colonial court to invoke the "presumption of innocence," in 1657, "in the eyes of the law everyone is honest and innocent unless it be proved legally to the contrary."[61] As Thayer put it:

> All who are brought before the tribunal "are taken, *prima facie, i.e.*, in the absence of evidence to the contrary, to be good, honest, free from blame, presumed to do their duty in every situation in life[,] so that no one need go forward, whether in pleading or proof, to show as regards himself or another, that the fact is so, but every one shall have it presumed in his favor.[62]

---

that Colorado not "offend a fundamental and deeply rooted principle of justice," because *Nelson* involved Colorado's "criminal process."

[59] Nelson, 137 S. Ct. at 1255 ("[O]nce those convictions were erased, the presumption of their innocence was restored.") (citing Johnson v. Mississippi, 486 U.S. 578, 585 (1988)).

[60] McCormick, Law of Evidence § 342.

[61] 16 Records of Massachusetts, III., 434, cited in Thayer, *supra* note 48, at 189.

[62] Thayer, The Presumption of Innocence, *supra* note 47, at 189. See also Jeffrey Thaler, Punishing the Innocent: The Need for Due Process and the Presumption of Innocence Prior to Trial, 1978 Wis. L. Rev. 441, 460 (1978) (quoting Thomas Starkie's influential 1832 treatise on the law of evidence for the principle that "the law always presumes in favour of innocence, as that a man's character is good until the contrary appear, or that he is innocent of an offense imputed to him till his guilt be proved)" The amicus brief submitted by the National Association of Criminal Defense Lawyers on behalf of Petitioners in the *Nelson* case has an extensive discussion of the historical precedents for this broader meaning of the "presumption of innocence."

This somewhat broader "presumption of innocence"—a "general rule of policy and sense" that *all persons* shall be assumed, in the absence of evidence, to be "good, honest, and free from blame"—is applicable in civil as well as criminal proceedings. It is related to the notion invoked by the American colonists in their anger over the Sugar and Stamp Acts of 1764–65,[63] and it runs, Thayer notes, "through all the law."[64] If the Court is signaling here that it is prepared to recognize this broader meaning, this may give the "presumption of innocence" a new and important role in the civil forfeiture arena.

V. Justice Thomas's Dissent

Finally, a word about Justice Thomas's dissenting opinion. He begins with the uncontroversial assertion that to prevail on her due process claim, Nelson "must first point to a recognized property interest in that money, under state or federal law"; you can't, in other words, be "deprive[d] . . . of . . . property without due process of law" unless that of which you have been deprived is *your* property—*that is*, unless you can show some "substantive entitlement" to it.[65] Conversely, if Nelson "do[es] *not* have a substantive right to recover the money—that is, if the money belongs to the State—then Colorado need not provide any procedure to give it back."[66]

And in this case, he goes on to say, the money Nelson seeks does indeed belong to the state. She does not have any substantive right, under state or federal law, to those funds—not anymore. The Colorado Supreme Court held, in the decision here under review, that

---

[63] "Taxation without representation" was the primary, but not the only, source of colonial anger against the two statutes. The "most onerous provisions of the [acts]" provided that merchants whose vessels were seized for alleged customs violations "bore the burden of proving that they were *not* involved in smuggling," which was "a constant source of irritation to the American colonists." Matthew P. Harrington, The Legacy of the Colonial Vice-Admiralty Courts (Part II), 27 J. Maritime L. & Comm. 323, 332–36 (1996) (emphasis added). See generally David S. Lovejoy, Rights Imply Equality: The Case Against Admiralty Jurisdiction in America, 1764–1776, 16 Wm. & Mary Quarterly, 459 (1959); Carl Ubbelohde, The Vice-Admiralty Courts and the American Revolution, 126-42, 154–58 (1960).

[64] Thayer, The Presumption of Innocence, *supra* note 47, at 189.

[65] Nelson, 137 S. Ct. at 1264 (Thomas, J., dissenting).

[66] *Id.* at 1263 (emphasis added) (internal quotation marks omitted).

"moneys lawfully exacted pursuant to a valid conviction become public funds . . . under Colorado law."[67]

The money that Nelson seeks, in other words, is not "her money" at all; it is Colorado's. It used to be "her money," and, when it was, the state could not deprive her of it without providing her with due process. It had done so—in her original criminal trial, where she received the full panoply of due process protections (trial by jury, proof beyond a reasonable doubt, etc.) before fees and costs were imposed on her. And once the money had been "lawfully exacted pursuant to a valid conviction,"[68] state law decreed that it became the state's money. Colorado could, if it chose, provide her with a mechanism to obtain reimbursement (as it had done in the Exoneration Act), but the Due Process Clause did not require it to do so.[69] Nor did the Due Process Clause limit the conditions—such as proof of actual innocence—it could place on receipt of those funds.

I admit that I initially found Justice Thomas's position here difficult to understand, or to square with his views as something of a civil-forfeiture hawk.[70] As I wrote shortly after the opinion was handed down:

> [It's] enough to send chills down the spine of any right-thinking libertarian out there, I would think. The state gets to define the conditions under which it can turn *your* property into *its* property; then, if you want to get it back (because you don't in fact fulfill the conditions that they set), the state doesn't have to prove that the seizure was lawful; you have the burden of proving (by clear and convincing evidence) that it was not!
>
> It's another way of saying: Once the state takes your money and calls it its own, we presume that it had a good reason for

---

[67] *Id.* at 1264.

[68] *Id.*

[69] *Id.* at 1266 ("In the absence of any property right under state law (apart from the right provided by the Exoneration Act, which petitioners decline to invoke) . . . Colorado is therefore not required to provide *any process at all* for the return of that money") (emphasis added).

[70] See *supra*, text accompanying notes 38–42.

doing so, and we'll give it back to you only if you prove that
it didn't have a good reason for doing so.[71]

That may have been overstating the case, and I now see that Justice Thomas's position has a logic, and even a certain elegance, to it. Where, after all, *does* Nelson's right to this money come from?

I think the answer to that question is this: from the "presumption of innocence," broadly conceived. The majority opinion says as much, albeit somewhat obliquely. Colorado may declare, as the dissent puts it, that "'moneys lawfully exacted pursuant to a valid conviction become public funds.'"[72] But "the convictions pursuant to which the State took petitioners' money were *invalid*, hence the State had no legal right to retain their money."[73] As the Court described:

> Colorado urges ... that the funds belong to the State because [Nelson's] convictions were in place when the funds were taken. ... *But once those convictions were erased, the presumption of their innocence was restored.* See, *e.g.*, *Johnson v. Mississippi*, 486 U.S. 578, 585 (1988) (After a "conviction has been reversed, unless and until [the defendant] should be retried, he must be presumed innocent of that charge."). ... Colorado may not presume a person, adjudged guilty of no crime, nonetheless guilty *enough* for monetary exactions.")[74]

The Court noted that

> under the Due Process Clause, [an individual] who has not been adjudged guilty of any crime may not be punished.[75]

---

[71] David Post, Whose Money Is It? Clarence Thomas and the Due Process Clause, Volokh Conspiracy, Wash. Post, Apr. 21, 2017, https://www.washingtonpost.com/news/volokh-conspiracy/wp/2017/04/21/whose-money-is-it-clarence-thomas-and-the-due-process-clause.

[72] Nelson, 137 S. Ct. at 1256 n. 11.

[73] *Id.*

[74] *Id.* at 1255–56 (emphasis added).

[75] *Id.* at 1255 n.8. See also Arkadelphia Milling Co. v. St. Louis Southwestern Ry. Co., 249 U.S. 134, 145 (1919) ("[A] party against whom an erroneous judgment or decree has been carried into effect is entitled, in the event of a reversal, to be restored by his adversary to that which he has lost thereby. This right, so well founded in equity, has been recognized in the practice of the courts of common law from an early period.").

As Justice Hood noted in his state-court dissent, "an invalid conviction is no conviction at all."[76] Colorado law must recognize, to the extent possible, that Nelson's conviction never happened, and that, once her convictions have been voided, she now stands, like any other citizen, before the tribunal as one who is "good, honest, and free from blame."[77] Colorado may not constitutionally declare that the funds Nelson paid owing to an *invalid* conviction belong to the state, because the "presumption of innocence" requires restoring her, to the extent possible, to the position she was in prior to her conviction, with all her rights, including her property rights, intact.

Conclusion

Nelson v. Colorado is in some ways a very small case, although I'm not sure I'd go quite as far as the commenter to one of my blog postings about the case, who wrote: "It took seven Supreme Court Judges (and how many lower court judges, and lawyers?) to conclude what is readily apparent to anyone with an ounce of common sense?" As I mentioned earlier, no state imposes as high a burden as Colorado did here on persons seeking a return of property that was taken from them as a consequence of a criminal conviction subsequently invalidated. So striking down Colorado's perhaps inadvertent attempt to do so will have little direct impact on the American legal ecosystem.

But at the same time, a small but not trivial number of people—several hundred, at least—have their criminal convictions overturned nationwide each year.[78] The decision may prove important to them, to the extent that it prohibits states from imposing "anything more than minimal procedures" on the return of their property.[79]

[76] Nelson, 362 P. 3d, at 1080 (Hood, J., dissenting).

[77] See *supra,* text accompanying notes 60–64.

[78] This is not intended as anything other than a very rough estimate. I'm not aware of authoritative statistics on the question; my guess is based on extrapolating from two studies, one in California and one in Colorado, showing an average of around 50 and 30 overturned convictions, respectively, in the two states. See The Chief Justice Earl Warren Institute on Law and Social Policy, Berkeley School of Law, Criminal Injustice: A Cost Analysis of Wrongful Convictions, Errors, and Failed Prosecutions in California's Criminal Justice System (2015), http://tinyurl.com/y9loqt8a. (California); Amicus Brief on Colorado Criminal Defense Bar In Support of Petition for a Writ of Certiorari, Nelson v. Colorado, No. 15-1256 (Jun. 10, 2016), http://www.scotusblog.com/wp-content/uploads/2016/06/CCDB-Amicus-Nelson.pdf (Colorado).

[79] Nelson, 137 S. Ct. at 1258.

Beyond that important, but relatively narrow, compass, if the decision presages a Supreme Court, or lower courts, more disposed to recognize a somewhat stronger, more muscular "presumption of innocence" outside the confines of the criminal process, that could have substantial consequences indeed for the law. For that, only time will tell.

Expressions Hair Design: Detangling the Commercial-Free-Speech Knot

*Mark Chenoweth**

As dads of daughters with long hair soon learn, one can spend quite a while detangling a particularly nasty rat's nest. Patience is the primary key to success. Working slowly to avoid further damage, combing through the problem area in sections, and using a large-tooth comb (never a broad brush) are other important steps to follow. The U.S. Supreme Court took a similarly painstaking approach to detangling the commercial-free-speech issues in the three credit-card-surcharge cases it reviewed during October Term 2016. It thereby straightened out the mess that the U.S. Court of Appeals for the Second Circuit had made of *Expressions Hair Design v. Schneiderman*, further clarified the law with its actions on other cases from the Fifth and Eleventh Circuits, and repaired an important area of First Amendment doctrine.[1]

Each of the three cases—*Expressions Hair, Rowell v. Pettijohn,* and *Dana's Railroad Supply v. Bondi*—posed the same basic question: Does it violate the First Amendment to force merchants who want to charge more for credit-card purchases to style their differential prices as a discount for cash rather than a surcharge for credit? Nearly everyone agrees in these cases that it would be fine to post one price as the regular price, charge that price for credit transactions, and give a discount to cash customers. Nearly everyone also agrees that it would be perfectly lawful to post two separate prices for each product: the cash price and the credit price. The problem arises when a merchant wishes to characterize the price difference as a "surcharge" for credit. Whether such a merchant wishes to explain why it charges

*Adjunct professor, Antonin Scalia Law School. The author wishes to thank Laura Scully Chenoweth and an anonymous reviewer for helpful feedback on earlier drafts of this article.

[1] Expressions Hair Design v. Schneiderman, 137 S. Ct. 1144 (2017).

more to its customers using credit cards, to deter credit purchases, or simply to be free from government dictates, the dilemma remains the same: Is this dispute about speech or merely conduct, and, if the former, does the First Amendment protect the merchant's speech?

Lest one think these are easy questions, a cursory review of the paths these three cases followed to the Supreme Court will dispel that notion—as well as any idea that this controversy is a proxy for some partisan fight. *Expressions Hair* saw the New York statute struck down at the district court level by a Democrat-appointed judge;[2] a three-judge panel of Republican appointees at the Second Circuit then reversed to uphold the statute.[3] In *Rowell v. Pettijohn*, a Republican-appointed district court judge upheld the Texas statute,[4] and a divided Fifth Circuit upheld that ruling with two Republican appointees in the majority over the dissent of a Democratic appointee.[5] Finally, in *Dana's Railroad Supply v. Bondi*,[6] a Democrat-appointed district judge upheld the Florida statute only to see a divided three-judge panel of Republican appointees at the Eleventh Circuit reverse and strike down the state law.[7] Such a tortuous path to the Supreme Court, escorted by a wide array of judges on all sides, does not bespeak a simple issue.[8]

Some quick-take commentators contended that *Expressions Hair* did not accomplish much because it ultimately left First Amendment

[2] Expressions Hair Design v. Schneiderman, 975 F. Supp. 2d 430, 444, 447 (S.D.N.Y. 2013) (Rakoff, J.).

[3] Expressions Hair Design v. Schneiderman, 808 F.3d 118 (2d Cir. 2015) (amending and superseding 803 F.3d 94 (2d Cir. 2015)).

[4] Rowell v. Pettijohn, No. A-14-CA-190-LY, 2015 U.S. Dist. LEXIS 40739 (W.D. Tex. Feb. 4, 2015).

[5] Rowell v. Pettijohn, 816 F.3d 73 (5th Cir. 2016).

[6] Dana's R.R. Supply v. Bondi, No. 14-cv-134 2014 WL 11189176 (N.D. Fla. Sept. 2, 2014); Dana's R.R. Supply v. Att'y Gen. of Fla., 807 F.3d 1235 (11th Cir. 2015).

[7] For good measure, the federal district court in the Ninth Circuit case Italian Colors Restaurant v. Harris, 99 F. Supp. 3d 1199 (E.D. Cal. 2015), appeal docketed, No. 15-15873 (9th Cir. Apr. 30, 2015), featured a Republican-appointed district judge who struck down California's law. Thus, across four district courts, one Republican appointee struck down a state statute (CA) and another upheld one (TX). Likewise, one Democrat appointee struck down a state statute (NY) and another upheld one (FL).

[8] Together with a fourth case from California that awaits decision by the Ninth Circuit, these cases represented state laws from the four largest U.S. states by population, totaling nearly one-third of the national population across them—an oft-overlooked indicator of the significance of cases like these.

analysis up to the Second Circuit on remand. Closer inspection reveals that the Court's cautious treatment of the three related credit-card-surcharge cases achieved quite a lot. Even within just the *Expressions Hair* opinion itself, the Court did some deft work. This essay proceeds by explaining what the Court held in that case and why that holding is both new and significant. Then it describes what the Fifth Circuit said in *Rowell*, what the Eleventh Circuit said in *Dana's Railroad Supply*, and what the high court did with them. Finally, the essay steps back to view this triptych of cases as a whole. By identifying the similarities and differences among these cases—and their outcomes—it teases out the greater significance of the Supreme Court's nuanced treatment of this subject and predicts what the Second Circuit will decide on remand in *Expressions Hair Design*.

I. State Anti-Surcharge Laws and Their Federal Roots

Some important (and relatively uncontested) federal statutory background explains why three credit-card-surcharge cases reached the Supreme Court at the same time. Congress enacted amendments to the Truth in Lending Act (TILA) in 1974 that prohibited credit-card companies from forbidding discounts for cash in their contracts with merchants.[9] Two years later, Congress amended TILA to forbid surcharges by merchants for use of credit cards. It also added definitions of "discount" and "surcharge." Then, in 1981, Congress passed the Cash Discount Act (CDA), which defined "regular price" as either the single price marked or as the credit price (if separate cash and credit prices were posted).[10] Because TILA defined a surcharge as "increasing the regular price," and the regular price was defined as the credit-card price, the CDA essentially made it so that the only way to violate the law was to mark a single price and then charge credit-card customers more than that marked price. The surcharge ban lapsed in 1984 and Congress has never revived it, but it lived on as the model for a dozen state-level copycat statutes.[11] That very

---

[9] Fair Credit Billing Act, Pub. L. No. 93-495, Tit. III, § 306, 88 Stat. 1515.

[10] Cash Discount Act, Pub. L. No. 97-25, Tit. I, § 102(a), 95 Stat. 144.

[11] Cal. Civ. Code § 1748.1(a); Colo. Rev. Stat. § 5-2-212; Conn. Gen. Stat. § 42-133ff; Fla. Stat. § 501.0117; Kan. Stat. Ann. § 16a-2-403; Mass. Gen. Laws ch. 140D, § 28A(a)(1)-(2); Me. Rev. Stat. tit. 9-A, § 8-509; Miss. Code Ann. § 31-7-9(d); N. Y. Gen. Bus.Law § 518; Okla. Stat. tit. 14A, §2-211; Tex. Fin. Code § 339.001(a); Utah Code Ann. § 13-38a-302 (2013), repealed by § 63I-1-213 (2014).

same year New York passed its version of the surcharge ban, borrowing the federal statute's prohibitory language, but leaving out the definition of "surcharge."

Predictably, credit-card companies resumed including anti-surcharge provisions in their contracts with businesses once the federal prohibition was no longer in effect. Because those agreements specifically prohibited businesses from describing any price difference as a surcharge for using credit, the state laws did not come into play at first. That is, state attorneys general had no need to enforce the statutes because the credit-card companies had contractual remedies available to enforce the prohibitions themselves. As part of an antitrust class-action lawsuit settlement reached in 2013, however, the major credit-card companies agreed to strike no-surcharge provisions from their contracts with merchants. This move awakened the long-dormant state laws at exactly the same time, so state attorneys general began to enforce them—presumably with some encouragement from the credit-card companies. Hence, once the credit-card companies dropped their contract clauses prohibiting surcharges, three cases reached the U.S. Supreme Court in quick succession.

In New York, Expressions Hair Design, Brooklyn Farmacy [sic] & Soda Fountain, and three other businesses (and their owners/managers) sued the New York attorney general and three district attorneys to enjoin enforcement of New York General Business Law § 518 as the only remaining barrier to discussing their prices freely with customers. These plaintiffs brought an "as applied" challenge to a single-sticker pricing regime in which a merchant quotes one price for a good or service and wishes to advertise a higher price for payment with a credit card. Specifically, they claimed that § 518 violates the First Amendment by controlling how they characterize the price differences they charge. In addition, they challenged the law as unconstitutionally vague because it assigns liability based on the hazy distinction between discounts and surcharges. They contended that the New York law did not make it sufficiently clear exactly what merchants could and could not say in relaying their prices.

II. Order of the Coif: The Supreme Court's *Expressions Hair Design* Decision

Chief Justice John Roberts coiffed a careful, albeit brief, opinion for the Court that Justices Anthony Kennedy, Clarence Thomas, Ruth Bader Ginsburg, and Elena Kagan joined in its entirety, while Justices Stephen Breyer, Sonia Sotomayor, and Samuel Alito concurred in the judgment. The heart of the decision first noted the limited nature of the petitioners' case. Although the court of appeals had treated their challenge to § 518 as a facial one, Roberts observed that petitioners had clarified at oral argument that they were bringing only an as-applied challenge to the single-sticker pricing format. The only challenged application of the law, the Court noted, is where a merchant "post[s] a cash price and an additional credit card surcharge, expressed either as a percentage surcharge or a 'dollars-and-cents' additional amount."[12]

Having thus narrowed the scope of the debate, the chief justice asked whether § 518 prohibits the petitioners' preferred pricing practice, as the court of appeals held, and he concluded that it does. The court of appeals had looked to the dictionary definition of "surcharge" because the New York statute (unlike its federal predecessor) fails to define the term. Because the appeals court's interpretation was not "clearly wrong," the Court followed customary practice and deferred to its interpretation of state law, finding that, "[w]here a seller posts a single sticker price, it is reasonable to treat that sticker price as the 'usual or normal amount' and conclude . . . that a merchant imposes a surcharge when he charges a credit card user more than that sticker price."[13]

Given that New York law so construed prohibits petitioners' desired pricing regime, the Court next considered whether it "unconstitutionally regulates speech."[14] The Second Circuit had

---

[12] Expressions Hair, 137 S. Ct. at 1149.

[13] *Id*. at 1150.

[14] Although the merchants also made a void-for-vagueness argument, the Court made short work of it. Even if the scope of the statute remains unsettled, the Court reasoned, the merchants' challenge sought only to vindicate one clearly forbidden pricing practice. Since "the law is not vague as applied to them," the merchants could not prevail. Expressions Hair, 137 S. Ct. at 1151–52 (citing Holder v. Humanitarian Law Project, 561 U.S. 1, 20 (2010) ("[A] plaintiff whose speech is clearly proscribed cannot raise a successful vagueness claim.")). By insisting at oral argument that they

concluded that § 518 does not implicate the First Amendment because the law regulates conduct rather than speech. It read the law to govern the mere relationship of the seller's sticker price to the price charged to credit-card customers, "requiring that these two amounts be equal."[15] Just as a law governing a single price does not regulate speech, it reasoned, so too a law governing how two prices relate to each other does not: "[P]rices (though necessarily communicated through language) are not 'speech' . . . when considered in relation to one another. Because all that Section 518 prohibits is a specific relationship between two prices, it does not regulate speech."[16]

But the Supreme Court recognized that "§ 518 is not like a typical price regulation."[17] Whereas typical price regulations dictate how much a store can collect for a good or service, New York's statute "tells merchants nothing about the amount they are allowed to collect from a cash or credit card payer."[18] Instead, it "regulate[s] . . . how sellers may communicate their prices."[19] "A merchant . . . may not convey that price any way he pleases" but rather "must display [the higher price charged to credit-card customers] as his sticker price."[20] While reiterating *Sorrell*'s admonition that "the First Amendment does not prevent restrictions directed at commerce or conduct from imposing incidental burdens on speech[,]" the Court did not consider the law's curbs on merchants' speech as a mere incidental burden accompanying primarily a conduct restriction.[21] To the contrary,

---

were bringing an as-applied challenge rather than a facial challenge, the plaintiffs essentially abandoned their void-for-vagueness claim. On the other hand, the plaintiffs might not have been able to win a facial challenge outright given both the confusion about what the statute required, which perplexed a large fraction of the Court, and the lack of a textual hook for the petitioners' surcharge/discount argument in the New York statute as compared to the laws from Florida and Texas. There has to be only one constitutional interpretation of the statute in order to survive a facial challenge, and there appears to be one available here, albeit it was not the interpretation that was enforced against these petitioners.

15 *Id.* at 1150 (citing 808 F.3d at 131).

16 Expressions Hair, 808 F.3d at 131.

17 Expressions Hair, 137 S. Ct. at 1150.

18 *Id.* at 1151.

19 *Id.*

20 *Id.*

21 Sorrell v. IMS Health Inc., 564 U.S. 552, 567 (2011).

the Court held, "[i]n regulating the communication of prices rather than prices themselves, § 518 regulates speech."[22]

Because the Second Circuit's resolution of the case sidestepped the First Amendment question, the Court next faced whether to analyze the constitutionality of New York's statute in the first instance. It declined. Even though the federal district court had reviewed the law under the First Amendment before striking it down, the court of appeals did not. So the Supreme Court begged off, as a court of review. In remanding the case with instructions to evaluate the statute as a speech regulation, the Court pointed out that the parties' briefs contested both the validity of § 518 under the *Central Hudson* test and whether it might be construed as a permissible mandatory disclosure statute under *Zauderer v. Office of Disciplinary Counsel*.[23]

Such a half-a-loaf holding did not come as much of a surprise. In fact, speculation ensued after oral argument that the Court might "DIG" the case entirely—that is, dismiss it as improvidently granted. The theory ran that several justices did not appear to be clear on the meaning of the statute and how it was being enforced in New York State. But instead of DIG-ing the case, the Court definitively held that the statute regulates speech rather than conduct, thereby requiring First Amendment analysis in this context.

Another reason this result did not surprise is that the Court did almost precisely what the solicitor general's brief recommended that the Court do. "The Court would provide an appropriate level of guidance on the question presented in this case by clarifying that Section 518 regulates speech. . . . The Court could then remand for the court of appeals . . . to determine the grounds on which respondents are defending Section 518 and to evaluate the statute's constitutionality in light of those defenses."[24]

---

[22] Expressions Hair, 137 S. Ct. at 1151.

[23] Central Hudson Gas & Elec. Corp. v. Pub. Serv. Comm'n of N.Y., 447 U.S. 557, 566 (1980); Zauderer v. Office of Disciplinary Counsel, 471 U.S. 626 (1985).

[24] See Brief for the United States as Amicus Curiae Supporting Neither Party at 34–35, Expressions Hair Design v. Schneiderman, 137 S. Ct. 1144 (2017) (No. 15-1391); see also *id*. at 19 ("Because Section 518 addresses the *communication* of an otherwise-permissible pricing scheme, rather than the pricing scheme *itself*, it is properly considered a regulation of speech.") (emphasis in original).

III. Running with Scissors: Bad Ideas in the Concurrences in Judgment

Justice Breyer's solo opinion concurring in the judgment reads more like a dissent. Given that he recently has been the Court's most ardent antagonist of commercial-free-speech rights, that position holds true to form.[25] Breyer's opinion interweaves three strands that bear analyzing more closely: *Lochner*,[26] former Yale Law School Dean Robert Post, and *Carolene Products*.[27]

Breyer's first concern surfaced at oral argument, where he put his objection starkly:

> [W]e are diving headlong into an area called price regulation. It . . . goes on all over the place in regulatory agencies. And so the word that I fear begins with an L and ends with an R; it's called *Loc[h]ner*. . . . Using the First Amendment as a tool to get at price regulation . . . [i]f you want to know what's worrying me, that's it.[28]

Breyer's invocation of the *Lochner* watchword signals his concern that respecting commercial-free-speech rights might somehow lead to judges' negating or supplanting legislative decisions regarding ordinary economic regulation—as he believes they did in the *Lochner* era—only now in the service of free speech rather than economic liberty or freedom of contract. As he put it later in the oral argument:

> [T]he Court should stay out of this under normal First Amendment standards. Because if we don't, we are going to discover all kinds of price regulation all over the place that suffers to greater or lesser degrees from this kind of problem, and you'll have judges all over the country substituting for regulators and others in trying to regulate.[29]

---

[25] See, Sorrell v. IMS Health Inc., 564 U.S., 580–81 (Breyer, J., dissenting); Reed v. Town of Gilbert, Ariz., 135 S. Ct. 2218, 2234 (2015) (Breyer, J., concurring in the judgment only).

[26] Lochner v. New York, 198 U.S. 45 (1905).

[27] United States v. Carolene Products Co., 304 U.S. 144 (1938).

[28] Transcript of Oral Arg. at 22, Expressions Hair Design v. Schneiderman, 137 S. Ct. 1144 (2017) (No. 15-1391).

[29] *Id.* at 47.

Breyer conceded at oral argument that he "may be the only one that . . . ha[s] this *Loc[h]ner* problem,"[30] but the discussion below will show that at least some lower courts share similar concerns.

To those who follow commercial-free-speech debates closely, Breyer's reference early in his opinion to Robert Post's scholarship provides the second clue to where he's coming from. An ongoing push by academics in the law schools, law journals, and the broader public square has sought to delegitimize commercial-free-speech rights. The origins and causes of that phenomenon fall outside the scope of the present article, but suffice it to say that Post has been perhaps the foremost protagonist in this drive to undermine First Amendment protection for commercial expression.[31] But the fact that no one else joined Breyer's opinion may well indicate that the Court will not bend to the winds of academe on this point.

Breyer assiduously prefers not to inquire whether a given regulation targets speech or conduct at all. He would just evaluate regulations by what kind of First Amendment interest they implicate, giving the greatest scrutiny where political discourse is involved, lesser scrutiny to commercial speech, and still lesser scrutiny where a mandatory disclosure simply seeks to prevent consumer deception. He is at pains to ensure that the First Amendment not interfere with applying a "permissive standard of review to 'regulatory legislation affecting ordinary commercial transactions.'"[32] He appears far less concerned about taking sides in the speech/conduct dichotomy than in embracing the *Carolene Products* side of the *Lochner/Carolene Products* dichotomy.

While still styling his opinion a concurrence in the judgment, Breyer agrees that § 518 governs speech only "because virtually all government regulation affects speech."[33] In other words, his agreement is in name only. He also endorses the majority's decision to

---

[30] *Id.* at 46.

[31] See, e.g., Gilad Edelman, The Supreme Court's First Amendment Problem, Yale Alumni Magazine, Vol. LXXX, No. 1, at 34 (Sept./Oct. 2016) (discussing Post's views at length); see also Martin H. Redish, The Adversary First Amendment: Free Expression and the Foundations of American Democracy at 29–74 (2013) (critiquing Post's participatory democracy conception of the First Amendment).

[32] Expressions Hair, 137 S. Ct. at 1152 (Breyer, J., concurring) (quoting United States v. Carolene Products Co., 304 U.S. 144, 152 (1938)).

[33] *Id.* at 1152.

remand the case to the Second Circuit but joins Justices Sotomayor and Alito's later (strong) suggestion that the appeals court certify a question to the New York Court of Appeals seeking clarification as to the statute's meaning. Ultimately, Breyer concludes that "it is not clear just what New York's law does" and so he offers conditional applications of the First Amendment depending on how the law gets interpreted.[34] Yet all those that he limns would apply standards deferential enough for the statute to survive review.

Justice Sotomayor's opinion concurring in the judgment, which slightly exceeds Chief Justice Roberts's opinion for the Court in length, takes issue both with the Second Circuit's failure to certify the statutory interpretation question to the New York Court of Appeals (the state's highest court) and her own Court majority's unwillingness to do the same—as well as its failure to resolve more than a portion of the case. Joined by Justice Alito, she advocates certification as the appropriate course of action, even on remand, seeing that as the only way to "permit the full resolution of petitioner's claims."[35]

Like Justice Breyer, Sotomayor suggests that "a federal court's resolution of the constitutional question may turn out to be unnecessary."[36] That is, if the New York Court of Appeals were to interpret the statute as simply requiring that cash and credit customers be charged the same price, then it would be an economic regulation subject only to rational-basis review. And so Sotomayor would have asked New York's highest court "What pricing schemes or pricing displays does § 518 prohibit?"[37] Even if certification did not avoid unnecessarily tackling the First Amendment question, she says, it "might have limited the scope of the constitutional challenge in the case."[38]

The fundamental problem with the Sotomayor/Alito approach is that the *Expressions Hair* petitioners brought an as-applied objection, so they already limited the scope of their constitutional challenge. Asking the state's highest court to identify all the schemes that the statute would prohibit is thus too broad a question, because it

[34] *Id.* at 1153.

[35] *Id.* at 1153 (Sotomayor, J., concurring).

[36] *Id.* at 1156.

[37] *Id.* at 1158.

[38] *Id.*

would be seeking an advisory opinion under these circumstances. The only statutory question properly before the Court—and the only one it might have been appropriate to certify—is whether the statute forbids the particular pricing scheme petitioners challenge. And the majority has now resolved that question in the affirmative, which is how it dispensed with the void-for-vagueness argument.

Inviting the Second Circuit on remand to come up with a different answer to this question (or advising it to certify that question to the New York Court of Appeals), as Sotomayor does, risks taking a knotty problem and making it worse. In theory, those courts might construe the statute "only as a price regulation" in such a way as to avoid the constitutional question, but there is likely an insurmountable obstacle to doing so.[39] Because longstanding practice and the aforementioned federal Cash Discount Act—which formed the background for New York's law—allow merchants to give a discount to cash customers, interpreting the New York (or Florida or Texas) statute to mean that merchants must charge identical prices to cash and credit customers is highly problematic.

Adopting such an interpretation would moot the Supreme Court's decision that New York General Business Law § 518 regulates speech and would postpone answering a First Amendment question simultaneously presented in two other certiorari petitions. The appeals court surely must recognize that undercutting the Supreme Court in that fashion would discredit the lower court as well. Hence, Justice Sotomayor's preferred approach might have made sense as an original matter, but it no longer does. Had the Second Circuit gone that route, or had the Supreme Court majority vacated the Second Circuit's opinion and instructed it to seek certification on remand (without deciding the speech/conduct question), that might have led to a satisfactory resolution of the case. But doing so at this juncture would only make a mess of things. Besides, even if the majority had gone this route, Sotomayor's solution would not have resolved the Fifth and Eleventh Circuit cases with the clarity that the majority's actions provided.

[39] *Id.*

IV. A Little Dab'll Do Ya: Why *Expressions Hair*'s Minimalist Holding Matters

Some commentators have slighted the Court's ruling in *Expressions Hair*, arguing that Chief Justice Roberts artificially manufactured unanimity by avoiding the central question in the case. That interpretation misreads what happened here. If the Court had wanted to sidestep, it could have followed Justice Sotomayor's suggested path. By instead eschewing the certification option and addressing whether state laws like New York's regulate speech, the chief justice's majority opinion broke new constitutional ground. Whether § 518 regulates speech or merely conduct was the central question this case presented, and the Court answered it directly. By deciding that "regulating the communication of prices . . . regulates speech," the Court did not answer whether this statute survives scrutiny under the First Amendment (or even what standard of review applies).[40] But that limited holding did accomplish several things.

First, the holding rescues commercial free speech from a tautology. Some lower courts, including the federal district court for the Western District of Texas in the *Rowell* case, have tried to sidestep any impact that credit-card surcharge laws have on the First Amendment by arguing that speech quoting an illegal price is unprotected. From the very beginning of commercial-free-speech doctrine, the Supreme Court has emphasized that speech concerning unlawful activity does not come within the ambit of First Amendment protection.[41] Indeed, the first prong of the *Central Hudson* test asks whether speech concerns lawful activity and is not misleading. Fail to satisfy that prong and the rest of the test does not matter.

If Congress or state legislatures could simply forbid speech about certain topics or, in this case, prevent describing a transaction in a particular way and then negate any First Amendment challenge to that ban on the rationale that the speech concerned illegal conduct, there would be very few speech restrictions that the First Amendment would preclude. "Congress shall make no law . . . abridging the freedom of speech" would mean little in the commercial-speech context. Fortunately, consistent with the strict scrutiny it applies to

---

40 *Id.* at 1146.

41 See Pittsburgh Press Co. v. Human Relations Comm'n, 413 U.S. 376 (1973).

content-based speech restrictions after *Town of Gilbert*, the Court's holding in *Expressions Hair* thwarts that source of mischief.[42]

Second, the Court's holding directly refutes the notion, propounded by the Second Circuit, that this statute governs conduct rather than speech. By establishing that regulating the communication of prices *does* regulate speech, the Court laid down an important marker. Contrary to Justice Breyer's view, it held that there *is* a line of demarcation between mere conduct and speech for the First Amendment to patrol. Although this decision does not specify where or how to locate that line, it countermands those lower courts that have behaved as though such laws simply do not regulate speech. In so doing, it throws a lifeline to citizens everywhere who confront statutes seeking to constrain them from uttering truthful and nonmisleading speech in the marketplace.

Just as important, the holding deprives lower courts of a shortcut to evade First Amendment scrutiny and compels them to analyze these laws under usual First Amendment tests, rather than the mere rational-basis review accorded to economic regulations. Likewise, legislators writing laws in this area now know that they cannot mischaracterize the regulation of speech as the regulation of conduct and thereby escape the Court's newly heightened scrutiny for commercial speech. In this way, *Expressions Hair* acts as a kind of backstop to *IMS Health* and *Town of Gilbert*.

Holding that this law governs speech (and not conduct) does not open the door to *Lochner*. Justice Breyer's concurrence in judgment does not repeat the concern that he voiced at oral argument, so perhaps he came to the same conclusion himself. At any rate, a sure sign that this decision does not list in *Lochner*'s direction is that Justices Ginsburg and Kagan joined it. To be sure, some academics from the "nudge" school of regulation urged the Court not to reject New York's statute.[43] But this holding does not foreclose all nudge-style

---

[42] As noted above, the federal district court in Texas employed this circularity in *Rowell*. Another federal court in Texas likewise discounted First Amendment objections to the Department of Labor's Fiduciary Rule. See Chamber of Commerce of the United States of America v. Hugler, 3:16-cv-1476, 2017 U.S. Dist. LEXIS 17619 (N.D. Tex. Feb. 8, 2017).

[43] See Brief for Constitutional, Administrative, Contracts, and Health Law Scholars as Amici Curiae in Support of Respondents, Expressions Hair Design v. Schneiderman, 137 S. Ct. 1144 (2017) (No. 15-1391).

regulation any more than it embraces *Lochner*. Rather, consistent with existing compelled-speech First Amendment jurisprudence, this ruling merely requires regulation that implicates the First Amendment to satisfy a level of scrutiny greater than rational-basis review. Or, if the government wishes to tip the regulatory scales in favor of one choice over another, it must do so through use of its own speech rather than commandeering or forbidding the speech of other actors in the marketplace in a content-discriminatory manner. Such a restriction on regulators promotes freedom and fidelity to longstanding First Amendment principles.

The final point to make about the Court's minimalist holding is that it may have helped assemble a somewhat unusual coalition. Chief Justice Roberts managed to sway Justices Ginsburg and Kagan to sign on to his opinion, both of whom joined Justice Breyer's dissent in *IMS Health* and merely concurred in the judgment (along with Breyer) in *Town of Gilbert*. At the same time, the chief justice lost Justices Sotomayor and Alito, both of whom had joined the majorities in *IMS Health* and *Town of Gilbert*. Because they did not write separately, any speculation as to why Ginsburg and Kagan joined the Court's opinion is uncertain at best. But the Court's choice to remand the question of how to apply the First Amendment to these facts may have papered over any differences these two justices have had with the Court's recent commercial-free-speech jurisprudence.

Moreover, judging by what these justices said at oral argument, they seem genuinely to perceive the statute to regulate the expression of prices rather than prices themselves. Justice Ginsburg observed, "It doesn't set any price at all. It lets the merchant set the price. And the question is how that price is described . . . New York is not regulating . . . the price of the goods."[44] Likewise, Justice Kagan observed, "So it does affect the way a seller communicates which price he's going to say is the regular price, is the list price. So why isn't that a speech regulation?"[45] In short, to them, because the statute dictates how a merchant can express prices, it regulates speech and thus is subject to First Amendment scrutiny. So they were on board with remanding the statute for such analysis. That these two justices in particular do not appear to be alarmed by the distinct

[44] Transcript of Oral Arg., *supra* note 28, at 49.
[45] *Id.* at 51.

possibility that appropriate First Amendment scrutiny will torpedo a regulation is a positive development for defenders of commercial speech.

V. Lather, Rinse, Repeat: Does the GVR in *Rowell* Have Separate Significance?

Having partially resolved the questions presented in *Expressions Hair* on March 29, five days later the Court granted, vacated, and remanded ("GVR'd") the certiorari petition filed in the Fifth Circuit's *Rowell v. Pettijohn* case. Like the Second Circuit, the Fifth Circuit panel had upheld the state statute it reviewed. Also like the Second Circuit, the Fifth Circuit had held that Texas's statute regulated conduct, not speech (or speech only incidental to an economic-conduct regulation)—allowing it to sidestep any elaborate First Amendment analysis. A third similarity is that both the New York and Texas statutes fail to define "discount" and "surcharge." In fact, the Fifth Circuit's reasoning tracked the Second Circuit's logic so closely (and quoted its language so extensively) that the Supreme Court had little choice but to remand *Rowell* in light of its *Expressions Hair* decision.

Nonetheless, a few key differences in the cases are worth noting. First, the Texas statute, unlike the New York one, is civil only. While that difference does not alter the First Amendment analysis much, it does affect the void-for-vagueness analysis, because the standard for deeming a statute overly vague that can only be enforced civilly is very high. Had the Supreme Court fully addressed *Rowell* on the merits, it would almost certainly have upheld the void-for-vagueness portion of the Fifth Circuit's judgment.

Rowell and *Expressions Hair* also differ in that the Fifth Circuit's decision appeared to turn in part on its determination that a surcharge and a discount are not the same thing. The appeals court seems to indicate that by banning surcharges and allowing discounts, the Texas law regulates only conduct. That is, because it rejects the Eleventh Circuit's view that a discount and a surcharge are two ways of referring to the same price difference, the Fifth Circuit treats those terms as regulating conduct rather than speech. Like the Second Circuit, the Fifth does not buy into the plaintiffs' complaints that their manner of talking about the price differences is restricted, but the court's reasoning turns in part on asserting a meaningful functional difference between a surcharge and a discount.

The third—and most significant—difference between *Rowell* and *Expressions Hair* is that the Second Circuit refrained from adjudging the constitutionality of a dual-pricing regime while in the Fifth Circuit "the parties concede dual pricing is allowed; the merchants simply object to their inability to characterize price differentials as a 'surcharge,' juxtaposed with a 'discount.'"[46] As the dissent observes, "The majority does not . . . explain how a law that affects merchants' ability to characterize legal price differentials as 'surcharges' rather than as 'discounts' is not a content-based restriction on speech subject to First Amendment scrutiny."[47]

Finally, as alluded to above, the Fifth Circuit upheld the trial court's granting of a motion to dismiss in this case. Unlike the Second Circuit, which reversed a trial court's striking down of New York's statute on substantive review, the Fifth Circuit may need to remand the case back to the trial court for a first shot at subjecting the Texas statute to First Amendment analysis.

In any event, by GVR-ing this case, the Supreme Court reversed both circuits that upheld state no-surcharge statutes. But there is a catch. Both the Second and Fifth Circuits also sidestepped the First Amendment question to a large extent. The Court let stand, without comment, the one court of appeals opinion that grappled with the First Amendment implications of these laws and struck down the state statute in question. While it is tempting to conclude that the Court reversed these two circuits because it believes both state statutes are unconstitutional, that reading goes too far. The most that can be deduced for certain is that lower courts must treat these kinds of regulations as speech regulations and must subject them to at least the intermediate scrutiny that traditional First Amendment analysis requires.

VI. If You Don't Look Good, We Don't Look Good: Why the Court Denied Cert in *Dana's Railroad Supply*

On the same day it GVR'd *Rowell*, the Supreme Court denied certiorari in *Dana's Railroad Supply v. Bondi*, having held onto the case for several months. This order of events further confirms the interrelated nature of these decisions from the Court's perspective. Court

---

[46] Rowell, 816 F.3d at 83.

[47] *Id.* at 85 (citing Sorrell v. IMS Health Inc., 564 U.S. 552 (2011)).

watchers normally caution not to read anything into a denial of certiorari. There can be vehicle problems or other cert-worthiness reasons why a case is denied that have nothing to do with the merits. Here, however, where three separate state statutes bearing a close resemblance to each other came before the justices at the same time, the Court's decision to let stand the Eleventh Circuit's ruling while almost simultaneously reversing and remanding two other circuit court judgments is probably significant.

The Eleventh Circuit is the only court of appeals to strike down a state credit-card surcharge statute to date, and it did so explicitly on First Amendment grounds. As related above, the Second and Fifth Circuits upheld the state statutes at issue without engaging the First Amendment issue at the heart of those cases. If the Court had thought that the Eleventh Circuit utterly bollixed up its handling of the First Amendment issue, it seems likely the Court would have said something more about the First Amendment to keep other courts of appeals from modeling their future work after the Eleventh Circuit.

Hence, a recap of what the Eleventh Circuit held might help forecast what the Second Circuit and other lower courts may do in forthcoming credit-card surcharge cases. The district court in *Dana's Railroad Supply* treated Florida's statute as a pricing restriction subject to rational-basis review and upheld it on those grounds. On review, the panel majority recognized that whether the statute was found to regulate conduct or speech would seal its fate, as laws that restrict speech are disfavored and presumptively unconstitutional.[48] The court determined that the statute does not ban dual-pricing regimes and does not appear to be designed to prevent bait-and-switch pricing tactics. Instead of banning particular pricing practices, which the court averred would be subject to rational-basis review, the statute splits hairs by restricting how stores may express the price difference between cash and credit purchases. Merchants can call the price difference a discount for cash but may not call it a surcharge for credit, even though the two things are identical under the circumstances. Thus, the Eleventh Circuit concluded that Florida's "'no-surcharge law' . . . is something of a misnomer. The statute targets expression

---

[48] See Dana's R.R. Supply, 807 F.3d at 1241–42 (citing United States v. Alvarez, 132 S. Ct. 2537, 2543–44 (2012)).

alone. More accurately, it should be a 'surcharges-are-fine-just-don't-call-them-that law.'"[49]

The Eleventh Circuit considered applying strict scrutiny to Florida's statute, as it saw the surcharge/discount issue as potentially treading on political issues, and it flirted with using the heightened standard of review called for in *IMS Health* and *Town of Gilbert* to evaluate content- or speaker-based discriminatory regulations. In the end, however, because it held that the statute could not survive intermediate scrutiny under *Central Hudson*, it did not evaluate the statute under more stringent standards.[50] In applying *Central Hudson*, the panel held that Florida's statute failed every prong of the test. Because it struck down the statute on First Amendment grounds, the panel did not reach the void-for-vagueness question except to hold that there was jurisdiction to address that question and that it was properly presented to the court.

If other circuits are going to follow the Eleventh Circuit's lead here, they should avoid replicating a couple of mistakes the majority made in *Dana's Railroad Supply*. First, the court treated the petitioners' challenge as a facial challenge to the statute when it was actually an as-applied challenge. Petitioners said theirs was an as-applied challenge in their briefs, and the litigation was prompted in part by cease-and-desist letters sent to the plaintiffs by the Florida attorney general. As the dissent pointed out, the prosecutor's interpretation of the statute would only be relevant to an as-applied challenge.

The second mistake the *Dana's Railroad Supply* majority made was to imply that a mandatory-disclosure regime would pass muster under *Zauderer* in the absence of consumer deception. Quite appropriately, the panel majority considered the applicability of *Zauderer* in the context of applying the *Central Hudson* test. The Second Circuit's questions for briefing on remand in *Expressions Hair Design* ask separately whether New York's statute would survive scrutiny under *Central Hudson* and whether § 518 could be deemed a valid disclosure requirement under *Zauderer*. Thus the Eleventh Circuit's recognition that *Zauderer* is really just a special case of applying the fourth prong of *Central Hudson* is a welcome development. Still, in saying in *dicta* that Florida "could require merchants to disclose to

[49] *Id.* at 1245.
[50] *Id.*

their customers the workings of their pricing policy," the majority overlooks the fact that charging customers a credit-card surcharge is not misleading in the first place.[51] Hence, even if Florida wanted to force a disclosure, it would first have to show that any such disclosure was "reasonably related to the State's interest in preventing deception of consumers."[52]

In any event, the Supreme Court's *Expressions Hair* decision resolved the circuit split on whether credit-card surcharge statutes regulate speech or conduct. Since only the Eleventh Circuit held that such statutes govern speech and evaluated it accordingly, there is not (yet) a circuit split on the question of how to apply the First Amendment to these statutes. The other circuits decided that it did not apply. The Supreme Court's minimalist holding resolved the split, and its remand of *Expressions Hair* and *Rowell* will permit the "how to evaluate no-surcharge statutes under the First Amendment" question to percolate further before the Court addresses it—if it ever does.

To be sure, a circuit split might still exist after the Second and Fifth Circuits complete their respective homework assignments from the high court. If so, it seems probable that the Court would revisit the First Amendment question that it forbore addressing in *Expressions Hair*. Of course, even if all of the other circuits now follow the Eleventh Circuit's lead, the Supreme Court might still take a cert petition from one of them. For example, the Court may have thought that the Eleventh Circuit was not on the right track but let the decision stand because that circuit had properly decided that the First Amendment applied and made a stab at scrutinizing the statute under the correct tests. The better guess is that the Second and Fifth Circuits should follow what the Eleventh did, rather than count too heavily on the high court's taking issue later with the First Amendment analysis of a case in which it denied cert.

VII. A Second Chance to Make a First (Amendment) Impression: Predicting the Second Circuit on Remand

On May 23, the Second Circuit issued an order recalling the mandate and reinstating the appeal in *Expressions Hair Design*. It further ordered both sides to submit letter-briefs addressing (1) whether § 518

[51] *Id*. at 1250 (citing Zauderer, 471 U.S. at 650–51).
[52] *Id*.

as applied to plaintiffs' pricing regime survives *Central Hudson* scrutiny; (2) whether § 518 is a valid disclosure requirement under *Zauderer*; and (3) what, if any, question the Second Circuit should certify to the New York Court of Appeals. The first two parts of this order track language at the end of Chief Justice Roberts's opinion ordering remand, while the third part asks whether to follow the certification suggestion made by the justices who concurred in judgment.

As of this writing, the Second Circuit has not decided whether to send part of the case to the New York Court of Appeals for resolution or whether it will hold oral argument, and its decision is still pending. Thus, it remains an opportune time to predict what the court might do on remand in this case. The short answer is that the court will evaluate, per the Supreme Court's instructions, whether § 518 can withstand First Amendment scrutiny. Multiple courts have evaluated these statutes accordingly, including the federal district court in this same case, so the panel has a road map (or several) to follow.

A. The Certification Question

Perhaps the first decision that the Second Circuit has to make is whether or not to certify a question to the New York Court of Appeals. None of the other courts examining these statutes certified a question, and the Second Circuit most likely will not do so either. Only the three justices who refused to join the Court's opinion recommended this course of action, and it would be a step at odds with the majority's holding in the case. Chief Justice Roberts's opinion already held that the statute regulates speech. If the Second Circuit certifies a question to the New York Court of Appeals, that court might interpret the statute *not* to regulate speech.[53] Then the Second Circuit would be a bit stuck. For the same reason that the Second Circuit itself won't follow the Breyer/Sotomayor suggestion and interpret the statute so as not to implicate the First Amendment, it will almost assuredly decide against certifying a question (and thereby running the risk of undercutting the U.S. Supreme Court's ruling).

---

[53] The Second Circuit might be able to fashion a question to certify to the New York Court of Appeals that would avoid this risk. But any question that forecloses that possibility would not be likely to give the Second Circuit any more information about the statute than it already has based on the Supreme Court's decision.

Besides, the Court already tried the *Pullman* abstention route the first time around to avoid deciding the state law question on how best to interpret § 518.[54] From the U.S. Supreme Court's perspective, the main thing that the Second Circuit got wrong the first time around was that it failed to recognize the statute as implicating the First Amendment. The appeals court won't make that same mistake again; the panel will take its cue from the majority opinion rather than the Breyer/Sotomayor/Alito concurrences in judgment and address the merits of the commercial-free-speech question directly.[55] It also will not want to further delay the case.

Another reason why the court of appeals will not certify a question is that the case remains an as-applied challenge where the specific set of facts—as the Supreme Court's ruling on the vagueness challenge underscored—is no longer in dispute. If this case were a facial challenge to the statute, seeking more information about how the statute applies might well be in order. But state supreme courts tend to balk at certifications anyway, especially to the extent that they see them as seeking advisory opinions. Here, the certification would almost explicitly be an advisory opinion, because further information on the metes and bounds of the statute are not necessary to resolve the as-applied challenge. Moreover, the New York Court of Appeals would probably prefer to opine in a case where it could also address the First Amendment question, not just to say how the statute applies and then return the case to the Second Circuit for the First Amendment analysis.

B. Central Hudson *Analysis*

Once the panel turns to analyzing the statute under First Amendment tests, there is every reason to think that the statute will fail

---

[54] See R.R. Comm'n of Texas v. Pullman Co., 312 U.S. 496 (1941).

[55] Certifying a question would also be in tension with having ruled against the plaintiffs on the void-for-vagueness argument. Justice Sotomayor's concurrence in judgment indicates oddly that this statute is not so vague as to create a due process problem but that it is ambiguous (that is, vague) enough to require certification. See Expressions Hair, 137 S. Ct. at 1155, note 3 ("The multiple available interpretations of § 518 do not render § 518 so vague as to violate the Due Process Clause. But they do render § 518 ambiguous enough to warrant asking the New York Court of Appeals to resolve the statute's meaning."). But if the Court cannot parse the statute without another court's help, how is an ordinary merchant subject to the statute's criminal penalties supposed to figure it out?

review. Although commercial speech has been the redheaded step-child of free-speech jurisprudence in most other lower courts, the Second Circuit has been a bright spot in recognizing commercial-speech rights.[56] As the court's briefing order portends, it will first consider how § 518 squares under the four-prong *Central Hudson* test, except that it will ignore the first prong because the Supreme Court has already decided that this speech concerns lawful activity and is not misleading.[57]

The second prong of *Central Hudson* asks whether the government's asserted interest in the regulation is substantial. As applied to a single-sticker pricing regime, it is hard to see what substantial interest the government would have in insisting that merchants de-scribe a price difference as a "discount" rather than a "surcharge." The panel offered some interests the first time around, implying they would survive rational-basis review (for example, to promote credit cards), but none would count as a substantial interest. The dissent in the Eleventh Circuit thought that preventing bait-and-switch tactics was a substantial interest, which it might be, but the majority there showed that the statute was not applied just to that narrow situation. The enforcement history in New York shows a broader pattern of enforcement as well, so the Second Circuit will not see a substantial government interest in play.

Central Hudson's third prong asks if the regulation directly ad-vances the government's asserted interest. Here, whatever that inter-est might be, it would be better served by regulating prices rather than communication about prices. For example, to prevent profiteer-ing, the state could cap the surcharge at the rate the merchant pays the credit-card company. Or the state could force merchants to dis-close exactly how they calculate their prices. Therefore, the Second Circuit will find that § 518 fails this prong too.

Finally, *Central Hudson* requires that the regulation be no more extensive than necessary to serve the government's inter-est—in other words, that it be narrowly tailored. New York's

[56] See, e.g., United States v. Caronia, 703 F.3d 149 (2d Cir. (2012)) (reversing the conviction of pharmaceutical sales rep for off-label speech).

[57] Just as the Eleventh Circuit considered analyzing Florida's statute under the heightened standards of review suggested by *IMS Health* and *Town of Gilbert*, so too the Second Circuit would have to consider whether § 518 can survive more stringent review if it were to hold that § 518 satisfies *Central Hudson*.

§ 518 cannot possibly satisfy this prong because there are far too many alternatives to advance the government's interest that do not involve restricting—indeed criminalizing—disfavored speech.

C. Zauderer *Analysis*

Having decided that the statute fails *Central Hudson* review, the Second Circuit might see if it can save the statute by construing it as a disclosure regime subject to *Zauderer*. As an initial matter, despite the passing reference to *Zauderer* in Roberts's opinion, it does not apply in this context. That test comes into play where the government has compelled speech, such as a disclaimer, that is designed to prevent consumer deception. New York's law does not compel any speech whatsoever. As applied, as Justice Ginsburg recognized at oral argument, a statute that "suppress[es] the actual cost of the credit card purchase" is not a disclosure regime.[58] Nor does it combat deception; if anything, it facilitates deception. Moreover, a disclosure statute would be clear about what a merchant must say to comply. This law includes no such affirmative guidance.

Finally, in legal terms *Zauderer* is not an altogether separate, standalone test that commercial-speech restrictions can satisfy in lieu of *Central Hudson*. Rather, *Zauderer* simply means that when governments try to narrowly tailor regulations to meet the fourth prong of the *Central Hudson* test, compelled disclaimers will pass muster where speech bans will not in order to prevent consumer deception. If the Second Circuit finds that § 518 fails any of the other prongs of *Central Hudson*, then *Zauderer* will not apply.

If, however, the Second Circuit misconstrues *Zauderer*, it might simply ask whether the New York statute means to track the former federal statute. If so, according to the solicitor general's brief, the former federal statute would have survived *Zauderer* scrutiny. One might then think that § 518 should satisfy *Zauderer* too. This theory founders on two points. First, the *Expressions Hair* plaintiffs have brought an as-applied challenge, and the enforcement history in New York is not consistent with construing the statute as identical to its federal precursor. Under the federal statute, the only way to violate it (because of the unique definition given to "surcharge" under that statute) was to list one price, call it the regular price, and

[58] Transcript of Oral Arg., *supra* note 28, at 59.

then charge credit-card customers more than that price. As long as a merchant listed both prices, he was free to call the higher price for credit-card customers a "surcharge." The same is not true under New York law.

Second, *Zauderer* applies a "purely factual and uncontroversial information" requirement to a particular disclosure.[59] Although one might construe New York's statute as allowing two different prices to be listed by those merchants who wish to charge separate prices to cash and credit customers, nothing in the statute *compels* that. So *Zauderer* would not seem to apply. Moreover, there is nothing deceptive about Expressions Hair Design's or the other plaintiffs' desires to list a single price along with a set percentage surcharge. Without the need to combat deception, again, *Zauderer* should not apply. Finally, even if *Zauderer* does apply, it is quite a stretch to contend that it's "uncontroversial" to disguise the cost of paying with credit.

The straightforward nature of the Second Circuit's order suggests that it does not plan to do anything very creative on remand. If that proves true, then the panel ought to eschew certifying a question to the New York Court of Appeals, strike down § 518 as unconstitutional under *Central Hudson*, and not apply *Zauderer* at all. If the panel does apply *Zauderer* (and/or *Central Hudson*) to uphold a dual-price regime under the statute somehow, then it will create a new circuit split between the Second Circuit and Eleventh Circuit on whether a no-surcharge statute survives *Central Hudson* review. The Second Circuit will then need to consider whether the statute must withstand heightened scrutiny under *IMS Health* and *Town of Gilbert*. If it rules that the no-surcharge statute does not withstand heightened scrutiny, then how it got there may not matter so much. But if the Second Circuit ultimately upholds the statute by adopting a First Amendment theory at odds with the Eleventh Circuit, this case may wind up back at the U.S. Supreme Court. If the circuit split was worth resolving once, the Court could well conclude it is worth resolving once and for all.

---

[59] *Zauderer*, 471 U.S. at 651.

VIII. Finishing Touches

When the three credit-card-surcharge cases arrived together on the Supreme Court's doorstep last year, they were a hot mess. Of course, circuit splits reach the Court with regularity, but it seldom happens that the cases causing the split reach the Court almost simultaneously.[60] The timing here was no mere coincidence.[61] Wisely the Court did not try to resolve all of the questions in the cases at once. Working patiently, the Court noted the limited question presented to it, undid the severe tangles left by the Second Circuit's bad *Hair* day, and sent that case back for a makeover. The Court then GVR'd the *Rowell* case and denied certiorari in *Dana's Railroad Supply*, letting stand the Eleventh Circuit's decision striking down Florida's no-surcharge statute on First Amendment grounds.

Avoiding a broad brush that might implicate *Lochner*, the Court issued a narrow but significant decision that no-surcharge statutes regulate speech, not merely conduct. Deeming such statutes economic-conduct regulations would have shredded the Court's commercial-speech jurisprudence. By not taking that shortcut, the *Expressions Hair* decision buttressed the Court's recent commercial-speech precedents. In holding that regulating the communication of prices regulates speech, the Court ensured that legislators at all levels will not find it easy to restrict merchants' speech in the future.

It will take another round of briefing in at least three different circuits—the Second, the Fifth, and the Ninth (in *Italian Colors*)—before the final fate of these various state statutes is known. Thus, although *Expressions Hair* did not deliver the sweeping victory that petitioners sought, the Supreme Court freed the Second Circuit's commercial-speech knot and straightened out an important area of commercial-free-speech doctrine.

---

[60] A cert petition was filed in *Expressions Hair Design* on May 12, 2016. A petition in *Rowell* was lodged on May 31, 2016, and the Florida attorney general filed one in *Dana's R.R. Supply* on June 6, 2016.

[61] Deepak Gupta serves as counsel to the targeted businesses in all four of the no-surcharge appellate cases discussed herein, which explains many of the similarities in the cases.

Looking Ahead: October Term 2017

*Christopher Landau and Sopan Joshi**

It's always a fool's errand to venture predictions about the Supreme Court. But it's an especially foolish fool who ventures predictions about the Supreme Court when a new justice arrives on the scene. We sincerely hope that's not why Cato asked us to pen these thoughts on the upcoming term, which will mark the Court's first full year with its newest member, Justice Neil Gorsuch. But in the interest of full disclosure, we offer this disclaimer: "Your *&$@! guess is as good as ours."[TM1]

The arrival of a new justice alters the Court not merely by one-ninth, but in its entirety. As in a chess game, such a move rearranges the entire board, as the other justices react and respond to the change. Consider, for example, what happened in October Term (OT) 1991, when the Court's most liberal member, Thurgood Marshall, was replaced by its most conservative member, Clarence Thomas, and the Court moved not to the right but to the left.[2] The lingering absence of Justice Antonin Scalia, who dominated discourse on the Court for almost three decades, only highlights the potential for surprise. Conventional wisdom simply substitutes Justice Gorsuch as a proxy vote for Justice Scalia while keeping all other inputs the same, and perhaps that theory will be borne out. But conventional wisdom—especially when it comes to the Supreme Court—is often wrong.

---

*Mr. Landau is a partner in the Washington office of Kirkland & Ellis LLP. He clerked for Justice Antonin Scalia in 1990–91 and Justice Clarence Thomas in 1991–92, and has argued nine cases before the Court. Mr. Joshi is an associate in the Chicago office of Kirkland & Ellis, and clerked for Justice Scalia in 2015–16 and Justice Samuel Alito in 2016. It goes without saying that the views in this essay are those of the authors, not Kirkland & Ellis or its clients.

[1] Cf. Matal v. Tam, 137 S. Ct. 1744 (2017).

[2] See, e.g., Planned Parenthood of S.E. Pa. v. Casey, 505 U.S. 833 (1992); Lee v. Weisman, 505 U.S. 577 (1992).

There tends to be a cycle in Supreme Court terms, with block-buster terms followed by lackluster ones, and vice versa. If that trend continues to hold, we should be in for quite a term, because it's hard to remember a term as anticlimactic as OT 2016. Many of the biggest cases of the upcoming term still remain unknown, as the Court has yet to fill four of its seven months of argument. As of this writing, the Court has 31 cases on its docket (versus 29 at this point last year, and 35, 39, and 47 at this point in the years before that). The granted cases include several that have the potential to be more consequential than any case decided last term. So while it's hard to predict just what kind of a term this will turn out to be, it's a safe bet to assume that it will turn out to be more significant than OT 2016. The following pages discuss some of the key cases, as well as several potentially significant cases in the pipeline.

I. Elections

It's sometimes surprising to discover that, in over 200 years, an important constitutional question has not been definitively answered by the Supreme Court. *Gill v. Whitford* presents such a question: is partisan gerrymandering unconstitutional? The Court has twice before addressed this question, but in neither case provided a clear answer.[3] Thus, although partisan gerrymandering is nothing new (Elbridge Gerry died in 1814), the law in this critically important area remains unsettled.

All of that could change as a result of *Gill*. In the wake of the 2010 census, the Wisconsin legislature (then, as now, controlled by Republicans) adopted a redistricting plan (Act 43) for state legislative districts. In 2012, under Act 43, the Republican Party received 48.6 percent of the two-party statewide vote share for Assembly candidates and won 60 of 99 seats in the Wisconsin Assembly. In 2014, under Act 43, the Republican Party received 52 percent of the two-party statewide vote share and won 63 Assembly seats.

A group of Wisconsin Democratic voters sued members of the Wisconsin Elections Commission. According to the complaint, Act 43 diluted Democratic votes statewide by (1) "cracking"—"dividing a party's supporters among multiple districts so that they fall short of a majority in each one," and (2) "packing"—"concentrating a

---

[3] See Vieth v. Jubilerer, 541 U.S. 267 (2004); Davis v. Bandemer, 478 U.S. 109 (1986).

party's supporters in a few districts where they win by overwhelming margins."[4] The plaintiffs alleged that these practices resulted in excessive "wasted" votes: votes cast either for a losing candidate (because of "cracking") or for a winning candidate (because of "packing"). They urged the court to adopt a new measure for assessing the discriminatory effect of partisan gerrymanders: the so-called "efficiency gap"—the difference between the parties' respective "wasted" votes in an election, divided by the total number of votes cast. The plaintiffs provided the following example:

> Suppose . . . that there are five districts in a plan with 100 voters each. Suppose also that Party A wins three of the districts by a margin of 60 votes to 40, and that Party B wins two of them by a margin of 80 votes to 20. Then Party A wastes 10 votes in each of the three districts it wins and 20 votes in each of the two districts it loses, adding up to 70 wasted votes. Likewise, Party B wastes 30 votes in each of the two districts it wins and 40 votes in each of the three districts it loses, adding up to 180 wasted votes. The difference between the parties' respective wasted votes is 110, which, when divided by 500 total votes, yields an efficiency gap of 22% in favor of Party A.[5]

The plaintiffs alleged that an "efficiency gap" of more than seven percent is presumptively unconstitutional insofar as it "treats voters unequally, diluting their voting power based on their political beliefs, in violation of the Fourteenth Amendment's guarantee of equal protection," and "unreasonably burdens their First Amendment rights of association and free speech."[6] They requested a declaration that Act 43—which produced an "efficiency gap" of 13 percent in 2012 and 10 percent in 2014—is unconstitutional, an injunction prohibiting further elections under the map, and the drawing of a new redistricting map.

A divided three-judge district court, per Seventh Circuit Judge Kenneth Ripple, ruled in the plaintiffs' favor[7]—and thereby became the first federal court to find an unconstitutional partisan gerrymander since the district court decision reversed by the Supreme Court

---

[4] Compl. at ¶ 5, Whitford v. Gill, No. 15-421 (W.D. Wisc.).

[5] *Id*. at ¶ 50.

[6] *Id*. at ¶ 2.

[7] Whitford v. Gill, 218 F. Supp. 3d 837 (W.D. Wis. 2016).

in *Davis v. Bandemer* more than 30 years ago. According to the majority, the test for an unconstitutional partisan gerrymander is whether a redistricting plan (1) "intended to place a severe impediment on the effectiveness of the votes of individual citizens on the basis of their political affiliation"; (2) "ha[d] that effect"; and (3) "cannot be justified on other, legitimate legislative grounds."[8] Act 43, the majority held, met each of these criteria: (1) partisan advantage was a "motivating factor" behind the plan, (2) the plan made it "more difficult for Democrats, compared to Republicans, to translate their votes into seats," as "corroborat[ed]" by the "efficiency gap," and (3) although the plan comports with neutral redistricting criteria (such as contiguity, compactness, and respect for political subdivisions), it is "possible to draw a map with much less of a partisan bent than Act 43."[9] In a subsequent remedial order, the court enjoined appellants from using Act 43 in future elections and ordered the state to enact a new plan for the 2018 elections by November 1, 2017.[10]

The Supreme Court noted probable jurisdiction over the case (because it involved a direct appeal from a three-judge district court, not a petition for certiorari) and, by a vote of 5-4, granted Wisconsin's request to stay the judgment pending disposition of the appeal.[11]

Gill, like previous partisan-gerrymandering cases, presents two major questions: (1) is a partisan gerrymandering claim justiciable at all, and (2) if so, under what standard? Those two questions are, of course, intertwined: a major rationale for deeming such claims nonjusticiable is the absence of any obvious objective standard for adjudicating them. In *Bandemer*, a majority of the Court held that such claims are justiciable but failed to produce a majority opinion on the relevant standard.[12] In *Vieth*, a plurality of the Court ruled that such claims are not justiciable,[13] but Justice Anthony Kennedy concurred in the judgment on the ground that he "would not foreclose all possibility of judicial relief if some limited and precise rationale

---

[8] *Id.* at 884.

[9] *Id.* at 884–927.

[10] 2017 WL 383360 (W.D. Wis. Jan. 27, 2017).

[11] 2017 WL 2621675 (June 19, 2017). Several of the authors' colleagues at Kirkland & Ellis filed amicus briefs supporting the state at the jurisdictional and stay stages.

[12] 478 U.S. at 118–27; *id.* at 127–43 (plurality op.).

[13] 541 U.S. at 277–306 (plurality op.).

were found to correct an established violation of the Constitution in some redistricting cases."[14] With the exception of Justice Thomas, all of the members of the *Vieth* plurality are gone. If the stay vote is any indication, *Gill* is likely to be a close case and (like *Bandemer* and *Vieth* before it) could well produce a fractured outcome. It is also one of those cases whose importance depends on its outcome. If the Court reverses, then the status quo continues and the case will be remembered only by election law mavens. But, if the Court affirms, it could fundamentally alter the nation's political trajectory. Act 43's challengers appear to believe that, in the "efficiency gap," they have found the holy grail of election law: a neutral, objective yardstick for courts to use in assessing whether partisan gerrymandering has crossed a constitutional line (and thus to satisfy the concerns that Justice Kennedy expressed in *Vieth*). If so, the 2015 *Chicago Law Review* article in which that concept was proposed will surely go down as among the most consequential of its kind in American history.[15] At a minimum, Supreme Court cognoscenti should expect to hear references to the "efficiency gap," "packing," and "cracking" in the months to come, and may wish to work those words into their cocktail-party vocabulary accordingly.

II. Foreign Relations/Immigration

A. Travel Ban

Unless our readers have been hiding under rocks for the last six months, they will be at least generally aware of the litigation over the travel ban that President Donald Trump abruptly announced by executive order during his first week in office. The order stated that "[n]umerous foreign-born individuals have been convicted or implicated in terrorism-related crimes since September 11, 2001, including foreign nationals who entered the United States after receiving visitor, student, or employment visas, or who entered through the United States refugee resettlement program."[16] To allow the federal government to reassess its visa and refugee programs, the order (1) suspended for 90 days immigrant and nonimmigrant entry into the

---

[14] *Id.* at 306 (Kennedy, J., concurring in the judgment).

[15] Nicholas Stephanopoulos & Eric McGhee, Partisan Gerrymandering & the Efficiency Gap, 82 U. Chi. L. Rev. 831 (2015).

[16] Exec. Order No. 13769, 82 Fed. Reg. 8977 (Jan. 27, 2017).

United States of all nationals of seven specified countries (Iran, Iraq, Libya, Sudan, Somalia, Syria, and Yemen), and (2) suspended for 120 days the U.S. Refugee Admissions Program, imposed a ban of indefinite duration on the entry of refugees from Syria, and limited the entry of refugees to 50,000 in fiscal year 2017.[17] The implementation of the order was—to put it mildly—rocky, and within hours batteries of lawyers had shown up at the country's major international airports and unleashed a torrent of lawsuits.[18]

The administration did not fare well in the initial round of litigation. A district court in Washington state granted a temporary restraining order (TRO) prohibiting nationwide enforcement of the executive order, and the Ninth Circuit—treating the TRO as an appealable preliminary injunction—affirmed.[19] The president responded by signing a revised executive order that reinstated the 90-day ban on the entry of nationals of six of the original seven countries (minus Iraq), and otherwise adjusted and provided further justification for the original order.

The revised order, which took effect on March 16, 2017, was again challenged across the country, and district courts in Maryland and Hawaii promptly entered nationwide injunctions against its enforcement. Those orders quickly made their way to the Fourth and Ninth Circuits, respectively, and both circuits mostly affirmed them.[20] The Fourth Circuit, sitting en banc in the first instance, affirmed by a vote of 10-3. The majority opinion, authored by Chief Judge Roger Gregory, concluded that the order violated the Establishment Clause because it was motivated by a discriminatory animus toward Muslims (based largely on the president's statements during the 2016 campaign), and essentially dismissed the order's national security concerns as pretextual.[21] Several judges concurred or concurred in the judgment, and three judges dissented. The dissenting judges

---

[17] Id.

[18] Several of the authors' colleagues at Kirkland & Ellis LLP have been involved in challenges to the travel ban.

[19] Washington v. Trump, 2017 WL 462040 (W.D. Wash. Feb. 3, 2017), aff'd 847 F.3d 1151 (9th Cir. 2017) (per curiam), reconsideration en banc denied, 853 F.3d 933 (9th Cir. 2017).

[20] Int'l Refugee Assistance Project (IRAP) v. Trump, 857 F.3d 554 (4th Cir. 2017) (en banc); Hawaii v. Trump, 859 F.3d 741 (9th Cir. 2017) (per curiam).

[21] IRAP, 857 F.3d at 588–604.

accused the majority of failing to follow *Kleindienst v. Mandel*, in which the Supreme Court upheld the exclusion of an alien for "facially legitimate and bona fide" reasons, and took particular aim at the majority's reliance on the president's statements during the campaign to impugn the validity of his official action.[22]

Meanwhile, across the country, a Ninth Circuit panel reached the same result, albeit for different reasons. Rather than ruling on constitutional grounds, the Ninth Circuit ruled on statutory ones: the court concluded that the president had exceeded his statutory authority. The key statute provides the following:

> Whenever the President finds that the entry of any aliens or of any class of aliens into the United States would be detrimental to the interests of the United States, he may by proclamation, and for such period as he shall deem necessary, suspend the entry of all aliens or any class of aliens as immigrants or nonimmigrants, or impose on the entry of aliens any restrictions he may deem to be appropriate.[23]

The Ninth Circuit concluded that the order did not make a sufficient "find[ing]" that the entry of all nationals of the targeted countries, and of refugees, "would be detrimental to the interests of the United States."[24] In addition, the court held that the order violated another statutory provision, which specifies that "[N]o person shall . . . be discriminated against in the issuance of an immigrant visa because of the person's . . . nationality,"[25] as well as a statute requiring the president to engage in "appropriate consultation" with Congress before setting the number of refugees to be admitted in any fiscal year.[26]

The government asked the Supreme Court not only to review both the Fourth and Ninth Circuit decisions, but in the meanwhile to stay the nationwide injunctions affirmed by those courts. In a *per curiam* order entered on the last day of last term, the Court granted the government's petitions for certiorari and directed the parties to address,

---

[22] *Id.* at 639–54 (Niemeyer, J., dissenting) (citing Kliendienst v. Mandel, 408 U.S. 753 (1972)).

[23] 8 U.S.C. § 1182(f).

[24] Hawaii, 859 F.3d at 769–74.

[25] 8 U.S.C. § 1152(a)(1)(A).

[26] 8 U.S.C. § 1157(a)(2).

in addition to the questions presented below, whether the disputed 90-day travel ban on nationals in the six targeted countries became moot on June 14, 2017—90 days after the revised executive order took effect.[27] Accordingly, the two travel-ban cases, *Trump v. International Refugee Assistance Project* and *Trump v. Hawaii*, have been scheduled for oral argument in the Court's October sitting.

In addition, the Court granted in part the government's request for a stay of the two nationwide injunctions, and stayed those injunctions insofar as they prevented enforcement of the revised executive order "with respect to foreign nationals who lack any bona fide relationship with a person or entity in the United States."[28] The Court took an unusual path to this Solomonic solution. Although the Court itself has previously characterized the first two factors in the multifactor test for granting (or staying) preliminary injunctive relief as "the most critical,"[29] the Court purported to bypass those issues (and the many contentious questions they implicated) to focus instead on the equities. As the Court noted, the injunctions at issue here extend well beyond the named plaintiffs, to encompass "foreign nationals abroad who have no connection to the United States at all." According to the Court, "the equities relied on by the lower courts do not balance the same way in that context." Thus, the Court held that either "a close familial relationship" or "a formal, documented" relationship "formed in the ordinary course, rather than for the purpose of evading [the order]" is required.[30]

Justice Thomas, joined by Justices Samuel Alito and Gorsuch, dissented on the ground that the injunctions should be stayed in full because, first and foremost, the government had shown a strong likelihood of success on the merits, as well as irreparable harm and a favorable balance of the equities. Justice Thomas also chastised the majority for "invit[ing] a flood of litigation . . ., as parties and courts struggle to determine what exactly constitutes a 'bona fide relationship,' who precisely has a 'credible claim' to that relationship, and

---

[27] Trump v. Int'l Refugee Assistance Project (IRAP), 137 S. Ct. 2080 (2017) (per curiam).

[28] *Id.* at 2087.

[29] Nken v. Holder, 556 U.S. 418, 434 (2009).

[30] IRAP, 137 S. Ct. at 2088.

whether the claimed relationship was formed 'simply to avoid [the executive order].'"[31]

Justice Thomas's predictions soon proved prescient, as the administration issued guidelines narrowly defining "a close familial relationship," which were promptly challenged in court. The district court in Hawaii rejected the administration's exclusion of grandparents, grandchildren, aunts, uncles, nieces, nephews, cousins, brothers-in-law, and sisters-in-law of would-be entrants, and the Supreme Court (again over the dissent of Justices Thomas, Alito, and Gorsuch) declined to intervene.[32]

So, after all of the legal drama surrounding the executive orders, where do things now stand? On the merits, it's hard to say. The Court's *per curiam* order partially lifting the stay successfully papered over whatever differences among the justices in the majority may have lurked beneath the surface. It also allowed the Court to reach a result that allowed both sides to claim victory—the president could claim that the Court (unanimously, no less) had largely upheld his orders, while the challengers could claim that the stay order left the injunctions intact in many, if not most, of their applications. Sure enough, both sides were promptly spinning the Court's stay order to their advantage. There remains considerable doubt as to whether the Court will ever reach the merits. As noted above, the ban on entry of nationals of six targeted countries was, by its terms, scheduled to last for only 90 days, and that time elapsed in mid-June, even before the Court granted review. Although other components of the executive order also have been challenged, most of those were scheduled to sunset too, and the Court may simply decide that the core of the cases is moot and dismiss them (presumably, but not necessarily, vacating the lower court opinions in the process). There is certainly risk to the administration in trying to push the issue: while three of the justices have staked out a clear position in the administration's favor on the merits, the other six have not, and it is by no means obvious that the administration can pick up the requisite two additional votes. Unless the administration decides to press its luck, these cases

---

[31] *Id.* at 2090 (Thomas, J., concurring in part and dissenting in part).

[32] Washington v. Trump, 2017 WL 2989048 (D. Haw. Jul. 13, 2017); 2017 WL 3045234 (Jul. 19, 2017).

may find their place among those that entered the Court to great public fanfare only to exit quietly.

B. Alien Tort Statute

It's not often that the exact same issue is briefed and argued twice on the merits in the Supreme Court. That is because, unless the Court divides evenly or dismisses a writ of certiorari as improvidently granted, it tends to render a merits decision on the issue presented. In *Kiobel v. Royal Dutch Petrol. Co.*, however, the Court departed from that norm.[33] The Court granted certiorari in that case to review the Second Circuit's conclusion that the Alien Tort Statute (ATS)[34] is categorically inapplicable to actions against corporations. After briefing and argument, however, the Court directed the parties to brief and argue an entirely different question: "Whether and under what circumstances the [ATS] allows courts to recognize a cause of action for violations of the law of nations occurring within the territory of a sovereign other than the United States."[35] The Court heard oral argument once again, and affirmed the judgment on the ground that the ATS does not apply extraterritorially, and none of the relevant conduct in that case touched and concerned the United States "with sufficient force to displace the presumption against extraterritorial application."[36]

That disposition left the Second Circuit in somewhat of an awkward spot. While the Supreme Court did not reject its per se rule against corporate liability under the ATS, neither did the Court provide a ringing endorsement of that rule by reaching out to decide the case on other grounds. One might have expected the Second Circuit to leave the matter at that by following the Supreme Court's lead and deciding subsequent cases on extraterritoriality grounds. But it did not. Instead, the appellate court went out of its way to decide a subsequent case based on its corporate-liability precedent in *Kiobel I*—while casting substantial doubt on that precedent—in an avowed effort to "clarify" the law in this area (that is, to wipe *Kiobel I* off

---

[33] 133 S. Ct. 1659 (2013).

[34] 28 U.S.C. § 1350.

[35] 132 S. Ct. 1738 (2012).

[36] Kiobel, 133 S. Ct. at 1669.

the books).[37] The panel all but invited the full Second Circuit or the Supreme Court to review its judgment applying *Kiobel I*, declaring that "we will leave it either to an en banc sitting of this Court or an eventual Supreme Court review to overrule *Kiobel I* if, indeed, it is no longer viable."[38]

The Second Circuit denied rehearing en banc by a vote of 10-3, and the three dissenters notably included two of the panel members.[39] Judge Dennis Jacobs, concurring in the denial of rehearing en banc, blasted the panel for having "steered deliberately into controversy" by resolving the case on corporate-liability rather than extraterritoriality grounds.[40] Judge Denny Chin, a member of the panel, wrote an opinion responding to Judge Jacobs, and Judge Rosemary Pooler wrote a separate dissent from the denial of rehearing en banc on the merits—in response to which Judge José Cabranes, author of *Kiobel I*, wrote yet another opinion concurring in denial of rehearing in banc.

If the Second Circuit panel sought to write its opinion in a way that would force the Supreme Court's hand, it achieved its goal: the Court granted certiorari in *Jesner v. Arab Bank, PLC*.[41] The petition presents the question originally presented, but not decided, in *Kiobel*: "Whether the Alien Tort Statute, 28 U.S.C. § 1350, categorically forecloses corporate liability." The significance of that question, in light of the Supreme Court's decision in *Kiobel II*, is open to question: as Judge Jacobs noted: "The principle of *Kiobel I* has been largely overtaken, and its importance for outcomes has been sharply eroded" by the extraterritoriality ruling of *Kiobel II*.[42] Indeed, extraterritoriality will clearly be "the elephant in the room" in *Jesner*, where the underlying offense against the law of nations is terrorism against Israeli citizens by four Palestinian terrorist groups that allegedly used accounts at branches of respondent Arab Bank in a score of countries (including a single U.S. branch, in Manhattan). If the Court is, once again, disinclined to address the corporate-liability question teed up

---

[37] In re Arab Bank, PLC Alien Tort Statute Litig., 808 F.3d 144 (2d Cir. 2015).

[38] *Id.* at 157.

[39] In re Arab Bank, PLC Alien Tort Statute Litig., 822 F.3d 34 (2d Cir. 2016) (order).

[40] *Id.* at 37 (Jacobs, J., concurring in the denial of rehearing en banc).

[41] Several of the authors' colleagues at Kirkland & Ellis represent the respondent, Arab Bank, PLC, in the Supreme Court.

[42] 822 F.3d at 35 (Jacobs, J., concurring in the denial of rehearing en banc).

by the Second Circuit, there appear to be ample grounds to rest a ruling on extraterritoriality grounds—or certainly individual justices may be tempted to do so. The merits of the corporate-liability question essentially boil down to the question of the level of generality at which "the law of nations" is incorporated into the ATS: is it incorporated only with respect to the underlying conduct prohibited, or it is incorporated with respect to both the underlying conduct and the status of the alleged perpetrator of that conduct? Although these questions will undoubtedly generate heated commentary in international law reviews, the practical effect of the Court's decision either way—should the Court even reach the issue—appears to be quite limited. If *Jesner* is "The Return of *Kiobel*," then *Kiobel* is returning in a far diminished state.

III. Religion

Back in the days when Justice Scalia cajoled the Supreme Court—and accordingly the Court's bar—to take history seriously as a tool of constitutional interpretation, we doubt he ever imagined that the following line would appear in a Supreme Court brief: "Cake making dates back to at least 1175 B.C." But there it is, right in the petition for certiorari in *Masterpiece Cakeshop, Ltd. v. Colorado Civil Rights Commission*, which the Court granted after distributing it for an eye-popping 19 conferences. While it is certainly possible that the justices were busy researching what qualified as a "cake" in the ancient world, it is more likely that they were divided over whether to grant review in a hot-button case that pits the rights of a gay couple, Charlie Craig and David Mullins, against the rights of a baker (and Masterpiece's owner), Jack Phillips, who declined to design and create a cake for their same-sex wedding.

After Phillips's refusal, Craig and Mullins filed charges of discrimination with the Colorado Civil Rights Commission, alleging prohibited discrimination in a place of public accommodation on the basis of sexual orientation. The commission ruled in their favor and issued a cease-and-desist order directing Masterpiece to (1) take remedial measures, including comprehensive staff training and alteration to the company's policies to ensure compliance with Colorado's anti-discrimination law, and (2) file quarterly compliance reports for two years that, among other things, document all instances in which patrons were denied service and the reasons therefor. Masterpiece appealed that order to the Colorado Court of Appeals, which af-firmed.[43] In so doing, the court rejected Masterpiece's argument that the application of Colorado's anti-discrimination law to require Phillips to design and create cakes for same-sex weddings violated his First Amendment rights to free speech and free exercise of reli-gion. According to the court, "Masterpiece does not convey a mes-sage supporting same-sex marriage merely by abiding by the law and serving its customers equally," and "the act of designing and selling a wedding cake to all customers free of discrimination does not convey a celebratory message about same-sex weddings likely to be understood by those who view it."[44] The court also rejected Masterpiece's argument that the anti-discrimination law was itself being applied in a discriminatory fashion, because the commission refused to penalize secular bakers who refused to design and create cakes with anti-gay messages.[45] By a divided vote, the Colorado Su-preme Court denied discretionary review.

At least on the surface, *Masterpiece Cakeshop* is an irresistibly com-pelling case because it appears to present a stark conflict between rights: the right to be free from discrimination, on the one hand, and the rights of free speech and the free exercise of religion, on the other. The Colorado Court of Appeals tried to sidestep this conflict by concluding that the acts of designing and creating a cake are not inherently expressive—especially where, as here, the baker declined to create the cake before any discussion of its design. Masterpiece counters that Phillips was exercising his First Amendment rights by refusing to design and create *any* cake to celebrate a same-sex wed-ding and notes that, in its landmark *Obergefell* decision, the Supreme Court acknowledged that "those who adhere to religious doctrines, may continue to advocate with utmost, sincere conviction that, by divine precepts, same-sex marriage should not be condoned."[46]

Precisely because it involves a clash of rights, it is very hard to pre-dict how *Masterpiece Cakeshop* will come out. The fact that there ap-parently were not four votes to grant certiorari until after the confir-mation of Justice Gorsuch suggests that the Court is closely divided.

---

[43] Craig v. Masterpiece Cakeshop, Inc., 370 P.3d 272 (Colo. App. 2015).

[44] *Id*. at 286.

[45] *Id*. at 289–93.

[46] Obergefell v. Hodges, 135 S. Ct. 2584, 2607 (2015).

As is often the case, it appears that Justice Kennedy's vote may be critical, and he has provided clues pointing in both directions. On the one hand, he has been the foremost champion of gay rights on the Court, authoring the majority opinion in *Obergefell* and other landmark cases that paved the path to that decision. On the other hand, he has arguably been the Court's staunchest defender of free speech, even when offensive or abhorrent. A critical issue may be the extent to which he, and the other justices, view the design and creation of a cake as an expression of the baker's views, as opposed to the client's views. The case may also provide an opportunity for the Court to revisit the elusive speech/conduct distinction and to clarify the level of constitutional protection owed to expressive conduct. Finally, the case may provide an opportunity for the Court to revisit its free-exercise jurisprudence, to address Masterpiece's argument that Colorado's facially neutral anti-discrimination law is being applied in a discriminatory manner because secular bakers have been allowed to decline to design and create cakes with an anti-gay message. For those who had never even contemplated the possibility that cakes could be "pro-gay," "anti-gay," "racist," "atheist," or "fascist," the case promises a delectable confectionary detour from the Court's ordinary fare.

IV. Arbitration

Hardly a term has gone by in recent years when the Supreme Court has not decided a case involving the Federal Arbitration Act (FAA). Such cases have tended to follow a familiar pattern: a lower court refuses to enforce an arbitration agreement on ostensibly neutral state-law grounds, and the Supreme Court reverses on the ground that those ostensibly neutral grounds are not neutral after all, but actually discriminate against or otherwise thwart federally protected arbitration rights. An important subset of these cases involves the enforceability of "class action waivers"—agreements that require bilateral arbitration, and prohibit classwide litigation or arbitration, to resolve disputes. In 2011, a closely divided Court held in *AT&T Mobility LLC v. Concepcion* that the FAA preempts state laws that deem such waivers categorically unconscionable or otherwise unenforceable. The Court reasoned that "[r]equiring the availability of classwide arbitration interferes with fundamental attributes of arbitration and thus creates a scheme inconsistent with the FAA."[47]

That observation, however, did not deter the National Labor Relations Board (NLRB) from ruling the following year that agreements between individual employees and their employers that require arbitration of work-related disputes on a bilateral (rather than collective or classwide) basis interfere with the employees' right to engage in "concerted activity" under the federal labor laws. That conclusion, the NLRB declared, did not conflict with the FAA because it did not discriminate against arbitration, but applied equally to agreements in which individual employees waived the right to pursue work-related claims against an employer in *court* on a classwide basis. The Fifth Circuit in 2013 rejected the board's approach because (1) the federal labor laws do not "contain a congressional command overriding application of the FAA," and (2) "use of class action procedures . . . is not a substantive right" under the federal labor laws.[48] The NLRB, however, continued to apply its approach in other cases (because, in light of the provisions governing judicial review of the board's decisions, it was not obvious that those decisions are subject to Fifth Circuit law).

In a trio of subsequent cases, the federal courts of appeals divided on the question whether the federal labor laws preclude the enforcement of class action waivers in arbitration agreements covering claims regarding wages, hours, and terms and conditions of employment. Both the Seventh and Ninth Circuits concluded that a class action is a form of substantive "concerted activity" within the meaning of the federal labor laws, and that any attempt to restrict that right is thus unlawful.[49] In light of that conclusion, those courts held that there was no conflict between the federal labor laws and the FAA, which does not require the enforcement of unlawful arbitration agreements. The Fifth Circuit, in contrast, reaffirmed its position that adjudicating work-related claims on a classwide or collective basis is not a substantive right protected by the federal labor

---

[47] 563 U.S. at 344.

[48] See D.R. Horton, Inc. v. NLRB, 737 F.3d 344, 357, 360–62 (5th Cir. 2013).

[49] Lewis v. Epic Sys. Corp., 823 F.3d 1147 (7th Cir. 2016); Morris v. Ernst & Young LLP, 834 F.3d 975 (9th Cir. 2016).

laws, and that a prohibition on class action waivers thus conflicts with the FAA.[50]

The Supreme Court agreed to review all three cases and consolidated them for oral argument. Thus, in *Epic Systems Corp. v. Lewis,* *Ernst & Young LLP v. Morris,* and *NLRB v. Murphy Oil USA,* the Court will analyze the relationship between the federal labor and arbitration laws. The core question is whether the right to pursue a work-related claim on a collective, as opposed to individual, basis is a substantive right protected by the federal labor laws. There is ample precedent in the context of Federal Rule of Civil Procedure 23 that the right to pursue a class action is purely procedural in nature, and indeed it could hardly be otherwise in light of the Rules Enabling Act.[51] But the asserted right to pursue a class action at issue here arises not from Rule 23, but instead from the federal labor laws. Thus, the Court will have to decide whether the right to engage in concerted activity encompasses a substantive right to adjudicate a claim on a collective or classwide basis, and, if so, how such a right can be reconciled with the FAA, given the Supreme Court's recognition that collective or classwide adjudication is fundamentally inconsistent with arbitration. Like *Masterpiece Cakeshop,* this trio of cases will require the Court to resolve a clash of federal rights, although the rights at issue here are statutory, rather than constitutional. Notably, the solicitor general—who had filed the petition on behalf of the NLRB seeking review of the Fifth Circuit's decision against the board—switched sides in the cases, and now urges the Court to hold that the FAA mandates enforcement of class action waivers, and that nothing in federal labor law is to the contrary.

In recent decades, arbitration has become a standard way for American businesses to try to insulate themselves from the vagaries of class action litigation. It is not surprising that the beneficiaries of class action litigation have pushed back hard. So far, those pushback efforts—which generally have relied on state law—have largely failed. The question now is whether federal law can defeat class action waivers where state law could not. Were the Court to uphold the NLRB's position, this trio of cases would represent the

---

[50] Murphy Oil USA, Inc. v. NLRB, 808 F.3d 1013 (5th Cir. 2015).

[51] See, e.g., Shady Grove Orthopedic Assocs., P.A. v. Allstate Ins. Co., 559 U.S. 393 (2010); 28 U.S.C. § 2072.

first major setback to arbitration rights in the Court in decades. And other disputes lurk in the wings: the Consumer Financial Protection Bureau has recently promulgated a new rule prohibiting class action waivers in consumer financial transactions under the Dodd-Frank Wall Street Reform and Consumer Protection Act. These cases could either mark the end of a golden era for arbitration at the Supreme Court or reaffirm the Court's commitment to bilateral arbitration.

V. Criminal Law and the Fourth Amendment

A. *Qualified Immunity*

It makes perfect sense to throw a wild and crazy house party when your lease is up; the landlord was probably never going to return that deposit anyway. But "Peaches," a.k.a "Tasty," is that rare, bold tenant who decided to move into a vacant house and throw a party *before* she had even signed a lease. And what a party! Officers responding to neighbors' complaints about "illegal activities" at the house arrived to the sight of "several women who were 'scantily dressed and had currency tucked into their garments.'"[52] The officers smelled marijuana. "There were candles set out, a few lights on, and normal plumbing."[53] (Sometimes extra details can confuse more than clarify.)

Officers eventually rounded up 21 partygoers, "including a man hiding in a closet," none of whom was Tasty/Peaches. When police finally reached her by phone, she confirmed that she had indeed invited the partygoers and that "she was 'possibly' renting" the house from the owner. "Possibly"? It turns out she wasn't; police called the owner, who informed them that Tasty/Peaches "had tried, but failed, to reach a lease agreement," and that "no one, including 'Peaches,' had permission to be there."[54] The police then arrested all 21 attendees for criminal trespass ("unlawful entry" in D.C. parlance), though prosecutors later decided not to pursue any charges.

Sixteen of the 21 arrestees filed a federal lawsuit under 42 U.S.C. § 1983, alleging that the officers lacked probable cause to arrest them. The district court granted summary judgment to the partygoers, and the D.C. Circuit affirmed. Under D.C. law, "unlawful entry requires

[52] Brief in Opp'n, D.C. v. Wesby 2–3, No. 15-1485 (O.T. 2017).
[53] Brief for Respondents, D.C. v. Wesby 3, No. 15-1485 (O.T. 2017).
[54] Brief for Petitioner, D.C. v. Wesby 3–5, No. 15-1485 (O.T. 2017).

proof that the accused 'knew or should have known that s/he was entering against the person's will,'" and "nothing about what the police learned at the scene suggests that the Plaintiffs" had or should have had such knowledge.[55] Nor were the officers entitled to qualified immunity. "[I]n the absence of any conflicting information, Peaches' invitation vitiates the necessary element of Plaintiffs' intent to enter against the will of the lawful owner. A reasonably prudent officer aware that the Plaintiffs gathered pursuant to an invitation from someone with apparent (if illusory) authority could not conclude that they had entered unlawfully."[56]

The D.C. Circuit denied rehearing *en banc*, but Judge Brett Kavanaugh dissented on the ground that the officers were entitled to qualified immunity. It's hard to summarize his position more vividly than he did himself:

> When police officers confront a situation in which people appear to be engaged in unlawful activity, the officers often hear a variety of mens rea-related excuses. "The drugs in my locker aren't mine." "I don't know how the loaded gun got under my seat." "I didn't realize the under-aged high school kids in my basement had a keg." "I wasn't looking at child pornography on my computer, I was hacked." "I don't know how the stolen money got in my trunk." "I didn't see the red light." "I punched my girlfriend in self-defense."

> But in the heat of the moment, police officers are entitled to make reasonable credibility judgments and to disbelieve protests of innocence from, for example, those holding a smoking gun, or driving a car with a stash of drugs under the seat, or partying late at night with strippers and drugs in a vacant house without the owner or renter present. . . .

> Under the circumstances, it was entirely reasonable for the officers to have doubts about the partiers' story and to conclude that there was probable cause to arrest the partiers for trespassing. The police officers are entitled to qualified immunity.[57]

---

[55] Wesby v. D.C., 841 F. Supp. 2d 20, 32 (D.D.C. 2012) (brackets omitted).

[56] Wesby v. D.C., 765 F.3d 13, 21 (D.C. Cir. 2014).

[57] Wesby v. D.C., 816 F.3d 96, 106–07, 109 (D.C. Cir. 2016) (Kavanaugh, J., dissenting from denial of rehearing en banc).

Judge Kavanaugh thought the officers were entitled to qualified immunity for the additional reason that no case had clearly established "that officers are required to believe the statements of suspected trespassers who claim that they have permission to be on the property."[58]

There's really not much more to say. Although the petitioners in *District of Columbia v. Wesby* gamely attempt to gin up some generalized legal questions ("Are officers entitled to disbelieve suspects?"), at bottom this is a heavily fact-bound case. Indeed, the petitioners spend only eight of the 35 pages of the argument section in their opening brief on qualified immunity; the other 27 are devoted to arguing that under the circumstances they in fact had probable cause to arrest the partygoers. You might as well stamp "fact-bound" on the cover.

It is, therefore, somewhat surprising that the Court granted review in the first place; denials of qualified immunity are generally the province of summary reversals, not plenary review.[59] And maybe that's where the case was initially headed; the petition was relisted eight times before finally being granted—no match for *Masterpiece Cakeshop*, perhaps, but impressive nonetheless. The unusually high number suggests that a justice may have been writing an opinion— either a potential summary reversal that ultimately failed to attract sufficient votes, or a dissent from denial of certiorari that eventually convinced a holdout to provide a fourth vote to grant plenary review.

Also worth remembering is Justice Thomas's separate opinion last term *Ziglar v. Abbasi*, in which he expressed his "growing concern with our qualified immunity jurisprudence."[60] "Instead of asking whether the common law in 1871 would have accorded immunity to an officer for a tort analogous to the plaintiff's claim under §1983, we instead grant immunity to any officer whose conduct 'does not violate clearly established statutory or constitutional rights of which a reasonable person would have known.' . . . We have not attempted

---

[58] *Id.* at 110.

[59] See, e.g., White v. Pauly, 137 S. Ct. 548 (2017) (per curiam); Mullenix v. Luna, 136 S. Ct. 305 (2015) (per curiam); Taylor v. Barkes, 135 S. Ct. 2042 (2015) (per curiam); see generally W. Baude, Foreword: The Supreme Court's Shadow Docket, 9 N.Y.U. J.L. & Liberty 1, 45 (2015) (cataloguing summary reversals by type of case).

[60] 137 S. Ct. 1843, 1870 (2017) (Thomas, J., concurring in part and concurring in the judgment).

to locate that standard in the common law as it existed in 1871, however, and some evidence supports the conclusion that common-law immunity as it existed in 1871 looked quite different from our current doctrine."[61] Justice Thomas concluded, "In an appropriate case, we should reconsider our qualified immunity jurisprudence."[62]

It's unlikely that *Wesby* will be that case; the parties have not briefed the issue at all. Amicus ACLU *has* briefed it, yet concludes by urging the Court to reconsider the doctrine "[i]n a *future* case."[63] And the Court will not lack for opportunities; there's at least one pending petition (and probably many more, if not now then soon) squarely asking the Court to abandon qualified immunity altogether.[64] All that said, qualified immunity is likely to survive for some time yet, and almost certainly to outlive *Wesby*. But it's something to watch out for—just in case.

B. Cell Phone Searches

Twice in recent years the Court has addressed how the Fourth Amendment's proscription on "unreasonable searches and seizures" applies to modern technology—specifically, the warrantless collection of data from mobile devices. *United States v. Jones* held that the Fourth Amendment prohibits warrantless GPS tracking of a suspect's car.[65] *Riley v. California* held that it also prohibits the warrantless search of an arrestee's cell phone.[66] On the surface, *Carpenter v. United States* appears to be a kind of amalgam of *Riley* and *Jones*; it asks whether the Fourth Amendment prohibits the warrantless search of historical cell phone records that could, through the analysis of cell-site (cell tower) data, reveal the movements of the cell phone (and therefore its user) over time. Yet *Riley* and *Jones* are unlikely to drive the decision in *Carpenter*, no matter how it turns out.

The reason is a complicating factor known as the "third-party doctrine": "[T]he Fourth Amendment does not prohibit the obtaining

---

[61] *Id.* at 1871.

[62] *Id.* at 1872.

[63] Brief for Am. Civil Liberties Union et al. as Amici Curiae 30, D.C. v. Wesby, No. 15-485 (O.T. 2017) (emphasis added); see also *id.* at 15–30.

[64] See Pet. for Cert., Surratt v. McClaran, No. 16-1492.

[65] 565 U.S. 400 (2012).

[66] 134 S. Ct. 2473 (2014).

of information revealed to a third party and conveyed by him to Government authorities, even if the information is revealed on the assumption that it will be used only for a limited purpose and the confidence placed in the third party will not be betrayed."[67] Applying the third-party doctrine, *United States v. Miller* held that the Fourth Amendment did not prohibit the police's warrantless search of the suspect's bank records.[68] Similarly, *Smith v. Maryland* held that the Fourth Amendment did not prohibit the warrantless use of a "pen register," a (now obsolete?) device that recorded every phone number the suspect dialed.[69] In each case the defendant had "voluntarily" given the information to a third party, and so forfeited any Fourth Amendment protection of that information. Or, put differently, by "voluntarily" providing the information to a third party, the defendant no longer had a reasonable expectation of privacy in that information.

Carpenter, as noted, involves "cell site location information," generally comprising the identities of each cell tower and directional sector to which the cell phone connected at the start and end of every call made or received. (A single cell site usually has multiple antennae, each pointing in a different direction, to cover "wedge-shaped sectors."[70] The directional sector thus provides more granular information about the location of the cell phone relative to the tower.) The information is not a perfect indicator of location, and can sometimes even be misleading, because cell phones do not always connect to the closest tower. Indeed, this was one of the key inconsistencies at the heart of the Adnan Syed case featured on the hit podcast *Serial*.[71] Nevertheless, the increasingly dense placement of cell towers (especially in urban areas) and the increasing frequency with which cell phones connect to towers (not just for phone calls, but for text messages, email, and other instances of internet access) mean that historical cell site location information can provide a fairly detailed picture of the user's whereabouts.

[67] United States v. Miller, 423 U.S. 435, 443 (1976).

[68] *Id*. at 443–44.

[69] 442 U.S. 735, 744–45 (1979).

[70] Pet., Carpenter v. United States 5 n.3, No. 16-402 (O.T. 2017).

[71] See Syed v. Maryland, No. 199103042–046, Pet. No. 10432 (Baltimore City Cir. Ct. June 30, 2016) (trial court order granting habeas relief based on unreliable cell tower data).

The prosecutors in *Carpenter* exploited this capability. Following a string of armed robberies in Ohio and Michigan, police sought Carpenter's historical cell phone records from MetroPCS and Sprint for the four- or five-month period over which the robberies occurred. They did so under the auspices of the Stored Communications Act, which instructs magistrate judges to authorize such disclosure without requiring a showing of probable cause.[72] The cell site location information revealed that Carpenter's phone had connected to cell towers near several of the robbery locations at the times of the respective robberies. In part on that basis, Carpenter was convicted of several counts of Hobbs Act robbery and associated firearms crimes. The district court denied Carpenter's motion to suppress the cell site location information, and a divided Sixth Circuit panel affirmed under the third-party doctrine.

Carpenter argues that the sheer quantity of data, often spanning months, is no different from the data in *Jones*. And an increasing "volume of warrantless requests for [cell site location information] and the ubiquity of cell phones" suggest that this type of warrantless tracking has morphed into precisely the "dragnet-type law enforcement practices" that the Supreme Court has decried and Judge Alex Kozinski feared was imminent.[73] The government contends that Carpenter has no ownership interest in the data, used by cellular-service providers "to find weak spots in their cellular networks and to determine whether to charge customers roaming charges for particular calls."[74] And, echoing the Sixth Circuit, the government also distinguishes "the content of personal communications," in which a suspect maintains a reasonable expectation of privacy, from "the information necessary to get those communications from point A to point B," in which he does not.[75]

But the government, like the Sixth Circuit, relies mostly on the third-party doctrine, which cares for none of this. All that matters is the information's having been voluntarily provided to a third party. There is no doubt that Carpenter's cell tower information was

[72] 18 U.S.C. § 2703(d).

[73] United States v. Knotts, 460 U.S. 276, 283–84 (1983); United States v. Pineda-Moreno, 617 F.3d 1120, 1126 (9th Cir. 2010) (Kozinski, C.J., dissenting from denial of rehearing en banc).

[74] Brief in Opp'n for United States, Carpenter v. United States, No. 16-402 (O.T. 2017).

[75] *Id.* at 18 (internal quotation marks omitted).

provided to MetroPCS and Sprint—they are the ones who gathered the information in the first place. (In fact, it's doubtful the information was ever provided to Carpenter himself.) But was the disclosure of this information "voluntary"? The word is in scare quotes for a reason; does anyone really *volunteer* to share such data? The Third Circuit, at least, thinks not: "A cell phone customer has not 'voluntarily' shared his location information with a cellular provider in any meaningful way. As the [amicus Electronic Freedom Foundation] notes, it is unlikely that cell phone customers are aware that their cell phone providers *collect* and store historical location information."[76]

Concurring in *Jones*, Justice Sonia Sotomayor somewhat presciently remarked that the third-party doctrine "is ill suited to the digital age, in which people reveal a great deal of information about themselves to third parties in the course of carrying out mundane tasks."[77] She went on:

> People disclose the phone numbers that they dial or text to their cellular providers; the URLs that they visit and the e-mail addresses with which they correspond to their Internet service providers; and the books, groceries, and medications they purchase to online retailers. . . . I for one doubt that people would accept without complaint the warrantless disclosure to the Government of a list of every Web site they had visited in the last week, or month, or year."[78]

As technology becomes ever more pervasive, the third-party doctrine will allow ever more data to be collected without a warrant on the ground that we have "voluntarily" provided the data to our service providers.[79] No surprise, then, that there are few scholarly defenders of the doctrine. In fact, there may be only one.[80] Nevertheless, for now, the doctrine lives on. The government asks the Court to leave it untouched; Carpenter, unsurprisingly, asks the Court to revisit it. It's possible, of course, that the Court could decide *Carpenter*

---

[76] In re Application of the United States for an Order Directing a Provider of Elec. Commc'n Serv. to Disclose Records to the Gov't, 620 F.3d 304, 317 (3d Cir. 2010).

[77] 565 U.S. at 417 (Sotomayor, J., concurring).

[78] *Id.*

[79] See generally Note, If These Walls Could Talk: The Smart Home and the Fourth Amendment Limits of the Third Party Doctrine, 130 Harv. L. Rev. 1924 (2017).

[80] Orin S. Kerr, The Case for the Third-Party Doctrine, 107 Mich. L. Rev. 561 (2009).

on the ground that cell site location information does not reveal the same sort of private information as that stored on a cell phone or the same precision of location-tracking as does a GPS device. But then it's hard to see why the Court granted review. "The judiciary risks error by elaborating too fully on the Fourth Amendment implications of emerging technology before its role in society has become clear."[81] *Carpenter*, rather, seems destined to reevaluate the third-party doctrine in gross.

C. Guilty Pleas(e)

Depending on your viewpoint, *Class v. United States* is either a dry criminal-procedure case or a sexy Second Amendment one (or at least the prelude to one). En route from Virginia to Pennsylvania, Rodney Class—a self-described "Constitutional Bounty Hunter" who roams the nation "to enforce federal criminal law against judges whom he believe[s] ha[ve] acted unlawfully"—stopped at the U.S. Capitol to get his "Commission by Declaration" as a "Private Attorney General" signed.[82] (The briefs, regrettably, do not explain where one can obtain such documents.) Unfortunately for Rodney, he unwittingly parked his Jeep in an employee parking lot on Capitol grounds, where a federal statute prohibits all weapons.[83] In the Jeep were a loaded 9mm Ruger pistol, a loaded .44 Taurus pistol, a loaded .44 Henry rifle, and some 200 rounds of ammunition.

Class, who lawfully possessed (under North Carolina law, at least) all of the weapons and ammunition, moved to dismiss the indictment in part on the ground that the federal statute violates the Second Amendment. After the district judge denied the motion, Class pleaded guilty and renewed his constitutional challenge on appeal. The question presented in *Class* is whether, by pleading guilty, Class waived his right to subsequently challenge the constitutionality of his statute of conviction.

At first blush, the question seems odd because such challenges are a staple of modern criminal law: a defendant will conditionally plead guilty but reserve the right to appeal the conviction on

---

[81] Ontario v. Quon, 560 U.S. 746, 759 (2010).

[82] Brief for United States, Class v. United States 2, No. 16-424 (O.T. 2017); Brief for Petitioner, Class v. United States 4–5, No. 16-424 (O.T. 2017).

[83] 40 U.S.C. § 5104(e).

grounds specified in writing.[84] That's exactly what happened in *Bond v. United States*; after losing her motion to dismiss the indictment, the defendant pleaded guilty but reserved the right to appeal her conviction on the ground that the statute of conviction violated the Tenth Amendment.[85] It's also a common path for Fourth Amendment cases to reach the Supreme Court; after losing a motion to suppress, a defendant will enter a conditional guilty plea to appeal the constitutionality of the search or seizure that yielded the incriminating evidence. But Class didn't enter a *conditional* guilty plea; nor did he waive his right to appeal. Instead, he pleaded guilty without explicitly preserving *or* waiving the right to challenge the constitutionality of his statute of conviction on direct appeal. What then?

The Supreme Court partially answered that question in a pair of cases from the 1970s, *Blackledge v. Perry*[86] and *Menna v. New York*.[87] *Blackledge* held that an unconditional guilty plea does not preclude a subsequent constitutional challenge "to the very power of the State to bring the defendant into court to answer the charge brought against him."[88] *Blackledge* distinguished challenges to garden-variety "antecedent constitutional violations . . . that occurred prior to the entry of the guilty plea"—which *are* waived—from assertions of "the right not to be haled into court at all"—which are not.[89] The federal habeas petitioner's claim that the state's filing the charge (to which he pleaded guilty) itself violated due process apparently fell in the latter bucket. Two terms later and relying on *Blackledge*, *Menna* held that an appeal challenging a conviction on double-jeopardy grounds likewise is not foreclosed by a guilty plea. "Where the State is precluded by the United States Constitution from haling a defendant into court on a charge, federal law requires that a conviction on that charge be set aside even if the conviction was entered pursuant to a counseled plea of guilty."[90] A guilty plea establishes only "factual guilt," and thus precludes only challenges to "constitutional violations not

---

[84] See, e.g., Fed. R. Crim. P. 11(a) (2).

[85] 564 U.S. 211 (2011).

[86] 417 U.S. 21 (1974).

[87] 423 U.S. 61 (1975) (per curiam).

[88] 417 U.S. at 30.

[89] *Id*. (internal quotation marks omitted).

[90] Menna, 423 U.S. at 62 (citing Blackledge).

logically inconsistent with the valid establishment of factual guilt.
. . . Here, however, the claim is that the State may not convict petitioner no matter how validly his factual guilt is established. The
guilty plea, therefore, does not bar the claim."[91]

Which brings us to *Class*. Is the (alleged) unconstitutionality of the
no-guns-on-Capitol-grounds statute merely an antecedent "constitutional violation not logically inconsistent with the valid establishment of factual guilt," or is it an infringement of Class's "right not be
haled into court at all"? The government and Class offer competing
accounts of Federal Rule of Criminal Procedure 11(a)(2), which describes the requirements to enter conditional guilty pleas, and the
application of *Blackledge, Menna*, and other cases; the parties generally treat the case as a dry procedural one. Viewed in this way, Class
seems to have a decent shot at victory. More than 100 years ago, the
Supreme Court concluded that a lower court lacks the "authority to
indict and try" a defendant "if the laws are unconstitutional and
void."[92] That sounds an awful lot like "can't be haled into court."

Yet it's hard to ignore the Second Amendment subtext. Class was
initially charged with violating D.C. Code § 22-4504(a), which prohibited carrying a pistol in public—until, that is, the ordinance was
held to be unconstitutional in another case.[93] And that *Class* involves
guns and gun rights can't be far from the justices' minds—not least
because this "constitutional bounty hunter," heavily armed and with
a vendetta against judges, parked his car just a few blocks from the
Supreme Court building.[94] With the possible exception of the non-
argued *per curiam* opinion in *Caetano v. Massachusetts*,[95] which simply
instructed the Massachusetts high court to come up with a better
explanation for upholding a ban on stun guns, the Court has stead-
fastly refused to hear a bona fide Second Amendment case since
McDonald v. Chicago in 2010.[96] Justice Thomas, invariably joined by
Justice Scalia (and now Justice Gorsuch), has taken to publicly

---

[91] *Id.* at 63 n.2.

[92] Ex parte Siebold, 100 U.S. 371, 377 (1880).

[93] See Palmer v. Dist. of Columbia, 59 F. Supp. 3d 173 (D.D.C. 2014).

[94] And just steps from the U.S. Capitol—especially salient after the recent shooting
at a congressional softball practice in Virginia. See M.D. Shear et al., G.O.P. Lawmaker
Shot Outside Capital, N.Y. Times, June 15, 2007, at A1.

[95] 136 S. Ct. 1027 (2016) (per curiam).

[96] 561 U.S. 742 (2010).

dissenting from the denial of cert in some of these cases.[97] In fact, Justice Thomas used his first (and so far only) remarks at oral argument in more than a decade to question the propriety of a misdemeanor conviction's depriving the defendant of his constitutional right to own a firearm.[98] Could *Class* eventually be the sleeper Second Amendment case he's been looking for?

Bond offers an intriguing parallel. The first time *Bond* reached the Court, the only question was whether the defendant had standing to challenge the constitutionality of her statute of conviction on federalism grounds. But that was merely a prelude to the *real* question: did the Tenth Amendment prohibit the Chemical Weapons Convention Implementation Act from criminalizing a jilted wife's spreading a chemical irritant on her husband's paramour's mailbox? That was the (far more interesting) question in the second *Bond* case.[99] Yet it's unclear whether, but for the first cert grant, the Court would have agreed to grant the second *Bond* petition at all. There was no clear split, and the question was not obviously one of recurring national importance. Stewart Baker once mused that "the Supreme Court is probably somewhat more likely to grant certiorari the second time around,"[100] and anecdotal evidence suggests that the Court does indeed have an affinity for hearing the same case multiple times. Examples from just the last few terms include *Horne v. Department of Agriculture*,[101] *Fisher v. University of Texas at Austin*,[102] *Kirtsaeng v. John Wiley & Sons, Inc.*,[103] and *Franchise Tax Board of California v. Hyatt*.[104]

---

[97] See, e.g., Peruta v. California, 137 S. Ct. 1995 (2017) (Thomas, J., joined by Gorsuch, J., dissenting from denial of cert.); Friedman v. Highland Park, 136 S. Ct. 447 (2015) (Thomas, J., joined by Scalia, J., dissenting from denial of cert.); Jackson v. City & Cty. of San Francisco, 135 S. Ct. 2799 (2015) (Thomas, J., joined by Scalia, J., dissenting from denial of cert.).

[98] Transcript of Oral Arg. in Voisine v. United States, No. 14-10154, at 35–39 (O.T. 2015).

[99] Bond v. United States, 134 S. Ct. 2077 (2014). Some of Bond's counsel in the Supreme Court are now, though were not at the time, the authors' colleagues at Kirkland & Ellis.

[100] Stewart A. Baker, A Practical Guide to Certiorari, 33 Catholic Univ. L. Rev. 611, 626 (1984).

[101] 135 S. Ct. 2419 (2015); 133 S. Ct. 2053 (2013).

[102] 136 S. Ct. 2198 (2016); 133 S. Ct. 2411 (2013).

[103] 136 S. Ct. 1979 (2016); 568 U.S. 519 (2013).

[104] 136 S. Ct. 1277 (2016); 538 U.S. 488 (2003).

So although *Class* presents a question about criminal procedure, history suggests that it could easily morph into a Second Amendment case—if not on this go-around, then on the next one. And that is reason enough to pay attention.

VI. Federalism

"What happens in Vegas stays in Vegas" isn't just a tourism motto, it's federal law—law that the consolidated cases *Christie v. NCAA* and *New Jersey Thoroughbred Horsemen's Association v. NCAA* hope to upend.[105] The 1992 Professional and Amateur Sports Protection Act (PASPA) makes it "unlawful" for a State to "authorize by law . . . betting, gambling, or wagering" on professional or amateur sports.[106] But PASPA's proscription "shall not apply" to any "betting, gambling, or wagering scheme in operation in a State" that existed "at any time during the period beginning January 1, 1976, and ending August 31, 1990."[107] This provision in effect grandfathers sports wagering in just four States—including, most notably, Nevada.[108]

New Jersey, however, is not one of those states, thus putting the lie to *Hamilton*'s assertion that "[e]verything is legal in New Jersey."[109] For decades, sports gambling in New Jersey had been expressly prohibited by statute.[110] (New Jersey has long had casinos in Atlantic City, and PASPA does contain an additional exemption for sports-wagering schemes "conducted exclusively in casinos" that were authorized within a year of PASPA's enactment.[111] But New Jersey never took advantage of this exemption.) Notwithstanding PASPA, in 2012 the New Jersey legislature authorized racetracks and Atlantic City casinos to enter, with a few exceptions for New Jersey-based teams

---

[105] Some of the authors' colleagues at Kirkland & Ellis represent the respondents in both cases.

[106] 28 U.S.C. § 3702.

[107] 28 U.S.C. § 3704(a)(1).

[108] The others are Delaware, Montana, and Oregon. See Brief in Opp'n for United States in Nos. 16-476 & -477, at 3 (O.T. 2017); see also NCAA v. Governor of the State of N.J., 730 F.3d 208, 216 (3d Cir. 2013); OFC Comm Baseball v. Markell, 579 F.3d 293, 297 (3d Cir. 2009).

[109] Lin-Manuel Miranda et al., "Blow Us All Away," Hamilton: An American Musical (Original Broadway Cast Recording) (Atlantic Records 2015).

[110] N.J. Stat. Ann. § 2A:40–1 (West 2011).

[111] 28 U.S.C. § 3704(a) (3).

and events, "the business of accepting wagers on any sports event by any system or method of wagering."[112] The NCAA and all four major professional sports leagues (NFL, MLB, NBA, and NHL) promptly sued to enjoin the state statute; among other defenses, the state argued that PASPA unconstitutionally "commandeers" the state.[113]

The constitutional "anti-commandeering" principle stems largely from a pair of cases in the 1990s, *New York v. United States* and *Printz v. United States*. *New York* held that, under the Tenth Amendment, "even where Congress has the authority under the Constitution to pass laws requiring or prohibiting certain acts, it lacks the power directly to compel the States to require or prohibit those acts."[114] So Congress may directly regulate the storage and disposal of radioactive nuclear waste, and it may "encourage" states to regulate the disposal of such waste generated within their respective borders, but it may *not* (as it had tried to do) compel state legislatures to enact statutes to regulate such disposal under pain of "taking title" to—being stuck with the very expensive problem of—the waste if they resist. Five years later, *Printz* extended this anti-commandeering principle to state executive officers; so Congress is free to require national background checks before firearms are transferred or sold, but it may not compel state law enforcement officers to conduct those background checks.[115]

According to New Jersey, *New York* and *Printz* rendered PASPA unconstitutional to the extent it prohibited the state from enacting legislation to authorize sports gambling. The Third Circuit disagreed, in large part because PASPA "does not *require* or coerce the states to lift a finger—they are not required to pass laws, to take title to anything, to conduct background checks, to expend any funds, or to in any way enforce federal law."[116] Instead, PASPA merely "prohibit[s] the states from taking certain actions."[117] Recognizing that "affirmative commands can be easily recast as prohibitions," the Third Circuit still held that PASPA was a garden-variety prohibition unlike

---

[112] N.J. Stat. Ann. §§ 5:12A-1, -2 (West 2012).

[113] See NCAA, 730 F.3d at 226–37.

[114] 505 U.S. 144, 166 (1992).

[115] 521 U.S. 898, 935 (1997).

[116] NCAA, 730 F.3d at 231.

[117] *Id.*

the laws in *New York* or *Printz*, and the court "d[id] not read PASPA to prohibit New Jersey from repealing its ban on sports wagering."[118]

In 2014 that's exactly what New Jersey did: it partially repealed its longstanding statutory ban on sports wagering, though only in casinos and at racetracks and with the same New Jersey-based limitations as in the 2012 law.[119] The 2014 statute expressly states that it is "not intended and shall not be construed as causing the State to sponsor, operate, advertise, promote, license, or authorize by law" sports wagering.[120] The NCAA and the four major professional sports leagues once again sued, and once again the Third Circuit ruled against the state.[121] First, the en banc court disavowed as "too facile" the previous panel's dictum that PASPA did not "prohibit New Jersey from repealing its ban on sports wagering."[122] "While artfully couched in terms of a repealer, the 2014 Law essentially provides that, notwithstanding any other prohibition by law, casinos and racetracks shall hereafter be permitted to have sports gambling. This is an authorization."[123] Having found that PASPA preempted the 2014 statute, the Third Circuit once again rejected the state's anti-commandeering arguments. "PASPA does not command states to take affirmative actions, and it does not present a coercive binary choice. Our reasoning in *Christie I* that PASPA does not commandeer the states remains unshaken."[124] Dissenting, Judge Thomas Vanaskie posited that no matter how the 2014 law is characterized, "PASPA was intended to compel the States to prohibit wagering on sporting events" and thus runs afoul of *New York*'s holding that Congress "lacks the power directly to compel the States . . . to prohibit [certain] acts."[125]

At the certiorari stage, both the sports leagues and the solicitor general (who filed a brief in opposition in response to the Court's call for his views) maintained that PASPA does *not* prohibit New Jersey

---

[118] *Id.* at 233, 232.

[119] S. Bill No. 2460, 216th Legis., 1st Sess. (N.J. 2014), reprinted at Pet. App. 218–22a.

[120] *Id.* § 2.

[121] NCAA v. Governor of the State of N.J., 832 F.3d 389 (3d Cir. 2016) (en banc).

[122] *Id.* at 396–97, 401.

[123] *Id.* at 397.

[124] *Id.* at 401.

[125] *Id.* at 406–07 (Vanaskie, J., dissenting).

from simply repealing its ban on sports wagering; it simply prohibits affirmatively *authorizing* sports wagering, and the 2014 law is really an authorization masquerading as a partial repeal.[126] This echoes the Third Circuit's understanding that a simple repeal, without more, would be *in*sufficient under New Jersey law (because of a complex interplay with a state constitutional provision) to allow sports wagering in the state.[127] That the 2014 law purported to allow sports wagering proved it was really an affirmative authorization, not merely a repeal of a ban.

So the ultimate question in the case seems to be: does PASPA prohibit state-sanctioned sports gambling (which is constitutional), or does it compel states to prohibit sports gambling (which is not)? As a practical matter, not much may turn on the answer to that question—either way, you can't walk into an Atlantic City casino and bet the over/under on the length of the National Anthem sung at the Super Bowl. (The over/under was 2:09 last year; singer Luke Bryan finished in 2:04.) But the case may reveal much about the Court's collective views of the anti-commandeering principle, which resists easy characterization or prediction. Thus, although *Printz* had a right-leaning political valence, the doctrine has emerged as one of the primary defenses of "sanctuary cities" who refuse to administer federal immigration law.[128] Any bet on the outcome in *Christie* would therefore be a risky wager.

---

[126] See Brief in Opp'n for the United States, NCAA v. Christie 15, Nos. 16-476 & -477 (O.T. 2017) ("If New Jersey wishes to repeal its prohibition on sports gambling altogether and thereby remain silent with respect to such gambling, or to adopt a partial repeal that is not a de facto authorization (by, for instance, lifting state penalties on informal or social wagering), PASPA does not stand in its way. But the 2014 Act's partial repeal—which is specifically tailored to facilitate sports gambling at state-licensed casinos and racetracks—is no different from a positive enactment authorizing such gambling."); Brief in Opp'n for NCAA et al., NCAA v. Christie 23, Nos. 16-476 & -477 (O.T. 2017) (similar).

[127] NCAA, 730 F.3d at 232.

[128] See, e.g., Order Granting [Plaintiffs'] Motions to Enjoin Section 9(a) of Executive Order 13768, at 39–41, County of Santa Clara v. Trump, Nos. 17-cv-574, -485 (N.D. Cal. Apr. 25, 2017) (granting a preliminary injunction in part under *New York* and *Printz*), ECF No. 82.

VII. Intellectual Property Law (but Really Constitutional Law)

Most readers' eyes glaze over when they see "patent law" or "Federal Circuit"—and Latin-sounding terms like *"inter partes* review" can't help either. But *Oil States Energy Services LLC v. Greene's Energy Group, LLC,* is actually a constitutional case about property rights and the separation of powers. Specifically, *Oil States* asks whether the patent agency, after granting a patent, can later take it away without providing the patentee a jury or an Article III forum. To fully understand the dispute, however, requires a little background on how patents are issued and canceled.

Let's begin with the Constitution, which grants Congress the "power . . . to promote the Progress of Science and useful Arts, by securing for limited Times to Authors and Inventors the exclusive Right to their respective Writings and Discoveries."[129] Congress wasted little time in enacting "An Act to promote the progress of useful Arts" in 1790, which authorized patents for up to 14-year terms for "any useful art, manufacture, engine, machine, or device, or any improvement therein not before known or used" that was "sufficiently useful and important."[130]

Congress quickly deleted the "sufficiently useful and important" part, which was deemed too high a barrier; only 55 patents had been issued in the three years since the 1790 act. A patentable item now needed only to be a "new and useful art, machine, manufacture or composition of matter, or any new and useful improvement on [the same], not known or used before."[131] This definition endures nearly verbatim today, the only meaningful addition coming in 1952, when Congress required the patented invention to be "non-obvious" "to a person having ordinary skill in the art" as well.[132]

Over time, some came to believe it was a little *too* easy to get a patent, particularly for software and "business methods."[133] Add to that concern "the *in terrorem* power of patent trolls" to extract large

---

[129] U.S. Const. art. I, § 8, cl. 8.

[130] 1 Stat. 109, 110 (1790).

[131] 1 Stat. 318, 319 (1793).

[132] 35 U.S.C. § 101; as amended by 66 Stat. 798 (1952), codified at 35 U.S.C. § 103.

[133] See, e.g., Bilski v. Kappos, 561 U.S. 593, 608–09 (2010); Timothy B. Lee, Software Patents Are a Disaster, Vox, www.vox.com/2014/12/31/7475317/software-patents-2014-review (Dec. 31, 2014).

settlements for dubious patents,[134] and it's no surprise that Congress eventually took action—though not, as it did in 1793, by changing the standards for patentability. Instead, Congress created procedures to allow patents to be revoked *after* they were granted.

Even the 1790 act permitted a district-court judge to repeal a patent within one year of its issuance upon a showing that it was "obtained surreptitiously by, or upon false suggestion."[135] But Congress eventually authorized more searching post-issuance review within the agency itself, not the courts. For example, the 1980 Bayh-Dole Act created "ex parte reexamination," under which "[a]ny person, at any time" can ask the agency to reexamine and potentially cancel a patent.[136] The agency itself can reexamine issued patents on its "own initiative" as well.[137] A patentee whose patent is canceled as a result of an ex parte reexamination may seek judicial review of the agency's decision.[138]

The 2011 Leahy-Smith America Invents Act created a parallel procedure called "inter partes review,"[139] under which any "person who is not the owner of the patent" can seek to invalidate any U.S. patent on the ground that it is either obvious or not novel.[140] Unlike ex parte reexamination, inter partes review is adversarial, so the petitioning party can participate in a trial-like proceeding. Both the patentee and the petitioner may appeal an adverse decision to the Federal Circuit.

And that brings us, finally, to *Oil States*. The petitioner claims that inter partes review is unconstitutional because it deprives a patentee of private property—his patent—without a jury, as required by the Seventh Amendment, and without an Article III tribunal, as required by, well, Article III. As in most such disputes, the parties start from different premises: the petitioner argues that a patent, once issued, is a private property right, whereas the government and the private respondent maintain that a patent is and remains a "public right."

---

[134] Commil USA, LLC v. Cisco Sys., Inc., 135 S. Ct. 1920, 1932 (2015) (Scalia, J., dissenting).

[135] 1 Stat. 111. The window for such a repeal was later increased to three years. See 1 Stat. 323.

[136] 35 U.S.C. §§ 301, 302.

[137] 35 U.S.C. § 303(a).

[138] 35 U.S.C. § 306.

[139] Pub. L. 112–29, 125 Stat. 284 (2011), codified at 35 U.S.C. §§ 300 et seq.

[140] 35 U.S.C. § 311.

The distinction is crucial. Since as early as the New Deal-era cases *Crowell v. Benson*[141] and *NLRB v. Jones & Laughlin*,[142] the Court has held that "public rights"—rights created by statute—may be adjudicated in a non-Article III forum and without a jury. (The full definition of public rights is a little more nuanced, but "created by statute" will suffice for this discussion.) The further expansion of the administrative state in the 1970s brought more cases reemphasizing this point, most notably *Atlas Roofing Company v. Occupational Health & Safety Review Commission*, which made explicit that "when Congress creates new statutory 'public rights,' it may assign their adjudication to an administrative agency with which a jury trial would be incompatible."[143] In other words, courts would essentially defer to Congress on the question whether a jury-trial right would impede the effective functioning of a statutory or regulatory scheme.

Moreover, the Seventh Amendment and Article III questions became somewhat intertwined over the years. *Crowell* held that even in disputes over *private* rights, an agency could conduct the initial fact-finding without a jury, subject only to deferential appellate review in an Article III court. (This is essentially how inter partes review works.) In other words, agency adjudication means no jury, even for private rights. And the flip side is also true: *Curtis v. Loether* held that a jury is required, even for disputes involving statutorily created rights, if the proceeding is heard in an Article III court. "[W]hen Congress provides for enforcement of statutory rights in an ordinary civil action in the district courts, where there is obviously no functional justification for denying the jury trial right, a jury trial must be available."[144]

So where do patents fit? "[T]he crucial question," said the Supreme Court in *Granfinanceria, S.A. v. Nordberg*, "is whether 'Congress, acting for a valid legislative purpose pursuant to its constitutional powers under Article I, has created a seemingly "private" right that is so closely integrated into a public regulatory scheme as to be a matter appropriate for agency resolution with limited involvement by the

---

[141] 285 U.S. 22 (1932).
[142] 301 U.S. 1 (1937).
[143] 430 U.S. 442, 455 (1977).
[144] Curtis v. Loether, 415 U.S. 189, 195 (1977).

Article III judiciary.'"[145] The *Oil States* respondents, unsurprisingly, argue that patents and inter partes review fit the bill. Not only are patents created and granted by statute, but inter partes review is just one piece of a massively complex "public regulatory scheme" into which the issuance and cancelation of patents are "closely integrated." The Federal Circuit agrees.[146]

Against this, the *Oil States* petitioner counters with some history. A patent-infringement suit has long been a traditionally "legal" cause of action heard in the English law courts. "[T]here is no dispute that infringement cases today must be tried to a jury, as their predecessors were more than two centuries ago."[147] And, setting aside invalidation because the patent was "obtained surreptitiously by, or upon false suggestion," the traditional way to invalidate a patent has always been to raise invalidity as a defense in an infringement suit. It follows that the adversarial inter partes review proceeding must also be conducted before a jury, in an Article III forum. By way of analogy, the petitioner points to copyright, also governed by a "public regulatory scheme"; yet copyright-infringement suits have also been "tried in courts of law, and thus before juries."[148] And like copyrights, patents are not "modern statutory rights unknown to 18th-century England."[149] Yet the analogy goes only so far. While "the common law" has long "recognized an author's right to prevent the unauthorized publication of his manuscript,"[150] patent rights, by contrast, have always "exist[ed] only by virtue of statute."[151] Nevertheless, as in *Curtis*, Congress has "provide[d] for enforcement of statutory [patent] rights in an ordinary civil action in the district courts," and "there is obviously no functional justification for denying the jury trial right."[152]

---

[145] 492 U.S. 33, 54 (1989) (quoting Thomas v. Union Carbide Agric. Products Co., 473 U.S. 568, 593–94 (1985)).

[146] See MCM Portfolio LLC v. Hewlett-Packard Co., 812 F.3d 1284, 1293 (Fed. Cir. 2015).

[147] Markman v. Westview Instruments, Inc., 517 U.S. 370, 377 (1996).

[148] Feltner v. Columbia Pictures Television, Inc., 523 U.S. 340, 348–49 (1998).

[149] *Id.* at 348.

[150] *Id.* at 349.

[151] Sears, Roebuck & Co. v. Stiffel Co., 376 U.S. 225, 229 n.5 (1964).

[152] Curtis, 415 U.S. at 195.

In the face of these competing narratives, the Court may well opt to sidestep the Seventh Amendment question. A further requirement for a jury, even for private rights, is that the sought-for relief be "legal," not "equitable." Because *inter partes* review offers no hope for monetary damages, the Seventh Amendment arguably does not apply regardless of whether patents are public rights. The petition gamely attempts to blunt this issue by arguing that the law-equity dividing line "can be difficult to draw" and so the jury "option must be open to patent holders and not foreclosed by *inter partes* review proceedings."[153]

Even setting aside the Seventh Amendment question, the petitioner urges that inter partes review violates Article III because only a court may deprive it of its lawful property (the patent). Long ago, in *McCormick Harvesting Machine Company v. Aultman*, the Court held that once a patent has been issued, "[i]t has become the property of the patentee, and as such is entitled to the same legal protection as other property."[154] An issued patent "is not subject to be revoked or cancelled by the President, or any other officer of the Government. . . . The only authority competent to set a patent aside, or to annul it, or to correct it for any reason whatever, is vested in the courts of the United States, and not in the department which issued the patent."[155]

That's a seemingly slam-dunk argument for the petitioner—had *McCormick* not been decided in 1898, long before the advent of the administrative state and the "public rights" doctrine. Subsequent cases, including the New Deal-era and 1970s cases discussed above, have arguably undermined *McCormick*. A line of bankruptcy cases, most recently *Stern v. Marshall*, has acknowledged that any right "integrally related to particular Federal Government action" may be adjudicated outside an Article III forum, especially if "resolution of the claim by an expert Government agency is deemed essential to a limited regulatory objective within the agency's authority."[156] And Congress's longstanding desire to have the agency reexamine

---

153 Petition, Oil States Energy Services LLC v. Greene's Energy Group, LLC 13 n.4, No. 16-712 (O.T. 2017).

154 169 U.S. 606, 609 (1898).

155 *Id*. at 608–09.

156 564 U.S. 462, 490–91 (2011).

issued patents, dating back to the creation of ex parte reexamination in 1980, places a heavy thumb on the functionalist scale.

Yet several justices have expressed unease with the powers of the modern administrative state and the lack of sufficient judicial oversight.[157] And the protection of property rights has long divided the Court.[158] Add to that the general track record of the Federal Circuit in the Supreme Court (read: not good), and the outcome of this case is anyone's guess.

VIII. Pipeline

If it's hard to predict how the Supreme Court will resolve the cases that it has agreed to review, it's even harder to predict what cases it will agree to review in the first place. Nonetheless, we feel compelled to highlight a few notable cases in the pipeline.

A. Union Fees

Last year, at a roundtable discussion on Justice Scalia's impact on the Supreme Court, the panelists were asked to recall their first thought upon hearing of his death. Without hesitation, one panelist responded, *"Abood* lives!" Sure enough, a little over a month after Justice Scalia's death, the Court issued a *per curiam* order in *Friedrichs v. California Teachers Association,* which was expected to be one of the landmark decisions of the term, affirming the judgment by an equally divided Court.[159] The issue in *Friedrichs* was whether the Court should overrule *Abood v. Detroit Board of Education,* where the Court upheld—against a First Amendment challenge—state laws that require public employees to pay "agency fees" to a union even if they want nothing to do with the union and disagree with its advocacy.[160]

---

[157] See, e.g., Perez v. Mortgage Bankers Ass'n, 135 S. Ct. 1199, 1213–25 (2015) (Thomas, J., concurring in the judgment); City of Arlington, Tex. v. FCC, 133 S. Ct. 1863, 1877–86 (2013) (Roberts, C.J., dissenting, joined by Kennedy & Alito, JJ.); Gutierrez-Brizuela v. Lynch, 834 F.3d 1142, 1149 (10th Cir. 2016) (Gorsuch, J., concurring).

[158] See, e.g., Murr v. Wisconsin, 137 S. Ct. 1933 (2017); Kelo v. City of New London, 545 U.S. 469 (2005).

[159] 136 S. Ct. 1083 (2016).

[160] 431 U.S. 209 (1977).

A majority of the Court sharply criticized, but stopped short of overruling, *Abood* in *Harris v. Quinn*.[161] Until Justice Scalia's death, the Court appeared poised to take that further step in *Friedrichs*. Like *Friedrichs* before it, *Janus v. American Federation of State, County, and Municipal Employees* presents the question whether *Abood* should "be overruled and public-sector agency fee arrangements declared unconstitutional under the First Amendment."[162] Given the Court's failure to resolve that issue in *Friedrichs, Janus* would seem a natural candidate for review. And why, one might ask, do passions run so high on this issue? For one, it involves compelled speech: laws forcing Americans to subsidize private activities with which they disagree. But it also involves money—and political power. If unions are unable to compel the payment of fees, it stands to reason that they will collect less money and hence exercise diminished political power. The stakes on this issue are very high and, if the Court were to grant review, this would unquestionably stand as one of the term's blockbuster cases.

B. Separation of Powers

Few issues excite separation-of-powers mavens more than statutory limits on the president's removal authority. President Andrew Johnson was impeached over a dispute arising from his attempt to remove his own Secretary of War, and an entire generation of lawyers has come of age reading Justice Scalia's dazzling dissent in *Morrison v. Olson* in law school.[163] Chief Justice William Howard Taft, after having served as president, authored the Court's decision in *Myers v. United States*, which broadly reaffirmed the president's exclusive authority to remove executive branch officials (and thereby repudiated the Tenure of Office Act that had led to President Johnson's impeachment).[164] But, scarcely a decade later, the Court limited *Myers* in *Humphrey's Executor* by upholding limitations on the president's authority to remove a member of the Federal Trade Commission, an "independent" agency that exercises executive power.[165]

---

[161] 134 S. Ct. 2618 (2014).

[162] No. 16-1466 (petition filed June 6, 2017).

[163] 487 U.S. 654, 697–734 (1988) (Scalia, J., dissenting).

[164] 272 U.S. 52 (1926).

[165] Humphrey's Executor v. United States, 295 U.S. 602 (1935).

In his *Morrison* dissent, Justice Scalia had some choice words for *Humphrey's Executor*, noting that it "was considered by many at the time the product of an activist, anti-New Deal Court bent on reducing the power of President Franklin Roosevelt," and gave "shoddy treatment . . . to Chief Justice Taft's opinion 10 years earlier in *Myers* . . . —gutting, in six quick pages devoid of textual or historical precedent for the novel principle it set forth, a carefully researched and reasoned 70-page opinion."[166]

The scope of *Humphrey's Executor* is now the subject of a case pending before the en banc D.C. Circuit, which has the potential to reach the Supreme Court this term (and, if not, almost certainly the following term). The Dodd-Frank Wall Street Reform and Consumer Protection Act created the Consumer Financial Protection Bureau (CFPB), headed by a single director, and specified that the president could remove the director only "for inefficiency, neglect of duty, or malfeasance in office."[167] Parties subject to the CFPB's regulatory authority challenged that provision on separation-of-powers grounds, and a divided panel of the D.C. Circuit in *PHH Corporation v. CFPB* sustained the challenge.[168] The panel distinguished *Humphrey's Executor* on the ground that the case involved an independent agency headed by *multiple* commissioners, whereas the CFPB is headed by only a *single* director.[169] The D.C. Circuit subsequently granted en banc rehearing, thereby vacating the panel decision. The full appellate court heard oral argument in May 2017, and as of this writing, the matter remains under submission. However the D.C. Circuit resolves the case, it will certainly present an attractive candidate for Supreme Court review. And—unlike the D.C. Circuit—the Supreme Court has the luxury of re-examining, as opposed to merely attempting to distinguish, *Humphrey's Executor*.

The flip side of the removal authority, of course, is the appointment authority. And a pending petition for certiorari raises an interesting question under the Constitution's Appointments Clause. *Raymond J. Lucia Companies v. SEC* seeks review of the D.C. Circuit's holding that administrative law judges (ALJs) who preside over enforcement

---

[166] Morrison v. Olson, 487 U.S. at 724, 725–26 (Scalia, J., dissenting).

[167] 12 U.S.C. § 5491(c) (3).

[168] 839 F.3d 1 (D.C. Cir. 2016).

[169] *Id.* at 13–36.

actions brought by the Securities and Exchange Commission (SEC) are not "inferior" officers of the United States, but instead mere employees who do not exercise "'significant authority pursuant to the laws of the United States.'"[170] The difference is one of constitutional dimension: under the Appointments Clause, "inferior" officers of the United States must be appointed by "the President alone, . . . the Courts of Law, or . . . the Heads of Departments."[171] The Clause promotes the separation of powers by preventing Congress from appointing persons who wield significant executive authority, and promotes accountability by identifying those responsible for appointing such persons. The petition appears likely to be granted: the Tenth Circuit has expressly rejected the D.C. Circuit's holding,[172] and the D.C. Circuit itself granted hearing en banc (thereby vacating the panel opinion), only to affirm the SEC's order by an equally divided court.

* * *

These are unconventional times, and the Supreme Court may be headed for an unconventional term. A single party now controls both the federal executive and legislative branches, and the new administration has expressed a willingness, if not an outright desire, to upend the established status quo. After eight years, however, the last administration left a strong imprint on the lower courts, and it is hard to imagine any substantial new initiative that will not face a legal challenge. The most momentous decisions of the upcoming term, thus, may arise in the context of motions for extraordinary relief, such as a motion to stay a lower-court injunction. In this regard, the travel-ban litigation may be most notable as a harbinger of things to come. It will be interesting, in this and coming terms, to see how the recent upheaval in Washington plays out in the polished marble corridors of One First Street Northeast.

---

[170] 832 F.3d. 277, 284 (2016) (quoting Buckley v. Valeo, 424 U.S. 1, 126 (1976) (per curiam)).

[171] U.S. Const. art II, § 2, cl. 2.

[172] Bandimere v. SEC, 844 F.3d 1168 (10th Cir. 2016).

Contributors

Thomas A. Berry is College of Public Interest Law Fellow at the Pacific Legal Foundation and a former legal associate in the Cato Institute's Center for Constitutional Studies. During law school, Berry interned at both Cato and Institute for Justice. His opinion pieces have appeared in popular outlets including *National Law Journal, National Review (Online),* and *The Federalist,* and his academic articles have been published in *Federalist Society Review* and *NYU Journal of Law and Liberty.* Berry holds a J.D. from Stanford Law School, where he was a senior editor on the *Stanford Law and Policy Review* and a Bradley Student Fellow in the Stanford Constitutional Law Center. He graduated with a B.A. in Liberal Arts from St. John's College, Santa Fe.

Jackson C. Blais is a research assistant to Prof. Richard Garnett of Notre Dame Law School. He is a graduate of Grinnell College and current J.D. candidate at Notre Dame Law School, where he is a Dean's Circle Fellow and serves as a staff editor on the *Notre Dame Law Review.*

Clint Bolick was appointed by Governor Doug Ducey in January 2016 to serve on the Arizona Supreme Court. Before joining the Court, Justice Bolick litigated constitutional cases in state and federal courts from coast to coast, including the U.S. Supreme Court. Among other positions, he served as vice president for litigation at the Goldwater Institute and as co-founder and vice president for litigation at the Institute for Justice. He has litigated in support of school choice, freedom of enterprise, private property rights, freedom of speech, and federalism, and against racial classifications and government subsidies. Justice Bolick received his J.D. degree from the University of California at Davis, where he has been recognized as a distinguished alumnus, and his B.A. *magna cum laude* from Drew University. He serves as a research fellow with the Hoover Institution. Among other honors, he was named one of the 90 Greatest DC Lawyers in the Last 30 Years by *Legal Times* in 2008, received a Bradley Prize in 2006, and was recognized as one of the nation's three lawyers of the year by *American Lawyer* in 2002 for his successful defense of school vouchers in *Zelman v. Simmons-Harris*. Justice Bolick is a prolific author of a dozen books and hundreds of articles. Among his most recent books are *Immigration Wars: Forging an American Solution* (2013), co-authored with former Florida Governor Jeb Bush; and *David's Hammer: The Case for an Activist Judiciary* (2007).

Clay Calvert is the Brechner Eminent Scholar in Mass Communication and director of the Marion B. Brechner First Amendment Project at the University of Florida. Calvert has authored or co-authored more than 130 law journal articles on topics related to freedom of expression. Calvert has filed, as counsel of record, multiple amicus briefs with the U.S. Supreme Court in cases such as *Elonis v. United States* and *Brown v. Entertainment Merchants Association*. Since 2015, his op-eds have appeared in *Fortune, Huffington Post, Newsweek, New Republic, Time* and *The Conversation*. Calvert is co-author, with Don R. Pember, of the market-leading undergraduate media-law textbook, *Mass Media Law,* now in its 19th edition, and is author of *Voyeur Nation: Media, Privacy, and Peering in Modern Culture* (2000). He received his J.D. with Great Distinction in 1991 from the University of the Pacific's McGeorge School of Law and then earned a Ph.D. in 1996 in Communication from Stanford University, where he also completed his undergraduate work in 1987. He is a member of both the State Bar of California and the Bar of the U.S. Supreme Court.

Mark Chenoweth has provided public service in all three branches of the federal government. He served as the first chief of staff to Congressman Mike Pompeo, as legal counsel to Commissioner Anne Northup at the U.S. Consumer Product Safety Commission, as an attorney advisor in the Office of Legal Policy at the U.S. Justice Department, and as a law clerk to Judge Danny J. Boggs on the U.S. Court of Appeals for the Sixth Circuit. Chenoweth has also worked as in-house counsel for Koch Industries, as a regulatory associate in the Washington office of Wilmer, Cutler & Pickering, as an adjunct professor at Antonin Scalia Law School, and as general counsel of Washington Legal Foundation. He is a graduate of Yale University and the University of Chicago Law School, where he co-founded the Institute for Justice Clinic on Entrepreneurship and became a Tony Patiño Fellow.

Nicole Stelle Garnett is the John P. Murphy Foundation Professor of Law at the University of Notre Dame. Her teaching and research focus is on property, land use, urban development, local government law, and education policy. She is the author of numerous articles on these subjects and of *Ordering the City: Land Use, Policing and the Restoration of Urban America* (2009). Her most recent book, *Lost Classroom, Lost Community: Catholic Schools' Importance in Urban America* (2014) represents the culmination of a major empirical research project with Professor Peg Brinig that examines the effects of Catholic school closures on urban neighborhoods. At Notre Dame, Garnett is also a fellow of the Institute for Educational Initiatives and the senior policy advisor for the Alliance for Catholic Education, a program engaged in a wide array of efforts to strengthen and sustain K-12 Catholic schools. Garnett is also a member of the editorial board of the *Cato Supreme Court Review*. From 2008 to 2010, she served as provost fellow at Notre Dame and has also been a visiting professor of law at the University of Chicago. Garnett received her B.A. from Stanford and her J.D. from Yale Law School. She clerked for Judge Morris S. Arnold of the U.S. Court of Appeals for the Eighth Circuit and for Justice Clarence Thomas of the U.S. Supreme Court. Before joining the Notre Dame faculty in 1999, she worked for two years as a staff attorney at the Institute for Justice.

Richard W. Garnett is the Paul J. Schierl/Fort Howard Corporation Professor of Law, with a concurrent appointment in the department of political science, at the University of Notre Dame. He teaches and writes about the freedoms of speech, association, and religion, and also about constitutional law more generally. He has published widely on questions regarding the role of religious believers and beliefs in politics and society and is the author of dozens of law-review articles and book chapters. His current research project, *Two There Are: Understanding the Separation of Church and State*, will be published by Cambridge University Press. Garnett is regularly invited to share analysis and commentary in national print and broadcast media, and contributes to several law-related blogs, including Mirror of

Justice and PrawfsBlawg. He is the founding director of Notre Dame Law School's Program on Church, State, and Society, an interdisciplinary project that focuses on the role of religious institutions, communities, and authorities in the social order. Garnett clerked for the late Chief Justice William H. Rehnquist and also for the late chief judge of the U.S. Court of Appeals for the Eighth Circuit, Richard S. Arnold. He is closely involved with a number of efforts to improve and strengthen Catholic schools and to reform education policy more generally. He served on the Notre Dame Task Force on Catholic Education, is a fellow of the University's Institute for Educational Initiatives, is a founding associate of the American Center for School Choice, and consults regularly with the Alliance for Catholic Education. He also served on the school board of St. Joseph Grade School in South Bend, Indiana.

David T. Goldberg joined Stanford Law School's Supreme Court Litigation Clinic in 2016. Before that, he taught for a decade at the University of Virginia, where he co-founded and co-directed that law school's Supreme Court Litigation Clinic. He has since 2006 been a partner in the firm of Donahue & Goldberg, specializing in complex public law matters in appellate courts. He has participated in roughly 150 cases in the U.S. Supreme Court, serving as counsel to parties in some 20 merits-stage cases, and is frequently asked to speak and write about the Court. Before establishing Donahue & Goldberg, Goldberg served on the legal staff of the NAACP Legal Defense Fund and before that, as law clerk to Justice David H. Souter and to Judge Ruth Bader Ginsburg, then of the U.S. Court of Appeals for the D.C. Circuit. Although civil rights law has been the principal focus of his practice, he has litigated cases under statutes appearing in 33 of the 53 titles of the U.S. Code and has represented a diverse array of clients, including the City of Chicago, the Western States Peanut Growers Association, Google, the Government of Canada, and James Brown, the late Godfather of Soul.

Sopan Joshi is a litigation associate in the Chicago office of Kirkland & Ellis. Joshi clerked for Justices Antonin Scalia and Samuel Alito of the U.S. Supreme Court, Judge Richard Posner of the U.S. Court of Appeals for the Seventh Circuit, and Judge Gary Feinerman of the U.S. District Court for the Northern District of Illinois. He graduated from Northwestern Pritzker School of Law and also holds B.S. and Ph.D. degrees in electrical engineering from Stanford University and the University of Illinois at Urbana-Champaign, respectively.

Thaya Brook Knight is associate director of financial regulation studies at the Cato Institute. She is an attorney with extensive experience in securities regulation, small business capital access, and capital markets. Before joining Cato, she co-founded and served as general counsel of CrowdCheck, a company providing due diligence and disclosure services in the online investing market. Following the recent financial crisis, she served as investigative counsel for the congressional oversight panel charged with overseeing the expenditure of Troubled Asset Relief Program funds. She also spent several years with the Washington office of the law firm WilmerHale, where her practice focused on securities litigation, securities enforcement defense, and corporate investigations. She holds a B.A. from Middlebury College and a J.D. from the University of Michigan Law School.

Christopher Landau is a senior partner in the Kirkland & Ellis appellate litigation practice, and was one of the founders of that practice almost 25 years ago. He has briefed and argued appeals involving a wide range of subject matters in courts all across the country, including the U.S. Supreme Court, every one of the federal courts of appeals, and many state appellate courts. Landau served twice as a law clerk at the Supreme Court, first to Justice Antonin Scalia (1990–91) and then to Justice Clarence Thomas (1991–92). Over the past two terms, the Court has granted review of five petitions in a row in which Landau served as counsel of record. In 2017, the chief justice appointed Landau to a three-year term as a member of the Judicial Conference Advisory Committee on Appellate Rules, which makes recommendations for changes to the Federal Rules of Appellate Procedure. When a group of federal judges decided to bring a lawsuit alleging that the Constitution does not allow Congress to withhold judicial salary adjustments previously established by law, they turned to Landau, and he succeeded in overturning prior binding precedent to vindicate the judges' constitutional claim. *See Beer v. United States*, 696 F.3d 1174 (Fed. Cir. 2012) (en banc).

Roger Pilon is vice president for legal affairs at the Cato Institute, the founding director of Cato's Center for Constitutional Studies, the inaugural holder of Cato's B. Kenneth Simon Chair in Constitutional Studies, and the founding publisher of the *Cato Supreme Court Review*. Before joining Cato he held five senior posts in the Reagan administration, including at State and Justice, and was a National Fellow at Stanford's Hoover Institution. In 1989, the Bicentennial Commission presented him with its Benjamin Franklin Award for excellence in writing on the U.S. Constitution. In 2001, Columbia University's School of General Studies awarded him its Alumni Medal of Distinction. Pilon lectures and debates at universities and law schools across the country and testifies often before Congress. His writings have appeared in both academic and popular journals and he appears often on radio and TV. Pilon holds a B.A. from Columbia University, an M.A. and a Ph.D. from the University of Chicago, and a J.D. from the George Washington University School of Law.

David G. Post is a former professor of law at the Beasley School of Law at Temple University, where he taught intellectual property law and the law of cyberspace. He is also a fellow at the Center for Democracy and Technology, a fellow of the Institute for Information Law and Policy at New York Law School, an adjunct scholar at the Cato Institute (where he is a member of the editorial board of the *Cato Supreme Court Review*), and a contributor to the Volokh Conspiracy blog. Professor Post is the author of *In Search of "Jefferson's Moose: Notes on the State of Cyberspace"* (2009), and co-author of *Cyberlaw: Problems of Policy and Jurisprudence in the Information Age* (2007) (with Paul Schiff Berman and Patricia Bellia), and numerous scholarly articles on intellectual property, the law of cyberspace, and complexity theory. He has been a regular columnist for the *American Lawyer* and *InformationWeek*, a commentator on the PBS News Hour, NPR's *All Things Considered*, BBC's *World*, and the PBS documentary *The Supreme Court*. His writings can be accessed online at www.davidpost. com.

Ilya Shapiro is a senior fellow in constitutional studies at the Cato Institute and editor-in-chief of the *Cato Supreme Court Review*. Before joining Cato, he was a special assistant/advisor to the Multi-National Force in Iraq on rule of law issues and practiced international, political, commercial, and antitrust litigation at Patton Boggs and Cleary Gottlieb. Shapiro is the co-author (with David H. Gans) of *Religious Liberties for Corporations? Hobby Lobby, the Affordable Care Act, and the Constitution* (2014). He has contributed to many academic, popular, and professional publications, including the *Wall Street Journal*, *National Affairs*, *Harvard Journal of Law & Public Policy*, *L.A. Times*, *USA Today*, *Politico*, *Weekly Standard*, *New York Times Online*, and *National Review Online*. He regularly provides commentary for various media—including an appearance on the *Colbert Report*—and is a legal consultant to CBS News. Shapiro has testified before Congress and state legislatures and, as coordinator of Cato's amicus brief program, has filed more than 200 "friend of the court" briefs in the Supreme Court. He lectures regularly on behalf of the Federalist Society, was an inaugural Washington Fellow at the National Review Institute and a Lincoln Fellow at the Claremont Institute, and has been an adjunct professor at the George Washington University Law School. In 2015 *National Law Journal* named him to its list of "rising stars" (40 under 40). Before entering private practice, Shapiro clerked for Judge E. Grady Jolly of the U.S. Court of Appeals for the Fifth Circuit. He holds an A.B. from Princeton, an M.Sc. from the London School of Economics, and a J.D. from the University of Chicago (where he became a Tony Patiño Fellow). Shapiro is a member of the bars of New York, D.C., and the U.S. Supreme Court.

Emily R. Zhang is a Ph.D. candidate in political science at Stanford University who graduated from Stanford Law School in 2017. She was a student in the Stanford Supreme Court Litigation Clinic during the fall of 2016, when she, along with Trevor Ezell, Samson Schatz, and Grace Zhao, worked on the merits briefs in *Packingham v. North Carolina*. Starting fall 2017, she will be a Skadden Fellow at the ACLU's voting rights project.

Cato Institute

Founded in 1977, the Cato Institute is a public policy research foundation dedicated to broadening the parameters of policy debate to allow consideration of more options that are consistent with the principles of limited government, individual liberty, and peace. To that end, the Institute strives to achieve greater involvement of the intelligent, concerned lay public in questions of policy and the proper role of government.

The Institute is named for *Cato's Letters*, libertarian pamphlets that were widely read in the American Colonies in the early 18th century and played a major role in laying the philosophical foundation for the American Revolution.

Despite the achievement of the nation's Founders, today virtually no aspect of life is free from government encroachment. A pervasive intolerance for individual rights is shown by government's arbitrary intrusions into private economic transactions and its disregard for civil liberties. And while freedom around the globe has notably increased in the past several decades, many countries have moved in the opposite direction, and most governments still do not respect or safeguard the wide range of civil and economic liberties.

To address those issues, the Cato Institute undertakes an extensive publications program on the complete spectrum of policy issues. Books, monographs, and shorter studies are commissioned to examine the federal budget, Social Security, regulation, military spending, international trade, and myriad other issues. Major policy conferences are held throughout the year, from which papers are published thrice yearly in the *Cato Journal*. The Institute also publishes the quarterly magazine *Regulation*.

In order to maintain its independence, the Cato Institute accepts no government funding. Contributions are received from foundations, corporations, and individuals, and other revenue is generated from the sale of publications. The Institute is a nonprofit, tax-exempt, educational foundation under Section 501(c)3 of the Internal Revenue Code.

CATO INSTITUTE
1000 Massachusetts Ave., N.W.
Washington, D.C. 20001
www.cato.org